THE A LIST

THE A LIST

The National Society of Film Critics'

100 ESSENTIAL FILMS

EDITED BY JAY CARR

DA CAPO PRESS

Designed by Jeffrey P. Williams
Set in 10.5 point Berkeley Book by Perseus Publishing Services

Cataloging-in-Publication data for this book is available from the Library of Congress.

First Da Capo Press edition 2002
ISBN 0–306–81096–4

Published by Da Capo Press
A Member of the Perseus Books Group
http://www.dacapopress.com

Da Capo Press books are available at special discounts for bulk purchases in the U.S. by corporations, institutions, and other organizations. For more information, please contact the Special Markets Department at the Perseus Books Group, 11 Cambridge Center, Cambridge, MA 02142, or call (800) 255-1514 or (617) 252–5298, or e-mail j.mccrary@perseusbooks.com.

1 2 3 4 5 6 7 8 9—05 04 03 02

Dedicated to the memory of

KATHY HUFFHINES

1943–1991

Contents

Introduction

PEOPLE LOVE MOVIES. People love lists. And so it is that the National Society of Film Critics for the first time in its history has chosen a list of the 100 movies you need to know to be film literate.

Readers should understand from the outset that no single member agrees with this list in its entirety. When a couple of members walked away from the project after films they thought should be included didn't make the final cut, I somehow felt we were on the right track. Our "A list" is a consensus that admits—OK, invites—dissent; I hope that our choices will engage you, or infuriate you, but in any event will sharpen your own critical approach to the movies—and just maybe add to your enjoyment of them.

Shrinking a century of films down to 100 titles means that there inevitably are omitted movies as worthy as the ones included. But while the selection process may have necessarily been arbitrary, it wasn't capricious. There are reasons why every last film was chosen. The only thing everybody agreed on is that it would be unforgivably parochial to limit the list to films made in the U.S. Obviously, no one standard was applied, which is why *Enter the Dragon* stands shoulder to shoulder with, say, *The Gospel According to St. Matthew.* Think of this collection of films as a grid, containing most of the significant kinds of film, whether by genre, or director, or star performance.

It also seemed more important than ever, given the perhaps inevitable stress on the contemporary, to supply perspective by citing landmark films of the past. There would have been no *Gone with the Wind,* for instance, if there hadn't been *Birth of a Nation. Les Vampires,* a silent French serial, set the pace for stylish criminality. Other films made the list simply because they represent the big pop myth in which Hollywood, at its best, excels—*The Wizard of Oz, Top Hat, Star Wars.*

Some films claimed a space for more than one reason. *Public Enemy* put on the map the kind of gangster movie *Pulp Fiction* reinvented. *Public Enemy* also put Jimmy Cagney on the map. He crackled with the kind of energy that drove hundreds of the urban movies that flew off America's big screens like fists, when cities believed in themselves with a populist vigor.

Many of the movies on the list define genres. And caused us to almost immediately break one of the few rules we had—such as one film, one director. *Vertigo* got in because it so deliciously was Alfred Hitchcock's psychic autobiography, and reminded us that there was a tough side to Jimmy Stewart that was just as pronounced as his aw-shucks persona. Hitchcock's *Psycho,* however, launched the slasher movie—a genre of arguable value, but too ubiquitous to be ignored. Billy Wilder, too. His *Double Indemnity* is one of the glories of film noir. But his *Sunset Boulevard* apotheosizes the Hollywood-on-Hollywood movie, reveling in its self-cannibalism while pretending to deplore it.

And don't think it didn't cause a pang or two to omit Wilder's *Some Like It Hot.* The temptation in compiling a book such as this one is to favor serious films. But it's a temptation that must be resisted, easy enough when you've got the likes of Buster Keaton, Charlie Chaplin, W. C. Fields, Woody Allen, and The Marx Brothers to pitch in.

The choices were, if anything, even more agonizing when it came to films from other countries. Italian neo-realism, the French New Wave, Bergman, Kurosawa, Satyajit Ray and others opened postwar America's eyes to the fact that it was a mistake to allow Hollywood alone to define film. Between the wars, Russian filmmakers built on the pioneering work of D. W. Griffith, inventing most of the rest of the film grammar Griffith didn't invent. German directors (Murnau, Lang, Pabst) brought Expressionism into the international mix, laying the basis for noir and a rich stratum of Hollywood films made by German-speaking exiles and refugees.

Some names—Renoir, Buñuel, Welles, Bresson, Scorsese, Coppola, Kubrick, Lubitsch, Spielberg—were locks. Others—Charles Burnett (*Killer of Sheep*), Theo Angelopoulos (*Landscape in the Mist*), Krzysztof Kieslowski (*The Decalogue*), were not, but their films are too important to remain uncelebrated. If this book is to be of special value, apart from warming the hearts of those gratified to find their favorites included, it will lie in leading people to insufficiently celebrated masterpieces. In the age of VCRs and DVDs, access to these films has never been easier. Today's dumbed-down cinema of sensory jolts and weekend grosses (apt word!) can use a few masterpieces. And a few laughs. They're in there, too. Enjoy!

JAY CARR
BOSTON, 2001

2001: A Space Odyssey (1968)

by James Verniere

SCREWING WITH AUDIENCES' HEADS was Stanley Kubrick's favorite hobby outside of chess, which is just another way of screwing with heads. One of the flaws of *Eyes Wide Shut* (1999), Kubrick's posthumously released, valedictory film, may be that it doesn't screw with our heads enough.

2001: A Space Odyssey (1968), however, remains Kubrick's crowning, confounding achievement. Homeric sci-fi film, conceptual artwork, and dopeheads' intergalactic joyride, *2001* pushed the envelope of film at a time when *Mary Poppins* and *The Sound of Music* ruled the box office.

As technological achievement, it was a quantum leap beyond *Flash Gordon* and *Buck Rogers* serials, although it used many of the same fundamental techniques. Steven Spielberg called *2001* "the Big Bang" of his filmmaking generation. It was the precursor of Andrei Tarkovsky's *Solaris* (1972), Spielberg's *Close Encounters of the Third Kind* (1977) and George Lucas's *Star Wars* (1977), as well as the current digital revolution. At the time of its release, *2001: A Space Odyssey* created a nationwide stir, in large part due to its willful opacity. Among numerical titles, only George Orwell's *Nineteen Eighty-four* and Joseph Heller's *Catch-22* compare to *2001* in terms of instant recognizability.

There are antecedents to *2001,* among them Georges Melies's pioneering *Voyage to the Moon* (1902), William Cameron Menzies's H.G. Wells–scripted *Things to Come* (1936), and George Pal's *Destination Moon* (1950), a surprisingly realistic film coscripted by popular science-fiction author Robert A. Heinlein (*Stranger in a Strange Land*).

Production of *2001,* an expansion of Arthur C. Clarke's 1951 short story "The Sentinel," began in December 1965 at MGM Studios at Boreham Wood, England. Shot in Super Panavision and released in Cinerama, the film premiered in New York City about a year before Neil Armstrong's historic walk on the moon.

The film opens about 3 million years in the past and ends in the eponymous 2001 with a sequence dubbed, with a wink and nod to the Age of Aquarius, "the ultimate trip." In between, *2001: A Space Odyssey* may be more of a series of landmark sequences than a fully coherent or satisfying experience. But its landmarks have withstood the test of time and repeated parody.

1

The first arrives in the wordless "Dawn of Man" episode, in which Kubrick dramatizes a crucial moment in human evolution, the sci-fi equivalent of Michelangelo's *The Creation of Adam*. After apelike creatures (costumed dancers and mimes) subsisting in a brutish wasteland encounter a mysterious black monolith, their leader picks up a bone, puzzles out how to use it as a tool/weapon (a small step for a man, a giant step for a man-ape), and smashes a warthog skeleton to pieces as Richard Strauss's "Thus Spake Zarathustra" thunders on the soundtrack.

After rejecting a score commissioned from Alex North (who was hired after Kubrick failed to lure composer Carl Orff to the project), Kubrick decided to use existing music, and he uses it brilliantly here, making Strauss's unexpectedly juxtaposed, anthemlike theme an indivisible part of the scene, perhaps the most famous Kubrick-arranged marriage of music and image.

That this landmark scene would be parodied, often hilariously in television commercials, on *Saturday Night Live* and in Carl Gottlieb's *Caveman* (1981) and Mel Brooks's *History of the World—Part 1* (1981) is only one indication of what a pervasive pop culture icon it soon became.

When the man-ape then tosses his newfound weapon/tool end-over-end and the tumbling bone turns into an orbiting satellite, Kubrick makes the cinema's most famous jump-cut and "eye rhyme." The subsequent "docking" sequence featuring a sleek spacecraft and a revolving space station, the much commented upon ballet mechanique sequence, suggests a link between Ezekiel and Freud. Johann Strauss's "Blue Danube Waltz," which we hear as the spacecraft makes its spiraling approach to the "wheel," becomes literal music of the spheres in this scene, celestial accompaniment to a cosmic, coital dance.

As this scene demonstrates, even more so than in *Dr. Strangelove or: How I Learned to Stop Worrying and Love the Bomb* (1964), technology is sexy (as it was to Kubrick, who loved gadgets, designed lenses, and collected cameras and electronic equipment). Kubrick's vision of space travel is sensual, obsessively detailed, and authentic: the sleek Space Shuttle–like orbiter; revolving "space wheel"; lipstick-red Olivier Mourgue space station lounges; the centrifugal hub of the *Discovery*, monitors and computer readouts; the "spine" of the *Discovery*, bug-like "space pods"; sarcophogilike hibernation units; and the Cyclopean HAL 9000 computer. Kubrick persuaded NASA, Boeing, IBM, and Pan Am among other aerospace and technology corporations to contribute designs and technical advisers to the film in exchange for planting their corporate logos on the screen, in this case for reasons that make aesthetic sense (Ridley Scott followed Kubrick's lead in the design of *Blade Runner* and *Alien*). *2001* also pokes fun at the future outer-space expansion of such franchises as Howard Johnsons and Hilton Hotels. A more prophetic vision of the new millennium might be hard to find.

More than authentic and prophetic, Kubrick's high-tech vision is beautiful. Some critics of the day complained of the film's "sterile" look. But Kubrick's minimalism is the correct aesthetic and engineering choice. *2001* bids farewell to the upholstered, gewgaw-choked interiors of Jules Verne.

Although almost a documentary of space travel, *2001* also operates on the level of a dream. Its comparative wordlessness—with an amazingly low ratio of dialogue to running time, *2001* is a virtual silent film—forces viewers to concentrate on the hypnotic blend of music and image. It often seems like a brain-teasing exercise in analogies: bone is to HAL as HAL is to monolith, etc. Its Escher- and Magritte-like images of *Discovery* crewmen Dave Poole (Gary Lockwood) and Frank Bowman (Kier Dullea) defying spatial logic as they move around inside the spacecraft, and the film's many ellipses and alignments, suggest the topsy-turvy, free-floating, free-associative landscape of a dream. Also contributing to the dreamlike pull are mirror images—the warthog skeleton and fossil-like design of the *Discovery*, the Gemini twins Poole and Bowman, etc.—and screens within screens. No wonder Federico Fellini listed *2001: A Space Odyssey* among his ten favorite films.

Kubrick biographer Vincent LoBrutto cites Louis Leakey's *Adam's Ancestors,* Robert Ardrey's *African Genesis,* and Joseph Campbell's *The Hero with a Thousand Faces,* which also would cast its shadow on George Lucas and *Star Wars,* among the influences on *2001*. But the greatest may have been the 1964 New York World's Fair with its multimedia exhibits—including films by Saul Bass and Charles and Ray Eames and a movie projected in an IMAX precursor called "Cinerama 360"—and its gadget-and-computer-driven "World of Tomorrow" outlook. It's as if Kubrick wanted the film to serve as a calling card for the human race in case aliens actually arrived.

Among the film's flaws are the bland characters and the final image of the "Space Child," which reaches for, but doesn't quite achieve, a metaphysical high note. The banality of Bowman and Poole, however, makes it possible for HAL (voice of Canadian actor Douglas Rain, who replaced Martin Balsam) to appear, to borrow a phrase from *Blade Runner,* "more human than human." In fact, HAL, the malfunctioning, killer computer, may be the "character" Kubrick identified with most closely and the one that makes the strongest impression on viewers.

The celebrated "Star Gate" sequence is impressive as technical achievement and light show (Monument Valley, the frequent setting of John Ford westerns, stands in as the alien landscape in these scenes). But it's more conceptual than visceral. Lucas would popularize, if not vulgarize, it in the leap into "hyper-space" and theme-park-ride-like "trench"-skimming attack on the Death Star in *Star Wars,* just as HAL would be transformed into the robot-servants C3PO and R2-D2.

While the storytelling lapses of *2001: A Space Odyssey* are undeniable, the film's ability to induce a sense of awe and wonder is unparalleled. In this regard, Kubrick, who obviously wanted to be declared a genius, may have been emulating not other filmmakers but the architects of gothic cathedrals.

The result is the polar opposite of the amiable, Saturday-matinee atmosphere of *Star Wars.* An aura of malice pervades *2001,* an aura of malice evident in most Kubrick films, as it is in the films of Alfred Hitchcock. The difference is that Hitchcock created Venus-flytrap movies, movies that are primarily exercises in seduction and entrapment, while Kubrick's works seem more like unassailable fortresses carved in ice.

Still, *2001* remains the most popular experimental movie ever made. That it was financed by one of the oldest, most conservative Hollywood studios is a priceless twist of fate.

In undertaking it, Kubrick mastered new technologies and refined and invented new techniques. His research was typically exhaustive. According to LoBrutto, before shooting *2001,* Kubrick insisted on screening every science-fiction film ever made. With *2001,* Kubrick in effect did to film what his monolith makers did to the human race: forced it along, made it evolve. Kubrick may have done the same thing to the young, slack-jawed baby boomers in the audience. *2001* was more than a vision of the future. It was a vision of the future of movies.

42nd Street (1933)

by Emanuel Levy

42ND STREET MAY NOT BE the best musical ever made, but it's certainly the definitive backstage musical and a breakthrough in that uniquely American genre. It's also one of the most enjoyable and enduring musicals: Its constant revivals, on Broadway and national tours, attests to its long-standing popularity with audiences of various generations. The outline of *42nd Street* has been copied numerous times, but seldom has the backstage atmosphere been so honestly and felicitously caught.

Satiated with a steady slate of screen musicals, usually in a revue format that was little more than a collection of staged numbers and a series of song cues, Warner had declared a moratorium on the genre, until production head Darryl Zanuck signed Rian James and James Seymour to write a more "substantial" musical grounded in the reality of the times.

Loosely based on Bradford Ropes's novel, *42nd Street* was released at the height of the Depression. It contains all the typical characters (which even then were cliches) we have come to expect in a backstage story: the aging and temperamental leading lady, the fresh and innocent ingenue, the cynical director who's desperate for a hit, the demanding financial backers. Even so, the film's plot was more substantial than previous or future efforts. The quality of the script, which was peppered with punchy lines, and the film's atmosphere gave *42nd Street* a distinctive freshness.

Mervyn LeRoy was originally assigned to direct, but he became ill and had to be replaced. The assignment was handed to Lloyd Bacon, a Warner contract director, who made the same year the James Cagney starrer, *Footlight Parade*. Bacon was a less ambitious and accomplished director than LeRoy, but he had a good sense of pacing. Compared with other musicals of the era, *42nd Street* moves at a brisk pace.

42nd Street is primarily known for four elements: Its corny plot, a glorious score by the team of Al Dubin and Harry Warren, splashy dance numbers choreographed by Busby Berkeley, and appealing cast, headed by the enormously likable Ruby Keeler.

By today's standards, the text, based on a tawdry backstage yarn, is insipid and even banal: Peggy Sawyer (Ruby Keeler), a naive understudy who wears puffed sleeves (signaling youthful innocence), steps into the star's shoes just hours before opening night and sets the world on fire. Warner Baxter plays a cynical Broadway producer-director who suffers from heart trouble amid pressures from backers. Baxter is mostly remembered for his memorable and much satirized speech. "You're going out a youngster," he tells the terrified ingenue, "but you've got to come back a star!"

The rest of the cast is also impressive: Bebe Daniels plays the elegant star who breaks her ankle; George Brent is her gigolo lover; Dick Powell is the singing twerpy juvenile; Ginger Rogers's Anytime Annie is the gold-digging chorine, known as the countess; Guy Kibbee is the sleazy sugar daddy who courts the leading lady.

Zanuck immediately recognized the talent of dance director Berkeley, whose work in *Whoopee* drew critical attention. To make sure that no other studio would benefit from his visual flair, he signed the inventive genius to a seven-year contract. With the studio's big budget (Hal Wallis's production cost a then mammoth $400,000) and technical facilities at his command, Berkeley overwhelmed audiences with his larger-than-life escapist entertainment. Berkeley's lavish, gaudy imagination was reflected in elaborately engineered, geometrically patterned dance routines.

It was at Warners that Berkeley developed his ribald yet erotic vision and the inimitable extravaganza of his choreography. His opulent numbers employed dozens of girls in a spectacular array of rhythmic movement, which one critic described as "kaleidoscopic patterns of female flesh, dissolving into artichokes, exploding stars, snowflakes, and water lilies."

However, it wasn't just the choreography that made Berkeley's numbers exciting. His use of the camera was daringly inventive, with dazzling diagonal angles, incredible traveling shots, and impeccable rhythmic cutting. Berkeley developed a monorail to give his camera greater mobility, devising a shooting technique that became known as the "Berkeley top shot." In pursuit of proper perspective for his complex shots, Berkeley drilled holes through stage floors and climbed to the ceilings of soundstages.

David Thomson sees an irony in the fact that, as the cinema was instituting its own morality in the 1930s, it also created a visionary like Berkeley who exploited film's lascivious disposition toward orgy, encouraging sexual daydreaming— Berkeley's camera had the thrust of a sexual act. Berkeley's Warners movies were much more outré and suggestive than his later musicals at MGM, a reflection of both changing times and tastes and studio interference. Women don't just dance in his production numbers: They are moving and evolving, making circles that are tightened or expanded, bursting forward and backward.

As for Keeler, in the 1930s, she starred in a string of Warner musicals that have since become classics (*Dames, Flirtation Walk*), but she's most intimately associated with *42nd Street*. Keeler always played variations of the same part: the sweet-natured girl picked from the chorus line at the last possible moment to replace a temperamental or ailing star. At the time, naive viewers thought that Keeler was romantically involved with Dick Powell, her costar, a notion that Warner's publicity machine obviously encouraged.

Considering that Keeler made only a dozen films, it's odd that she's so widely remembered as the pert girl of Warner musicals. Keeler's dancing was clunky and her line delivery amateurish, yet she was extremely amiable. Her charisma largely depended on her ordinary looks, the fact that she was not glamorous. As a screen presence, she combined sweet naivete and strong ambition, embodying the fantasies of stage-struck girls during the Depression.

42nd Street was one of the first movies to use a full backstage narrative. Structurally, though, the film is flawed for two reasons: There are not many song-and-dance numbers, and they all appear in the last reel. Bits and pieces of musical numbers (mostly "42nd Street") are heard in rehearsal early in the film. And one song, "You're Getting to Be a Habit With Me," is performed on a bare stage. But they mostly serve as preparation for the three big production numbers, stacked together at the end.

As scholar Martin Rubin has observed, there is little in the film's numbers that could not be presented within the confines of a realistic stage. The scale and spectacle of the final numbers are relatively restrained and stagebound: The effects of "Shuffle Off to Buffalo" are conceived in terms of the stage's limitations. The one notable exception is "Young and Healthy," which utilizes uniquely cinematic devices: Overhead shots, through-the-legs tracking shot, the use of frameline to conceal the chorus behind Dick Powell and his costar after they kiss. But, as in "Shuffle Off to Buffalo," a scene shift is handed via a theatrical device: A prop bench sinks below the floor and becomes part of a revolving platform.

It's in the climactic title number, "42nd Street," that the film strains against the confines of a realistic stage show, as in the trick cut, that moves a dancing Keeler from the apron of the stage to a taxicab, and a continuously expanding stage space. The camera's tightness and fluidity were ahead of the times. In this number, sweeping crane shots depict vignettes of life on the "naughty, bawdy" street with speed and smoothness, setting up dazzling transitions and dizzying patterns that would become a signature of Berkeley's unique vocabulary.

There are shifts in scale and perspective, as when the chorus holds up cutouts to form the skyline of Manhattan, or when the camera moves horizontally across the stage, looking up at Keeler and Powell as they kiss atop a skyscraper. Powell then pulls down a miniature asbestos curtain that fills the frame and ends the number.

42nd Street boasts the strongest, most "serious" plot and characterizations of any 1930s musical. Indeed, the narrative, with its references to unemployment and other social ills, maintains an emotional pull that prevents the film from being overwhelmed by Berkeley's numbers. While the sketchy plot of other Warner musicals are easily eclipsed by Berkeley's spectacular numbers, *42nd Street* possesses a dramatic drive that counters Berkeley's effects. The overall impact is based on the link of the characters to a recognizable reality and the relative restraint of Berkeley's numbers.

Even so, it would be unfair to describe *42nd Street* as an "integrated" musical in the way that MGM/Minnelli musicals (*Meet Me in St. Louis, The Band Wagon*) were in the 1940s and 1950s. It did help, though, that the songs were similar in tone to the narrative and therefore didn't call too much attention to themselves. As Rubin pointed out, this may be the reason why *42nd Street* stands high in the pantheon of classic musicals, but not as high in the canon of Berkeley's work.

Like most pictures, *42nd Street* reflected the zeitgeist, which was manifest in the film's harsh tone: Competing for jobs, the chorus girls are tough and aggressive. In the title song, a woman is stabbed, then the camera swoops up to a second-story window, from which playboy Powell looks down, singing nonchalantly, while his valet mixes a cocktail in the background. Like most musicals, the movie embodied the ideological contradictions inherent in the American Dream. It's tempting to perceive Keeler's Peggy as an Horatio Alger heroine, who's rewarded not only for hard work but also by fate—the leading lady's injury. Depression audiences must have been starved for such rags-to-riches and overnight success stories.

Similarly, the epilogue wasn't only powerful but also ambiguous, depicting a depressive and exhausted Julian Marsh, sitting alone almost unappreciated in the alley outside the theater, where his show has just been declared a hit. It's the kind of ending that showed the gap between personal and collective happiness. At the time, viewers probably remembered the happy collective finale rather than the personal misery, though in recent classroom screenings, most of my students single out the uncharitable, often ruthless manner in which the characters manipulate each other almost up to the end.

The 400 Blows (1959)

by Peter Brunette

FEW YOUNG PEOPLE TODAY, even those who pride themselves on their knowledge of movies, seem even to have heard of François Truffaut, and that's a real shame. For it was he and his rebellious critical colleagues at the legendary French film magazine *Cahiers du Cinéma* who, after deciding to become directors themselves, brought a glorious new *joie de vivre* to international filmmaking in the late 1950s and early 1960s. Fed up with what they saw as the stultifying, always *très correct* "tradition of quality" in French cinema, where classy literary adaptations and high production values reigned supreme, Truffaut, Jean-Luc Godard, Claude Chabrol, and their pals left the well-provisioned studios and went directly into the streets instead. There they shot their movies with little-known actors in a refreshingly awkward, semi-documentary style that drew heavily upon the neorealism that had dominated Italian cinema just after the war, a decade or more earlier. The incredible, almost embarrassing paucity of their cinematic means was more than made up for by their sincerity, imagination, and passionate belief in the movies as personal statement, something more than mere entertainment.

No film of what came to be known as *la nouvelle vague* (the New Wave) embodies these features more than Truffaut's first full-length effort, *The 400 Blows* (1959). The archetypal expression of the misunderstood and unloved teenager, it is guaranteed to warm the cockles of any thirteen-year-old's heart, even today. In one of the great turnabouts in cinema history, Truffaut, who, owing to his intemperate critical attacks on the French film industry, had been refused press accreditation at the Cannes film festival in 1958, won the director's prize there for *The 400 Blows* a year later.

First, a note on the title. It's undoubtedly befuddled countless American film-goers for the last four decades, but it's simply a literal (and lazy) translation from the French title, *Les 400 Coups,* which of course is meaningless in English. It derives from the phrase *faire les 400 coups,* which means, simply, to raise hell. And that's exactly what Truffaut's alter ego, Antoine Doinel, sets out to do. Played by the lifelong Truffaut stand-in, the edgy Jean-Pierre Léaud, seen here in the first of a string of incarnations of this same character, Antoine Doinel is an unwanted bastard child for whom his mother and stepfather have little time. One day, while playing hooky from school with his grand buddy, the equally neglected René, he spots his mother in the arms of another man. Hurt and frustrated, torn between his bitchy mother and his more sympathetic but feckless father, he is caught in a series of increasingly serious mishaps and misunderstandings that eventually lead to incarceration in a juvenile facility, from which he ultimately escapes.

But only in a manner of speaking. At the end of the film, he has reached the sea, his geographical, psychological, and symbolic goal, only to have to turn back suddenly from the pounding surf when it becomes impossible to run any further. In the final shot of the film, Truffaut brilliantly catches Antoine in a freeze-frame (in one of the first dramatic uses of that now worn-out, banal advertising technique), as he turns, trapped, back toward the audience. The final abrupt dolly-in on Antoine's stunned face is unforgettable.

Much of the film's power derives from the fact that it's so overtly autobiographical. Like most first-time novelists and filmmakers, Truffaut turned to his own life for inspiration, and the frustration and bitterness of his own depressing childhood imparts a powerful personal charge to the movie. The genius of this film, though, lies in the director's ability to transcend his own individual suffering to mount a devastating critique of the casual brutality of his society's routine treatment of children. The opening scene in Antoine's French class—so clearly reminiscent of Vigo's *Zéro de Conduite* and so influential on Fellini's subsequent film, *Amarcord*—is remarkable for both its nastiness and its humor. The clear message of the film is that school and other institutions are prisons and represent the death of the spirit, while the cinema (which Antoine and his family attend during one happy but brief interlude) is joyful life. In fact, what's perhaps most striking about the juvenile detention center Antoine ends up in is how little it differs from his original classroom. It is the originality and intensity of this critique that also redeems the film's occasional lapse into romantic sentimentality (a life-long tendency of Truffaut's that would quickly alienate his more severe *Cahiers* colleagues), as when Antoine peers out from behind the grillwork of the police wagon and the director bulls his way in for a shameless close-up to catch those superfluous tears streaming down Antoine's face.

But there's infinitely much more to the film than bitterness and sentimentality. Inspired by his Italian master Roberto Rossellini, whom he idolized, Truffaut captures the textures and sounds of the streets of Paris, especially the less savory, but lively *quartiers* like Pigalle and Montmartre, which are so palpably present that they assume the importance, almost, of additional characters. Even in the credits, the Eiffel Tower, that quintessential signifier of Paris, is visually discovered over and over again. In 1959, the sheer joy of these celebratory urban interludes was something new to the movies.

As in much subsequent European cinema, many scenes take place in real time, such as when Antoine takes out the garbage or chugs a stolen bottle of milk, or, quintessentially, when he goes to an amusement park and is swirled around one of those antigravitational rides that hold riders up by centrifugal force. Rather than use a quick montage to merely suggest the experience, Truffaut shoots the whole thing, partly from Antoine's swirling point of view, to allow us to feel what his young hero does, this combination of glorious joy and frustrated entrapment that is also his life. (As critic Annette Insdorf has pointed out, Truffaut, in a characteristic personal touch, can himself be spotted on the ride.) The director also employs symbolic means for expressive purposes—note the long tracking shot that seems to trap Antoine during what he thinks is his escape and the plethora of bars and cages that surround him throughout the film—to further help us get under his character's skin but also to add thematic heft to the movie. In one powerful, improvised scene in the juvenile home, Antoine speaks directly to an unseen female psychiatrist (and to us, of course) about his sad life. What's perhaps most interesting about this scene is that we learn completely new details about his background that we haven't seen dramatized (a screenwriting "mistake" in the Hollywood system), thus suggesting even further that what we're dealing with here is a real human being who, even in the best of circumstances, can never be fully known or understood.

Truffaut's legendary talent for directing children starts here, but *The 400 Blows* is not just for kids. Or rather it's addressed to that child, still searching for that impossible combination of freedom without loneliness, that abides in all of us.

All About Eve (1950)

by Peter Travers

IT WAS A BUMPY NIGHT on March 29, 1951, as Joseph L. Mankiewicz's theater fable *All About Eve,* with fourteen Academy Award nominations (a record until *Titanic* tied it in 1997), vied with Billy Wilder's Hollywood parable *Sunset Boulevard* for the best picture prize. After all, it was hard to forget Norma Desmond, the silent screen diva indelibly played by Gloria Swanson, railing against the tyranny of talk. "Words! Words! Words! You made a rope of words and strangled this business," said Norma in a tirade against the writers of talkies. And then there was Mankiewicz—his older brother Herman had cowritten *Citizen Kane* with Orson Welles—who had elegantly strung together a rope of words to create *All About Eve,* a vivid feat of comic verbalization that skewered the pretensions of star egos. One could almost picture poor Norma Desmond checking out the career-defining performances of Bette Davis, Anne Baxter, and George Sanders in *All About Eve* and noting in horror that when they opened their mouths all that came out was "talk, talk, talk!"

Ah, but what talk. Even now, a half century after *All About Eve* took home the best picture Oscar, along with dual statuettes for Mankiewicz for writing and directing, lines from the script fly off the screen with their sting intact. In the post *Star Wars*–era, movies have again lost the knack of polished speech, and *All About*

Eve—glib though it may be in patches—takes unapologetic glee in the shimmer and sophistication of its language.

Take the opening scene in which nearly the entire cast is gathered to watch Eve Harrington (Anne Baxter) collect the Sarah Siddons award for distinguished achievement in theater acting. Milton Krasner's camera provides close-ups, but Mankiewicz gives us voiceover narration from drama critic Addison DeWitt, a role oozed by George Sanders (he deservedly won the Oscar as best supporting actor) in a posh voice dipped in acid: Wielding a cigarette holder like a Zulu warrior would brandish a weapon to blow poison darts, the critic instructs: "To those of you who do not read, attend the theater, listen to unsponsored radio programs or know anything of the world in which you live—it is perhaps necessary to introduce myself. My name is Addison DeWitt. My native habitat is the theater— in it I toil not, neither do I spin. I am a critic and commentator. I am essential to the theater as ants to a picnic, as the boll weevil to a cotton field. . . . "

And so we're off. Addison will introduce the dramatis personae: the producer Max Fabian (Gregory Ratoff), the director Bill Sampson (Gary Merrill), the playwright Lloyd Richards (Hugh Marlowe), and the playwright's wife Karen (Celeste Holm). But these are secondary figures, paralleling the secondary awards that have just been presented. Says Addison: "Minor awards are for such as the writer and director—since their function is merely to construct a tower so that the world can applaud a light which flashes on top of it."

Those lights are two: The supernova is the veteran actress Margo Channing (Bette Davis), introduced by Addison as "a star of the theater. She made her first appearance at the age of four in *A Midsummer Night's Dream*. She played a fairy and entered, quite unexpectedly, stark naked. . . . Margo is a great star. A true star. She never was or will be anything less or anything else." A cue for a close-up if there ever was one. The camera studies the face of Margo, meaning Davis, whose performance never was or will be anything less than a magnificent showcase for a star's art. Davis can act with her eyes hooded, her head down, and her mouth shut. She seemed to intuit that Margo would be her last great glamour role before *Whatever Happened to Baby Jane,* however entertaining, would consign her to playing hags in horror films. Here, though, Davis's face possesses something beyond beauty: it has grandeur and wit. Watch her as Addison tells us that "the part for which Eve Harrington is receiving the Sarah Siddons award was intended originally for Margo Channing." Margo pours herself a stiff drink of Scotch. Addison offers some soda to dilute it, prompting her to look at the bottle, and at him, as if it were a tarantula and he had gone mad. The conflict between Margo and Eve is set up in a gesture and a glance. Ms. Davis, in case you may have forgotten, knows how to execute a close-up.

Which brings us to Anne Baxter as Eve. Many people believe Davis lost a much-deserved third Oscar (Judy Holliday was a surprise winner for *Born Yesterday*) because Baxter put herself in contention against Davis as best actress instead of settling for the best supporting actress category, which she surely would have won. But this is awards silliness. It only seems fitting that Davis would do battle against the actress who played her bete noire in the film. For who could be more calculating than Eve, the "kid" who worms her way into Margo's life and then tries to steal her man—suitably, a director of Hollywood films—and her career? Baxter never had a meatier role or one she could invest with such dramatic flourish and subtle toxicity. "Eve," intones Addison, pouring oil over that single syllable until the name ululates with a Garden of Eden-like premonition of doom. "You know all about Eve. . . . what can there be to know that you don't know . . . ?"

All that's left, after that brilliant Mankiewicz prologue, is to let the story unfold through the point of view of three narrators: Addison, Karen, and Margo. The conflict between Margo and Eve is the heart of the film, but the script brims over with character and incident. There's the terrific Thelma Ritter as Birdie, Margo's all-seeing maid, who is onto Eve's sob-sister stories from the beginning: "Everything but the bloodhounds snappin' at her rear end." And the young Marilyn Monroe appears as Miss Caswell, introduced by Addison as "a graduate of the Copacabana School of Dramatic Arts." Monroe is on screen for only a few minutes but holds her own even in this school of sharks. "Why do they always look like unhappy rabbits?" she asks when she spies a producer at Margo's party. Monroe reads the line in a baby voice tinged with prescient sadness.

The party is the film's centerpiece. "The general atmosphere is very Macbethish," Lloyd observes correctly. Margo has had it with Eve and is about to explode. "Fasten your seat belts, it's going to be a bumpy night." The line is famous, but it's Davis who makes it so. It's a lesson in acting to watch her build up to those words, stopping first to belt down her martini, swoop up a staircase, and turn midway—eyes flashing—until the guests are all at attention. A bumpy night, indeed.

The main bump in Mankiewicz script comes in Margo's speech to Karen about being a female. "In the last analysis, nothing is any good unless you can look up just before dinner or turn around in bed—and there he is. Without that, you're not a woman." Of course, *All About Eve* predates the feminist movement, but those words turn to ashes in Margo's mouth, and in Davis's (though she married

Gary Merrill after filming was completed). Perhaps Mankiewicz meant us to believe that Margo was kidding herself, her words a momentary reaction to turning forty. The scene certainly plays better if seen that way. And an earlier moment at the party validates that interpretation as Margo talks about males and aging: "Bill's thirty-two. He looks thirty-two. He looked it five years ago. He'll look it twenty years from now. I hate men."

Above all, *All About Eve* is a tale of theater folk. "We are a breed apart from the rest of humanity," says Addison, whose affair with Eve is less an exercise in sentiment than sado-masochism. When Eve threatens to leave him for Lloyd and laughs at his possessive attitude, Addison slaps her sharply. Eve goes to the door, opens it, and orders him out. Addison, ever the critic, offers a withering retort: "You're too short for that gesture." He also offers a list of what they have in common: "a contempt for humanity, an inability to love or be loved, insatiable ambition—and talent. We deserve each other."

Funny thing about great movies. Age only makes them seem fuller and richer. Mankiewicz would never again achieve such a pitch-perfect blend of wit and rueful wisdom. In the last scene, Eve becomes victimized by Phoebe (Barbara Bates), a young actress with a killer instinct to match hers, and the circle of vanity continues. In 1970, *All About Eve* became a rather diluted Broadway musical called *Applause,* in which Margo, played by Lauren Bacall, sings of the theater as a place where "painted trees and flowers grow/and laughter rings fortissimo/and treachery is sweetly done." The treachery of the theater has never been as sweetly or artfully done as it is by Mankiewicz and his cast of a lifetime in *All About Eve.* They know that true satire must draw blood as well as laughter. Take Margo's last words to Eve: "You can always put that award where your heart ought to be." Ouch.

Silence. Curtain.

Annie Hall (1977)

by Jay Carr

WHEN THEY WALK INTO A BOOKSTORE, she wants books about cats, he wants books about death. She, of course, is Diane Keaton as Annie Hall. He, of course, is Woody Allen, playing himself, sort of, yet dancing around some deft artistic contrivances in one of the great never-the-twain-shall-meet comedies.

Sweet, funny, rueful, bittersweet, *Annie Hall* draws upon the on-again, off-again relationship of Keaton and Allen in so-called real life. But it's as much about the limits of art as it is about the limits of their love affair. Allen's Alvy Singer and Keaton's Annie Hall end up apart. So, in the film, do life and art—the first with its inevitable disappointments, the second with its consolations—a dichotomy that Allen has explored repeatedly, often wistfully trying, as he says in *Annie Hall,* to get things to come out perfectly in art, because they usually don't in life.

Annie Hall is full of artful artlessness. Allen begins and ends the film by framing it with a pair of old Borscht Belt jokes. They're more than the security blanket of an artist who began performing as a stand-up comedian. In *Annie Hall,* Allen steps off confidently as a filmmaker, in charge of his material, knowing what he wants to do with it. As in his earlier film, *Play It Again, Sam,* he talks directly to the audience. After the parodies of *Sleeper* and *Love and Death,* his subject again is himself, but he's ready to explore it more deeply and deftly—and does, with more self-confrontation and less *shtick.*

The opening joke, the one about the woman complaining that a Catskills hotel's food is so terrible and the portions are so small, aptly mirrors his view of life. The last, about the man who says he can't afford to talk his deluded brother out of the belief that he's a chicken because the family needs the eggs, speaks to Allen's belief that we need our illusions—a belief that love can happen, a belief that art can happen, or both. The poignant joke in *Annie Hall* is that for Alvy, Allen's alter ego, love could have happened, but he's too insecure to allow it to. And Keaton's Annie is too neurotic to stand up under his vacillations.

Keaton launched a fashion mode in her men's hat, vest, tie, and slacks. But Annie plays against the assertive mannishness Hollywood had previously associated with women dressed as men. Unable to complete a sentence, speaking in self-deprecating fragments, smiling her way out of the verbal corners she paints herself into with what was to become her trademark "La-di-da," Keaton is the anti-Dietrich. Meanwhile, in his stammering but somehow always forward-pressing way, Allen became the new paradigm of the sexy leading man, a nerd who routed Hollywood's traditional he-men. Suddenly wit and sensitivity were what was sexy in a man. In the wake of such actors as Al Pacino and Dustin Hoffman supplanting the Rock Hudsons and Cary Grants, Allen not only was plugged into the zeitgeist; he became one of its shapers.

What comes through in repeated viewings is that Alvy *noodged* the relationship to death—and is unsparing enough of himself to say so. He's always at Annie, pecking away, questioning, urging her to improve herself. Apart from her insecurities, she puts up with him because he's bright. Once they get past their funny scene in which subtitles tell us how they're actually sizing one another up sexually as they exchange gassy pseudo-esthetic badinage about photography, he never lets up. It's almost inevitable that her first choice in the bookstore is going to be a book about cats. It's a subject she knows he can't control, a choice of subject she knows at some level will render him speechless. As in all great screwball comedies—and *Annie Hall* is one of them—an unpredictable woman upends a stuffy man.

That someone who looks and sounds like Allen would even have a serious chance at a relationship with someone like Keaton's Annie would have been unthinkable in a comedy of previous generations, despite the occasional romantic successes of a Buster Keaton or Charlie Chaplin. The scene in which Annie takes Alvy home to her family in Wisconsin, and he's convinced he's being stigmatized for his Jewishness, is a classic. But it's also at the root of the therapeutic influence Alvy represents. Unlike Alvy's Jewish family, featuring table talk at which everything and everybody were aired and bared, Annie's WASP family is repressed. One result is her brother Duane's barely contained rage, expressed in his violent fantasies, which give rise to the hilarious driving-to-the-airport-in-the-rain sequence, the hilarity arising from Alvy's deer-in-the-headlights expression behind the sweep of the windshield wipers as Duane looks murderously clenched and Annie looks oblivious.

Again and again, you want to yell at the screen and tell Alvy to just let up a little and leave Annie alone and things will go much better. But the stony avoidance of anything but banalities at the Hall dinner table is the reason Annie is such a neurotic mess, or, rather, the reason she's the kind of neurotic mess she is. She wants to be a singer but is too inhibited to fill her songs with the kind of emotion great singers summon. Her first performance of "Seems Like Old Times" rides a small, tentative voice, so quavery and exposed and naked that you writhe for her. At the end, Allen shows how Annie has grown in confidence by reprising Annie's vocal of "Seems Like Old Times." The song underpins the melancholy nostalgia of the ending, where Alvy and Annie meet as friends, not lovers. The second time Annie sings it, her voice has more confidence and poise. It's a barometer of her growth, if also a self-compliment to Alvy, the implication being that the relationship with him has helped free her.

Allen's final version of the script eliminated several surreal fantasy scenes in favor of the down-in-the-trenches flavor of what transpired between Alvy and Annie. He keeps the focus on Alvy's rueful surfeit of awareness and self-awareness. Audiences were charmed by *Annie Hall*, partly because of Allen's affection for New York (an affection that was to reach its apotheosis in *Manhattan*). Nobody mistook it for a sentimental romantic comedy, though. It's too complex, too bleak.

Even when it's being funny, as when Allen needles his own ego by stopping people in the street and talking to them about his love life, as if they know all about it, and care, *Annie Hall* remains true to its pessimism.

Extolling love even as he elbows it away, proclaiming the healing power of art even as he scorns its devices and artifices in the act of using them, Allen has it both ways. In conversationally engaging us in seemingly spontaneous asides about what we're to see, as if it's up for grabs, Allen and *Annie Hall* go Luigi Pirandello one better. The Italian playwright stood outside his work and commented on it in *Six Characters in Search of an Author. Annie Hall* is one character in search of an author—and finding him by looking into the mirror, then looking into the lens.

Ashes and Diamonds (1958)

by Peter Keough

HE SEIZES THE SCREEN as soon as he appears, and he knows it. Zbigniew Cybulski, "the Polish James Dean," lolls by the roadside taking in the pleasant morning, a smile on his baby face, his eyes shut, a machine gun and a pair of dark glasses by his side, waiting to kill. As Maciek, the playfully nihilistic antihero of Andrzej Wajda's 1958 *Ashes and Diamonds,* he embodies everything irresistible and awful about youth, romanticism, Polish history, and the movies. Wajda's alter ego, Cybulski burns brightly in what is the seminal masterpiece of Polish cinema and one of the greatest films of all time.

His moment in the sun is brief, for their target approaches. "I am used to waiting for greater things," Maciek mutters, not for the last time, and springs into action. Those greater things, it would seem, have already been accomplished. Based on a controversial 1948 novel by coscreenwriter Jerzy Andrzejewski, the film takes place on May 8, 1945: Germany has surrendered, Poland has been liberated by the Soviets, peace reigns in Europe. But Maciek and his commanding officer Andrzej (Adam Pawlikowski) are among the last remnants of the Home Army, the anticommunist underground for whom this is no victory, for whom fighting to the death against the new tyranny is all that matters. Their legacy is that of the cavalry lancers who charged invading German Panzers in 1939: recklessly courageous, anachronistic, doomed, and absurd.

So the war rages on. In a brutal, nearly surreal sequence they ambush a car they believe to be carrying Szczuka (Waclaw Zastrzezynski), the Soviet-trained commissar appointed to take charge of the region. One of the survivors, a terrified young man, flees to a nearby church, pounding on the locked door. Grinning demonically, Maciek empties his weapon on him. The youth's back bursts into flame, the door opens, and he falls dead inside.

Wajda savors such ironies. The killings, for example, prove pointless, even by the perpetrators' benighted standards. They killed the wrong man. This futility, though, only intensifies the desperate, evanescent beauty of the scenario, and the grotesque violence establishes motifs repeated throughout the film. Wajda illustrates the existential tragedy that unfolds over the next eighteen-hour period with images of fire and destruction, with Christian iconography and symbols of Poland's tortured past and crumbling traditions, with emblems of death, redemption, and rebirth. They spring into the foreground and background of Krzysztof Winiewicz's deep-focus, black-and-white cinematography like troubled thoughts. And at their center is the fallen angel face of Cybulski.

Unaware of their mistake. Maciek and Andrzej head to town to rest and celebrate at the Monopol, a fleabag Grand Hotel where people come and go and most are carrying weapons and agendas. As Andrzej in close-up phones in news of the mission's success to their superior, we see Maciek clowning around in the middle distance while in the far corner, emerging from the doorway like their worst nightmare, enters the unscathed Szczuka. Maciek, though, has the presence of mind to book a room adjacent to their intended victim. That night the local officials are joining their Soviet allies in a banquet at the hotel celebrating the war's end. In the drunken confusion at the end of the party, Maciek will finish the job.

He used to wait for greater things. Sometimes, though, great things come unexpectedly. Like Krystyna (Ewa Krzyzewska), the pretty barmaid whom Maciek teases as he and Andrzej kill time. He's just flirting, and he knows it has no future, but he makes her promise to drop by later that night during her break, just squeezing her in before he has to "do his man." He promptly forgets, and when she does in fact make the rendezvous, Maciek must discreetly hide some stray ordnance before getting down to the business at hand.

Their postcoital moment, lying on the bed and talking with dreaminess and dread of what could be but probably won't, is one of the few sequences in the film in which Wajda allows close-ups unchallenged by expressionist intrusions into the frame. Of course, this privileged space disintegrates. The hobbling footsteps of the victim returning to his room interrupt their sweet nothings. A wounded bear of a man, an antifascist veteran who fought as a Polish volunteer in the

Spanish Civil War, Szczuka wants all the more to reconcile the internecine factions of postwar Poland because his own son fights for the other side. Their neighbor's disquiet destroys the illusion of love and peace, reminding Maciek of his murderous duty only hours away.

Not that there is any shortage of such reminders. Earlier at the hotel, Maciek pours shots for each of his fallen comrades and sets them alight; lost in reminiscence, he turns around, and the tiny flames in the foreground form the same pattern on his back as those on the poor man he had executed in the film's opening scenes. Then there is Szczuka's problem with matches; he never seems to have any, and whenever he fumbles to light up a cigarette Maciek always seems to be on hand to provide. This running routine culminates with a macabre turn on the old "three on a match" superstition and one of the most baleful fireworks displays in movies.

The centerpiece of these mementi mori takes place when Maciek and Krystyna have escaped from the hotel only to run into a rainstorm. They seek shelter in a ruined church, this time unlocked, and separated by one of the ugliest crucifixes in human history, a gothic horror hanging upside down from the ceiling, Maciek almost confesses to Krystyna his dilemma, assuring her that he can "change" some things. She finds an old inscription on the wall and, aided by his light, reads the poem by the nineteenth-century Polish émigré Norwid that gives the film its title and ends with the lines:

> . . . will the ashes hold the glory of a starlike diamond
> The morning star of everlasting triumph?

Probably not, since moments later the smitten pair discover that the church is a crypt in which the assassins' victims lie in state. Everyone loves a glorious loser, however, especially one as sexy as Cybulski, and if the truth be told Wajda himself, though deftly chiding the nationalist side's delusions and arrogance ("in the Colonel's house we can forget the ugliness outside," says a dinner guest at Maciek and Andrzej's superior's house, though a china set visibly rattles from the Soviet tanks rumbling on the street), he might be rooting a little for the home team. His father, after all, was a cavalryman and apparently one of the thousands of Polish officers massacred by Soviets in the Katyn Forest in 1939.

And so the images one recalls from this film do not inspire moderation and practicality and compromise with the powers that be, but the sublimity of lost causes and quick deaths. A white steed, a specter of those lancers lost defying the Nazi blitzkrieg, steps out of nowhere into a rainy alley and is ignored (such a horse will have the starring role in Wajda's next film, *Lotna*). A hand emerges from behind a clothesline and blood oozes over the sheet: it is the red and white Polish flag, it is the shadow and light of a movie screen. When Maciek flees across a field of garbage to catch a train (as would Cybulski himself in real life in 1967; he would fall between the cars, dead at forty), we don't think of him as discarded on the ash heap of history but as crystallized into a starlike diamond, the everlasting triumph of art.

L'Atalante (1934)

by Terrence Rafferty

JEAN VIGO, WHO DIED IN 1934 at the age of twenty-nine, was one of the greatest artists in the history of the movies—and probably the most tantalizing. His body of work consists of a pair of short documentaries, a forty-seven-minute fiction film (*Zero for Conduct*), and one full-length feature—all told, less than three hours of finished film. The feature, *L'Atalante,* was released in Paris in September 1934 (just three weeks before Vigo's death), in a version the filmmaker had never seen: the distributor had cut the movie by almost a third, added a mediocre popular song, and then, for good measure, retitled the picture *Le Chaland Qui Passe,* after the new tune. *L'Atalante* was largely restored in 1940, but it has retained over the years the aura of something fragile and patched up, and that quality of seeming slightly damaged is perhaps what has made it for many viewers an object of special devotion: it's a movie that people see again and again and love in ways they find difficult to explain. Now *L'Atalante* has been given another major renovation. This version, prepared by Pierre Philippe and Jean-Louis Bompoint, adds about nine minutes of footage not included in the previous reconstruction, and the restorers discovered in the archives of the British Film Institute a pristine nitrate print of a cut of the movie that obviously preceded the distributor's intervention; *L'Atalante* now looks and sounds better than ever. (The prints that have been circulating for the last fifty years are uniformly atrocious.) Thanks to Philippe and Bompoint, we can see all the lucid beauties of Boris Kaufman's cinematography, rather than have to struggle to imagine them, and hear Maurice Jaubert's lovely score without distortion; we can even make out the dialogue, which in previous prints was often just a low rumble of undifferentiated sound. But the best thing about this shiny new *L'Atalante* is that for all the restorers' diligence, the film is still messy, imperfect, defiantly incomplete. Like everything Vigo did, like his frustratingly brief career, *L'Atalante* is an unfinished product, unsuitable for framing: even in its current spruced-up condition, it's essentially a collection of inspired fragments, the sketchbook of an artist whose imagination was, and will forever remain, gloriously immature.

This movie was, in part, Vigo's attempt to "grow up" as a filmmaker—to make a conventional commercial picture. His previous film, *Zero for Conduct,* about a revolt in a boys' boarding school, was a celebration of the pure freedom of children's imaginations, a stirring expression of resistance to the forces of authority and order—to anything that would impose discipline on the diverse, unruly energy of play. *Zero for Conduct* isn't constructed like an ordinary movie; Vigo evidently considered the discipline of narrative a form of repression, too, and his indifference to it has a lot to do with why *Zero for Conduct* still seems, almost six decades later, like one of the few truly subversive movies ever made. And the French censors—as alert to insubordination as the dwarf headmaster and the malevolent instructors who rule the world of Vigo's schoolboys—banned the movie from public exhibition. For *L'Atalante,* Vigo agreed to work within the constraints of a simple and apparently innocuous story (from an original scenario by an undistinguished writer named Jean Guinée). Jean (Jean Dasté), the captain of a river barge named *L'Atalante,* marries Juliette (Dita Parlo), a girl from one of the villages on the barge's route. As the newlyweds travel down the river, Juliette becomes increasingly restless and disenchanted; she has escaped from her village, but all she's seeing of the world is riverbanks, the inside of cramped cabins, and her husband and his odd crew—a rambunctious old salt called Père Jules (Michel Simon) and a quiet cabin boy (Louis Lefèvre). Bored and impatient, she sneaks off to see the sights of Paris, but when she returns to the place where the barge was docked she discovers that Jean has shoved off without her. She wanders on the shore, he drifts downstream on the boat, and the separation makes them both miserable. Finally, they find each other again; life resumes its intended course.

The miracle of *L'Atalante* is that Vigo keeps breaking free of the story's ordained course: he's incapable of simply riding that dull, even current and making only the scheduled stops. He treats the story the way a jazz musician treats a popular song, improvising on the melody by plunging into its carefully sequenced chords and predictable rhythms and taking them apart to see what they're made of. He hits notes that we had never dreamed were there but that seem, once we've heard them, pure and essential, like pearls dredged from far beneath the smooth, lulling flow of the song. In one of the film's most sublime sequences, Jean, aching from the absence of Juliette, dives off the barge into the river because his bride once told him that you see the face of the one you love when you look under the surface of the water. Jean has tried the trick a couple of times before, jokingly and unsuccessfully, but this time—now that he is abandoned, mad with grief, reckless—he sees her luminous in her wedding dress, and laughing with an unforced, innocent joy that looks like the sweetest of invitations, the promise of every kind of pleasure. The floating images of Juliette superimposed on Jean's desperate, searching face are reminders of some of our earlier views of her and especially of a ghostly image of the bride in her white dress walking slowly along the top of the barge as it glides down the river at twilight. In the underwater sequence, Jean seems, at last, to be seeing his wife the way Vigo has seen her from the start—as an ordinary woman who becomes radiant when she is looked at with desire. This sequence tells us most of what we need to know about Vigo's eroticized approach to the art of moviemaking: he forgets his orders, immerses himself in the ordinary beauties of the sensual world, and summons up visions that shine with the possibilities of earthly pleasure.

The other key to Vigo is his attraction to chaos, clutter, sheer profusion—a quality that is, in a sense, just another side of his eroticism. The toys and gadgets and bric-a-brac that fill his movies are played with and caressed by the camera with such loving attention that they seem like fetishes. And there are so *many* of them—so many objects to divert us from the implacable responsibilities of living, so many beautiful distractions. Père Jules's cabin, overrun by cats and jammed with bizarre mementos that are the residue of a full and gleefully disorderly life, is the image not only of its inhabitant but also of its creator. This museum of useless things—with which, in a long and brilliantly sustained sequence, the old sailor enchants Juliette—is Vigo's world in miniature, a place where something to tickle the imagination or to stir memories or simply to gaze at in wonder is always ready to hand. And the character itself, as it is conceived by Vigo and played by the magnificently peculiar Simon, is the presiding spirit of the movie: Père Jules is a comic metaphor for the diversity of the world's riches; he is—in his demented, random way—a living encyclopedia. At one point, he gets excited, and all sorts of strange stuff bubbles out of him with startling alacrity: Indian war whoops, bullfighting moves, snippets of songs and dances from Russia, Africa, the Orient. (He takes us around the world in about eighty seconds.) His body is covered with crudely drawn tattoos, and in one of the most welcome of the newly restored shots he amuses Juliette by making a face tattooed on his belly appear to smoke by putting a cigarette in his navel. Père Jules is, of course, a child, both splendid and monstrous, and there is, too, something profoundly childlike about the way the character is conceived: only a very innocent eye could see this crazy old drifter as the epitome of worldly experience.

Vigo may have been trying, with some part of himself, to make a "normal" movie—one conventional enough, at least, to get past the censors and into the commercial cinemas—but L'Atalante shows how hopelessly, wonderfully unsuited he was to popular moviemaking. His storytelling is still casual, almost perfunctory: the narrative will slow to a languorous drift, then abruptly begin chugging forward, then stop to give us a long look at some unanticipated marvel off in the distance, then lurch irritably ahead again. And his approach to composition and editing is so personal that audiences expecting an ordinary movie might become disoriented: shots are taken from unexpected angles, are held longer than usual, are juxtaposed with other shots in unprecedented ways. Vigo was helplessly original; he seems at times to be speaking a different language from other filmmakers. (On seeing Vigo's work for the first time, James Agee wrote, "It is as if he had invented the wheel.") He is the most playful and the least rigid of the great film artists; he had the liveliest eye and, perhaps, the freest imagination. Everything he shows us looks mysteriously new, full of possibilities, and so encourages us to linger on it, investigate it, dream it, have our way with it.

In a sense, the restorers' work on L'Atalante springs from impulses like those—from the feeling, evoked at virtually every moment in Vigo's films, that there's something more for us to discover. The latest version of L'Atalante is new only in the sense that this movie has always seemed new; it isn't changed in any fundamental way. The footage added by Philippe and Bompoint is just extra stuff, beautiful and inessential and thus fully in keeping with the movie's expansive spirit. They've given us a few more glittery things to hoard in our imagination and fondle in our memories when life gets a little dull. In Jean Vigo's movies, greater profusion only creates stronger desire: his images seduce us with the promise of a larger, richer world and unbounded freedom to roam in it—the promise, that is, of endless stimulation, inexhaustible sensations. There can be no definitive L'Atalante, because the world of Vigo's films subverts the very idea of definition. This extraordinary movie will always elude our attempts to grasp it and keep it in its place: we'll never see everything in Père Jules's cabin; the image of the woman in the water disperses when we try to embrace it, then forms itself again and leads us on.

The Bank Dick (1940)

by Henry Sheehan

"DON'T BE A LUDDY-DUDDLY. Don't be a moon calf. Don't be a jabber-now. You're not those, are you?"

That's not an excerpt from a Joycean interior monologue, but a line of criminal seduction from *The Bank Dick,* a 1940 comedy written by and starring W.C. Fields. Fields delivers the line in the person of a slovenly bank guard named Edgar Sousé, pronounced not "souse" but "sou-zay, accent grave on the 'e'" as he painstakingly and repeatedly points out. Everything about Sousé is as misleading and inflated as that accent, though very little of it could be called grave. A middle-class homeowner despite his apparent lack of a job, he spends his days at the bar of the Black Pussy Café (yes, you read it right), a refuge from his household harridans, wife, mother-in-law, marriageable daughter, and younger daughter (who routinely throws bottles at the back of her father's head).

Sousé's—and Fields's—very appearance was a Groszian-sized exaggeration of middle-class complacency. Always fat, at this late stage in his career Fields was as round and heavy-looking as a beachball filled with cement. His nose was bulbous to an extraordinary degree and his eyes swum in rheum damned behind a permanent, fleshy squint.

Despite all that, Edgar and his creator are immensely likable. Somehow, they have become victims of that very bourgeois complacency that was supposed to buoy them up. Yet Edgar prospers only through luck and the very quick appropriation of it. He only got his job, for example, because a bank robber ran into the bus-stop bench he was occupying at the time and his future son-in-law mistook his tumble for a flying tackle.

More important, Edgar is a relatively honest man. All he really wants is to be left alone to drink and get drunk (his alcohol abuse is almost shocking by today's standards). But all around him, middle-class cupidity runs rampant. The women in his house want him not just to make more money but to achieve the respectability that comes along with it. No sooner does Edgar land his job than he's targeted by a smooth-talking con man, J. Frothingham Waterbury (Russell Hicks), who wants to unload some worthless stock on him.

It's that crooked smooth talk, plus the pressure to succeed, and his own desire to live out the life of a wealthy, work-free drunk, that finally provokes Edgar into jabberwockian pleading quoted above.

Today, Fields is probably the least appreciated comedian in Hollywood cinema, a condition he himself lived to endure. But at one time, he was one of the biggest figures in show business, with a Dickensian background to rival that of Charlie Chapin.

Born to a pushcart fruit peddler who had immigrated to Philadelphia from England, Fields (born William Claude Duckenfield or Duckinfield), ran away from home at age eleven. He had been abused as a child, and it's not clear whether the cause of his running away was that he hit his father with a shovel or his father hit him. At any rate, he had already formed his ambition to be the world's greatest juggler, and he practiced for years as he lived in the streets, getting into scrapes with the police and enduring beatings from toughs. Fields would say later that his nose was as swollen as it was thanks to a particularly savage pummeling.

By fourteen, Fields was juggling professionally and by twenty-two was touring Europe and appearing before England's royal family. He made his Broadway debut in 1915, became one of the headlining mainstays of the annual Ziegfeld Follies, and, in 1923, starred in the Broadway hit *Poppy*. Along the way, the comic patter Fields used to accompany his juggling took over his persona, and the juggling became a humorous, if marvelous, ornament to his comedy.

In 1925, after having appeared in a couple of shorts, Fields brought *Poppy* to the movie screen as *Sally of the Sawdust,* directed by no less than D.W. Griffith. Most of the themes and characterizations that would appear in Fields's films (at least the many he wrote under a variety of obvious pseudonyms; the credit on *The Bank Dick* reads "Mahatma Kane Jeeves") were already present in *Sally.*

Fields played a con artist in that one, a role he would sometimes broaden to include shady circus owners. Yet, veteran vaudevillian that he was, Fields had a healthy distrust of his middle-class audience and did not cede them the moral high ground. Fields apparently lost a lot of money in various financial schemes pressed on him by respectable types, and he disdained what he considered the hypocrisy of a greedy, grasping middle class. What could have been just healthy contempt, though, had a bitter tinge to it, one irrigated by the alcohol he consumed more and more often.

Fields's alcoholism is mostly treated as a biographical detail, an important cause in his decline from the leading man in a D.W. Griffith production, with stops at first-class studios (Paramount, MGM), before declining to the status of minor attraction at Universal, at the time a B-studio (and which soon pushed Fields aside in favor of Abbott and Costello, at that).

But Fields's boozy temperament and consciousness are at the very heart of his best pictures: *The Bank Dick*, *The Old-Fashioned Way* (1934), *Never Give a Sucker and Even Break* (1941), and maybe especially *It's a Gift* (1934). It's been observed that the episodic nature of Fields's films follows the skit structure of the Ziegfeld Follies and, to a lesser extent, a vaudeville bill. The theory goes that Fields incorporated this structure into his own movies.

But Fields didn't produce those pictures; he appeared in them. Why not say he was just as influenced by the formal structure of his biggest stage success, *Poppy*? In fact, Fields's most personal, most scattered-seeming comedies do have a structure, albeit a surreal, internalized, and heavily inebriated one.

The Bank Dick's seventy-two minutes, for example, open with Edgar Sousé making a fairly theatrical entrance, coming down the stairs of his home after we've watched the women in his life pick over his faults over breakfast. As he enters the scene, he performs one of his physical routines, using only his tongue to flip a lit cigarette into his mouth and hide it from his wife (later, he'll show other cigarette tricks to a bunch of children, the only scene in the movie in which he doesn't show outright hostility to children).

He goes out, ambles down to the Black Pussy, has a conversation with the bartender and his bottle of whiskey ("Take your hat off in the presence of a gentleman," he mutters as he uncorks it), and, after a few drinks, regales a man with stories of his career in show business. His audience turns out to be a production manager for a film on location (the action takes place in Lompoc, a real California town), and before you know it, Edgar has been hired to fill in for a drunken director named A. Pismo Clam.

The movie itself turns out to be a weird effort, with a six-and-a-half-foot-tall leading man and a four-foot-tall leading lady in evening dress turning up for shooting on Lompoc's dusty streets. Edgar decides to improvise a college football picture out of it, but before he can put his plans into effect, a series of mishaps—some perpetrated by his family—cost him the job. It's then that he repairs to the bus-stop bench where he luckily encounters the fleeing bank robbers.

Though probably unintentionally, these scenes recapitulate Fields's career: He runs away from his family (though wife and mother-in-law rather than father), he entertains some folks with his verbal dexterity (though at a bar rather than on a stage), then somehow finds himself directing a movie on which the director is treated like a maharajah. Then, thanks to some mishaps not entirely of his own making, he loses his job and then wins another, albeit less prestigious, one.

As wild as the material is, it's treated in a matter-of-fact way. *The Bank Dick's* director, Edward Cline, was a former Mack Sennett Keystone Kop and slapstick two-reeler director (as was another frequent Fields collaborator, director A. Edward Sutherland) and his style was, to put it nicely, simple and straightforward—almost primitive.

While this didn't exactly elevate Fields's comedy, a study of it does put the lie to the critical truism that Fields's comedy was primarily verbal. Fields's comedy started first and foremost with his own bulbous appearance (one of Fields's best directors, Norman Z. McLeod, was a former animator, used to working with such caricatured shapes). The contrast between his appearance and other, sometimes equally caricatured figures, is his first line of comic attack. Then throw in the ever-present bits of physical business—he was forever fooling with his hat—and you have laughs before you ever have dialogue. Cline's simple, medium-shot, extended-take approach resulted in perfect, squared-off framing for Fields's unique humor. It's an approach very much in keeping with Charles Dickens or an illustration by Phiz.

After Edgar gets the bank job, the movie's plot really flies. Edgar has semi-innocently lassoed his would-be son-in-law and bank teller, Og Oggilby—played by that lisping, six-foot-tall pile of putty, Grady Sutton—into his stock scheme, a misstep that sends Edgar into a vortex of complications. The best involve a bank examiner played by the wonder-comic character actor Franklin Pangborn, whom Edgar momentarily sidelines with a Mickey Finn.

But Edgar's misdemeanors always pale next to the felonious nature of middle-class life. Edgar asks a physician how business is, and the man of medicine harrumphs wistfully, "Fair, fair. I don't suppose we'll ever get a whooping cough epidemic again."

That Fields can sweeten this bile enough to make us laugh is the miracle of his comedy. Perhaps it's best not to worry about how he does it and take his—or Edgar's—advice: "I'll do the worrying. Be happy, I say."

The Battleship Potemkin (1925)

by Roger Ebert

THE BATTLESHIP POTEMKIN HAS BEEN SO FAMOUS for so long that it is almost impossible to come to it with a fresh eye. It is one of the fundamental landmarks of cinema. Its famous massacre on the Odessa Steps has been quoted so many times in other films (notably in *The Untouchables*) that it's likely many viewers will have seen the parody before they see the original. The film once had such power that it was banned in many nations, including its native Soviet Union. Governments actually believed it could incite audiences to action. If today it seems more like a technically brilliant but simplistic "cartoon" (Pauline Kael's description in a favorable review), that may be because it has worn out its element of surprise—that, like the 23rd Psalm or Beethoven's *Fifth*, it has become so familiar we cannot perceive it for what it is.

Having said that, let me say that *Potemkin*, which I have seen many times and taught using a shot-by-shot approach, did come alive for me the other night, in an unexpected time and place. The movie was projected on a big screen hanging from the outside wall of the Vickers Theater in Three Oaks, Michigan, and some 300 citizens settled into their folding chairs in the parking lot to have a look at it. The simultaneous musical accompaniment was by Concrete, a southwestern Michigan band. Under the stars on a balmy summer night, far from film festivals and cinematheques, Sergei Eisenstein's 1925 revolutionary call generated some of its legendary rabble-rousing power.

It's not that anybody stood up and sang "The Internationale." The folding chairs for this classic exercise in Soviet propaganda were on loan from the local Catholic church. Some audience members no doubt drove over to Oink's in New Buffalo afterward for ice-cream cones. But the film did have headlong momentum, thrilling juxtapositions, and genuine power to move—most especially during the Odessa Steps sequence, which had some viewers gasping out loud.

The movie was ordered up by the Russian revolutionary leadership for the twentieth anniversary of the Potemkin Uprising, which Lenin had hailed as the first proof that troops could be counted on to join the proletariat in overthrowing the old order.

As sketched by Eisenstein's film, the crewmembers of the battleship, cruising the Black Sea after returning from the war with Japan, are mutinous because of poor rations. There is a famous close-up of their breakfast meat, crawling with maggots. After officers throw a tarpaulin over the rebellious ones and order them to be shot, a firebrand named Vakulinchuk cries out, "Brothers! Who are you shooting at?" The firing squad lowers its guns, and when an officer unwisely tries to enforce his command, full-blown mutiny takes over the ship.

Onshore, news of the uprising reaches citizens who have long suffered under czarist repression. They send food and water out to the battleship in a flotilla of skiffs. Then, in one of the most famous sequences ever put on film, czarist troops march down a long flight of steps, firing on the citizens who flee before them in a terrified tide. Countless innocents are killed, and the massacre is summed up in the image of a woman shot dead trying to protect her baby in a carriage—which then bounces down the steps, out of control.

That there was, in fact, no czarist massacre on the Odessa Steps scarcely diminishes the power of the scene. The czar's troops shot innocent civilians elsewhere in Odessa, and Eisenstein, in concentrating those killings and finding the perfect setting for them, was doing his job as a director. It is ironic that he did it so well that today the bloodshed on the Odessa Steps is often referred to as if it really happened.

News of the uprising reaches the Russian fleet, which speeds toward Odessa to put it down. The *Potemkin* and a destroyer, also commanded by revolutionaries, steam out to meet them. Eisenstein creates tension by cutting between the approach fleet, the brave *Potemkin*, and details of the onboard preparation. At the last moment, the men of the *Potemkin* signal their comrades in the fleet to join them— and the *Potemkin* steams among the oncoming ships without a shot being fired at it.

The Battleship Potemkin is conceived as class-conscious revolutionary propaganda, and Eisenstein deliberately avoids creating any three-dimensional individuals (even Vakulinchuk is seen largely as a symbol). Instead, masses of men move in unison, as in the many shots looking down at *Potemkin's* foredeck. The people of Odessa, too, are seen as a mass made up of many briefly glimpsed but starkly seen faces. The dialogue (in title cards) is limited mostly to outrage and exhortation. There is no personal drama to counterbalance the larger political drama.

Eisenstein (1898–1948) was a student and advocate of Soviet theories of film montage, which argued that film has its greatest impact not by the smooth unrolling of images but by their juxtaposition. Sometimes the cutting is dialectical: point, counterpoint, fusion. Cutting between the fearful faces of the unarmed citizens and the faceless troops in uniform, he created an argument for the people against the czarist state. Many other cuts are as abrupt: After *Potemkin's* captain threatens to hang mutineers from the yardarm, we see ghostly figures hanging there. As the people call out, "Down with the tyrants!" we see clenched fists. To emphasize that the shooting victims were powerless to flee, we see one revolutionary citizen without legs. As the troops march ahead, a military boot crushes a child's hand. In a famous set of shots, a citizen is seen with eyeglasses; when we cut back, one of the glasses has been pierced by a bullet.

Eisenstein felt that montage should proceed from rhythm, not story. Shots should be cut to lead up to a point and should not linger because of personal interest in individual characters. Most of the soundtracks I've heard with *Potemkin* do not follow this theory and instead score the movie as a more conventional silent drama. Concrete, the Michigan band (Boyd Nutting, Jon Yazell, Andrew Lersten), underlined and reinforced Eisenstein's approach with an insistent, rhythmic, repetitive score, using keyboards, half-heard snatches of speech, cries and choral passages, percussion, martial airs, and found sounds. It was an aggressive, insistent approach, played loud, by musicians who saw themselves as Eisenstein's collaborators, not his meek accompanists.

It was the music, I think, along with the unusual setting, that was able to break through my long familiarity with *Battleship Potemkin* and make me understand, better than ever before, why this movie was long considered dangerous. (It was banned at various times in the United States and France, and for a longer time than any other film in British history; even Stalin banned it, at a time when mutiny was against the party line.)

The fact is, *Potemkin* doesn't really stand alone but depends for its power upon the social situation in which it is shown. In prosperous peacetime, it is a curiosity. If it had been shown in China at the time of Tiananmen Square, I imagine it would have been inflammatory. It was voted the greatest film of all time at the Brussels, Belgium, World's Fair in 1958 (ironically, the very year *Citizen Kane* had its great re-release and went to the top of the list for the next forty years). The Cold War was at its height in 1958, and many European leftists still subscribed to the Marxist prescription for society; *Potemkin* for them had a power, too.

But it suffers when it is seen apart from its context (just as *The Graduate,* by striking the perfect note for 1967, strikes a dated note now). It needs the right audience. In a sense, the band Concrete supplied a virtual audience; the loud, passionate, ominous music by the three young musicians worked as an impassioned audience response does, to carry and hurry the other watchers along. *Battleship Potemkin* is no longer considered the greatest film ever made, but it is obligatory for anyone interested in film history, and the other night in that small-town parking lot I got a sense, a stirring, of the buried power it still contains, awaiting a call.

The Birth of a Nation (1915)

by Dave Kehr

WHEN D.W. GRIFFITH'S *The Birth of a Nation* was re-released in 1921, only six years after its premiere, the advertising posters proclaimed it an "American

Institution." It has been one ever since, for better—in that it gave birth to the movies as an industry, a cultural force, and a social power—and for worse, in that the film contains perhaps the most virulently racist imagery ever to appear in a motion picture.

Griffith's Civil War epic cannot be forgiven for its portrayal of African Americans as sex-crazed animals, the Radical Republicans who led the Reconstruction as their deluded patsies, and the Ku Klux Klan as an army of heroes, gallantly riding to the defense of the nation.

But neither can Griffith's great artistry be denied. When Woodrow Wilson famously declared that *The Birth of a Nation* was "like history written with lightning," he captured something essential about Griffith's filmmaking: here is a work that crackles with electricity, that that eschews the three-act dramatic form of the Victorian stage in favor of a strikingly modern, nonliterary form of narration, founded in an ebb and flow of energy, an expansion and dilation of space, a rush of images and a cascade of emotion that quite clearly transcend the broken-backed plot, the stereotypical characters, and the melodramatic situations.

The Birth of a Nation put an end to a certain kind of popular theater and elevated in its place a medium that had, until then, been largely a novelty attraction headed from vaudeville theaters to sideshows. An industry grounded in one- and two-reelers was transformed within a couple of years into an industry of feature films; storefront nickelodeons grew into lavish movie palaces, and movies became the preferred entertainment to the emerging American middle class—all because of Griffith's film.

Born in 1875 in La Grange, Kentucky, Griffith was the son of a Civil War veteran, a former colonel who enjoyed recounting his wartime adventures to his son. Among the more than 500 short films he made for the American Biograph Company between 1908 and 1913 are several Civil War dramas, in which Griffith can be seen developing the contrast between epic scale and intimate drama that would inform *The Birth of a Nation* and set the formula for most of the epic film-making that came after it.

The film was based on a hoary stage play which the Reverend Thomas F. Dixon Jr. had adapted from two of his novels, *The Clansman: A Historical Romance of the Ku Klux Klan* and *The Leopard's Spots*. Griffith enlisted the help of his old Biograph associate Frank E. Woods in "arranging" the story, as the opening credits put it—Griffith himself being notorious for working without a finalized scenario. By keeping the structure of the film in his head, and by being able to constantly revise and improvise as he worked with his actors on location, Griffith achieved a spontaneity and vivacity that few of his contemporaries could equal and none could surpass.

The Birth of a Nation is structured as a series of oppositions. On the epic, historical level, Griffith posits North vs. South, the Union vs. the Confederacy, war vs. peace, and black vs. white. On the intimate, dramatic level, similar oppositions are played out in interpersonal terms: the contrast of North and South becomes the contrast between the Stoneman family, intellectuals who live in stuffy, book-lined quarters in urban Washington (the character of Austin Stoneman, played by Ralph Lewis, is based on the Radical Republican senator Thaddeus Stevens), and the Camerons, plantation owners who live in the idyllic small town of Piedmont. The political tension between the Union and the Confederacy becomes the interpersonal tension that develops between romantic couples, notably Elsie Stoneman (Lillian Gish), the senator's daughter, and Ben Cameron, the eldest of the three Cameron sons, who has seen Elsie only in a photograph but has fallen hopelessly in love with her.

For Griffith, war is associated with the aggressive North, personified by the arrogant, cigar-smoking Ulysses S. Grant in the historical tableaux, and on the personal level by Congressman Stoneman's conniving assistant Silas Lynch, a power-crazed mulatto who intends to plunder the defeated Confederacy.

Peace is the province of the South, where an intertitle announcing "Hostilities" is followed by a shot of kittens and puppies wrestling. (Suggestively, Elsie is also associated with a kitten on her first entrance, foreshadowing her suitability as a mate for Ben.) It takes only one shot for Griffith to establish the tranquility and stability of Southern life: a view down the tiny main street of Piedmont, with the local church dominating the background and the Cameron mansion, a modest affair with a brace of white columns in front, dominating the right side of the screen. The left side of the screen belongs to the dirt road, which bears a traffic of happy slaves, presumably on their way to a pleasant day's work picking cotton.

Most commentators place the black/white opposition at the center of The Birth of a Nation, and it is certainly its most conspicuous component. But behind it lies another contrasting pair—the opposition of male and female. Griffith's "blacks," many of whom are played by Caucasians in burnt-cork makeup, are predominantly large, stocky men—not for Griffith is the feminized slave culture of Gone with the Wind, where the black population seems to consist of round, motherly women, bent old men, and irresponsible children. For Griffith, blackness is associated with male sexual power, with violence, and with rape.

Griffith's white Southerners, on the other hand, are predominantly feminine. The Camerons appear to be a matriarchal clan, dominated by a strong-willed, independent woman, Mrs. Cameron (Josephine Crowell), who takes the initiative to go to Washington to search for the wounded Ben in a government hospital while her biblically bearded husband, Dr. Cameron (Spottiswoode Aitken), stays behind, too weak to leave his easy chair. Ben's two younger brothers, Wade (George Beranger) and Duke (Maxfield Stanley) are barely more than boys; the dominant siblings are the two daughters, Margaret (Miriam Cooper), the eldest and an elegant embodiment of "the manners of the old school," and Flora (Mae Marsh), a wide-eyed innocent with blonde curls and an irrepressible, childlike energy.

By right, Ben Cameron should be the dashing, manly hero of the piece, but instead Griffith has made him a strangely effeminate figure, played by the diminutive, delicate Henry B. Walthall. Nicknamed "The Little Colonel," he is first presented as a dandy wearing a top hat and twirling a cane. Injured in battle, he is later found lying back in a hospital bed, a large white bandage covering a symbolic head wound. Ben only regains his stature and potency when he puts on the flowing white robes of the Klan.

Duke, the youngest Cameron brother, bonds with the junior Stoneman through some blatantly homoerotic horseplay and hugging; later, they will die together on the battlefield in each other's arms, kissing each other on the lips. This is not to suggest any homophobia on Griffith's part—such physical expressions of affection are common in early films and these characters are, in any case, among the film's most positive.

But there is a sense on Griffith's part of a masculinity that desperately needs to be curbed—a masculinity brutally represented by Gus (Walter Long), the liberated slave who attempts to rape Flora (she jumps to her death rather than submit to him). Gus's Northern counterpart is the mulatto Silas Lynch, who is encouraged by Congressman Stoneman's speeches on the equality of the races to believe that he has a right to the hand of Stoneman's daughter. Stoneman, for his part, appears to have a sexual relationship with his mulatto housekeeper, Lydia Brown (Mary Alden), an affair described in an intertitle as "the great leader's weakness that is to blight a nation."

The most famous single sequence in *The Birth of a Nation* comes as Ben Cameron, at the climax of the film's central battle sequence, charges across the field, a Confederate flag raised above his head. The camera, looking down on Ben from an overhead mount, rushes ahead of him and stops abruptly when Ben reaches the Union lines. In a spectacular, truly thrilling gesture, he rams the pole of the Confederate flag down the barrel of a Union cannon, demonstrating not only exceptional courage and theatrical flair but also a sense of mastered, controlled sexuality—a virility contained and put to service at an appropriate moment, rather than allowed to sow the chaos that we will see among the broadly caricatured liberated blacks of the Reconstruction scenes.

The double weddings that end the film—Ben Cameron to Elsie Stoneman, and Phil Stoneman to Margaret Cameron—seal, of course, the union of the North and the South and symbolize the resolution of many of the thematic oppositions Griffith has built into the overriding conflict of the war. Here is "the birth of a nation," in the sense that a new ruling paradigm has emerged, one that channels male sexual energy not into the violence of rape and war but into the gentle, controlled sexuality of monogamous marriage. With war over and the anarchy of sex channeled into positive creation, America can finally begin is true business— which, as we know, is business.

Blow-Up (1966)

by Andrew Sarris

MICHELANGELO ANTONIONI'S *Blow-Up* is the movie of the year, and I use the term "movie" advisedly for an evening's entertainment that left me feeling no pain (or Antonioni) whatsoever. It is possible that this year's contributions from Ford, Dreyer, Hitchcock, Chabrol, and Godard may cut deeper and live longer than Antonioni's mod masterpiece, but no other movie this year has done as much to preserve my faith in the future of the medium. If you have not yet seen *Blow-Up* see it immediately before you hear or read anything more about it. I speak from personal experience when I say it is better to let the movie catch you completely unawares. One of its greatest virtues is surprise, and the last thing you want is to know the plot and theme in advance. Unfortunately, most of the reviewers have given the show completely away. Judith Crist coyly conceals the plot gambit in *Gambit,* but she spills the beans in *Blow-Up* with no qualms whatsoever. Why? I suppose she considers *Blow-Up* too esoteric for audiences to enjoy in the course of mindless moviegoing. It's a pity since, purely on a plot level, *Blow-Up* provides more thrills, chills, and fancy frissons than any other movie this year.

The excitement begins with the opening credits, which are stenciled across a field of green grass opening into a pop blue rhythm-and-blues background of dancing models perceived only partially through the lettering, which, among other things, implicates Antonioni in the script and heralds Vanessa Redgrave, David Hemmings, Sarah Miles, and a supporting cast of unknowns. The billing is misleading. Miss Redgrave and Miss Miles make only guest appearances in what amounts to a vehicle for David Hemmings and Antonioni's camera. *Blow-Up* is never dramatically effective in terms of any meaningful confrontations of character. The dialogue is self-consciously spare and elliptical in a sub-Pinteresque style. Fortunately, the twenty-four-hour duration of the plot makes it possible for Antonioni to disguise most of the film as a day in the life of a mod photographer in swinging London town. What conflict there is in *Blow-Up* is captured in the opening clash between vernal greens on one plane and venal blues, reds, yellows, pinks, and purples on another. The natural world is arrayed against the artificial scene; conscience is deployed against convention.

The film itself begins with more obvious contrasts. A lorry loaded with screaming revelers made up in garishly painted mime faces. Cut to derelicts trudging silently out of flophouse with bundles and belongings. One would suspect Antonioni of facile Marxist montage in his cross-cutting between mimes and derelicts, between noisy merriment and quiet morning afterment, but one would be wrong. The mimes are merely an Italianate mannerism in London, and the derelicts are simply the grubbier side of a photographer's visual concerns. Nevertheless, the cross-cutting functions by itself without any explicatory dialogue or commentary. Even the protagonist is identified for us only by degrees. Antonioni can afford a leisurely exposition for two reasons. First, we are going to be looking at Hemmings all through the movie, and a slightly mysterious materialization will not hurt him at the onset. Secondly, the emphasis throughout is not so much on the protagonist himself as on what he and his camera see and on how well he blends in with the background. Gradually we are filled in not so much with a plot as with a routine—a day in the life of a candid cameraman.

Blow-Up abounds with what Truffaut calls "privileged moments," intervals of beautiful imagery while nothing seems to be happening to develop the drama or advance the narrative. Very early in the film, the camera confronts the photographer's long black convertible head-on at a crossroads. Suddenly the entire screen is blotted out by a blue bus streaking across from right to left, followed quickly by a yellow truck. That sudden splash of blue and yellow defines Antonioni's mood and milieu better than any set of speeches ever could. Wherever Antonioni's camera goes, doors, fences, poles, even entire buildings seem to have been freshly painted for the sake of chromatic contrast or consistency. Part of Antonioni's ambivalence toward his subject in *Blow-Up* is reflected in the conflicting temptations of documentary and decoration. After painting the trees in *The Red Desert* a petrified gray, Antonioni feels no compunctions about painting an outdoor phone booth in *Blow-Up* a firehouse red. If reality is not expressive enough, a paintbrush will take up the slack. This theory of controlled color is carried about as far as it can go in *Blow-Up* before its artistic limitations become too apparent. Antonioni is heading in a dangerous direction, but the Pirandellian resolution of the plot saves him on this occasion from the stylistically bloated decadence of *The Red Desert*.

The ultimate beauty of *Blow-Up* is derived from the artistic self-revelation of the director. *Blow-Up* is to Antonioni what *Lola Montes* was to the late Max Ophuls, what *Ugetsu* was to the late Kenji Mizoguchi, what *Contempt* was to Godard, what *French Can-Can* was to Renoir, what *Limelight* was to Chaplin, what *Rear Window* was to Hitchcock, what *8 1/2* was to Fellini—a statement of the artist not on life but on art itself as the consuming passion of an artist's life. As David Hemmings moves gracefully through off-beat sites in London, his body writhing to meet the challenge of every new subject, we feel that Antonioni himself is intoxicated by the sensuous surfaces of a world he wishes to satirize. Curiously, he is more satisfying when he succumbs to the sensuousness than when he stands outside it. The unsuccessful sequences—the rock 'n' roll session, the marijuana party, the alienation conversations between Hemmings and Vanessa Redgrave in one scene and Sarah Miles in another—all suffer from the remoteness of cold chronicles recorded by an outsider. Antonioni is more successful when be forgets his ennui long enough to photograph a magnificent mod fashion spectacle that transcends the grotesquely artificial creatures that lend themselves to the illusion. Even more spectacular is the teeny bopper sandwich orgy that digresses from the main plot. An entire generation of miniteasers and inhibited exhibitionists are divested of their defenses in a frenzied choreography of bold beauty and heartrending contemporaneity. The stripping away of pink and blue leotards may explain why the Metro lion has decided to skulk away from the opening credits like a timid pussy cat scared of the Production Code.

The fact that Antonioni can be entertaining even when he is not enlightening makes the eruption of his plot all the more stunning. It starts simmering in the midst of apparent aimlessness. The photographer-protagonist wanders out of an antique shop, drifts by chance into a park where he ignores a grotesquely sexless park attendant jabbing trash with her pike, passes by a tennis court where two children are playing a clumsy brand of tennis, photographs pigeons afoot and in flight, then stalks a pair of lovers up a hill. At a distance, it looks like a tall girl pulling at an older man in what later will be recalled in retrospect as a spectacle of carnal Calvary. Here Hemmings becomes a weak-kneed voyeur as he scurries behind fences and trees with his telescopic lens. This is raw, spontaneous Life in an ominously leafy setting. Vanessa Redgrave, she of the incredibly distracting long legs and elongated spinal column extended vertically through an ugly blue-plaid minisuit making her look at a distance like a seven-foot girl guide, in short, Vanessa Redgrave via Antonioni rather than Karel ("Morgan!") Reisz, runs up to Hemmings to plead for the pictures, but everything in the movie has been so fragmented up to this time that we accept her trivial invasion of privacy argument at face value. Hemmings refuses to return the negatives and later tricks her into accepting bogus negatives while he develops and "blows up" the real ones. What seemed like a tryst in a park is magnified into a murder. Death, which has hovered over Antonioni's films from the very beginning of his career, makes its grand entrance in a photographer's studio through the eyes of a camera that sees truth whereas the eyes of the photographer only see reality. This then is the paradox of Antonioni's vision of art: The further we draw away from reality, the closer we get to the truth. Vanessa Redgrave, an irritating, affected personality in her "live" scenes, comes to life with a vengeance in the "blow-up" of her photos.

From the moment of his artistic triumph, the protagonist becomes morally impotent. He has discovered truth, but is unable to pass judgment or secure justice. He returns to the scene of the crime that night and finds the corpse of the murdered man. He visits a neighboring artist and mistress only to find them furiously flagrante delicto. He returns to his studio and discovers the theft of his blow-ups. He is physically frightened when he hears footsteps and begins to cower in a corner of his decor. It is only the artist's mistress (Sarah Miles) treading as beautifully as ever on her cat feet and in her transparent dress. He tells her about the murder, but she is too preoccupied with her own problems to give him much help. The rest of the film threatens to degenerate into one of Antonioni's shaggy-dog Odysseys to futility when the photographer returns to the scene of the blown-up crime. The wind is blowing. The body is gone. The leaves flutter with chilling indifference. Then suddenly the mime revelers from the opening sequence reappear in their loaded lorry and disembark at the tennis court. Two mimes play an, imaginary game with somewhat clumsy gestures while the others watch with silent, swivel-headed concentration. Antonioni's camera begins following the action of the imaginary ball back and forth across the net until it is "hit" over the fence near where the photographer is standing. He walks back to the spot where the "ball" has landed and throws it back. He then begins swiveling his head back and fourth and even hears the ball bouncing. He smiles at his own susceptibility, but suddenly an expression of pain flashes across his face. The camera cuts to an overhead shot of the photographer, a self-judgment of both contempt and compassion. Antonioni, the ex-tennis player who once sold his trophies to live, has come out in the open with a definitive description of his divided sensibility, half-mod, half-Marxist. Unlike Fellini, however, Antonioni has converted his confession into a genuine movie which objectifies his obsessions without whining or self-pity. As befits the classical tradition of moviemaking, *Blow-Up* can be enjoyed by moviegoers who never heard of Antonioni.

Bonnie and Clyde (1967)

by Richard Schickel

MEMORY DECONSTRUCTS MOVIES. We remember them mainly in fragments—an image or two, a bit of dialogue, a star's attitude. *Bonnie and Clyde,* to take a convenient example, is most immediately recalled by most of us—certainly by me—as a funny old car bucketing through a lonesome Dust Bowl landscape, its bank robber passengers shaking with gleeful laughter as they outrun the fruitlessly pursuing cops. The policemen intend, if they can, to kill the fleeing miscreants; at the very least they want to put them in jail and throw away the key. But those cars—and there are several of them, since there are several chase sequences in the movie—are inescapably comic. You can't quite believe that anything so silly looking could contain such deadly potential.

You also can't quite believe that a movie so jaunty and genial can achieve the deadly weight it attains in its signature sequence—the one that we tend to remember much more specifically than we do its comic car chases. That sequence is, of course, the death, by inordinate gunfire, of its principals at the end of the film. Their little outlaw band has been decimated, and they have taken refuge on a farm owned by the father of C.W. Moss, their dim-witted wheelman. They have been to town for supplies. As they return, their host, apparently fixing a flat tire on his truck, hails them. They stop to help. It's a pretty spot, which Bonnie's expression registers. Then there's a rustle in the bushes. Some startled birds take flight. Their betrayer dives for cover under his truck. Clyde and Bonnie exchange looks of incredible poignancy: Puzzlement, fear, love, a sad acceptance that they have arrived at the end from which there is no escape, chase across their faces. And then the incredible firepower of the ambush rips into their bodies. We see the bullets tearing into them. We see their bodies bounce and twitch in slow-motion response to the impact.

The sequence, no matter how often you reencounter it, tears your heart out. It is also based on historical truth. In their research, the filmmakers discovered that 1,000 rounds were fired when the real Bonnie and Clyde were ambushed. It also had, according to the film's director, Arthur Penn, a very self-conscious contemporary reference—to the excesses of munitions then being expended on the effort to pacify Vietnam. When one of the bullets rips a piece of Clyde's head off, we were supposed to recognize, too, the reference to Bobby Kennedy's assassination.

It is a curious fact that none of this was noted by reviewers at the time. That's probably because the argument over the film was largely framed by Bosley Crowther, the veteran lead critic of the *New York Times*. He was a tiresome old fud, and people had long since wearied of his cluelessness, especially when it came to all the new ways of cinematic seeing that had been arriving in the United States from abroad for something like a decade. Now he proved himself equally blind to American innovation. He didn't care a rap about Penn's truthful visualization of Bonnie and Clyde's end. He was, in fact, outraged by the claims to "a faithful representation" of historical fact that the film's publicists apparently put forward—as if such faithfulness was something the movies routinely offered when they took up historical subjects. He was even more angry over the way the film blended farce and tragedy, which he deemed "as pointless as it is lacking in taste"—as if that were not its very point, the main reason for making it.

But besides missing the obvious references to Vietnam at the end of the film, he also failed to see that the whole movie was pitched toward youthful America's general feelings of victimization at that time. Oddly enough, Pauline Kael—Crowther's opposite in every way—also missed those points in her lengthy consideration of *Bonnie and Clyde,* published in the *New Yorker* a couple of months later. She saw its originality and its power, but, somewhat irrelevantly, she spent much of her space comparing it to older movies about outlaw couples on the run, making some dubious connections between it and *The Manchurian Candidate* and somewhat peevishly picking away at flaws that were more visible to her than to others.

No matter, perhaps. Within a year Crowther was out at the *Times,* Kael was permanently in at the *New Yorker* and *Bonnie and Clyde* gained ten Academy Award nominations. Partly as a result of them it became a huge hit in a re-release campaign that Beatty indefatigably masterminded. More important, it became a touchstone film, one of those rare movies that seems to signal a seismic shift in the sensibilities both of moviemakers and moviegoers.

Looking back at the movie now, I think perhaps the reviewers, whatever their overall judgement of the film, were right to ignore its political and social meanings. The whole Vietnam controversy seems like ancient history now, but *Bonnie and Clyde* remains remarkably fresh and gripping, a movie you don't have to damn with faint praise of that deadly (and medicinal) phrase, "historically important." The reason for this may lie in the way it examines two things no one had quite thought to take up in the movies before: the links between sexuality and the American way of death, the links between celebrity and martyrdom.

Think for a minute about the scene, early in the picture, where shy, sly Clyde completes his seduction of bored, golden Bonnie. They are standing outside a gas station, sucking on soda pops. He has confessed his criminal past, but she doesn't quite believe his boast that he did time for armed robbery. Now, though, he slides an enormous gun out from beneath his coat. She touches it reverently, sexually. But still she asks: Does he have the nerve to use it? Or is it just a boastful boy's toy, more useful for impressing girls than it is for impressing victims?

Clyde's answer is to stroll across the street, stick up a grocery store, and steal a car. Off the two of them go, buckety-buckety, laughing all the way. Soon thereafter he confesses his impotence. Soon after that, having taken refuge in an abandoned farmhouse—it has been foreclosed by the bank—they are lending their guns to the displaced farmers to take potshots at the bank's "Keep off" signs. It is not much of a revenge; it is, indeed, a childish one, but it is what Clyde Barrow and Bonnie Parker have to offer.

It is all they ever have to offer in the way of social concern and comment. But it is enough for them to gain Robin Hoodish status among the Dust Bowl's downtrodden and dispossessed. They are pretty—prettier in the movie than they were in life—but they are not too bright. Especially Clyde. He's always pretending to have thought things out, but basically his career in armed robbery is ad hoc, improvised, childlike.

Take for example, the moment their frolicsome ways are tainted by murder. By now they have recruited the rest of their gang—besides Michael J. Pollard's C.W. Moss, they include Clyde's good-ole-boy brother (Gene Hackman) and his perpetually hysterical bride, Blanche (Estelle Parsons, the only performer to win an Oscar for this film)—and they have hit a relatively rich bank. But C.W. doesn't park outside it, motor running. Instead he finds a tight, *legal* parking space down the street, from which he has trouble extricating his vehicle when his confederates exit the bank. This delay gives the bank manager time to leap on their running board. Unthinking, Clyde kills him with a shot to the head—the blood blossoming like a flower unfolding.

The movie is now darkened by death and so is Clyde. Later, he chastises C.W. for his stupidity in a movie theater while the chorines warble "We're in the

Money." But yet the murder doesn't seem to score Clyde. More killings will, indeed, follow, but Clyde remains optimistic and infinitely distractible. He is his own best cheerleader. Had things broken differently for him one can easily imagine him as another sort of All-American figure, the good-natured social chairman of a second-tier frat house at some third-tier college. Be that as it may, Beatty's weightless playing of this figure—his utter heedlessness of consequence—is one of the movie's permanent ornaments.

Faye Dunaway is no less good as Bonnie. She begins the movie hot and naked and looking for any action that will relieve the boredom of her waitress's life. But yet she is self-conscious as no one else in the movie is. She desperately wants Clyde to claim his manhood with her (the movie very sensibly avoids two historical speculations, both of which Kael rather wished it had explored—a homosexual attachment between Clyde and C.W., a straight relationship between C.W. and Bonnie), and she's alternately encouraging and petulant on that point.

What's more interesting is her growing sense of doom. As the takings at the banks dwindle (even Clyde complains that they're doing a lot of work for not much gain), as their escapes from the police become narrower and more perilous, a sense of gloomy portent settles on her. It is the function of the sequence where the gang takes Gene Wilder and Evans Evans for a joyride to bring these feelings to the surface. Everyone—outlaws and squares alike—gets along famously until Wilder's character casually admits that he's an undertaker by trade. Immediately Bonnie orders the car stopped and the puzzled pair dumped on a lonesome road. His profession reminds her too vividly of the end she alone among the Barrow Gang can see.

Then there's the doomy Parker family picnic she insists they attend. I think Penn's use of diffusion filters on the scene is his only directorial mistake in this film—its softness jerks us out of the reality that is elsewhere so brilliantly sustained. But there's an encounter with Bonnie's mother that is chilling. The old woman knows she will never see her daughter again and as much as says so, Clyde tries to reassure her—he can run circles around the cops. Mrs. Parker doesn't buy that for a minute. "You'd best keep on running, Clyde Barrow," she says. And the look on her daughter's face acknowledges the grim truth she has spoken.

Maybe it is her foreboding that inspires Bonnie's muse. But it is not long before she is scribbling "The Ballad of Bonnie and Clyde" in a notebook. It is a taunt and a boast and finally an elegy:

Someday they'll go down together;
   They'll bury them side by side;

> To few it'll be grief—
> To the law a relief—
> But it's death for Bonnie and Clyde.

Proud Clyde sends this effusion off to a newspaper. It is printed and reprinted, and his delight in his lady's gift knows no bounds. Also, he senses in it the beginnings of a new kind of celebrity—a kind that no other backwoods bank robber has ever known—and, magically, Clyde is restored to potency. Or maybe he's not restored; maybe this is a first-time thing.

It's a terrific narrative stroke—so much more interesting than merely drawing a comparison between success with your gun and success with your member. But the newspaper in which Bonnie and Clyde have been reading her work blows away across a fallow field—one the many things Penn was good about was contrasting the bouncy violence of his action with the empty serenity of his bucolic landscapes. The shot portends their ending, which follows soon enough.

The movie itself portends something else—a new attitude toward crime and death in the American cinema. Prior to *Bonnie and Clyde,* as Kael observed, it was possible for movies to elicit a certain sympathy for doomed criminals, especially when they were lovers. But as society's victims—people who had not been given the education or the economic means to avoid the criminal life, we, in the audience, were encouraged to bear a certain amount of guilt for the bad, but morally satisfying ends, they came to.

In the previous history of the movies only James Cagney, often as careless and attractive in himself as *Bonnie and Clyde* was as a movie, sometimes hinted that crime might pay in ways that conventional moral accountancy could not calculate. You often had a feeling that, gripped by his demonic energy, some of his gangsters would have been crooks had they been born in mansions and gone to Yale, so strong was the force of his motiveless but good-natured malignity.

At some point in preproduction it was proposed to Beatty, Penn, and the writers, Robert Benton and David Newman, that *Bonnie and Clyde* be made in black and white, as a period piece. They rejected the idea. They didn't want to put that distance between their work and their audience. They wanted to make a color movie, in which the past was shown to be—cars and costumes aside—indistinguishable from modern America. More important, I think they must have wanted to propose, in addition to everything else, the very modernist notion that we live in an indeterminate universe, to suggest that criminal life was just an unlucky accident. Clyde meets Bonnie when he happens upon her mother's car and thinks to steal it. Suppose he had gone after a different auto. Suppose Bonnie had not been home to spot him. She might have remained a waitress. And he might have been just another small-time crook. Or even have gone straight—as, perhaps, the night manager in a convenience store. Instead, a tinkly legend grew up around them. Can you imagine how thrilled Bonnie and Clyde would have been by *Bonnie and Clyde?* Except, of course, their legend required their martyrdom.

Think, too, about the people they murdered. Had they been standing a couple of inches to the left or right they might have been spared. Had they decided to cash their check a little later or a little sooner, they might have been spared the rigors of a bank robbery. In other words, this movie pioneers the concept of a chance universe. And that's a concept that has animated most of our best crime movies since—*Pulp Fiction,* for one, or *Fargo.* "I don't deserve this," a much older Gene Hackman croaks to Clint Eastwood at the conclusion of *Unforgiven.* "I was building a house," he adds, conveniently omitting the more sadistic criminal activities he hides beneath his pious mask. "Deserve's got nothin' to do with it," says Eastwood's Will Munny as he prepares to drop the trigger on his helpless antagonist.

That phrase is an emblem of our time. It was the most profound business of *Bonnie and Clyde* to bring it to popular consciousness, no matter what its creators thought about the war in Vietnam (although now we have begun to see that as the most terrible accident in our political history). In this it succeeded most wonderfully—immortally so, in my still bedazzled opinion.

Breathless (1960)

by David Sterritt

> *Everything can be put into a film.*
> *Everything should be put into a film.*
> **—JEAN-LUC GODARD, 1967**

"ALTHOUGH I FELT ASHAMED OF IT AT ONE TIME," said Jean-Luc Godard in a 1962 interview, "I do like *Breathless* very much, but now I see where it belongs—along with *Alice in Wonderland.* I thought it was *Scarface.*"

Godard was speaking of his first major film, released in 1960. Like countless other Godard statements, this one teeters between the sincere and the sardonic, refusing to pin down where the filmmaker stands vis-à-vis his film.

And that, of course, is the point. "I want to restore everything, mix everything up and say everything," he remarked four years later, summing up one of his basic attitudes: Film is as unlimited as life itself and just as resistant to categories and pigeonholes. No movie is a monolith, and a work as rich and mercurial as *Breathless* may well be a fantasy and a *policier,* a mobster flick and a social critique, an occasion for shame and a cause for pride, a godchild of Howard Hawks and Lewis Carroll at one and the same time. Starting with his first feature, the most revolutionary he ever made in terms of sheer impact on world cinema, Godard mixed everything up with a vengeance.

Based on a scenario by François Truffaut, another key member of the New Wave filmmaking group, *Breathless* is the story of a gangster and his girl. The former is Michel Poiccard, played by Jean-Paul Belmondo in the defining performance of his career. The latter is Patricia Franchini, played by Jean Seberg in the performance that rescued her from oblivion after the failure of *Saint Joan* and *Bonjour Tristesse,* the Hollywood pictures that were supposed to make her a star. Michel is a small-time thug who finds big-time trouble when he steals a car, goes for a joyride, and kills a cop who chases him. Patricia is an American student who casts flirtatious eyes around Paris when she isn't busy hanging out with Michel, peddling newspapers on the Champs-Elysées and attending an occasional class at the Sorbonne so checks will keep arriving from her parents back home.

After jumping to an explosive start with Michel's burst of violence and flight from capture, the movie settles into an edgy yet oddly unhurried ramble as he dodges the police, hunts for an accomplice who owes him the cash he needs to get out of town, and pesters Patricia for sex, sympathy, and a promise that she'll flee to Rome with him when his money comes in. Meanwhile the cops tighten their dragnet, making the city a gigantic trap for our increasingly nerve-jangled protagonists. All of which becomes moot when Patricia abruptly picks up the phone and betrays Michel to the police, who gun him down in the street outside the apartment where he's been hiding. His final dash toward freedom seems almost perfunctory—by now he's fed up, played out, "at the end of breath," to translate *A bout de souffle,* the film's French title—and he expires under Patricia's eyes, mumbling about how disgusting the whole affair has been. She gives Godard's camera a last enigmatic gaze before the movie fades to black, leaving us to wonder if love and loyalty have simply eluded this particular pair or have become irrelevant illusions unsuited to our existentially anguished age.

Breathless takes its title partly from Michel's ultimate exhaustion, but more from the hyperactive style Godard employs to tell his story. That style, along with the formula-jolting narrative twist provided by Patricia's betrayal, is what gave the movie its extraordinary influence on a generation of filmmakers. Cinematically speaking, *Breathless* represents a remarkable blend of inventive maneuvers that build upon the best of film's then-recent past while anticipating a newly free-wheeling future.

Godard's fascination with motion picture history grew from his 1950s training as an obsessive cinephile and a critic for *Cahiers du Cinéma,* the French journal edited by André Bazin, a legendary supporter of reality-based film. Bazin's notions of mise-en-scène helped form the predilections and rebellions of Godard, Truffaut, and other protégés who developed the *auteur* theory—calling for directors to "write" with their cameras as personally as poets write with their pens—and later sparked the New Wave movement. Like his mentor and colleagues, Godard greatly admired the Italian neorealists of the late 1940s and early 1950s, who turned away from studio artificiality and movie star glamour in favor of naturalistic stories with authentic settings. Godard followed their lead, shooting his first feature in streets, apartments, offices, and cafés genuine enough to make the film as much a documentary about Paris as a fiction about two (sometimes) likable losers.

Realism was only one factor in Godard's innovative equation, however. He also reveled in cinematic expression for its own sake, rejecting the dominant "classical Hollywood style" that plays down the signs of creative filmmaking—editing, camera movement, and so forth—in order to absorb spectators in the story's emotional and psychological values. Godard careened in the other direction, placing cinematic pyrotechnics at the center of the moviegoing experience. During the process of shooting *Breathless,* the camera glided with unprecedented freedom as Godard propelled cinematographer Raoul Coutard through the action in a wheelchair and a mail cart; during the editing process, Godard spliced together disparate shots and yanked out extraneous frames with an improvisatory gusto that relied—like the behaviors of his characters—less on rules and customs than on the unfettered impulses of the moment.

The results of this combination seemed insufferable to traditionalists, who questioned not just the worth of this proudly subversive movie but the competence and perhaps the sanity of the upstart who had slammed it together. Their distaste for its style was matched by their disdain for its content, and Godard added fuel to the fire by proclaiming *Breathless* the "anarchist film" he had dreamed of directing, raising questions as to what sort of anarchism he intended to represent via such incorrigibly aimless characters. "This rebel is far from being a leftist," complained the respected critic Georges Sadoul about what he saw as Godard's penchant for knee-jerk nonconformity at any price. "The anarchist [Michel] is part of the same group that writes 'Death to the Jews!' in the corridors of the subway," wrote Louis Séguin in *Positif,* an anti–New Wave journal, "and makes spelling mistakes in doing so." The lack of evidence for such right-wing fanaticism (even if Michel does say he "likes cops" at one point) was apparently irrelevant to its infuriated critics. Godard's scorn for what an admiring reviewer called "the rules of film narrative" had struck a nerve—many nerves—and angry members of France's film establishment minced no words in expressing their outrage.

Others recognized the vast possibilities held out by Godard's highly original techniques and the vigorous ways in which *Breathless* mirrored the increasingly volatile tone of the period when it was made. This period encompassed the end of the 1950s, marked on both sides of the Atlantic by a tendency to evade social and political problems (relating to war, race, poverty, etc.) that stubbornly refused to go away, and the start of the 1960s, when pressures generated by those problems built toward an impending eruption of volcanic proportions. Filmmakers of this era modified their methods a bit, expanding the classical style—more color productions, new widescreen formats, looser censorship codes—to shore up theatrical film against television's rising threat. But such efforts proved too timid for growing numbers of young people who questioned conventional notions of authority and propriety in art and politics alike. Artists in many fields began echoing and amplifying this trend, from Alain Resnais and Jean Anouilh in Paris to Edward Albee and Robert Rauschenberg on the American scene. It's no coincidence that the jazzed-up writing of the Beat Generation authors reached a pinnacle in 1959, embodying a spur-of-the-moment sensibility that's uncannily close to Godard's own. *Breathless* was a movie of its richly precarious time, plugging into the cultural zeitgeist with incontestable energy.

The impact of *Breathless* was augmented by Godard's position as a founding member of the New Wave group, which zoomed to prominence in 1959 when Truffaut's masterly drama *The 400 Blows* stormed the Cannes International Film Festival, earning its maker the best director prize. Truffaut became an instant superstar, and his associates—Godard plus Jacques Rivette, Claude Chabrol, and Eric Rohmer—were perfectly positioned to capitalize on their fame by association, since all had recently put their filmmaking careers in motion. The timing couldn't have been better for *Breathless,* which appeared at just the right moment to ride the New Wave's swelling surf yet had more than enough personality of its own (too much, detractors howled!) to strike a truly distinctive note. Along with other signature pieces of the early New Wave period—subsequent Truffaut films, Rivette's moody *Paris Belongs to Us,* and Chabrol's peripatetic *Les Bonnes Femmes* among them—it had a literally eye-opening effect on filmmakers in Hollywood and elsewhere who scrambled to emulate its blend of photographic realism, stylistic exuberance, and performances perched on a razor-thin line between Brechtian self-consciousness and B-movie brio.

In the decades since its premiere, *Breathless* has stood as an appropriately scruffy monument to the eminently Godardian values of aesthetic freedom, cinematic spontaneity, and profoundly personal expression. While this is entirely justified, there's a certain irony in the canonization of such a zestfully anarchic work from such a strenuously uncategorizable director. Influenced by the Existentialist philosophy of Jean-Paul Sartre and his ilk, *Breathless* takes it for granted that existence precedes essence—that is, human realities seem preordained but are actually mutable, unstable, and shaped by the choices we make in the moment-by-moment flow of experience. Godard directed the film in precisely this spirit, spurning the security of studio production for off-the-cuff shooting from a scenario so sketchy that Godard had to call out the dialogue to his actors as the camera rolled, dubbing in the sound of their voices after filming was over.

This doesn't mean his protagonists are models of psychological self-determination. Quite the opposite, they are creatures of the sociocultural scene in which they find themselves, as Michel obliquely acknowledges late in the story when he reels off a veritable catalogue of behavioral stereotypes—"squealers squeal, burglars burgle, killers kill, lovers love"—that describe him and his girlfriend all too well, nailing them as no more unfettered or free-spirited than the pop-culture character clichés that swirl through their media-saturated society. Godard's goal was to capture that society on its own exasperating/exhilarating terms, at once mirroring it, dissecting it, savoring it, and exploding it. In later films of the 1960s he did for other genres what he did for the gangster movie here—the political thriller in *The Little Soldier,* the musical comedy in *A Woman Is a Woman,* the war movie in *Les Carabiniers,* the science-fiction fantasy in *Alphaville,* and so on—before turning to a drastic form of scorched-earth cinema (starting with films like *Weekend* and *La Chinoise, ou Plutôt à la chinoise*) that carried his increasingly radical ideas to their logical (or illogical) conclusions.

But that, to quote one of Godard's favorite taglines, is another story. *Breathless* remains his most frequently watched film, his most deeply influential film, and the film that brought the most international attention to the most tumultuously protean figure to emerge from European cinema in the second half of the twentieth century. It has left audiences breathless since the day it hit the screen.

Bringing Up Baby (1938)

by Morris Dickstein

DESPITE THE HARDSHIPS OF THE DEPRESSION and the variety of film genres that became popular then—gangster movies, backstage musicals, dance films, costume dramas, fables of social misery—the comedies have held up as the least dated, best remembered films from the classic period of the 1930s. When the censorship imposed by the Production Code took hold in 1934, it became almost impossible for Hollywood movies to deal directly with sex and love. Ironically, this led to our greatest era of romantic comedy, as directors combined slapstick and farce with sophisticated dialogue to trace the pitfalls and pratfalls of adult relationships. The zany effervescence of screwball comedy, with its buoyant, anarchic energy and rapid-fire dialogue, became a suggestive way not only of countering depression but of making movies about sex without any sex in them. Perhaps the greatest, certainly the wildest of these movies was Howard Hawks's *Bringing Up Baby* (1938). Though Hawks had directed *Twentieth Century* a few years earlier, based on a hit Broadway comedy by Ben Hecht and Charles MacArthur, he would always be best known for his hard-boiled action films. Yet his comedies have the same stripped-down, unsentimental qualities.

In *Bringing Up Baby* Hawks brought together Katharine Hepburn and Cary Grant in a zany tale that proved too much for Depression viewers but has grown in stature ever since. Hepburn, after a checkered film career with RKO all through the 1930s, had just scored a great success in *Stage Door* as a headstrong aristocrat who gets her first taste of real life and wins her spurs as an actress. Grant, after several false starts, had just perfected the part of the debonair and sardonic ladies' man that he would play from then on. In *The Awful Truth* he blithely alienates his ladylike wife, played by Irene Dunne, but wins her back on the brink of their divorce. With his high spirits he injects pure mayhem into her life, disrupting on her dull and conventional romance with the cloddish Ralph Bellamy.

Bringing Up Baby adapts the plot and heightens the frantic narrative rhythm of *The Awful Truth* but reverses the sexes (which would be switched back in Hawks's next comedy, *His Girl Friday*, where a hyperkinetic Grant again faces off against the dubious domestic appeal of Ralph Bellamy). In *Bringing Up Baby*, Grant, playing against type, is a staid paleontologist who, with his fiancée, is completing the reconstruction of the skeleton of a brontosaurus. Behind his round, horn-rimmed glasses and sober scientific air, we suspect, is the dapper Grant we know, the sleeping prince who needs to be awakened. Hepburn has fallen for him, and she takes on Grant's earlier role as the troublemaker, the exuberant life-force, loony and spontaneous, wreaking havoc on his orderly plans. To this woman in love he is fair game, to be stalked, captured, and rescued from an imminent marriage to "Miss Swallow," his grimly serious colleague at the Museum of Natural History. As he awaits the final bone that will lock the fossil (and his future) in place, Miss Swallow informs him, to his mild distress, that their marriage will be all business—no children, no frivolity, no honeymoon, "no domestic entanglements of any kind." At this point the movie looks too much like a live-action cartoon to be convincing on any level.

Into this safe and predictable world, like a whirlwind, comes Hepburn as the dizzy rich girl, a role Carole Lombard had patented in movies like *My Man Godfrey*. Step by step she involves Grant in infinite complications, most of them having to do with a pet leopard named Baby. We soon realize that behind the farcical and seemingly anarchic plot, the movie itself is enormously complex and cunningly constructed, a riot of off-color references, double-entendres, and correspondences on which critics have feasted for decades. The movie begins and ends with that huge dinosaur, whose cage-like skeleton suggests the kind of death-in-life that lies in store for Grant. Hepburn and her leopard, on the other hand, represent the irrepressible energy of the life-force itself—sex, spirit, and fun—and the baby that Miss Swallow will never permit Grant to have.

The breakneck speed of the movie and its teasing mockery of the censor exemplify this life-affirming thrust. Long before Robert Altman made it a hallmark of his style, Hawks accelerated the comic action with overlapping dialogue, training his actors to bite off the ends of each other's lines. Grant is an egghead, but the movie draws him into a zany atmosphere of inspired madness that cracks open his shell. As he tries frenetically to follow Hepburn's logic and keep up with her antics, Grant, with an almost continuous slow burn, wonderfully conveys the mounting exasperation of a man losing his mind and, just underneath, loving every minute of it. "It never will be clear as long as she's explaining it," he tells someone, yet this is just what he needs to save him from dry rational clarity. This pair are made for each other but, as in all screwball comedy, one or both of them will be the last to know.

One model for screwball can be found in Shakespeare's mature comedies such as *Much Ado About Nothing* and *As You Like It*, with their haughty, self-sufficient men, strong women, and fierce combat of words and wits. Just as Shakespeare's battling couples slough off their fixed identities when they withdraw from the court and get entangled in the forest, so Grant and Hepburn transport their leopard up to the wilds of Connecticut, where nature itself will help bring them together. This is a delicious joke, for Connecticut is hardly the Forest of Arden, let alone a primitive jungle. "There aren't any leopards in Connecticut, are there?" asks Major Applegate (Charlie Ruggles), the meek big-game hunter, whose expert imitations of wild mating calls attract the warm admiration of Hepburn's feisty Aunt Elizabeth (May Robson). To add to the complications, a "bad" leopard, who looks very much like Baby, has escaped from the circus and is repeatedly mistaken for his tame double. This creature has mauled people and needs to be put down, as if to acknowledge that nature can be violent and destructive as well as sexy and life-giving, while showing that the two can easily be confused.

This doubling effect demonstrates how pervasively Freudian the movie can be, even as it mocks the vogue for psychoanalysis that began to take Hollywood by storm in the 1930s. In one of many good character parts, Fritz Feld does a classic caricature of an obtuse Germanic analyst even as he is given lines that express the movie's central themes. With awesome self-importance, he explains the psyche to a fascinated Hepburn: "The love impulse in man reveals itself in terms of conflict." This conflict is at the heart of screwball comedy, and Hepburn will do her best to exacerbate it. Thanks to Freud the movie is also loaded with jokes and symbols that make an end-run around the censor, starting with Miss Swallow and "Mr. Bone," the name Hepburn bestows on Grant when she's trying to conceal his identity, while doing everything she can to break it down. "My future wife has always regarded me as a man of some dignity," he tells Hepburn pompously. With relentless brio she levels this dignity, liberating the person trapped behind it. This is slapstick with a social message. When she breaks his glasses she says, "You look much handsomer without them." Deprived of his clothes, he is forced to don first a frilly woman's robe (I "went gay," he tells her incredulous aunt), then an ill-fitted riding outfit of her own horsey set. "I'm not myself today," he adds, as if taking note of the meltdown of his own rigid personality. This is an echo of a great early scene when *she* was exposed, with her dress ripped open and underwear showing; then Grant had shielded her gallantly by gluing himself to her rear in a slightly obscene mating dance that anticipates the whole movie. Now the woods of Connecticut give full play to her creative chaos. "I'm a victim of your unbridled imagination," he complains to Hepburn, as her aunt insists that there are already enough lunatics in the family. Her friend Major Applegate mistakes the call of a leopard for a loon. By enmeshing Grant in such lunacy, Hepburn exposes him to love. "In moments of quiet I'm strangely drawn to you," he tells her, "but, well, there haven't been any quiet moments." Hawks later regretted he hadn't put anyone normal into the movie, if only for scale. As in Shakespeare, sex, madness, and imagination seem closely allied.

This is not the Freud who saw a tragic conflict between civilization and impulse but the popular Freudianism of the 1920s and 1930s, pitting spontaneity and instinct against Victorian shackles of repression. But the movie is so free of gush that the single moment resembling a love scene is when they sing together, in very rough harmony, the only song that can lure their leopard down from the psychiatrist's roof: "I can't give you anything but love, baby." This sounds like the wisdom the good doctor himself had grandly delivered, but when he hears it warbled under his window, he assumes the singers are delusional and must be quietly locked up. In the great farcical climax, everyone in the movie has been clapped in jail except the "bad" leopard, liberation's evil twin. Only Hepburn, with her sublime innocence and determination, proves able to haul him in and put him behind bars, aided finally by a now-fearless Cary Grant. To drive this change home, Hepburn confronts her man as he takes refuge behind the dinosaur skeleton, the last thing that can come between them. In a final moment of inspired mischief, she brings the fossil crumbling to its knees as they huddle together on the exposed scaffold. This giddy climax is as much out of William Blake as of Freud: "Drive your cart and your plow over the bones of the dead."

Casablanca (1942)

by Jay Carr

IT'S STILL THE SAME OLD STORY. Maybe more so. *Casablanca* was never a great film, never a profound film. It's merely the most beloved movie of all time. In its fifty-year history, it has resisted the transmogrification of its rich, reverberant icons into camp. It's not about the demimondaines washing through Rick's Cafe Americain—at the edge of the world, at the edge of hope—in 1941. Ultimately, it's not even about Bogey and Ingrid Bergman sacrificing love for nobility. It's about the hold movies have on us. That's what makes it so powerful, so enduring. It is film's analogue to Noel Coward's famous line about the amazing potency of cheap music. Like few films before or since, it sums up

Hollywood's genius for recasting archetypes in big, bold, universally accessible strokes, for turning myth into pop culture.

It's not deep, but it sinks roots into America's collective consciousness. As a love story, it's flawed. We don't feel a rush of uplift when trenchcoated Bogey, masking idealism with cynicism, lets Bergman, the love of his life, fly off to Lisbon and wartime sanctuary with Paul Henreid, while he strolls into the mist toward Brazzaville with his corrupt French police pal, Claude Rains, drawling, "Louis, I think this is the beginning of a beautiful friendship." Part of what's wrong is that you believe Bogart: Although you certainly believed his earlier bitterness came from pain, you're now quite convinced that he and Rains will have a good time, trading ironic repartee, understanding one another fully, neither making uncomfortable demands on the other.

Apart from the fact that Paul Henreid's Victor Laszlo is such a saint that he's irritating, you don't want to see Bergman's Ilsa Lund go off with him. She's so obviously strong—and strong-willed—that you're disappointed to see her just knuckle under and go off and do what she's supposed to do. Her appeal is precisely that she'll let her feelings lead her to what she's not supposed to do, namely, love Bogey's Rick Blaine. Ilsa's pain adds to her poignancy. But mainly you're feeling more than a little let down by her genuflection to idealism. You feel passion is being subordinated to an abstraction. You want her to second-guess Rick and not go. *Casablanca* leaves the heart feeling cheated. And it's hardly Bergman's greatest role. Even though her face mirrors real ambivalence (she didn't know which man Ilsa would wind up with until almost the end of shooting), she's more complex and psychosexually interesting in Hitchcock's *Notorious*. And Rick is a little too accepting of the idea of losing her.

So if *Casablanca* really can't be said to be one of film's great love stories, what is it? Several things. When it opened, late in 1942, *Casablanca* was said to be a lucky movie, its popularity ascribed to topicality and timing—with insufficient credit given to the way creative lightning could strike under chaotic conditions any time a studio gathered under its roof a band of combustible creative types. The Allies' successful North African offensive, launched at Casablanca in November, caused Warners to move up the premiere. Shortly afterward, Roosevelt and Churchill held a summit conference there. So the real Casablanca, by staying in the news, fed the resonances of the film. But patriotism is only the most obvious of several powerful claims *Casablanca* has made on audiences.

Movies, so central to American life, shaped the American mind, and *Casablanca* is as much about movies as about romantic adventure. It taps our love of movies, our involvement with them, our dreamy bondage by them. Some movies innovate. *Casablanca* culminates. It brings to a peak the between-the-wars imperative that one was obliged to live life with a sense of style. The style at work in *Casablanca* is marked by witty poise, by the sophistication of cafe society between the wars, with its white linen suits and baccarat in private rooms—and also its helplessness before corruption, its impotent sleekness. One of the many extraordinarily potent resonances comes when we notice that the croupier at Rick's is played by Marcel Dalio, the same Dalio who played the nervous aristocrat dancing on the edge of a crumbling world in Jean Renoir's *Rules of the Game* in 1939. There are more than a few homages to French films of the period.

But it's the insistence of *Casablanca* on the importance of style, exemplifying it in the character of Rick, that has caused *Casablanca* to tilt toward Bogart over the years. That and his way of standing outside institutions and calling his own shots to his own moral code—which, as the film quickly makes clear, includes some bravely defiant idiosyncrasies, such as okaying IOUs but refusing to cash the check of an obviously solvent Berlin banker. And after the film's revival—to an audience with its collective ear cocked to the winds of existentialism emanating from the Deux Magots on Paris's Left Bank and the alienated howl of the American Beats—it was revelation. Bogey single-handedly solved the biggest problem facing any young generation: how to keep your integrity and still be cooler than everyone else in sight. Even when making light of fighting for the right losing causes in Spain and Ethiopia, he stays cool—replying, when asked his nationality, "I'm a drunkard."

It's his controlled exterior that makes Rick's wild romanticism acceptable. With his pouchy, watchful eyes, perpetual cigarette, black bow tie, and white dinner jacket, his cynical crust fooled nobody—least of all Bergman's Ilsa. He talked a good game of noninvolvement, but obviously he was nuts about her, still wounded deeply by her abandonment of him after their fling in Paris (the flashbacks were skilled montages by Don Siegel, who went on to become a well-known director in his own right). His is the emotion you feel when they meet up again in his club, over Dooley Wilson's piano—that source of so much garbled legend.

Neither he nor Ilsa ever said "Play it again, Sam" to Wilson. What she says, after entering the club with her Resistance-hero husband, whom she believed dead when she took up with Rick in Paris, is, "Play it once, Sam, for old time's sake. Play it, Sam. Play 'As Time Goes By.'" Rick, rushing over, says, "Sam, I thought I told you never to play it." Then he notices Ilsa. They exchange a long look. Later, when Rick is sitting at a table after hours (muttering, "Of all the gin joints in all the towns in the world, she walks into mine"), he masochistically asks

Sam to play: "You know what I want to hear. You played it for her. You can play it for me. If she can stand it, I can. Play it!"

Max Steiner, the film's musical director, didn't want the song. It was there only because Murray Bennett, the teacher who wrote the unproduced play (with Joan Alison) on which the film is based, liked it. Steiner wanted to drop it and may have succeeded—except that Bergman had already cropped her hair for her next film, *For Whom the Bell Tolls,* and retakes were impossible. So it stayed.

Actually, Wilson—the only cast member ever to have played the real city of Casablanca—couldn't play the piano. He was a singing drummer. (Studio musician Elliott Carpenter dubbed the piano-playing.) Wilson and Bogart were the only American-born members among the leads. There's evidence on both sides, but on the whole it leans away from the story that Ronald Reagan was Jack Warner's first choice for the role of Rick. George Raft—who made the mistake of turning down roles that Bogart capitalized on in *High Sierra* and *The Maltese Falcon*—campaigned for the role, but it was Bogey's from the start.

Producer Hal Wallis first considered Ann Sheridan for the female lead, then Hedy Lamarr. French actress Michelle Morgan was Warner's first choice. But she wanted $55,000, and Warners got Bergman from David O. Selznick, who owned her contract, for $25,000 plus the use of Olivia de Havilland's services for one film. Philip Dorn was Paul Henreid's only serious competition for the role of her freedom-fighting husband. Rains, Peter Lorre, and Sydney Greenstreet had a lock on their high-profile, corruption-tinged roles, but Otto Preminger was Wallis's first choice for the role of Major Strasser, the Nazi officer played by Conrad Veidt. Even Wilson was an afterthought. Wallis first thought of women—Lena Horne, Ella Fitzgerald, and Hazel Scott—before settling on Wilson.

Workhorse Michael Curtiz, himself a refugee from Hungary, and the director of forty-two Warners films in a decade, was assigned the film after William Wyler, Vincent Sherman, and William Keighley turned it down. When Howard Koch, one of the writers, pointed out inconsistencies to him, Curtiz is reported by Koch to have answered, "Don't worry what's illogical. I make it go so fast nobody notices." It was more a case of nobody making much of the flaws, the biggest of which has the precious exit visas everybody's chasing bear the signature of Resistance mainstay Gen. Charles de Gaulle—a name not likely to be cherished by the collaborationist Vichy government running Casablanca. When the film won best picture, best director, and best screenplay Oscars, Curtiz's broken English rose to the occasion. He said: "So many times I have a speech ready, but no dice. Always a bridesmaid, never a mother. Now I win. I have no speech."

Many writers contributed to the script. Oscar winners Koch and brothers Julius and Philip Epstein figured most prominently in a lineup that included Aeneas McKenzie, Wally Kline, Jerry Wald, Casey Robinson, and Wallis himself, who wrote Bogey's curtain line. Most of the best-known and most-quoted lines came from the Epsteins—"Round up the usual suspects." And the exchange between Bogart and Rains: "I came to Casablanca for the waters." "Waters? What waters? We're in the desert." "I was misinformed." Or Rains's: "I like to think you killed a man. It's the romantic in me."

Somehow there was something fitting about *Casablanca* being born in a kind of chaos that paralleled that coursing through the flossy raffishness of Rick's Cafe. *Everybody Comes to Rick's* was the title of the original play, with its crossroads-of-the-world atmosphere. These days, everybody writes about Rick's. The movie's flaws never did matter. What mattered then, and matters even more resonantly now, is its evocation of a yeasty, corrupt atmosphere from which self-respect could somehow be won, or won back. The cynical Rick would have loved the result of an experiment by writer Chuck Ross in 1982, detailed in *American Film* magazine. Changing its name back to *Everybody Comes to Rick's,* Ross sent the story to 217 agencies. Most returned it unread. Of the eighty-five who did read it, only thirty-three recognized it. And yet, as an example of potent iconography under pressure, it has seldom been matched and never been surpassed. First, last, and always, *Casablanca* remains a triumph of stance.

The Chant of Jimmie Blacksmith (1978)

by Joe Morgenstern

COMING UPON *The Chant of Jimmie Blacksmith* can be a shattering experience even now, a quarter-century after it was made; few films have been as unsparing in their depiction of the violence engendered by racial hatred. But tracking it down can be frustrating, since few great films are as little known or as hard to find. Unavailable in the United States on video, let alone on DVD, Fred Schepisi's national epic about an Australian aborigine caught between two cultures at the turn of the twentieth century was a critical success around the world after its release in 1978, but it was a commercial flop at home, where audiences weren't ready to confront the racist horrors of their nation's past. (At the time of its release, the production was Australia's most expensive ever, with a budget of $1.6 million.) These days the best chance of seeing *Jimmie Blacksmith*—and seeing it as it should be seen, in all of its widescreen splendor—is at occasional screenings at repertory theaters, festivals, or museum archives. Wherever you may find it, though, the film will richly reward the search.

The Chant of Jimmie Blacksmith is based on a 1972 novel of the same name by Thomas Keneally, who is best known as the author of *Schindler's List*; Keneally collaborated with Schepisi on the screenplay. The book, which became a metaphor of Australia's racial divide, fictionalized the life of Jimmy Governor, a red-headed black man—half-white, half-aborigine—who went on a murderous rampage in New South Wales after trying and failing to assimilate into white society. The hero of the film, Jimmie Blacksmith, is played by Tommy Lewis, a mixed-blood aborigine from the Northern Territory who was still in his teens when Schepisi spotted him at an airport and offered him the part.

"Blasted blacks!" Those are the film's first words, spoken by a scornful white man. Yet Jimmie, with his slightly hunched shoulders, darting eyes, quick smile, and pomaded black hair, wants ardently to be accepted by those who consider him—when they notice him at all—as subhuman and who use him as they use all aborigines, casually and ruthlessly, as disposable help. Jimmie chooses to think his prospects for prosperity and freedom are good; he was, after all, taken in and taught to read and write by a Methodist minister and his wife. That makes it all the more painful to see him rebuffed or exploited at every turn—as a semiskilled laborer sinking posts and building fences, as a would-be sidekick to a drunken lout of a local constable, as a farmhand with a pregnant white wife.

Today we're surfeited with stories of indigenous peoples exploited and their cultures wrecked, of radicalizing events that unleash uncontrollable forces. But *The Chant of Jimmie Blacksmith,* which predates multicultural chic and political correctness by at least a decade, feels remarkably fresh and uncontrived. The film doesn't seem to be plotted—though of course it is, with some slightly intrusive didacticism toward the end—as much as played out spontaneously and inevitably. When Jimmie explodes, and then takes his terrible revenge on those who've starved and betrayed him, we understand instantly all we need to know about how he reached the breaking point and why.

I spent several months in Australia the year *Jimmie Blacksmith* came out, and I remember the shockwaves it caused. The country was in the midst of a cinema renaissance that produced such memorable features as Bruce Beresford's *Breaker Morant,* Gillian Armstrong's *My Brilliant Career,* and *The Last Wave,* Peter Weir's surreal, mystical evocation of the aboriginal presence in contemporary Australian life. But *Jimmie Blacksmith,* which had been stunningly well photographed—by Ian Baker—across the vastness of the island continent, was something else, a relentless tragedy of obvious importance that was just as obviously doomed to fail as popular entertainment. (Fred Schepisi, whose name is pronounced "Skep-see," has made a number of other superb films, including *Roxanne, The Russia House, Six Degrees of Separation,* and *A Cry In the Dark,* another drama set in Australia but one that is happily and readily available in your local video shop.)

As I watched *Jimmie Blacksmith* again recently, on a muddy conversion of an Australian videotape that won't play on American VCRs, I also remembered a story told to me by Michael Caulfield, a white Australian—with an aboriginal half-brother, if I'm not mistaken—who coached the indigenous actors in the cast. These were men, Caulfield said, who understood perfectly well what movie acting meant and who wanted very much to perform their roles well. One day, though, while the cast and crew were waiting for camera tracks to be laid for a scene in a forest, one of the aborigine actors, noticing a bird circling overhead, picked up a rock, casually flung it aloft, and knocked the bird out of the sky. It's not for nothing that the blacks in *The Chant of Jimmie Blacksmith* strike us as fascinating aliens, as if from another planet; the actors, too, were astraddle two worlds.

The movie's fame has come to rest mainly on its prescient politics; type the title in an online search engine and you're quickly confronted by scores of earnest, tedious essays in which scholars or critics explicate the whole thing to death. ("The character of Jimmie Blacksmith materializes the anxieties associated with searching for one's identity . . . ") What's just as admirable, though, and a lot more enjoyable, is the ineffable beauty, as well as that wonderful strangeness, of a film about partly primitive blacks that was, after all, written and directed by two eminently cosmopolitan white men.

Jimmie uses his youthful energy and his native optimism—native to his personality, though maybe also to his race—to keep a lid on his feelings as long as possible. The fences he builds are straight and true, and the pride that he takes in them brightens his handsome face. He stands waiting outside in a yard near a chicken coop while his wife is giving birth inside the farmhouse—both his maleness and his blackness keep him outside—but the moment he hears his baby's first, faint cry he does an exquisite little dance, part of a private ritual that keeps us outside too. That the graceful dancer soon becomes a vengeful killer is certainly shocking, but not, given what we learn, surprising. *The Chant of Jimmie Blacksmith* is a stirring tale of uncontainable rage.

Children of Paradise (1945)

by Jay Carr

MARCEL CARNÉ'S *Children of Paradise* isn't just one of France's great love stories—it's one of film's. Think of Bogey standing on the tarmac in *Casablanca,* bereft of Ingrid Bergman. Think of Vivien Leigh's Scarlett at the end of *Gone with the Wind,* determined to make Clark Gable's Rhett Butler frankly give a damn. Then think of Jean-Louis Barrault's Pierrot, hurling himself at a carnival throng, trying to swim upstream and catch the retreating coach widening the gap between him and the love of his life, Garance, played by actress Arletty with devastating poise. It's every bit as much a classic. Like all great love stories, it's awash in yearning. Back in the days when art houses served espresso, this was the finale that made a generation of Americans fall in love with Arletty and with French film.

Now *Children of Paradise* [has returned] in its restored, 188-minute length (American distributors did what occupying Germans couldn't do at the time it was made; they sliced thirty-eight minutes out of it). Although in some ways a period piece, it's psychically and emotionally timeless.

When it opened, in 1945, it was hailed as a triumph of French culture over the Nazis, who had just fled, and under whose noses it had been made. (Had they remained, they almost certainly would have jailed director Carné and screenwriter Jacques Prévert.) It's a celebration of theatricality in general and of nineteenth-century French theatricality in particular. But it also has a subtext that no intelligent onlooker of the 1940s could have missed—a subtext that for years afterward threatened to relegate it to the merely timely but that today makes it urgent once more.

In the independence of its heroine—Arletty's worldly Garance, deftly preserving her integrity as she negotiates a course around some dangerous and powerful suitors—it wasn't hard to see a surrogate for wartime France itself. And the spectacle of the sensitive mime, Jean-Louis Barrault's Baptiste, sublimating his experience and his love for Garance into art (she was forty-six when it was filmed, he was twelve years younger), spoke to French citizens who felt immobilized by powerlessness. Nor was it a big stretch to read into its assassination of an oppressive and powerful aristocrat by a dandified criminal a gesture of defiance against the Nazis who occupied France for four long years. Finally, the loathing of the film's characters for a ragpicker who acts as an informer mirrored the attitude of many French toward collaborators. In the film, the hateful old man is furious when Baptiste steals his identity and symbolically kills him night after night in a sketch.

As the production shuttled between Paris and Nice, interrupted by wartime exigencies, legends grew around it, especially stories of the way Resistance leaders hunted by the Gestapo would hide out in the film's crowd scenes. Not that a certain ambivalence didn't cloud *Children of Paradise,* too, just as it clouded the French civilian population. Carné ran into postwar trouble simply because he chose to stay in France and work during the Occupation. (His perhaps disingenuous justification was that he thought it best to stick to his post and give employment to French film workers.) Nor did his friendship with Arletty help. Ironically, this personification of La Resistance was under arrest the night the film premiered, her crime being an affair of several years' duration with a Luftwaffe colonel.

Unlike the leading male characters, all modeled on historical personages, the character of Garance was modeled in large part on Arletty herself. A cool, composed free spirit true to her own imperatives, she's the motor of the film—and the reason it reemerges in the postfeminist 1990s as so utterly modern. The frankly sexual Garance is the power in the film; her four suitors all practice emotional avoidance in one form or another. The reasons she seems so compelling and seductive today are her emotional intelligence and the grace with which she sidesteps all the agendas men try to project onto her—including the man she loves, the myopic Baptiste, who insists on putting her on a pedestal (and in the film does, making her look as ridiculous as she feels, turning her from statuesque into statue).

During an unconsummated bedroom scene, she tells Baptiste gently but firmly not to mythify her, to accept her as she is. Unable to deal with her sexuality, he stares at the moon and goes on sublimating and idealizing. Baptiste is based on a real figure, Jean-Gaspard Debureau, famed for the dreamlike hold of his expressive miming. The other larger-than-life performer, Pierre Brasseur's Frederic Lemaitre, was a leading romantic actor. He's worldly and playful but self-centered and emotionally shallow: After his love scene with Garance, she politely tells him to shut up, aware that he's more in love with the sound of his own voice than with her. But the expansiveness and generosity with which Brasseur plays him render him likable. If Baptiste is the moon, Lemaitre is the sun.

The murderous dandy, Pierre-Francois Lacenaire, is the subject of a fascinating recent film by Francois Girod. It depicts Lacenaire, among other things, as a man who lives for the spotlight and a great media manipulator during his trial for murder. The Lacenaire we see in *Children of Paradise*, compellingly played by Marcel Herrand, is filled with icy rage, and Arletty's Garance spots it early on. When he propositions her, she deflects him, remarking that his head is too hot for her and his heart is too cold and that she's afraid of draughts. Possibly, it's that she senses his homosexuality (mirroring Carné's), which emerges more tangibly during his showdown in a Turkish bath with the arrogant aristocrat whom Garance is forced by circumstances to accept as her protector (though she won't allow him to possess her).

The resonances and intertwinings go on and on in *Children of Paradise*. They've been spelled out in detail in studies by Georges Sadoul and Robert Chazat and, recently, with the most elaborate working out of the movie's Freudian patterning, by MIT professor Edward Baron Turk. Turk also points out that students of painting will notice the use Carné makes of Georges Ingres. When Arletty is being harassed by bullying police, who condescendingly refer to her as a painter's model, scarcely disguising their use of the term as euphemism for prostitute, she replies that she posed for Ingres (the real-life Arletty posed for Matisse and Braque). After aping Ingres's odalisque poses in the film's first half, she seems imprisoned in costumes derived from Ingres's society portraits during her bird-in-a-gilded-cage phase.

Time has dealt more generously with *Children of Paradise* (the title refers to the proles in the theaters' cheapest, uppermost balcony seats) than it has with Carné, who never recaptured the magic of his collaborations with Prévert during the 1930s and 1940s. In predictable fashion (following the Oedipal imperatives outlined by Turk), New Wave critics and filmmakers excoriated Carné and his generation. But François Truffaut, one of Carné's sternest critics, later seemed to forge an unconscious bond in his own Occupation melodrama, *The Last Metro,* when he fictionalized the fascist critic Lucien Rebater, who under the Nazis wielded enormous power in the collaborationist paper, *Je Suis Partout.* And it is Pierre Renoir, Jean's elder brother, who plays the sleazy informer in *Children of Paradise*—he was hurried into the role when Carne's first choice, Robert Le Vigan, fled after it became apparent the Allies were going to win and Le Vigan's collaborationist leanings would be held against him. (They were—he spent four years in prison.) Ironically, the real Debureau looked more like the man who would have played the role had Barrault not been able to schedule around his Comedie Francaise appearances—Jacques Tati.

But if *Children of Paradise* transcends its time and place, it would be a mistake to discount either. Wartime tensions influenced the shoot just as surely as Carné's—and Prévert's—psychic agendas. Film's great love stories end with the lovers apart, clutching emptiness. None seem more empty-handed than Barrault's anguished Baptiste. The pain on his face as his body strains toward the ever-elusive Garance stands for the suspension in which the film itself is steeped—frozen, eternally poised between consummation and flight, like all timeless romances. Garance's frank stare into the camera reminds us that happy endings are banal, that unfinished business is what keeps love alive.

Chinatown (1974)

by James Verniere

CHINATOWN, ONE OF THE BEST FILMS of one of the best decades in American movie history, is a grinning skull of a movie lewdly murmuring those incantatory, seesawing fragments, "My sister, my daughter, my sister, my daughter," into our ears. A 1974 film noir set in Depression-era Los Angeles, it's a fiendishly clever merging of Raymond Chandler, Franz Kafka, and Sophocles. It is both a definitive American film and distinctly un-American-like, especially by today's industry standards.

Its controversial ending in which Faye Dunaway's beautiful, fetishized face is transformed into a death's head by a fluke pistol shot would never pass muster among today's marketing experts, although Alfred Hitchcock, whose influence is also palpable, probably loved it. With its doom-laden fatalism, ably enhanced by composer Jerry Goldsmith's "lonely horn," its oddly ominous, gently bobbing camerawork by John A. Alonzo (who replaced the legendary Stanley Cortez), its sense of history as a recurring nightmare, and its Polish-Jewish film school graduate and Holocaust survivor director Roman Polanski, Chinatown is an art-house movie in American mainstream drag. Seldom since Hitchcock's prime had a director displayed such a facility for making a commercial movie that is also a work of art.

An example of Hollywood's tradition of cultivating foreign filmmakers, Polanski's Chinatown was independently produced by Paramount production head Robert Evans (Love Story, The Godfather, etc.) and is even more accomplished than Polanski's first American triumph, his 1968 adaptation of Ira Levin's Rosemary's Baby, which Evans had overseen at Paramount.

Based on a screenplay by Robert Towne, a screenplay over which Towne and Polanski battled fiercely (in Towne's version, the evil tycoon dies and the heroine lives), *Chinatown* is a fact-based tale about the role greed played in the evolution of modern-day Los Angeles and, of course, Hollywood.

Polanski's antagonist is another randy devil, in this case sinister Noah Cross, a tycoon who has had an incestuous relationship with his daughter and whose name sounds both biblical and like a negation of Christianity. The plot involves a scandal, two murders, a family secret, two femmes fatales and a conspiracy at the highest levels of L.A. society to enrich itself even more by transforming the arid valley into valuable real estate and incorporating it into the City of Los Angeles.

The film is a virtual catalogue of the Seven Deadly Sins, beginning with Lust in a comic scene in which the jaded private detective and former policeman J.J. Gittes (Jack Nicholson) sits languidly smoking while his client Curly (Burt Young) gasps in anguish at photographs of his wife screwing a male stranger (in this scene, Jake casually refers to his office's new venetian blinds, the signature prop and visual trademark of film noir).

The dirty joke will soon be on Jake and the viewers. Jake, the dandified, slightly disreputable private investigator of Towne's script, springs from the same gumshoe gene pool as Chandler's Philip Marlowe and Hammett's Sam Spade, but with crucial twists. Jake's insolence, his lack of respect for police and social superiors, is informed as much by Vietnam/Watergate-spawned irreverence and iconoclasm as pulp-noir conventions.

And unlike most fictional detectives, Jake is never seen with a gun in his hand. When Jake, the noir knight errant, finds that he has failed miserably to thwart the forces of darkness, it cues one of the screen's most memorable lines: "Forget it, Jake. It's Chinatown." The word "Chinatown," with its echoes of the Far East, where the United States had been mired in an unpopular war, is L.A. cop code for a mystery one can never solve or even fully grasp, an absurdist-existentialist synonym for Fate.

Although set in Los Angeles in the late 1930s, the film reeks of Old World pessimism and post-Vietnam disillusionment and despair: a pervasive sense of rot flourishing just beneath California's cloudless skies, hilltop mansions, manicured gardens, and jeweled sunsets. Not since Rene Clement's French-language hit *Purple Noon* (1960), a sun-splashed Italian Rivera–set film noir featuring color photography by the great Henry Decae, had evil enjoyed such, uh, clement weather.

Although producer Evans suggested a black-and-white retro look for the film, Polanski insisted on Panavision and color, arguing in his autobiography that he wanted "a film about the '30s seen through the camera eye of the '70s," and the color imagery, especially for a period and a genre we associate with black-and-white, is stunning: the sun-drenched yellows and browns and tanned Los Angeleno faces, Evelyn Mulwray's cream-colored Packard, her hazel eyes, auburn marcelled hair, blood-red lipstick and nail polish. In a foreshadowing similar to an earlier shot of a pocketwatch with a shattered face, Jake breaks the ruby lens of Evelyn's taillight and then in his car trails the glowing, damaged white "eye" in the distance.

Polanski's own morbid sensibility percolates throughout. As a child, Polanski was smuggled out of the Krakow ghetto and found refuge, if not love or kindness, in various foster homes. He narrowly avoided death twice, once when a Nazi soldier took a potshot at him, and again much later when his pregnant wife and several of their friends were stabbed to death by members of Charles Manson's so-called family in their Benedict Canyon home in 1969 while Polanski was abroad. Polanski would emerge from seclusion after the Tate–La Bianca murders to transform Shakespeare's *Macbeth* into a cinematic bloodbath.

Although deeply traumatized by the murders, Polanski had already demonstrated a fondness for psychological and gothic horror, variations on themes of sex and death, in such previous films as *Knife in the Water* (Poland, 1962), *Repulsion* (Great Britain, 1965), *The Fearless Vampire Killers or: Pardon Me, But Your Teeth Are in My Neck* (Great Britain, 1967) and *Rosemary's Baby* (1968). In a typically kinky twist, Polanski cast himself in *Chinatown* as the pint-sized thug with an Eastern European accent who symbolically castrates Jake, whom he addresses as "kitty cat," by slitting his nose with a knife, an act anticipating the mutilation of Evelyn Mulwray's face.

In a rehearsal for her own grisly death, Evelyn Mulwray rests her head on her steering wheel in another scene, inadvertently sounding her horn. When Evelyn later helps Jake escape in her car from two thugs (including Polanski's "midget"), a pistol is fired at them, leaving a hole in Evelyn's windshield. In the very next moment, Evelyn gently touches her fingers to her left eye as if brushing away a particle of glass. It's the same eye in which Jake will detect a "flaw" and that will be destroyed by a final bullet.

In another scene, Jake waits outside the office of L.A.'s new Water and Power Chief Engineer (John Hillerman) and just under his breath sings and hums the 1936 Dorothy Fields–Jerome Kern standard "The Way You Look Tonight," a macabre touch. In light of all this fatal momentum, no other ending was possible.

Nicholson, the hugely charismatic veteran of the Roger Corman biker-horror-movie school of filmmaking, established a following with his killer smile and widely mimicked, ironic line delivery in such films as *Easy Rider* (1969), *Five Easy Pieces* (1970) and *Carnal Knowledge* (1971). He received his third Academy Award nomination for his role in the Towne-scripted *The Last Detail* (1973). Faye Dunaway, who had failed to find a worthy follow-up to star-making turns in *Bonnie and Clyde* (1967) and *The Thomas Crown Affair* (1968), tangled with Polanski on the set but was cast in spite of pressure to hire Jane Fonda. With her sculpted cheekbones, applied eyebrows, haughty demeanor, and wounded sexuality, Dunaway's Evelyn Mulwray is mysterious and erotic, a "flawed" art deco goddess who can barely muster the nerve to pronounce the word "father" out loud. Both Dunaway and Nicholson give career-defining, Academy Award–nominated performances (both lost).

Polanski and Evans cunningly cast veteran actor-director John Huston in the role of incestuous tycoon Noah Cross. Rawboned and with a deep, sepulchral voice, Huston's Cross relishes fish served with their heads attached, and with his back to Jake, he gives the camera an unforgettable, fish-eyed look when he realizes Jake knows he's not telling him the truth about his murdered son-in-law and former partner Hollis Mulwray (Darrell Zwerling). "You may think you know what you're dealing with, but, believe me, you don't," he warns Jake. Huston's Cross is majestic and loathsome, Lord Death. Huston was, of course, also the son of great American screen actor Walter Huston and was the writer-director who made history with his 1941 screen version of Dashiell Hammett's *The Maltese Falcon*. Humphrey Bogart played Sam Spade in Huston's film and was a 1960s antiestablishment icon and obvious inspiration for Jake Gittes.

In what would have been a notably incestuous development, Polanski and Nicholson, in whose home Polanski would allegedly commit the crime he remains accused of (sex with a minor), reportedly toyed with the idea of casting Anjelica Huston, Nicholson's lover at the time, as Cross's daughter Evelyn.

"See, Mr. Gittes, most people never have to face the fact that in the right time and the right place they're capable of anything," is Cross's explanation for his relationship with his daughter Evelyn, and it sounds prophetic in light of Polanski's subsequent legal predicament. Although the Hustons wisely vetoed the casting idea, the scene in which Cross asks Jake if he is sleeping with his daughter remains creepily resonant.

Chinatown has roots in such film noir masterworks as *Murder My Sweet* (1944), *The Big Sleep* (1946) and *Touch of Evil* (1958) and yet also anticipates the scandal-mongering, celebrity-obsessed cynicism of Curtis Hanson's *L.A. Confidential* (1997). John Boorman's *Point Blank* (1967) and Robert Altman's *The Long Goodbye* (1973). The period was a fruitful one for film noir experiments and revisions.

But none was as perfect as *Chinatown* (production designer Richard Sylbert and costume designer Anthea Sylbert, who was married to Richard Sylbert's identical twin brother Paul, made monumental contributions to the film). Another grace note in the film is the way Asian faces haunt the edges of Polanski's frame (and Jake's world): the Mulwrays' husband-and-wife butler (James Hong) and maid (Beulah Quo), their vexed Japanese gardener (Jerry Fujikawa), who mutters the line, "Bad for glass," meaning "Bad for the grass," tipping Jake off to saltwater in the Mulwrays' pond, and a lewd joke about "a Chinaman" Jake tells his coworkers. Most evocative of all are the numerous, nameless Asian faces drawn irresistibly to the carnage at the end. Like Homeric shades drawn to spilled blood, they are the audience's ghostly, rubbernecking stand-ins, and like them, all we can do is stare in silence at the horror.

Citizen Kane (1941)

by Godfrey Cheshire

IT IS NOW NOT ONE, but two. *Citizen Kane* strides forward, shadowed closely by the doppelganger: *"Citizen Kane."* The first is a movie directed by Orson Welles and released by RKO Radio Pictures in 1941, to considerable critical acclaim but disappointing box-office returns; at the Oscars it won only best screenplay (for Welles and Herman Mankiewicz). The second is the reputation: "the greatest film ever made." That superlative, which coalesced into critical orthodoxy in the 1960s, has its own history and of course can be, worse than an absurdity, an impediment. Truth be told, there are times when it seems *"Citizen Kane"* has wholly eclipsed *Citizen Kane.* We have to strain to see the movie behind the monument.

Viewers who encounter it in the age of the computer should be cautioned to crank their expectations downward, to give *Kane* the chance it deserves—and needs. In the decades after its release, Welles's film inspired a generation of young European filmmakers to unleash an explosion of cinematic modernism that valued obliqueness, quietude, indirection, ambiguity. *Kane* exhibits few of those qualities itself. A Hollywood picture determined to outstrip Hollywood, it is hectic, bombastic, overdetermined, brassy with self-importance. Its psychology and social comment are leagues less sophisticated those that achieved by Henry James, among others, decades earlier, and even its celebrated visual vocabulary now looks fustian. In the 1940s, Welles's dramatic chiaroscuro, low-angled shots that revealed ceilings, crystalline depth-of-field, and so on, appeared powerful, modern, hyperarticulate. Today the same thing can seem not just baroque but dinky. Seen on TV, or a modern movie screen not shaped for its squarish picture, its proscenium is quashed to puppet-show size; its people resemble miniatures, not giants.

The most likely way for a newcomer to be impressed, then, may be to ignore the possibility. Forget the reputation. Sit back, experience it as a souvenir of the studios' golden age. Above all, give it several viewings. Allow time to absorb its flashy tricks—some extraordinary, some trite—until you begin to glimpse some of the ineffables behind them: the epic collision of talent and ambition, the sometimes inchoate paradoxicality, the strange soulfulness.

In *Kane,* form determines content more than the other way around, and the key to the film's form (if a single one can be pinpointed) is radio. Welles was twenty-four, a Broadway boy-wonder, when he came west to take up his Hollywood contract, and one thing that seldom receives comment is how terribly anxious he must have been, behind the bluster and hype. With *tout* Hollywood waiting for him to land smack on his face, he took his time and covered himself well, bringing in many colleagues from his Mercury Theater group (including Joseph Cotten, Agnes Moorehead, and John Houseman), and relying, for both inspiration and example, on paradigms offered by his successes in radio: those included the newsreel show *The March of Time,* a cinematic equivalent of which opens *Kane,* launching us into a pseudojournalistic investigation of the death and life of just-expired newspaper magnate Charles Foster Kane.

Imagine *Kane* as a radio play "set to images" and you have a useful angle on its central creative dynamic. In perhaps no other great movie does the sound "lead" the picture as it does here. The film's much-lauded "musical" structure, its use of syncopation, elaborate aural cues, and overlapping dialogue: all these owe to radio. So do things that seem primarily visual. Involving the most elaborate use of flashbacks seen in a Hollywood (or any?) movie till then, *Kane* recounts Kane's life via the shifting, not always reliable testimonies of five former intimates, a technique Welles called "prismatic." No doubt the device has numerous precedents and parallels in theater and the novel, but in those forms, such dreamily interwoven voices are exceptional; in radio drama, they're standard.

Given the way that *Kane's* narrative seems to blossom from seeds of monologue and memory, radio no doubt deserves credit for much about the film's visual plan.

If you're to illustrate a time-shifting tale spun from many heightened, overheated subjectivities, the straightforward formulas of realism just won't do, will they? Radio, when the mind vivifies its most suggestive images, tends to conjure an exaggerated, gothic/expressionist theater of the imagination, a bedazzled world of shadow and light, yawning with wide-angle distortions and fairytale architectures and perspectives so extreme as to induce vertigo. Such is the hot-house realm summoned up, Prospero-like, by Welles, using a photographic arsenal supplied (and in some cases created) by the great Gregg Toland.

Here's where that paradoxicality—the battle (or ballet) between *Kane* and "*Kane*"—begins to show. The film's style was originally hailed as "realistic." Today, most viewers would judge it as hallucinatory as *The Cabinet of Dr. Caligari.* Which judgment is correct? Weirdly, the film makes a case that both are. Though utterly phantasmagoric by current codes of realism, *Kane* holds fast to its own notion of realism, and we have to admit its point: it is, at the least, a documentary of the inside of someone's mind.

Paradox also infuses current appraisals of the film's story, where a zestfully elaborated superficiality pretends toward, and glancingly attains, a kind of profundity. Sweeping from the late nineteenth century across most of the twentieth century's first half, through the corridors of politics, media, show biz, big money, and high society, *Kane*'s vision of America is more operatic than analytical and surely no more incisive than could be found in the era's better novels or magazines. Yet it became so iconic as to be accepted as cinema's testament to the collective memory, while other sources have been forgotten. In any case, the film is not really about backdrops; its country, finally, is the vast heartland known as Charles Foster Kane.

He is least interesting considered as a satiric portrait—or vicious caricature, the acid mostly supplied by Mankiewicz—of right-wing press baron William Randolph Hearst, who hated the film and tried to stop its distribution. Welles obviously was after something grander in any event: a Shakespearean Everymogul, one large enough to sustain his own decades-spanning, rafters-shaking, expertly overblown performance while also digging into modern America's fears of loneliness and loss. Kane, after all, is the man who gains the world only to lose his soul; who builds an empire and a castle but forfeits the love of everyone around him, most movingly his oldest and best friend, the stoic newspaperman Jed Leland (Cotten).

Why the unstoppable trajectory toward that bitter end: dead in his mansion surrounded only by junk and servants? A pop-psychological mystery, *Kane*, like *Gatsby*, circles ever-backward looking for a reason and locates one finally in childhood trauma: Kane was wrenched from his mother at age eight. Though Welles and Mankiewicz both disowned that event's poignant symbol—the little sled with the tender, vernal name—"Rosebud" by now has passed from cliche to archetype and survives, happily, as one of the film's most poetic and inspired touches. *Kane,* in any case, cautions us that it may not explain anything after all.

Concerning Kane, perhaps it doesn't. Concerning Welles, however, it asserts a connection to his own abruptly interrupted childhood and the epochal effort to entertain the world that followed. Such biographical linkages may be irrelevant to the worth of most movies, but in this one they end up being central. For *Citizen Kane* is nothing if not the great proof and paradigm of *self*-expression in the cinema. One may quibble with or even deride its view of America, or human nature, or cinematic technique, but there's no contesting this: Until Orson Welles did it, no one—no *artist*—had come to Hollywood in the sound era and (co)written, directed, and starred in *his own* studio movie, much as a novelist, a playwright, or a composer conceives and controls a creative project.

Modern cinema, the era of the *auteur* and the art film, begins with that audacity, which forever after remains its primary symbol and holy text. Yet *Kane* continues to excite, impress, amuse, and astound (and, occasionally, exasperate) today not because of its landmark status but because it still exudes the wonder and thrill of artistic discovery, the giddiness of high-stakes daring, the narcissistic pull of power, fame, and youthful self-regard. Beyond its many paradoxical fusions (of expressionism and realism, fairytale and reportage, projection and autobiography), it lets you sense what it must have felt like to be a boy genius suddenly let loose in the vast dream factory of Hollywood; the film's encyclopedic ambitions, its air of trying to cram everything (and then some) into a single movie, stem from the terror and possibility of that freedom.

As for how the movie turned into the superlative: it is a fascinating tale that runs from the rediscovery of American cinema in post–World War II Paris to battles over auteurism in America in the 1960s and beyond. Enterprising cinephiles should be urged to launch their own voyages through the astonishing galaxy of opinion that, in illuminating *Kane,* comprises "*Kane.*" Read, among others, André Bazin, François Truffaut, Andrew Sarris, Pauline Kael, Peter Bogdanovich, Joseph McBride, Jonathan Rosenbaum, and David Thomson. Ultimately, it's no secret that *Citizen Kane* became "the greatest film" by being, without question, the greatest *critic's film.*

Close Encounters of the Third Kind (1977)

by Matthew Seitz

AS A CHILD GROWING UP IN suburban Phoenix, Arizona, during the 1950s, Steven Spielberg was fascinated by the concept of UFOs and life on other worlds. His youthful obsession bore spectacular fruit decades later; this movie- and TV-crazy suburban boy grew up to become an expressive director whose first three features, *Duel, The Sugarland Express*, and *Jaws*, coupled precision-tooled suspense narratives with an uncanny understanding of how middle-class Americans thought, felt, and dreamed. His nautical horror film *Jaws*, released in the summer of 1975, went on to become the top grossing film of the 1970s. It was succeeded two years later by the space fantasy *Star Wars*, directed by his old friend and future coproducer, George Lucas.

Spielberg's own 1977 release, *Close Encounters of the Third Kind*, about the effects of extraterrestrial contact on a handful of middle-class Indiana suburban- ites, didn't unseat Lucas's high-tech cliffhanger, but it was arguably the decade's most complex, moving, and mysterious blockbuster—a spectacle that deployed the latest in optical and sound effects to suggest not just what extraterrestrial life might look like but how proof of its existence might make us *feel*. The film's unof- ficial sequel, *E.T.*, a rapturously intense kids' movie about the friendship between a fatherless suburban boy and a stranded alien botanist, did topple *Star Wars* from its box-office perch, establishing Spielberg not just as the most technically fluent and financially successful director of the modern age but also the most emotion- ally intuitive.

Close Encounters begins with a black screen backed by ominously shapeless chords by Spielberg's longtime collaborator, John Williams; the music rises in pitch, climaxing with a burst of music and blinding white light. Thus does the director summarize, in a few brilliant seconds, the keys to his own artistic strat- egy: the opposing poles of mystery and certainty, darkness and illumination, fear and reassurance. Audaciously invoking fairy tales and miracles (including clips from the 1956 version of *The Ten Commandments* and a Warner Bros. cartoon with Marvin the Martian, and overheard snippets of "When You Wish Upon a Star" from Disney's *Pinnocchio*), Spielberg dares to take extraterrestrial visitation seri- ously, portraying its life-altering effect on the lives of everyday Americans.

In the first act, the film's hero, Roy Neary (Richard Dreyfuss), a suburban electrician and family man, crisscrosses the Indiana countryside in his battered pickup, attempting to restore order (light) to a state plunged into chaos (darkness) by UFO visitations. At a crossroads, his truck is nuked by otherworldly light so intense that it sunburns half his face. Tracking the saucers via radio reports, Roy crosses paths with a suburban single mom, Jillian (Melinda Dillon), who's chasing her five-year-old son, Barry (Cary Guffey), a wide-eyed moppet lured from his spacious woodland home by unseen visitors. Roy, Jillian, and Barry witness a flyby visitation from starships that roll through the air like Christmas tree ornaments. Imprinted by the aliens with visions of a flat-topped mountain, these ordinary folks become hopeless seekers, groping after a truth that's more emotional than scientific.

Although Spielberg is frequently accused of sugarcoating the fantastic, the second act of *Close Encounters* depicts these same everyday visionaries as the secular equivalent of religious pilgrims whose glimpse of infinity wrecks their lives. (*Taxi Driver* screenwriter Paul Schrader, who did uncredited work on the film's script, envisioned the heroes' encounter with a higher life-form as a biblical event akin to Paul's revelation on the road to Damascus.) Jillian's son is kidnapped by the visitors for an unknown purpose (seeing the lights tumbling down from lighting-spackled storm clouds, the grinning kid cries, "Toys!"), then spends the rest of the film attempting to reunite with him. Roy tries to physically re-create his subconscious vision, spiraling into derangement and driving away his wife and kids. (The visitation turns workaday Americans into artists; Jillian draws sketches of her dream, while Roy makes sculptures.)

A newscast about a chemical spill at Devil's Tower, Wyoming, puts longitude and latitude to Roy and Jillian's dream of the heavens descending upon a mountaintop; they make their way West (the classic American journey) but are captured by the military, which concocted the chemical-spill story to keep civilians from intruding on the government's first meeting with the aliens. (The chief UFO researcher, Lacombe, is played by the French New Wave figurehead François Truffaut, a movie critic turned autobiographical filmmaker whom Spielberg considered a hero; by casting Truffaut, the young director instantly gave a populist sci-fi movie the art-house equivalent of street cred—and implied that even expensive Hollywood blockbusters could be personal.)

Undaunted, they escape government custody, make their way to the other side of the mountain to a state-constructed landing strip, and are rewarded with a biblically fantastic sound-and-light show in which a sky full of UFOs serves as a mere curtain-raiser. After a moment of ominous silence, the mothership rises up from behind Devil's Tower, like a demon disgorged from the earth. Spielberg's concise, abstract opening is elaborated upon in the film's finale, which has the mothership darkening all who gaze upward at its majesty, then illuminating every corner of the screen with music and light before releasing several decades' worth of abductees, including Barry. The man-child Roy, divested of everything but his desire to leave this earth, is tapped as the aliens' only human passenger on the return home—faith and innocence rewarded. Throughout the finale, Spielberg cloaks the aliens in ethereal light and presents them in suggestive flashes. Like characters in a dream, their motives and actions are never explained—yet the director's beatific images and increasingly sweet music tell us they mean no harm and that humanity is elevated by their presence.

Released five years later, *E.T.*, about a stranded alien with nearly Christlike powers befriending and mentoring a fatherless boy named Elliott (Henry Thomas), might have played like a storybook addendum to *Close Encounters*. Yet Spielberg's awesome command of darkness and light—and his deep-seated conviction that sentient beings everywhere were basically decent—transcended science fiction and fantasy, plugging into moviegoers' collective fantasy of secret missions and imaginary friends and their wish for paternal rescue from fear, loneliness, even death. Spielberg and screenwriter Melissa Mathison repeated *Close Encounters* tropes (including government scientists who seemed evil on first glance but had our best interests at heart) while enlarging the former movie's intense desire for love, escape, and deliverance. Set largely in a spooky green forest primeval (a setting Spielberg revisited, with much less clarity, in 2001's broken-backed robot parable *A.I.*), it was a fairy tale full of eye-popping storybook images: a wilted flower springing to life, an airborne bicycle silhouetted against a blinding full moon.

As always, the director repeatedly plunged his audiences into darkness, then blinded them with light, yet for most viewers, the strategy seemed liberating rather than bullying—the surehanded tricks of a master showman. E.T., a long-necked, waddling robot puppet whose gibbering language was voiced by movie star Debra Winger, seemed an unlikely candidate to melt hearts, but he did exactly that. By turns a freak, a clown, a brother, and a Jesus figure that could heal by touch, this squat amphibian erased a divorce-wracked family's emotional scars, then resurrected himself before ascending heavenward. Watching it, one is reminded that a diverse array of Spielberg films—from *Always* and *Jurassic Park* to *Schindler's List* and *A.I.*—have showed people, animals, and sometimes entire cultures being raised from the dead. Directors love to play God, but only Spielberg makes a career of it—and makes the act seem not blasphemous or cynical, but playful and divine.

Closely Watched Trains (1967)

by Richard Schickel

IT IS PERHAPS TOO EASY TO FORGET, on those rare occasions when we consider cultural objects produced in Czechoslovakia, that that country's national epic is—uniquely—a comic one: Jaroslav Hasek's *The Good Soldier Schweik*. So it was, in the late 1960s, when, suddenly, happily, we were obliged to conjure with the work of what amounted to the "New Wave" of filmmakers that had somehow crawled out from under the Stalinist overcoat—actually it was more of a winding sheet—to delight the world with their subversive cheek.

These movies, arriving in our theaters more or less simultaneously, seemed something of a miracle. They were small in scale. They were typically about ordinary, unglamorous people, who were generally regarded with a humorous and humane eye. They were also different in tone from the national cinemas that had earlier caught our attention—Italian Neorealism, for example, or the French *Nouvelle Vague*. There was a wryness about them, a gently stated sense of the absurd, that suggested (as *Schweik* had) that for a small, geopolitically disfavored nation a certain sly cunning, an ability to speak in humanistic metaphors about political matters, was perhaps the only way to resist its surrounding bullies.

The national portrait presented in the films of this new generation—their attitudes formed during the Nazi occupation of World War II, sharpened by the Stalinist dictatorship of the postwar period—was what we might now call a slacker Nirvana, a place where private problems always took precedence over public issues, where ideological pomp was ever subverted by the imp of personal perversity.

There was something delightfully casual about the manner of these films, too. Loosely structured, often shot in the streets and on provincial back roads, frequently acted by amateurs, their lack of formal pretense seemed all the more remarkable since they were, after all, the products of an Iron Curtain country.

Czech Spring or not, Dubcek or not, we still wondered how the chief figures of this renaissance, all graduates of FAMU, the famous state film school—got away with it. Obviously it required a certain courage to go their own, largely apolitical, largely comical ways even in a slightly looser cultural climate. Therefore, our gratitude for their efforts was conditioned by admiration for their determination to speak in the tongue of humanity. Mostly, however, we were simply grateful and welcoming when, in the late 1960s, Forman's *Loves of a Blonde*, Passer's *Intimate Lighting*, and Menzel's *Closely Watched Trains* appeared in the United States.

None was more successful than Menzel's marvelous film. From Bosley Crowther to John Simon, every major American reviewer recognized its merits. It went on to gain the fond regard of sophisticated audiences and the Academy Award as the best foreign film of 1967.

One always returns to such a widely hailed and beloved film with a certain trepidation. So often our initial enthusiasm is betrayed by the passing years. We wonder, especially with films that are so immediately likable, if we were taken prisoner by people carrying false papers, whispering seductive nothings in our ears. That's not the case with *Closely Watched Trains*. If anything, it seems to me more poignant than it did when it first appeared more than thirty years ago.

I think we were all somewhat misled by it at first. A lot of us treated the tragic end of the film, as no more than a *coup de theatre,* a sudden lurch toward seriousness that the director and the writer (novelist Bohumil Hrabal) somehow pull off without spoiling the film's overall sense of fun.

There's some truth in that argument. But what struck me most strongly when I recently returned to the movie was how cleverly the filmmakers lead us to believe they're just kidding around, that their aim is nothing more than a sort of chucklesome and offhand geniality. It is only when the movie is over that we discern a certain inevitability in the fate of its central figure, Trainee Milos Herma (Vaclav Neckar). We ought perhaps to perceive that in the scheme of this movie, its most passive and clueless figure has to become its victim-martyr. This development nails down the movie's main point. Which is that in a chancy universe unlikely figures have as good a chance of ending up heroes as the more visibly promising ones.

An apt alternative title for the movie might be *Closely Packed Frames,* for despite its relatively short running time—it is just a little over an hour and a half long—and despite the fact that it rarely strays beyond its principle setting, a sleepy, small-town railway station, it is uncommonly rich in character and comic incident. Given the modest volume of its traffic, each and every member of the station's staff has plenty of time to pursue his or her interests, all of them irrelevant to the great drama—World War II—that is proceeding, as it were, just up the tracks from them.

The stationmaster dreams futile dreams of promotion while he and his wife devote most of their energy to raising pigeons, geese, and rabbits in the backyard.

Hubicka, the train dispatcher (wonderfully played by Josef Somr) has a feckless air about him, which belies his success as a womanizer. Indeed, the sequence in which he seduces the telegrapher, is, I think, one of the most original such scenes in all of movie history, involving, as it does, a succession of rubber stamps applied with increasing erotic hilarity to the wriggling thighs and bottom of his eagerly giggling partner.

Passing through the station from time to time are the imperious local countess, the outraged mother of the seduced telegrapher, some Nazi soldiers intent on having their way with a carload of nurses whose train has been sidetracked near the station. The most significant of the station's visitors is the clueless Quisling, Councilor Zednicek (played with a sort of weary menace by Vlastimil Brodsky), who is in charge of making the trains—especially the "closely watched" ones (those carrying munitions to the German army) run on time. He always has a map with him and is always eager to employ it to show the strategic brilliance of the latest German retreat. He is, of course, treated with varying degrees of silent contempt by the gang at the station. Passionate ideologues bemuse and slightly puzzle them.

For most of the movie Trainee Herma is the passive observer of their little symphony of self-absorption, searching it for the clues that might help him to become a successful adult. This is not a status that we, watching him watching them, have much confidence he will attain. A cheerful train conductor (Jitka Bendova) has her eye on him, but when she takes him away to her uncle's house for a night of romantic frolic, he fails her—premature ejaculation. This leads him to attempt suicide. A kindly doctor (played by Menzel himself) advises him to find a patient, older woman to properly initiate him in the art of love. This, naturally, leads the lad to ask virtually every woman he encounters if she would oblige him.

That's funny. But it turns out that Dispatcher Hubicka is no more a political layabout than he is a sexual one. He is in touch with the resistance and ready to aid it in blowing up an ammunition train as it passes through the station. It's representative, known by the obvious *nom de guerre* as Victoria Freie (Nada Urbankova) arrives bearing the bomb Hubicka requires. Better still, she's the older woman Milos has been looking for. Encouraged by Hubicka, she sweetly, genially makes a man of him (as we used to say).

More of a man, it turns out, than anyone bargained for. The next day, as the ammunition train approaches the station, Councilor Zednicek and his retinue arrive to investigate the charges of illicit rubber-stamping brought against Hubicka. It is a wonderfully absurd moment, given the complicity of his "victim" and the ludicrous nature of his "offense." Still, the hearing—which ends with him charged not with a sexual offense but with desecration of the German language with which the rubber stamps were inscribed—requires his presence. But not Milos's. He eases the bomb out of its desk-drawer hiding place, eases himself out of the station to a platform overhanging the tracks. He is, remember, a new man, charged with hubris and, perhaps, after so many years of vulnerability, a new sense of *invulnerability.*

The train appears. He drops his deadly package. Some offscreen sentries see and shoot him. He falls off his perch on to the train. And blows up with as it disappears around a curve in the track. The force of the blast blows his hat back toward the station where his conductor-girlfriend picks it up as it rolls past her feet.

Just before this final burst of well-staged action occurs, Councilor Zednicek appears trackside to vent his disgust with the ridiculous hearing over which he has just presided. He's a busy man. With important duties to attend. And these Czechs are, he says, nothing more than "laughing animals."

Well, Hubicka does laugh as the explosion reverberates through the railway yard. But it is a laugh of triumph. Of unlikely victory. It is also says that any kind of animal, but especially the human animal, can be dangerous when tormented or wronged or simply not taken seriously enough. Most important, this concluding sequence turns the entire movie into a metaphor for Czechoslovakia itself. It says that pleasant, pleasure-loving little country, so often occupied, so often *pre*occupied by its own survivor's *Schweik*-ishness, is more dangerous than it looks. It is, after all, the country that assassinated Heydrich in World War II and endured the reprisal for that act at Lidice. It is also the country that, not a year after *Closely Watched Trains* was released, endured a terrible punishment for its cheekiness, its ironic-satiric spirit—Soviet tanks in Wenceslas Square, the reimposition of the Iron Curtain mentality on its free and easy spirit.

Of the great figures of the Czech movie renaissance, only Menzel stayed on in Prague. Forman, of course, went on to a major international career, which included two directorial Academy Awards. Passer went on to a more minor one, as did many another émigré Czech film worker.

Menzel, according to the standard reference books, continued working as an actor and director on the Prague stage but was obliged to denounce the "errors" of the Czech new wave before being allowed to return to the cinema. Of the many features—well over a dozen of them—that he made after *Closely Watched Trains*—only a handful achieved very limited distribution in the West, some only after long delays imposed by the Stalinoid cultural bureaucracy. Of them all, only *My Sweet Little Village,* nominated for a best foreign language film Oscar in 1986, was widely seen. It is a film very much in the spirit of *Closely Watched Trains*, and brave enough in its criticism of a clumsy state bureaucracy, but nowhere near as memorable satirically or tragically.

Maybe Menzel is one of the many victims of twentieth-century megapolitics, yet another artist on whose art the difficult business of surviving in a totalitarian society imposed too much of a distorting strain. Maybe, on the other hand, he is essentially a man capable of just one great, near-perfect work. I suspect that the former is the case, since the descriptions one reads of his many unseen works are so appealing. One would give anything to see those films, to be in touch with the full career of this insinuating filmmaker. Perhaps . . . someday. In the meantime, we do have *Closely Watched Trains,* as fresh and potent as it ever was and a film that continues to reward many a close rewatching.

Close-up (1990)

by Jonathan Rosenbaum

A WATERSHED BOTH IN THE HISTORY of Iranian cinema and in the career of Abbas Kiarostami, one of its major filmmakers, *Close-up* (1990) also goes a long way in defining the Iranian New Wave by exemplifying and helping to clarify three of its most characteristic traits—a use of nonprofessional actors and natural locations, an exposition of the barriers between movies and ordinary people established by social class and the media, and a breakdown between what usually distinguishes fiction from non-fiction. One reason why this film went on to become the most influential feature of the Iranian new wave is that it not only epitomizes the special status and importance movies (and art in general) has in Iranian life but also highlights the philosophical and humanist dimensions of Iranian art films in general. It seems significant that during the same period when Iranians virtually became the most demonized people on the planet, they also gradually became known for producing the most ethical and humanist cinema, incidentally affording audiences glimpses into their culture that the news media generally denied them by harping on fundamentalist and terrorist stereotypes.

Before *Close-up* was made, Iranian films were rarely seen or discussed outside their home turf—not always or necessarily because they were too localized, but often because outsiders simply weren't paying close enough attention. *The House*

Is Black—an astonishing short documentary about a leper colony by Forough Farrokhzad, one of the greatest Persian poets, in 1962—won a prize at a German film festival but then was basically forgotten until the mid-1990s; and the first Iranian feature I ever saw myself, in London in the mid-1970s—Parviz Kimiavi's *The Mongols,* a modernist satire about Western views of the Middle East—still awaits rediscovery. But *Close-up* received wider recognition, especially in Europe, helping to launch Iranian cinema as an exportable commodity as well as a viable concept in the world at large.

Like the plot of *Six Degrees of Separation,* with which it shares a few striking similarities, *Close-up* is based on a true story. An impoverished bookbinder and film freak in his thirties named Hossein Sabzian, sitting next to a middle-class housewife named Mrs. Ahankhanh on a bus in Tehran, claimed to be Mohsen Makhmalbaf—then and now one of the most famous artists in Iran, a former fundamentalist and terrorist against the shah in his teens who first became a playwright, then an increasingly skeptical and adventurous filmmaker whose best known films by the late 1980s included *The Cyclist* and *Marriage of the Blessed.* Continuing his impersonation, Sabzian was invited to the woman's home and befriended her husband and two grown sons, offering to cast them all in his next film and proposing to use their house as a location. Then, after he borrowed money from the Ahankhanhs that he failed to return, he was eventually exposed as a fraud and arrested.

Ready with a film crew to shoot another feature, Kiarostami, who was pushing fifty at the time—having made principally films for and about children over the past twenty years—read a story about the Sabzian incident in a weekly magazine and immediately decided to shift his plans and make a film about this subject instead. What kind of film? Sort of a docudrama, but with all the real people playing their own parts in a restaging of some of the events—not only the meeting between Sabzian and Mrs. Ahankhanh on the bus and his subsequent arrest and trial but also Kiarostami's own visit to Sabzian in jail, when he asked the bookbinder to play himself in a picture. (At the restaged trial, where the turbaned judge agrees to play himself as well, two cameras are used—one of them reserved for close-ups of Sabzian, the other employing a zoom lens that roves more freely around the courtroom.)

In some cases, including the film's very first scene, major events are restaged from unexpected vantage points: after a reporter from the weekly magazine is alerted that Sabzian is about to be arrested at the Ahankhanhs' home, we accompany him and the two policeman in a cab to the designated house, but once we get there, we perversely remain outside with the driver, who picks flowers from a pile of leaves nearby, dislodging an aerosol can that he distractedly kicks across the road. (Sabzian himself is barely visible when he gets into the cab with the two policemen, and it might be argued that the driver, reporter, and even the spray can—later kicked again by the reporter while searching for a tape recorder from the Ahankhanhs' neighbors—are more important at this stage of the plot.)

Much later in the film, we finally get to see the same scene from the vantage point of the Ahankhanhs and Sabzian inside the house. And still later we're present at a brand new scene arranged by Kiarostami himself: Sabzian, after his release from jail, meets the real Mohsen Makhmalbaf for the first time and climbs on the back of his motorbike so they can jointly pay a visit to the Ahankhanhs, picking up a conciliatory bouquet of flowers for the family en route.

The more we watch these events unfold, the more mysterious as well as unexpected everything becomes. In the first scene, it's the giddiness of the reporter anticipating a scoop that's emphasized. We don't get to the restaged meeting of Sabzian and Mrs. Ahankhanhs on the bus until the middle of the trial, when it occurs as a sort of impromptu flashback, and even the question of whether the participants are always furnishing their own dialogue is less than obvious. (The scene looks rehearsed, and assuming that their memories diverge at all, we can't tell whose version of this scene prevails.) Kiarostami generally remains offscreen or viewed from behind, and the degree to which he functions as ringmaster or as simple witness isn't spelled out. Even in the final sequence, when it appears that a failure in the sound equipment prevents us from hearing all of Sabzian's conversation with Makhmalbaf on the motorbike, there is good evidence that this problem is being faked—as well as some more recent evidence from critic Godfrey Cheshire, who has researched this film in detail, that the technical problems were genuine. (Interestingly enough, Kiarostami deliberately and pointedly turned off the soundtrack near the end of his previous documentary—a monumental feature about schoolboys, *Homework*, made the same year—with similarly effective results.)

Everything, in short, gets thrown into question; the veracity of what we see and hear remains uncertain, and that's really the point: the closer up we get, the farther away we feel from grasping this simple story with any confidence. What none the less comes across loud and clear is that there's some of Sabzian in all of us and that documentaries are every bit as constructed as fiction films. This doesn't mean that what we're watching is "only a movie," as the Hollywood-derived expression would have it; for Sabzian, we quickly learn, movies are a matter of life and death, and the reverence for art and poetry held throughout Iranian society—which is partly what made Sabzian's impersonation possible in the first place—is an important part of what gives *Close-up* and countless films derived from it (by Kiarostami and Makhmalbaf themselves as well as by many others) particular pungency. Film, as we see it, is what enables people to cross class barriers—in their imaginations when they watch films and, in this case, in life when a poor man impersonates a famous film director. It becomes an instrument of empowerment as well as a double-edged sword: Sabzian goes to jail for impersonating someone else, but Kiarostami gets prizes and recognition for persuading Sabzian, the Ahankhanhs, the reporter, the judge, and others to impersonate themselves. Without being in the least bit pretentious, *Close-up* offers us a profound site of contemplation on the subject of what movies ultimately mean to ordinary people and some further thoughts about what they do to us.

Dance, Girl, Dance (1940)

by Carrie Rickey

WE SPEAK OF "SEMINAL" FILMS such as *Citizen Kane*, *Casablanca*, and *Spartacus*. Let us now praise an "ovular" film: Dorothy Arzner's *Dance, Girl, Dance*, a 1940 movie as subversive and unconventional as the woman who made it. Arzner's picture is a peppy little number that bounces, along with stars Lucille Ball and Maureen O'Hara, from burlesque to ballet, settling finally on a type of dance—and of woman—that need not undress itself to express itself.

The lone female studio director during Hollywood's golden era, Arzner was along with George Cukor and Mitchell Leisen one of a handful of feminists who not only directed movies about women but did so expressly from the heroine's point-of-view. Alas Arzner's *Dance, Girl, Dance*—released the same year as *The Grapes of Wrath*, *Rebecca* and Cukor's own *The Philadelphia Story*—initially met with critical drubbing and commercial disdain, losing RKO Studios some $400,000.

But like *It's a Wonderful Life*, a humiliating critical and commercial failure in its own time, *Dance, Girl, Dance* was rediscovered during the 1970s. Disgruntled that contemporary Hollywood did not reflect the aspirations of the emerging woman's movement, 1970s feminists found a foremother in Arzner, all of whose films challenge the implicit assumption that the spectator of films is male and the sexual spectacle female. A sequence on the burlesque stage, in which O'Hara confronts leering men salivating at her dishabille, expressly challenges and critiques standard Hollywood practice.

The O'Hara character, aspiring ballerina Judy, keeps body and soul together by pirouetting daintily on the boards to whet audience appetite for the provocative bumps and grinds of Bubbles, the burlesque queen played not just to the hilt, but to the cleavage, by Ball.

One night, the strap on Judy's bodice snaps—and so does she. Exasperated by being Bubbles's stooge—on stage as well as in her romantic life—Judy steps out of performance and confronts the spectators in the vaudeville house—and, by extension, the movie theater—with a forthrightness brash as Manet's *Olympia*. "Go ahead and stare," she chides the drooling men in the audience perceiving her merely as sexual object. "I know you want me to tear my clothes off so you can look your 50 cents' worth. Fifty cents for the privilege of looking at a girl the way your wives won't let you? . . . What's it for? So you can go home when the show is over . . . and play at being the stronger sex for a minute? I'm sure [your wives] see through you just like we do."

For the 1970s generation galvanized by theories advanced by John Berger and Laura Mulvey about classical art's and cinema's presumption of the active, powerful male observer and passive, powerless female observed, *Dance, Girl, Dance* was an object lesson in resisting objectification, a revelation, revolutionary. Just as it was also a kick, in every meaning of the word.

Contract director Roy Del Ruth was originally slated to make this unassuming B movie based on a story by Vicki Baum of *Grand Hotel* fame. Disappointed with Del Ruth's footage, producer Erich Pommer replaced him with Arzner. She was a twenty-year Hollywood veteran who had worked her way from studio typist to become a much-admired editor of the silent classics *The Covered Wagon* and *Blood and Sand* to become the one "femme megger" (so dubbed because directors wielded megaphones) in the studio system. (Though in its infancy the movies had almost as many female directors as male, by the time of the industry consolidations of 1920, most of the founding mothers of film had been marginalized.)

Arzner made one immediate, and crucial, change to the script. She replaced the dance teacher, in the Del Ruth version a male mentor named Basiloff, with Maria Ouspenskaya as Basilova, a female mentor more sensitive to the ideals and necessities of her charges. She explicitly modeled Basilova, with her man-tailored suits and ties, on herself and Bubbles on the popular entertainer "Tex" Guinan. (On the basis of Arzner's butch manner of dress and her longtime companion, choreographer Marion Morgan, most observers assume that she was lesbian.)

With Arzner behind the camera, *Dance, Girl, Dance* was rechoreographed as a study in conflicts, most of them neatly mediated by the finale. We have the struggle between high culture (ballet) and low (burlesque), that between innocence (O'Hara's Judy) and experience (Ball's Bubbles), that between working class (Judy and Bubbles) and leisure class (Jimmie, the millionaire fancied by both, played by Louis Hayward), and finally, that between the romantic (Judy) and the pragmatist (Bubbles). Arzner comes not to judge but to celebrate this diversity of women, work, and art.

In a sly subversion of the Hollywood Production Code—commandments prescribing that promiscuity be punished by the final reel and virtue rewarded—Arzner's movie suggests two ideas transgressive for female characters of the time. One is that Judy's sexual inhibitions inhibit her progress as a dancer and compound her powerlessness. The other is that Bubbles's sexual appetite and shamelessness gives her power over men, whether potential employers or lovers. As Arzner's most eloquent analyst, film scholar Judith Mayne, observes, "Women may be objectified through performance, but they are also empowered."

Only when Judy, erotically charged by her crush on Jimmie and sick of prostituting her talent in burlesque, challenges the audience with her analysis of the power dynamic between spectator and spectacle, does she find her own power. It earns her the admiration of the modern dance impresario, Steve Adams (Ralph Bellamy), who admires Judy for her fluency both in the formal ballet and vernacular burlesque. It moreover earns her the admiration of Adams's female assistant, who applauds Judy's outburst and reminds us that there are women on both sides of the stage, and that—as Mayne notes—"they take pleasure in looking at each other."

The Decalogue (1988)

by Michael Wilmington

KRZYSZTOF KIESLOWSKI'S *The Decalogue* was the masterpiece of an exemplary stubborn man, both a great 1988 Polish film and a testament of its time. Shot during the collapse of the old Soviet bloc, largely unknown to the public because of its unusual length (almost ten hours) and spotty distribution, it remains an unforgettable, dauntingly ambitious work: one of the major achievements of the whole postwar era.

Most initially striking about *The Decalogue* is its form. It's an epic—but an intimate one. Set in a modern Warsaw apartment complex, composed of ten episodes (each inspired by one of the Ten Commandments), and acted with searing intensity by a virtual "Who's Who" of Polish actors (staunch Daniel Olbrychski, magnetic Grazyna Szapolowska, comical Jerzy Stuhr, intense Boguslaw Linda, and dark-eyed Maja Komorowska), *The Decalogue* is a rare film work mixing high ambition and near faultless achievement. Few directors would have undertaken such a massive, risky project. Fewer still could complete it with such stunning success.

Kieslowski and his scenarist, Krzysztof Piesiewicz, wrote the script during a period of extraordinary national ferment. But, unlike Andrzej Wajda, earlier in *Man of Iron,* they don't chronicle change or upheaval directly. Instead, they make *Decalogue* a vast fresco of private emotions and moral conflicts. At first glance, their canvas seems very small: that mundane Warsaw complex, several buildings facing each other across a barren courtyard. Within those buildings live most of the important characters of *The Decalogue*: a largely middle-class mix of doctors and teachers, taxi drivers, and postmen. Most know each other only casually. And though the stories move outside to the city and countryside, Kieslowski always returns to those towering walls and monotonous windows. There, he implies, if you look closely enough, you can see many of life's dramas unfold.

In order, these are the episodes:

Decalogue 1: (I am the Lord thy God; Thou shalt not have other gods before me.) The life of a university teacher who implicitly trusts computers is shattered when his child falls through ice on a lake that was measured as safe.

2: (Thou shalt not take the name of the Lord thy God in vain.) An elderly doctor must decide whether to deceive the pregnant, desperate young wife of a man whose cancer may be incurable.

3: (Remember the Sabbath day, to keep it holy.) On Christmas Eve, a married taxi driver's old mistress takes him on a wild-goose chase through Warsaw.

4: (Honor thy father and thy mother.) An acting student who lives with her father discovers a letter from her dead mother, which may reveal long-buried family secrets about her parentage.

5: (Thou shalt not kill.) (Released in expanded form as *A Short Film About Killing*.) A seemingly psychopathic young drifter-killer from the provinces, his brutal cab-driver victim, and the lawyer who will argue his capital case in court cross paths on two days of death: the murder and the execution.

6: (Thou shalt not commit adultery.) (Released in long expanded form as *A Short Film About Love*). A shy young postman-milkman regularly spies through his telescope on the affairs of a promiscuous young woman across the courtyard. He falls in love; she discovers him.

7: (Thou shalt not steal.) A beautiful, melancholy young woman whose illegitimate daughter has been raised by the woman's mother as her own daughter kidnaps her child and tries to establish their true ties.

8: (Thou shalt not bear false witness against thy neighbor.) A famous, elderly professor of ethics encounters a young Jewish woman she first met decades ago during World War II, when she refused to help hide the little girl from the Nazis.

9: (Thou shalt not covet thy neighbor's wife.) A once-philandering doctor, whose sex life has ended because of illness, becomes racked with jealousy over his wife's affair with a younger man.

10: (Thou shalt not covet thy neighbor's goods.) Two brothers—a punk rocker and a family man—discover that their recently deceased father kept a fortune in stamps in his flat. As swindlers gather around them, they become obsessed with their unusual inheritance.

Initially shown on Polish TV as a series, the ten episodes can all be appreciated independently. (Decalogue Five and Six are the peaks.) But they gain immensely when seen together. Themes recur and develop. Major characters in one tale reappear as background people in another. And the episodes are linked by a mysterious figure: a silent young blond man with intently observant eyes who keeps reappearing at crucial moments.

Overall, through the ebb and flow of the separate dramas, *The Decalogue* keeps building into a rich, multifaceted chronicle of a deeply flawed society, the bleak moral flotsam of a materialist world adrift, seen throughout with a cool, seemingly dispassionate eye. Kieslowski began as a highly critical documentarian (1969's *From the City of Lodz* and 1975's devastating *Personnel*), and, like Ken Loach, he carries a reportorial approach into his fictional dramas—even when his stories (*Blind Chance* or *No End*) veer into fantasy. Nowhere is that blend more potent than in *The Decalogue*. Backed by composer Zbigniew Preisner's spare score, the film maintains a tone of pure, haunting melancholy, and unbearable truth. Only one of the ten episodes, the last, is comical. But it's dark comedy indeed: a satiric view of crumbling Polish society in the new age of greed.

I first saw *The Decalogue* at a special "détente" retrospective of modern Eastern European and Russian cinema assembled by Ken Wlaschin for Los Angeles's 1991 AFIFEST, and though there were many great films and discoveries at that series— the whimsical fantasy of Slovakia's Juraj Jakubisko, the mordant gaze of Alexei

Gherman—*The Decalogue* towered above them all, as it still towers over the rest of Kieslowski's filmography (including *Three Colors: Red, White, Blue*) and much of post-1970s world cinema.

His work, various yet integral, moves rigorously through three distinct periods and styles: the mostly black-and-white documentary years (1969–1978), some of his best, least-seen work; the second phase (1979–1988) of acerbic social dramas (*Camera Buff*), which culminates in *The Decalogue*; and the third (1991 to his death, when he became a canonized international art-film maker and devotee of French screen beauty—piquant Irène Jacob, ravishing Julie Delpy, and radiant Juliette Binoche, three "colors" to stoke your dreams). All those films lead to and away from *The Decalogue*. And throughout all those years, Kieslowski, a fiercer moralist than Ingmar Bergman, remained at odds with his own society.

Is there a strict religious significance in his choice of the Ten Commandments? Kieslowski denied it—perhaps breaking the Eighth Commandment when he did. Using the laws, he continually forces a reexamination of his little world. Why do we live? Why do we suffer? What brings us joy? Pain? How, in the face of a world full of cruelty, can we be decent to each other? Most modern films wouldn't bother to ask those questions. And if they did, it would be in heavily clichéd terms. But Kieslowski's beautiful, sad, clear-eyed *Decalogue*—an overwhelming psychological and spiritual epic for our times—faces the darkness, sends out a prayer (of sorts) against the storm.

Diary of a Country Priest (1951)

by Henry Sheehan

DIARY OF A COUNTRY PRIEST (*Le Journal d'un curé de campagne*) (1951) was the fourth film made by Robert Bresson though, in some sense, it marked a beginning for the forty-four-year-old filmmaker. It was, for example, the first in which he used a mostly nonprofessional cast. It was also the first in which, employing a cinematographer (L.H. Burel) whose career began in 1915, Bresson turned away from the conventionally "beautiful" look of his previous film, *Les Dames du Bois de Boulogne,* to relying on harsher, less velvety images. Some observers have called this look flat, perhaps because they find it a useful prologue to comparing Bresson's image-making to icon-painting.

But *Diary* does not sport a flat or primitive look, and neither would any of Bresson's ten forthcoming films. Bresson was indeed influenced by painting, but he wasn't enthralled by any particular age's techniques. While many of his films do sport shots that look like the flat, iconic portraits of saints made in the Middle Ages, the filmmaker is more than happy to break his images into multiple fields when it suits his purpose. Contrary to even laudatory critics, Bresson is not some artifact from the past or an oddball wrapped up in the intricacies of obscure Catholic philosophy. Although his movies are distinctly religious, they are also extremely modern, bound up in examining men and women's place in an indifferent society driven by profit and retaining ancient social structures even as it makes technological advances. Bresson's tendency could no longer be ignored in 1977 when he made *The Devil Probably*, which centered around a group of long-haired university students involved, with Bresson's obvious approval, in environmentalism.

Diary of a Country Priest offers no such easy clues as to its specific modernity. Based on a novel by Georges Bernanos, which the militant, antifascist, anticommunist Catholic novelist finished shortly before World War II, the action takes place in the cold, wet countryside of Artois, the very northernmost region of France. It's unclear exactly when the action takes place at first, though eventually it's clear that the setting is contemporary with the production.

But Bresson isn't in pursuit of timelessness, so much as realism. You could say the same about drama; Bresson does everything he can to avoid it, and he does so in pursuit of the same realism. Take the movie's third or fourth shot, in which we see the young priest (an emaciated but smooth-faced Claude Laydu) standing for the first time in front of the weathered rectory of his new parish. Already, he's seen the local aristocrat, a middle-aged count (Jean Riveyre) with a young woman who, we'll discover, is his daughter's governess and his lover. But though we see them in close-up, it's part of a series of shots that mostly show the priest walking his bike against a larger panorama of the countryside. And then, we get to that shot of him in front of the rectory, and on the soundtrack the noise of a large, horse-drawn wagon overwhelms the silence.

In 1975, Bresson published a collection of aphorisms called *Notes on Cinematography*, a key to his filmmaking philosophy. Among the longer observations is this: "The exchanges that are produced between images and images, sounds and sounds, images and sounds, give the people and objects in your films their cinematographic life and, by a subtle phenomenon, unify their composition."

The seen and the seeing, the noise and the offscreen noisemaker, have all combined to show us an enormous amount of social detail in what has always been considered an "interior" drama. We know we're in a land of ruling cliques and peasants (some quite miserly, as we discover in the very next scene), of natural beauty and human ugliness. Standing at its axis is the priest, physically unprepossessing but, in a face that Bresson will dote over, beautiful in an ethereal way.

Bresson insists: The priest is in the world, our world. He doesn't transcend it, nor does he even try. Suffering from physical and spiritual injury, he follows the dictates of the church as best he can. Along the way, he delivers a woman from bitterness and anger against God to a holy, satisfying reconciliation, yet finds that his good work is widely misinterpreted. Far from a good man, he's considered a largely ineffectual one, a meddler and a drunkard. He does nothing—purposely—to rehabilitate his reputation and suffers his own spiritual alienation along the way. Yet he adheres to his duties with a strange fervor so that, as a nearby avuncular priest, the Pastor of Torcy (Andre Guibert), recognizes, the young priest is a saint in the making.

The brilliance of *Diary*—its "subtle phenomenon"—is that we are able to maintain a double-vision of the priest as both bungler and saint-in-the-making. This happens even though Bresson complicates the issue by having his spiritual protagonist find his greatest victory not, fashionably, among the poor and downtrodden but among the privileged.

The Countess (Marie-Monique Arkell) has lost herself in reveries of a son who died in boyhood. Her indifference to the world around her has been something of a contributing factor (though not an excuse) to her husband's philandering. It's certainly a prime cause of her nearly grown daughter Chantal (Nicole Ladmiral), who has rebelled with such emotional violence against her parents that, as she tells the priest, she can't wait to sin.

We can't tell how the poison we bear within us will infect others, the priest tells the Countess at the beginning of an evening session that ends with the woman weeping on her knees. If you expect that time in between to be filled with melodramatic gesturing, you can be excused, for that's usually the approach of "religious" films. But Bresson refuses to let his actors "act." He demands that they strip themselves of gesture and facial expression, that they move with deliberation and speak in something close to a monotone.

Oddly ("subtle phenomenon" again), this increases both the emotional impact of the confrontation between the Countess and priest and, in its general application, of the rest of the film and of Bresson's work. Bresson despised conventional acting, along with conventional cinema technique, as "screens." They distracted us, he has written, from peering into the soul of his characters—or, rather than "characters," "people," since Bresson's style lends to erase the boundaries between player and played.

The priest and Countess's argument over her soul in subdued, almost muffled tones is a brilliant proof of Bresson's insight. Inevitably, we're drawn to the two faces, especially the priest's, which becomes illuminated with an intense spirituality. At the same time, throughout the scene, there's a persistent noise on the soundtrack, which sounds like a knife on a whetstone but turns out to be the scratch of a rake. It's a reminder not that the world intrudes into the spiritual, or the other way around, but that any sense of boundaries between the two is artificial. We have souls, but there in our bodies that are in the world, and this sets the condition for our salvation.

Bresson doesn't endorse a generalized spirituality; he is very definitely Catholic—and French Catholic at that. Throughout the movie, the priest suffers from such stomach cramps that he can only ingest bits of stale bread and cheap red wine that he sugars himself. The diet, of course, leaves him open to charges of alcoholism, and it's not entirely clear that the priest doesn't succumb to wine's inebriative effects from time to time.

Worse, this physical problem seems tied to the priest's inability to pray. Although he celebrates the mass every day (even when the Count's mistress is the only one who shows up for it) and performs the sacraments, he personally cannot pray. Instead, he confides his innermost thoughts and reports of his daily routine to his journal. We see him and, in voiceover, hear him make his entries, which range from dry descriptions of humiliations to the desperate request that he be able to pray once more.

The priest is asking for that multidefined divine gift, grace, that which unites individuals with God. In a twist that haunts many of Bresson's characters (in *Mouchette* and *Une Femme douce* most of all), the priest has received grace but doesn't have the ability to see it. What he does have is the determination to press on with his priestly duties. As the Pastor of Torcy tells him, he's one of those who "hold on" no matter what—even though holding on to what is unclear.

Bresson has a fierce admiration for those who hold on, and the closest he comes to contempt is for those who once had hold but let go. In this case, the contempt is visited on an old friend of the priest, Louis Dufrety (Bernard Hubrenne), whom he visits in his most dire moment of need. Louis has left the priesthood and taken up with a woman after suffering from a body- and faith-battering encounter with tuberculosis. But the priest saves his anger not for Louis's sexual wanderings but for his purported interest in "the intellectual life." This is apostasy plain and simple, the rejection of a belief in both the material and spiritual for a preoccupation with something that is neither.

Bresson's beliefs have never been very popular. He disdains both materialism and bloodless spirituality in ways that should alienate the contemporary world's mainstreams. It's his greatness as an artist that reaches out to all and everyone and convinces us, at least for the duration of his films, that he is exactly right.

Diner (1982)

by Peter Rainer

IF I HAD NOT BEEN PRIMED IN ADVANCE, I would not have expected much from writer-director Barry Levinson's *Diner.* If there's one thing we don't need now it's another 1950s rite-of-passage movie, complete with the obligatory buddy-buddyisms and a sound track of Golden Oldies. Levinson, who co-wrote . . . *And Justice For All* and *Inside Moves* as well as, among other credits, *The Carol Burnett Show,* and Mel Brooks's *High Anxiety* and *Silent Movie,* has in the past demonstrated a wacky, uneven flair. But nothing in his previous work gives any indication of the depth in *Diner,* which also marks his directorial debut. He's accomplished a minor miracle—a movie that, on the surface, is thoroughly familiar and yet, because of its artistry and perception, seems totally fresh.

The movie opens on Christmas night 1959 in Baltimore. There's not a whole lot of plot; essentially, we follow for a few days the lives of five guys in their early twenties—ex-high-school buddies—as they try to come to terms with their encroaching adulthood. In conventional terms, nothing much "happens" in this movie. It's a multicharacter study, and we quickly sort out the characters: There's Eddie (Steve Guttenberg), a fervid Colts fan who's about to get married—but first his wife must pass a football quiz; Billy (Timothy Daly), Eddie's prospective best man, who, in town from grad school, discovers that his sort-of girlfriend Barbara, a local TV-studio engineer (Kathryn Dowling), is pregnant; Shrevie (Daniel Stern), who appears to prize his record collection more than his wife Beth (Ellen Barkin); Fenwick (Kevin Bacon), a hard-drinking college dropout on the bum from his upper-class family; and Boogie (Mickey Rourke, the arsonist in *Body Heat*), a soft-spoken ladies man and gambler who works in a beauty parlor—with his oily pompadour and smart jackets, he's like a hood-prince. (There's also a sixth character—Paul Reiser's Modell—who's used in his brief appearances as the group's comic foil.)

None of these characters are quite what they first appear to be. Eddie swaggers a lot, but he overdoes it; he has the fast, clipped speech of someone who's trying to fortify himself against uncertainties. Billy has a clean-cut handsomeness that bespeaks blandness, but he has surprising reserves of vehemence. In a strip-joint/bar with Eddie one night, he shouts down the lagging house band and then sprints up to the stage to pound out some boogie-woogie—it's as if Bobby Rydell turned into Jerry Lee Lewis. Fenwick at first comes across as a spoiled-brat goof-off with the scary, gruff voice of a premature alky but he, too, shows unexpected depths of feeling, as well as smarts (watching *College Bowl* on TV, he consistently blurts out the correct answers ahead of the Ivy League eggheads). Shrevie, the only married member of the group, is never at a loss for words with his friends, but he has nothing to say to his wife, or she to him. When Eddie, nervous about the upcoming wedding, talks to him about what married life is like, Shrevie comes across as small-spirited, unfeeling. He sees marriage in almost purely sexual terms—as a way of ensuring regular nookie. And Shrevie is dispirited by that regularity. Domesticity depresses him.

Because he acts out, or pretends to act out, the boys' erotic fantasies, Boogie is the group's unspoken leader. Boogie, like the others, is more complex than he at first appears. He may be a smooth-talking con-man with women, but he's a *heart-felt* con-man; his soft-soothing patter is a clue to some essential tenderness. Of all the boys, he's the only one who is able to really talk to women, to level with them. "If you don't have good dreams, you have nightmares," he says, and he means it. At times, he has the blasted look of someone who's trying to shuffle off bad dreams, but, when his life connects with his fantasies—when, for example, he spots a vision of loveliness cantering on her horse in the countryside—he has a satyr's gleam in his bright eyes. He's the most poetic character in the film because, despite all his bull, he's the most open to the emotional possibilities in life.

It's rare to see a movie where the friendships seem as real, as lived-in, as they do here. This is partly due to Levinson's reverberant script and direction, and partly a result of the fine ensemble acting. The performances are uniformly superlative. The actors have reimagined their roles, which on the surface seem so familiar from other movies, as completely as Levinson has. When the boys congregate at the shiny, art deco Fells Point Diner on the edge of town, we can see immediately why they're friends. Inside the diner, with its harsh, white light—like stage lighting—they take turns being on; they're like a round-robin of stand-up (or sit-down) comics, and their actions crystallize their characters. Nothing that they do inside the diner is quite real; the affections and hostilities that fly through the air don't really lead anywhere. They're stage routines, and yet they provide a more heady interaction for the boys than anything on the outside (in the same way that many theatrical performers claim to be most alive when they're on stage). When some real life butts into this bright fantasy world—when Eddie, alone with Boogie, drops the mournful news that he's a virgin—the moment cuts though the atmosphere like a shiv.

The world that the diner insulates these boys from is the last dregs of the 1950s—a time when young men and women were beginning to really question their relationship to each other. What they're going through is a faint prelude to the social upheavals of the 1960s; the people in *Diner* are the last shock troops of the old order. They accept the rigid social confines of their lives, but it doesn't sit too well with them. The women in this film feel excluded from the men's lives without really wanting to take part in their rituals. Eddie tells Billy that the two of them share secrets his future wife "will never know," but he says so with false bravado. These people are sensitive and intelligent enough to register, however subliminally, a sense of missed emotional connections. And, finally, that sense of loss is tragic. Even if they don't feel the loss, we do. The modern perspective that Levinson gives *Diner* makes it seem, despite its considerable humor, ineffably sad—even the soundtrack, with up-tempo standards like Elvis Presley's "Don't be Cruel" and Fats Domino's "Whole Lotta Loving," carries an echo of regret.

If the young men in this film believe that marriage primarily means missing out on things, that's because they don't know what to say to women. That's why Eddie puts his fiancée through a multiple-choice/true-false football quiz; if she passes, then they can marry and at least he'll have something to talk about with her. *Diner* gets at the psychological roots of buddy-buddyism. For guys like Eddie or Shrevie, their lives will never have the vibrancy as before they were married; they can still hang out together, but it won't be the same. (Their slang word for a gorgeous woman is—revealingly—"death," as in "she's death.") Billy, who is meant, I think, to be a precursor of a "liberated" man—he actually thinks his girlfriend's TV-studio job has value—may have a more hopeful future. So may Boogie, if he's lucky. Fenwick seems primed for dissolution; so does Beth, as long as she's with Shrevie. *Diner* reveals its people for who they are and also what they will become. The perspective of time gives us a double-image. And, because the future of these people seems for the most part as muted and drained of color as the look of their present (as photographed by Peter Sova), we want to hold onto them while there's still some vitality left. After the movie has ended, the closing credits come on, and we hear again on the soundtrack for several minutes the joyful, animated voices of the guys in the diner, ribbing and taunting each other. At the screening I attended no one got up to leave until the voices had faded away.

Do the Right Thing (1989)

by David Sterritt

SPIKE LEE'S MOST FULLY REALIZED FILM, *Do the Right Thing*, is urban and American down to its bones. This helps explain why reaction to it was so mixed at the Cannes International Film Festival, where I saw its world premiere in 1989 with an audience of international critics and journalists. Spectators applauded at the end, but their clapping seemed driven more by duty than enthusiasm, as if it were *de rigueur* to cheer a maverick movie by a spunky black filmmaker even if his message seemed cranky or cryptic. Europeans wondered if its subject was timely—racial unrest is "very 1960s," a West German critic told me—and some Americans criticized it for stirring up discontents that seemed, well, unnecessary in the late 1980s.

Initial reaction in the United States was also mixed. Many hailed the film's energy and complexity, while others criticized its characterizations—are these well-rounded individuals or stereotypical stick figures?—and some accused it of presenting a sanitized portrait of ghetto life.

While the characters of *Do the Right Thing* are certainly etched in bold strokes, I find them as fleshed out as they need to be for this densely structured film. And whatever one thinks of the movie, it can't be accused of irrelevance. Tensions between blacks and whites have diminished but hardly ceased in the years since Lee wrote and directed it, and the root causes of this friction—including poverty, unequal schooling, and police persecution—are inextricably tied to the long tradition of American racism. That tradition is the context in which Lee wrote *Do the Right Thing*, drawing on such highly publicized New York incidents as the death of a graffiti artist in police custody and the harassment of African Americans by white rioters in the Howard Beach neighborhood of Queens. (The film is dedicated to four then-recent black victims of white power.)

But there's more to the movie than muckraking anger. One way to approach its deeper meanings is to recall Lee's previous picture, *School Daze*, and especially the very unusual ending of that very unusual musical. *School Daze* weaves several seriocomic storylines into a complicated fabric, tracing various aspects of life and love in a black American college. When the time arrives for a resolution of the action, Lee gives us something different. One character rouses the others out of bed and assembles them in a group, shouting at them—and at the audience in the theater—two forceful words: "Wake up!"

Do the Right Thing begins with those very same words, and they're a key to Lee's intention as a filmmaker, not only in these movies but in his career as a whole. He's not after entertainment for its own sake. Rather, he wants to wake us and shake us into awareness of the racism and misery that are embedded in contemporary urban society. At times his good intentions lead him into simplistic storytelling, as when he becomes a sort of cinematic social worker in parts of *Mo' Better Blues* and *Jungle Fever*, and at times his ideas take on such excess energy that they careen almost out of control, as in overstuffed yet exhilarating epics like *Summer of Sam* and *Bamboozled*. But at his best he has an extraordinary ability to rethink social and cultural issues in strikingly original motion picture terms.

That's why *Do the Right Thing* dodges the formulas and patterns of conventional Hollywood cinema. Its characters are often abrasive; its language is floridly foul; and it takes a skeptical view of easily articulated solutions to race-related violence. Yet it's an attractive and even beguiling film in many ways, enriched by humor and intelligence from beginning to end. And for all its iconoclasm, it shows a canny consciousness of the more inventive and freewheeling tropes that Hollywood has come up with in the past, as when a black character gives his own street-smart version of the "love vs. hate" routine enacted by Robert Mitchum in Charles Laughton's classic movie, *The Night of the Hunter.*

The more good-natured aspects of *Do the Right Thing* have been a target for its less sympathetic critics. In particular, Lee's portrait of Brooklyn's poor Bedford-Stuyvesant neighborhood has been panned as a *Sesame Street* version of ghetto life, too clean and polite to be believed. I think this criticism has its own tinge of racism. On any given day in even the worst urban neighborhoods, most folks are just living their lives, not stealing or overdosing or wallowing in dirt and crime. It's true that Lee's characters have more than their share of challenges to meet, and years of ingrained poverty have taken such a toll that some have lost the knack of coping with reality: Check out the three men who sit forever on the corner, commenting on the action like a Greek Chorus with a four-letter vocabulary. There's no reason for Lee to exaggerate their plight by throwing in hackneyed views of inner-city misery, though. Their situation speaks for itself, and what it reveals is a credible perspective on slum life that never lapses into shock tactics or cheap sentimentality.

Do the Right Thing takes place in and around Sal's Famous Pizzaria, operated by the eponymous Italian American businessman and his two grown sons. It's the hottest day in anyone's memory, and tempers are likely to flare over trifles. That's what happens when a young man named Buggin' Out feels a flare of anger at Sal for not hanging pictures of African American celebrities on the Italian-only "Wall of Fame" that decorates the pizza joint. Add a few more provocations—especially the blaring boombox that music freak Radio Raheem carries everywhere he goes—and you have the ingredients for serious trouble. Sure enough, violence erupts before the day is over, through an intricately structured series of events in which the character meticulously constructed as the "trustworthy" black guy (the delivery man Mookie, played by Lee himself) touches off an incendiary spark that explodes the accommodating attitudes of his black friends along with the smug complacency of his white neighbors.

The climax of *Do the Right Thing* has gotten more attention than any other part of the movie, and from some contemporaneous reviews you'd think Lee's film is as gruesome as a standard Hollywood action picture. In fact, its violence is mild compared with the mayhem unleashed by countless thrillers, westerns, and other genre movies since Sam Peckinpah and company upped the bloodletting ante in the 1960s; and it's not uncommon for such films to have racial implications a lot less progressive than the views embedded in Lee's work.

Nor does *Do the Right Thing* end with violence. Its outbreak of mayhem is followed by a denouement that doesn't resolve the story but offers a series of dialectical propositions that grow out of it. White cops attack a black man. Then infuriated blacks attack the pizzeria. Then the black man who escalated the violence has a partial reconciliation with the pizzeria owner, surprisingly complex in its emotional dynamics. Then two quotations appear: one from Martin Luther King Jr. saying violence is always self-defeating, and another from Malcolm X saying violence in self-defense may be necessary. These images and words offer no definitive answers to racial problems, any more than the film's title tells us what the "right thing" is supposed to be. They *do* open the door to thought and dialogue, which is a far more constructive contribution for a movie to make than simply adding to the pile of skin-deep polemics already produced by the culture industry.

The last scenes of *Do the Right Thing* call to my mind the distinction between two kinds of violence drawn by social philosopher Paul Goodman in his book *Drawing the Line*. In his view, "natural" violence may be dreadful and destructive, but it's rooted in human nature and erupts spontaneously out of deep-seated drives and emotions—the violence of parents defending their family against physical attack, for instance. By contrast, "unnatural" violence is stirred up artificially from the outside, as when a government incites public frenzy against a distant country that poses no immediate threat. The destruction of property in *Do the Right Thing* seems distressing but altogether "natural" to me. This doesn't mean it's good. But as narrative it's true to past experience in real urban ghettos, and as psychology it's true to the imperfections of human nature when confronted by the short-term stress of immediate provocation and the long-term misery of poverty-plagued urban life. While it's not a pretty picture, it's hardly a despairing one, either.

As perceptive critics have observed in the years since its release, *Do the Right Thing* is a deeply dialectical film in many ways, from its self-questioning conclusion to its inventive use of basic narrative film techniques. Its music, for instance, is a three-part tapestry that vividly conveys three kinds of consciousness in the Bed-Stuy mix: Rap songs represent the hardcore street folks; romantically inclined string tunes (anticipating the Aaron Copland score of *He Got Game*) evoke the sophistication of American folk culture; and the jazz/soul/rhythm-and-blues records spun by the disc-jockey character (Mister Señor Love Daddy) carve out an eclectic middle ground between them. The film's visual style does similar things, as when Lee chooses sharp *cuts* to separate shots of Sal and Radio Raheem during their disastrous boombox feud—suggesting the formidable gulf that separates these two characters—but uses quick-swinging *pans* to depict Radio Raheem's crank-up-the-volume contest with a Hispanic man, suggesting that these two inhabit the same psychological world even if their shared interests are often expressed through contrast and competition.

Much more could be said about the film's many layers of interest, from its use of interruptive techniques that Bertold Brecht would have praised to its clever deployment of the Aristotelian narrative unities (place: Sal's joint; time: the hottest day of the year; action: the inexorable growth of specific race-based animosities). With its ingenious camera work, expressive music score, brash yet indomitable humor, and smartly dialectical structure, *Do the Right Thing* is the richest and most thought-provoking portrait of underclass experience yet painted by an American fiction film.

La Dolce Vita (1959)

by Roger Ebert

I HAVE HEARD THEORIES THAT Federico Fellini's *La Dolce Vita* catalogs the seven deadly sins, takes place on the seven hills of Rome, and involves seven nights and seven dawns, but I have never looked into them, because that would reduce the movie to a crossword puzzle. I prefer it as an allegory, a cautionary tale of a man without a center.

Fellini shot the movie in 1959 on the Via Veneto, the Roman street of night-clubs, sidewalk cafes, and the parade of the night. His hero is a gossip columnist, Marcello, who chronicles "the sweet life" of fading aristocrats, second-rate movie stars, aging playboys, and women of commerce. The role was played by Marcello Mastroianni, and now that his life has ended we can see that it was his most representative. The two Marcellos—character and actor—flowed together into a handsome, weary, desperate man, who dreams of someday doing something good but is trapped in a life of empty nights and lonely dawns.

The movie leaps from one visual extravaganza to another, following Marcello as he chases down stories and women. He has a suicidal fiancée (Magali Noel) at home. In a nightclub, he picks up a promiscuous society beauty (Anouk Aimee), and together they visit the basement lair of a prostitute. The episode ends not in decadence but in sleep; we can never be sure that Marcello has had sex with anyone.

Another dawn. And we begin to understand the film's structure: A series of nights and dawns, descents and ascents. Marcello goes down into subterranean nightclubs, hospital parking lots, the hooker's hovel, and an ancient crypt. And he ascends St. Peter's dome, climbs to a choir loft, and to the high-rise apartment of Steiner (Alain Cuny), the intellectual who is his hero. He will even fly over Rome.

The famous opening scene, as a statue of Christ is carried above Rome by a helicopter, is matched with the close, in which fisherman on the beach find a sea monster in their nets. Two Christ symbols: the statue "beautiful" but false, the fish "ugly" but real. During both scenes there are failures of communication. The helicopter circles as Marcello tries to get the phone numbers of three sunbathing beauties. At the end, across a beach, he sees the shy girl he met one day when he went to the country in search of peace to write his novel. She makes typing motions to remind him, but he does not remember, shrugs, and turns away.

If the opening and closing scenes are symmetrical, so are many others, matching the sacred and profane and casting doubts on both. An early sequence finds Marcello covering the arrival in Rome of an improbably buxom movie star (Anita Ekberg) and consumed with desire. He follows her to the top of St. Peter's, into the bowels of a nightclub, and into the Roman night, where wild dogs howl and she howls back. His pursuit ends at dawn when she wades into the Trevi Fountain and he wades after her, idealizing her into all women, into The Woman; she remains forever just out of reach.

This sequence can be paired with a later one where children report a vision of the Virgin. Marcello races to the site, which is surrounded by TV cameras and a crowd of the devout. Again, we have an idealized woman and the hope that she can solve every problem. But the children lead the faithful on a chase, just as the Ekberg character led Marcello around Rome. They see the Virgin here, and then there, as the lame and the blind hobble after them and their grandfather cadges for tips. Once again everything collapses in an exhausted dawn.

The central episodes in *La Dolce Vita* involve Steiner, who represents all that Marcello envies. Steiner lives in an apartment filled with art. He presides over a salon of poets, folk singers, intellectuals. He has a beautiful wife and two perfect children. When Marcello sees him entering a church, they ascend to the organ loft and Steiner plays Bach while urging Marcello to have more faith in himself, and finish that book. Then follows the night of Steiner's party and the moment (more or less the exact center of the film) where Marcello takes his typewriter to a country trattoria and tries to write. Then comes the terrible second Steiner scene, when Marcello discovers that Steiner's serenity was made from a tissue of lies.

To mention these scenes is to be reminded of how many other great moments this rich film contains. The echo chamber. The Mass at dawn. The final desperate orgy. And of course the touching sequence with Marcello's father (Annibale Ninchi), a traveling salesman who joins Marcello on a tour of the night. In a club they see a sad-faced clown (Poidor) lead a lonely balloon out of the room with his trumpet. And Marcello's father, filled with the courage of champagne, grows bold with a young woman who owes Marcello a favor—only to fall ill and leave, gray and ashen, again at dawn.

The movie is made with boundless energy. Fellini stood here at the dividing point between the neorealism of his earlier films (like *La Strada*) and the carnival visuals of his extravagant later ones (*Juliet of the Spirits, Amarcord*). His autobiographical *8 1/2*, made three years after *La Dolce Vita*, is a companion piece, but more knowing: There the hero is already a filmmaker, but here he is a young newspaperman on the make.

The music by Nino Rota is of a perfect piece with the material. It is sometimes quasiliturgical, sometimes jazz, sometimes rock; lurking beneath is the irreverence of tuba and accordions, and snatches of pop songs ("Stormy Weather" and even "Jingle Bells"). The characters are forever in motion, and Rota gives them music for their processions and parades.

The casting is all typecasting. Anita Ekberg might not have been much of an actress, but she was the only person who could play herself. Lex Barker, a one-time movie Tarzan, was droll as her alcoholic boyfriend. Alain Cuny's severe self-confidence as Steiner is convincing, which is why his end is a shock. And remember Anouk Aimee, her dark glasses concealing a black eye; the practical, commonsensical Adriana Moneta as the streetwalker; Alain Dijon as the satanic ringleader at the nightclub; and always Mastroianni, his eyes squinting against a headache or a deeper ache of the soul. He was always a passive actor, and here that quality is needed: Seeking happiness but unable to take the steps to find it, he spends his nights in endless aimless searching, trying to please everyone, the juggler with more balls than skills.

Movies do not change, but their viewers do. When I saw *La Dolce Vita* in 1960, I was an adolescent for whom "the sweet life" represented everything I dreamed of: sin, exotic European glamour, the weary romance of the cynical newspaperman. When I saw it again, around 1970, I was living in a version of Marcello's world; Chicago's North Avenue was not the Via Veneto, but at 3 A.M. the denizens were just as colorful, and I was about Marcello's age.

When I saw the movie around 1980, Marcello was the same age, but I was ten years older, had stopped drinking, and saw him not as a role model but as a victim, condemned to an endless search for happiness that could never be found, not that way. By 1991, when I analyzed the film a frame at a time at the University of Colorado, Marcello seemed younger still, and while I had once admired and then criticized him, now I pitied and loved him. And when I saw the movie right after Mastroianni died, I thought that Fellini and Marcello had taken a moment of discovery and made it immortal. There may be no such thing as the sweet life. But it is necessary to find that out for yourself.

Double Indemnity (1944)

by Matthew Seitz

"I NEVER KNEW THAT MURDER COULD SMELL LIKE HONEYSUCKLE."

That's a confession by the narrator and hero of *Double Indemnity,* a hard-boiled insurance man named Walter Neff (Fred MacMurray) who died because he fell for a great pair of legs. Walter Neff narrates quite a bit of this 1944 Billy Wilder classic, laying out the story of how a routine sales call somehow turned into a steamy adulterous affair with one Phyllis Dietrichson (Barbara Stanwyck), a black-widow blonde who wanted to kill her husband for the insurance money and needed an expert to help maximize her profit. Remarkably enough, he thought he was in love with the woman—and thanks to the doomed romantic charge passing between MacMurray and Stanwyck, audiences nearly believed the feeling was mutual.

Their story takes the form of an extended deathbed confession by the fatally shot hero. He spills his guts (so to speak) into a recorded message to his colleague and buddy, Barton Keyes (Edward G. Robinson), a veteran insurance man who claims he can spot lies with the help of a little man in his belly.

"Suddenly it came over me that everything would go wrong," Walter says. "It sounds crazy, Keyes, but it's true, so help me. I couldn't hear my own footsteps. It was the walk of a dead man."

James M. Cain's novel wasn't a mystery but a seamy drama about a man's self-deception; the film version, adapted by Wilder and mystery novelist Raymond Chandler, preserved and enlarged the idea of Neff investigating himself—not just as criminal or a patsy but as a man. Of course it exemplifies the movie genre that came to be known as "film noir." A post–World War II offshoot of the 1920s German Expressionist school of filmmaking, *noir* depicted nightmarish scenarios (sometimes just plain nightmares) in a dark, stylized, antirealistic way, serving up heaping helpings of murder, thievery, conspiracy, and extramarital sex disguised as cautionary tales. Though the evildoers were always punished—with privately appointed censor Will Hays waving his scissors in Hollywood's direction in the 1930s and 1940s, the stories couldn't end any other way—noir films were still deeply subversive affairs. Cynicism trumped optimism; naive or generous characters existed mainly to be taken advantage of, or to remind us of how far the hero had fallen from anything resembling decency. The genre singlehandedly contradicted and undermined the optimistic attitude of most Hollywood features, which were designed to strengthen audiences' faith in America and her institutions.

But even as it satisfies genre requirements, *Double Indemnity* stands apart from its genre and in some ways transcends it. With its shadow monochrome photography, adultery-and-murder plotline, and unstinting view of man's corruptibility, Wilder's film is arguably his sexiest, bleakest portrait of corruption; unlike *Some Like It Hot, Sunset Boulevard,* even *The Apartment* (in which MacMurray reprised his heel routine), its seductive power is undiluted by the intrusion of "innocent" major characters, and it's chock full of touches so playful that it's as if the movie is winking at the audience. (After disposing of Phyllis's husband's body, the murderers' car won't start—a twist Wilder improvised on the spot when his own car had engine trouble.) The three central characters—Walter, Phyllis, and Keyes—

are types, but the actors' gloriously hard-boiled performances suggest that the characters know they're types and enjoy playing parts in this turgid little melodrama.

"You'll be here, too?" asks Walter, plotting another clandestine meeting with his beloved.

"I guess so, I usually am," Phyllis says.

"Same chair, same perfume, same anklet?"

"I wonder if I know what you mean."

"I wonder if you wonder."

The characters seem deeper and more complex than the usual noir protagonists, not just because of the leads' aggressively colorful performances but because Walter, Phyllis, and Keyes form a strange sort of love triangle. Walter, who is neither as smart nor as stubborn as he thinks, is caught between the temptress Phyllis (who seduces him into deceiving his employer and violating several of the Ten Commandments). The cigar-chewing crook-trapper Keyes takes the place of the "good girl" typically spotlighted in films of this type. Like Walter, Keyes is a hard-boiled grownup who has been conditioned by his job to expect the worst of people. Yet his detective's instinct isn't moralistic; like Sherlock Holmes, he treats evil almost as a value-neutral puzzle, an equation to be solved for "X." (In one of the film's most memorable scenes, he recites the different types of death for which actuarial numbers are available.) In this film, moral behavior is viewed not as something to be embraced for its own sake but as a dull but preferable alternative to getting caught and going to the gas chamber. Walter's opening confession squelches our expectations of a whodunit, focusing our attention on the dirtball hero's struggle to avoid capture—and the efforts of Keyes, the better angel of his nature, to get to the bottom of a claim that makes his stomach hurt.

Where other noirs treat forbidden sex as a plot device, Wilder's film understands it on an emotional level. On a superficial level, Neff's story is a familiar one about a smart aleck who got outsmarted by a ruthless dame. But peek beneath that brass-hard surface and you find a perversely involving story of a romance that didn't work out—a tragedy about two doomed heels in love. The lead actors play Neff and Phyllis not merely as a patsy and his manipulator but as sexy beasts, so knowingly cynical that they practically taunt each other into bed. "When they met it was murder!" screamed the film's advertising tagline. Nearly sixty years after its release, *Double Indemnity* is still a killer.

Duck Soup (1933)

by William Wolf

WHEN PARAMOUNT RELEASED *Duck Soup* in 1933, the reviews were mixed and the film's lack of commercial success ended the Paramount–Marx Brothers relationship. Yet appreciation for this anarchic, hilarious movie has grown through the years, and many justifiably regard *Duck Soup* as the ultimate Marx Brothers work, the film that best reveals the essence of their talent and originality.

No matter how much we laugh at *A Night at the Opera* and *A Day at the Races,* or subsequent Marx Brothers films, we would never see another that captures their comic style with the utter abandon and purity found in *Duck Soup*. The film represented a fork in the road in their careers, which veered into a more structured, commercial environment under the aegis of MGM's "boy-wonder," producer Irving Thalberg. He apparently believed that the brothers could be packaged with broader appeal if their antics were occasionally relieved by un-Marxist musical production numbers.

But did the brothers Marx really need the singing of Allan Jones and Kitty Carlisle? Did they need the racist dance number that intrudes upon *A Day at the Races* and is an embarrassment when we watch it now? Artistically, if not commercially, it was a mistake to mold their free spirit into more of a Hollywood formula. A mistake, but hardly surprising.

When we revisit *Duck Soup* we can appreciate anew the unfettered brand of comedy that made Groucho, Harpo, and Chico unique. (This was the last film in which Zeppo, never more than an adjunct, appeared.) Besides featuring the kind of horseplay that made the brothers stage stars before they became film stars, *Duck Soup* is rich in political satire, a rare commodity in Hollywood at the time, and not all that frequent even at the millennium. No matter what wars are being waged around the world, when we watch the crazy-quilt war enveloping the mythical Freedonia, we are reminded to be ever-skeptical of whatever reasons politicians and statesmen trumpet to justify the carnage.

In a 1976 interview with me, Woody Allen called *Duck Soup* "probably the best talking comedy ever made." But some, including Allen, have rejected the idea that it was intended as political satire. Whatever the intent, the satire is certainly there.

The comedy makes a shambles of a government going to war and depicts a zany battleground of total chaos.

While the comedy appears freewheeling, there was nothing haphazard about the film's creation. Many contributed, including Bert Kalmar and Harry Ruby, who collaborated on the screenplay, with additional dialogue credited to Arthur Sheekman and Nat Perrin. Herman Mankiewicz, who received no credit, spent a brief turn as supervisor but was fired. Kalmar and Ruby also did the music and lyrics that enhanced the satire with pertinent numbers quite different from the diversionary music and lyrics used in the subsequent MGM concoctions.

At the insistence of the Marx Brothers, the director hired for *Duck Soup* was Leo McCarey, whom they wanted because of his experience directing some of the best silent comedies of Laurel and Hardy. He was reluctant at first. The Marx Brothers had a reputation—not unjustified—of being difficult on the set. But he accepted, and Groucho later credited McCarey with giving *Duck Soup* its antiwar aspect. McCarey also worked out the classic scene in which Groucho thinks he's looking at himself in a mirror when he's really looking at Chico in disguise, with Harpo in a similar disguise showing up for a topper. Hans Dreier and Wiard B. Ihnen teamed to create the imaginative art direction that enhanced the visual inventiveness, complemented by Henry Sharp's black-and-white photography.

Duck Soup, virtually nonstop in its deflation of pomposity, authority, or any semblance of order, has a framework not to be dignified by anything as specific as plot. Groucho as Rufus T. Firefly is appointed the ruler of the mythical Freedonia (with Zeppo as his aide) by the wealthy Mrs. Teasdale, played with delightful aplomb by Margaret Dumont, the inimitable grande dame of Marx Brothers films and straight-woman to so many of Groucho's disrespectful lines. The essence of their repartee can be found in the following exchange:

Mrs. Teasdale: The future of Freedonia rests on you. Promise me you'll follow in the footsteps of my husband.
Firefly: How do you like that? I haven't been on the job five minutes and already she's making advances to me. Not that I care, but where is your husband?
Mrs. Teasdale: Why, he's dead.
Firefly: I'll bet he's just using that as an excuse.
Mrs. Teasdale: I was with him to the very end.
Firefly: Huh! No wonder he passed away.
Mrs. Teasdale: I held him in my arms and kissed him.
Firefly: Oh, I see. Then it was murder . . .

The film's musical numbers play a major satirical role. Groucho was a Gilbert and Sullivan fan, and the affinity is present in the early production number in which Firefly sings: "The last man nearly ruined this place/He didn't know what to do with it. If you think this country's bad off now/Just wait till I get through with it." A later number, "Freedonia's Going to War," gets wilder as it satirizes the way governments create a popular hysteria: "Oh, hi-de, hi-de, hi-de, hi-de, hi-de, hi-de-ho/To war, to war, to war we're gonna go . . . They got guns/We got guns. All God's chillun got guns . . ." The sequence winds up with a square dance.

Louis Calhern, in other venues usually a more serious actor, makes the perfect villain as Trentino, the scheming, ever-thwarted ambassador from the rival power Sylvania. Trentino plots to marry Mrs. Teasdale, who holds Freedonia's purse strings, and enlists the aid of dancer Vera Marcal (Raquel Torres) to help undermine Firefly. He assigns Chicolini (Chico) and Pinky (Harpo) to spy on him.

When Firefly slaps Trentino with his gloves, it doesn't mean a duel. It means war. There are two lines that go to the heart of what happens when matters between countries get out of hand to the point of no return:

Trentino: I am willing to do anything to prevent this war.
Firefly: It's too late. I've already paid a month's rent on the battlefield.

This is probably the only war ever fought primarily indoors, mostly from a farm-house kitchen, Firefly's command center. But this is a war without logical boundaries. When Pinky isn't parading with a sandwich board reading, "JOIN THE ARMY AND SEE THE NAVY," Firefly is commanding Chicolini: "Now, go out in that battle-field and lead those men to victory. Go on, they're waiting for you."

Chicolini: I wouldn't go out there unless I was in one of those big iron things that go up and down like this. What do you call those things?
Firefly: Tanks.
Chicolini: You're welcome.

Or an exchange such as the following:

Firefly: "Chicolini, your partner's deserted us, but I'm still counting on you. There's a machine-gun nest near Hill 28. I want it cleaned out."
Chicolini: "All right, I'll tell the janitor."

Every fan of *Duck Soup* has favorite lines or situations. One of the prized non-sequiturs is the appearance of Mr. Slow Burn himself, Edgar Kennedy, operating a lemonade stand and involved in comic shtick with Harpo and Chico. Among the lines I recall fondly is Groucho's rallying battle cry invoking Mrs. Teasdale: "Remember, you're fighting for this woman's honor, which is probably more than she ever did." Or Firefly telling Mrs. Teasdale: "All I can offer you is a Rufus over your head."

And who can forget Harpo on his Paul Revere ride, interrupted when he sees a blonde in a window? Or the scene with Harpo popping up in a bathtub together with the husband he is fleeing, none other than Edgar Kennedy?

What's thoroughly captivating about *Duck Soup* is the total lack of any effort to be logical even though barbs are thrust at a subject as serious as warfare. The mayhem is allowed to run rampant in service of the Marx Brothers' talent for the ridiculous. Prior to *Duck Soup* a similar approach was evident, of course, in their Paramount films *The Cocoanuts* (1929), *Animal Crackers* (1930), *Monkey Business* (1931), and *Horse Feathers* (1932), but each of those had more plot. With *Duck Soup,* in reaching the apex of their free-form comedy of the absurd, the Marx Brothers demonstrated the latitude that could be taken with cinema as an art form. Their work could even be related to the surrealism of Luis Buñuel and Salvador Dali in their *Un chien andalou* (An Andalusian Dog), made in France in 1928. Playwright Eugene Ionesco, the renowned practitioner of the Theater of the Absurd, said that the three greatest influences on him were Groucho, Harpo, and Chico.

In the years that followed there would be some wonderful Marx Brothers comedy in *Room Service, At the Circus, Go West, The Big Store,* and to a lesser extent in *A Night in Casablanca* and *Love Happy.* But there's a certain sadness when one reflects on *Duck Soup* and wonders how much the creativity of the Marx Brothers was stifled by trying to blend their talent with Hollywood box-office requirements to make them more marketable to a broader audience. We'll never know.

We can trace their influence on such successors as Woody Allen, Mel Brooks, and Monty Python. But one speculates how far they might have gone in experimenting with new forms instead of reworking their familiar territory. Would they also have been drawn to more topical satire? It's noteworthy that Mussolini was angry enough with *Duck Soup* to ban it. Groucho mused in a 1946 interview with Mary Morris of the newspaper *PM:* "The movies don't recognize any real heavies in the world. You don't dare make a joke that implies anything wrong with Franco. The poor public is smothered under tons of goo."

Not with *Duck Soup* it wasn't.

Easy Rider (1969)

by William Wolf

JACK NICHOLSON, DENNIS HOPPER, PETER FONDA, drugs, hippies, the open road, protests, long-hair, nonconformity, backlash. *Easy Rider* picked up the beat of the 1960s at the end of that turbulent decade. It also fueled a developing urge to make personal films that could be done on budgets low enough to deal with subjects of little or no interest to conventional Hollywood.

The French New Wave already had its influence and now it was the turn of American filmmakers. True, a major Hollywood company, Columbia, released *Easy Rider,* but the deal was struck only after the independent venture had been completed. Independent filmmakers in succeeding decades owe a debt to *Easy Rider* as one of several 1960s films that inspired others to work out of the mainstream.

The film was the brainchild of Dennis Hopper and Peter Fonda, who brought their idea to Bert Schneider and Bob Rafelson, whose Raybert Productions coproduced the film with the Pando Company. The budget was a mere $400,000. With Hopper, Fonda, and Jack Nicholson in the cast, the film had potential. But would they finish it? Some would-be backers had their doubts.

Hopper directed, Fonda produced, and both Hopper and Fonda collaborated on the screenplay after a draft had been written by Terry Southern. By the standards of the time, the low-budget film was a meaningful financial as well as critical success, grossing nearly $20 million, according to the trade publication *Variety.* At least for a while producers looked for directors to make them "another *Easy Rider.*" The awards were numerous. The Cannes Film Festival cited it as best film by a new director. Nicholson was named best supporting actor by both the National Society of Film Critics and the New York Film Critics Circle, and the National Society also gave a special award to Dennis Hopper.

Looking back on the film today is like entering a time warp. Were Nicholson, Hopper, and Fonda ever *that* young? Although he had ample experience, Nicholson had yet to have a breakthrough. As George, the doomed lawyer who befriends two drug-dealing, freedom-loving bike riders, he gave a performance that became the turning point in his career. Peter Fonda as Wyatt and Dennis Hopper as Billy, with their long hair recalling the trappings of free expression that characterized the era, embodied the period's drug culture. Those were no fake joints that they smoked onscreen.

The journey of the trio characterizes the clash between such liberated souls and a society that looks askance at nonconformists. In ironic symbolism Wyatt's motorbike is decorated with the stars and stripes, with a safety helmet to match. Wyatt also has an American flag replicated on the back of his leather jacket. At the outset Wyatt and Billy make a drug buy in Mexico. They are seen carefully sniffing coke to make sure it's the real stuff, as does "The Connection" (Phil Spector) to whom they sell some of it at an airport.

Both men are decent guys, not intending to harm anyone and just wanting to enjoy roaming the country. Billy is pretty well stoned most of the time. The man in charge at a second-rate motel, taking in their long-haired biker look, refuses to even open the door. A hitchhiker to whom they give a lift leads them to a commune, where more of the film's spirit—and that of the sixties—comes into play. Relaxed living, friendly women, yet not without male jealousy.

As they continue their trip, playfully riding uninvited behind a school band in a parade gets them busted in New Mexico. In jail they meet George, who hasn't done anything. He comes from a prominent family, is a lawyer, and is sleeping off a drunk. George acquaints them with the facts of life prevalent in that part of the country:

Well, they got this here—see-uh-scissor-happy "Beautify America" thing goin' on around here. They're tryin' to make everybody look like Yul Brynner. They used-uh-rusty blades on the last two long-hairs that they brought in here and I wasn't here to protect them. You see-uh—I'm a lawyer. Done a lot of work for the ACLU.

George helps them get out of the clink before they can get worked over and now two become three. George has a card that he says was given to him by the governor of Louisiana advertising "Madame Tinkertoy's House of Blue Lights," in New Orleans, reputed to be "the finest whorehouse in the South." Off they go on the next leg of their trip with George riding on the back of Wyatt's bike.

There's a funny scene when they sleep outdoors and his new companions try to teach George how to smoke grass. In retrospect, the idea of Nicholson not knowing how to use the weed and inhale properly becomes even funnier. George protests that he has enough problems with the booze. The scene exudes a feeling of camaraderie as well as humor.

George is the one with the speeches that underscore what the film is about: "This used to be a helluva good country. I can't understand what's gone wrong with it." It's not the long hair or the way they dress that upsets people, he tells Billy and Wyatt "What you represent to them is freedom." He warns: "'Course don't ever tell anybody—that they're not free, 'cause then, they're gonna get real busy killin' and maimin' to prove to you that they are."

We can predict that the trio will run into trouble en route, and indeed, they do, first at a roadside cafe where the long hair of Wyatt and Billy proves an irritant. They're needled by a local deputy and his cronies, extra resentful because several young girls are attracted to the travelers. Later, while they are sleeping in a swamp area, a group of men beat them brutally, killing George. The distraught survivors continue, determined to reach New Orleans. At Madame Tinkertoy's emporium they become friendly with Karen (Karen Black) and Mary (Toni Basil), who agree to join them in the Mardi Gras, which is in full blast.

A hallucinatory sequence follows, as the women and men wander into a cemetery, pop pills, and make love. It's a mind-blowing binge before the storm, and afterward Wyatt and Billy take to the highway once again. Two men in a passing truck taunt the outsiders and one aims a rifle at Billy, who responds by giving him the finger. Billy is gunned down. Wyatt first tries to stanch the bleeding, then rides for help. He too is shot. The camera pulls back to encompass a view of the victims and the countryside with the "Ballad of Easy Rider" providing the coda.

In effect the shooting marks an epitaph for an era. The Kennedy assassinations. The Martin Luther King Jr. assassination. The killing of Malcolm X. The Chicago riots. The protests against the Vietnam War. The 1960s were over, but the pain, including the growing opposition to the war, would carry over into the 1970s.

Easy Rider is more visual than verbal. There is a feeling of spontaneity in various scenes, and the cinematography of Laszlo Kovacs and the settings add to the impression of authenticity. The scenes of the countryside through which the protagonists travel are exhilarating, offering a loving look at the beauty of the land. To get actual footage of a Mardi Gras, the event was shot in advance of the rest of the film, in fact before the script had even been completed. Once the filming of the story began, the shooting was done in sequence. *Easy Rider* became the on-the-road experience of its makers who were living out their own take on the 1960s through their project.

As for the title, Fonda explained its origin in a 1969 interview in *Rolling Stone* with writer Elizabeth Campbell: "'Easy rider' is a Southern term for a whore's old man, not a pimp, but the dude who lives with a chick. Because he's got the easy ride. Well, that's what's happened to America, man. Liberty's become a whore, and we're all taking an easy ride."

The film holds up for its overall impact, although the pace lags occasionally and some of the dialogue is banal or pretentious. The music, an added "character" in the film, provides an important element in setting the right tone. The soundtrack is rich with numbers by such groups and performers as Steppenwolf, the Byrds, The Band, The Jimi Hendrix Experience, Little Eva, The Electric Flag, Bob Dylan, and Roger McGuinn, who composed and performed the title song "Ballad of Easy Rider."

Today the film is best viewed as an artifact of the period in which it was made. For those who didn't live through the 1960s, *Easy Rider* tells us much about the dynamics and attitudes of the decade and what kind of music was popular. There's also the pleasure of seeing early Nicholson, Hopper, and Fonda, who would all go on to further important work, and we see Karen Black before her acclaimed performance in Rafelson's *Five Easy Pieces.*

The film is also a nostalgic reminder of the continuing ups and downs of the independent filmmaking movement in the United States. The excitement engendered when a nonmainstream film succeeds inspires other work, but the limited opportunities leave room for only a few financial success stories. The talent often moves into the mainstream of big-budget films, and the struggle persists with newcomers trying to make their mark with their personal visions. But there aren't many easy rides. There is, however, an *Easy Rider* as a perpetual reminder of what's possible.

Enter the Dragon (1973)

by Michael Sragow

IN ENTER THE DRAGON, a Shaolin Temple priest and a Western intelligence agent persuade a suburban Hong Kong phenom named Lee (played by *Bruce* Lee) to attend a gangland chieftain's kung fu tournament. It's actually an audition for potential thugs to fill an underworld army. But Lee disdains the suggestion that he might need military help. He's an old-fashioned Chinese individualist; his body makes him super self-sufficient. *Enter the Dragon* is basically a revenge fantasy: the henchmen of Lee's mobster-enemy (Shih Kien) hounded Lee's sister to her death. But along with its tension (and its camp), the film is suffused with sympathy for outcasts and underdogs. One of Lee's allies is an American black (Jim Kelly) who escapes to the kung fu match after practicing on a pair of racist cops. (When crossing the Hong Kong harbor he mutters, "Ghettos are the same all over the world—they stink.") Add a debt-ridden white gambler (John Saxon), who knew Kelly's Black Power black belt in Vietnam, and you've got a three-man shock troop for the Rainbow Coalition. When this film premiered, extremists were telling slum kids to get their hands on guns; Lee's message was that angry young men of all colors possess "the fire next time" within.

Lee died on July 20, 1973, six weeks before this $600,000 "epic" debuted and went on to gross $150 million worldwide. It's a gaudy, gimcrack construction that's also a whirling piece of legendry. (The new print restores three minutes of dialogue spelling out the ethos of Lee's celluloid myth.) Lee coined his own action-film iconography out of flying fists and feet. Twenty-five years later he still excites the audience from the moment he appears, in wrestling briefs that drape his buttocks like the cheekiest, chicest Calvin Kleins. It's less a matter of sexual attraction than transcendent awe. He's reed-thin and feather-delicate, and when he goes on the attack there's no macho cool about him. He vibrates with concentrated energy, like a spindle. You fear his intensity will crack your skull. He takes you so far into his gladiator's psyche that you *feel* his moves and countermoves even when he gyrates too quickly for you to understand them. He could be giving himself whiplash as he shakes his head clear for the next step; more than thinking on his feet, he thinks on his bobbing toes. Because he was so incredibly quick and light, I once called him the Fred Astaire of kung fu, making martial arts look easy. But you could say he's the Baryshnikov, exercising midair scissors cuts as complex as Balanchine ballets, or the Savion Glover, conjuring improvisational dance from his rattling kinetic rhythm.

The opening match in *Enter the Dragon* is a warm-up for novices: Chop Sockey 101. He wins it with ease and without preening. Of course, Lee choreographed all the fights in the film himself. But he makes them appear spontaneous—no, inspired—and as selfless as the work of a completely engaged athlete. Lee fills the movie with acrobatic wonders. Vaulting into a tree he appears to be reversing gravity; more than in any *Superman* film, you believe a man can fly.

Lee's triumph is one of personality and vision, not just physical performance. At rest, his slightness, the light timbre of his voice, and his unlined features are disarmingly boyish. Lee also has a boy's furtive cunning. He has as much control over his facial muscles as he does over his biceps—we know that his occasional blankness is an act of will, a camouflage against prying eyes. At sport he doesn't pander to sadistic fantasies; he plays by strict, fair rules. But in a grudge match, his very being alters. His lungs expand like bellows, filling his body with new weight. His muscles ripple like electrified barbed wire. And his face takes on the aspect of a demon. It's tantamount to seeing the Incredible Hulk emerge without special effects.

Lee communicates instantly with teenagers and children because he seems to have just straddled adolescence himself. Most of the time, he's stoic, but when his family honor is at stake, and his private essence challenged, he allows himself to go tantrum-crazy. In his Hulk act he lets loose a primal scream. Lee refutes the notion that we grow up and out of youthful sentiments, jettisoning them in stages, like rockets. Lee holds them in equipoise—and assumes a suave, wry maturity. He shows that childish emotions need not be retrogressive; they can be downright restorative for adults.

You can't predict how Lee will react from moment to moment, yet his personality hangs together. His shifts in accent from the slurred and breathy to the ultra-deliberate and Mr. Moto–esque ("con me" becomes "khan me") somehow merge to seem pleasing and refined. His mystique is magnetic. He's never just "an inscrutable Oriental." He betrays enough of his inner workings to compel our curiosity. The Lee figure is a rebel without a portfolio. But he does have a cause, which is nothing less than authenticity. Near the beginning of *Enter the Dragon*, he urges a boy at the Shaolin Temple to kick him with "emotional content." The boy holds back, reluctant to attack an understanding older-brother figure. Lee doesn't condescend or coddle; instead, he slaps the kid repeatedly, catalyzing fighting passion. What Lee is trying to teach isn't a bag of tricks or an ethereal ritual but an *organic* discipline. He's putting flesh on the Force. He wants us to be so attuned to our emotions and abilities that we can set them loose in controlled torrents—floods of feeling coursing through physical floodgates.

In the 1979 kung fu movie *Circle of Iron*, made from a script Lee was developing at the time of his death, TV's martial arts master, David Carradine, taught a surly neophyte Lee's special Spartan strain of Zen. Carradine instructed the boy to distrust abstract religious values and to respect justice—not arbitrary rules. The overriding theme was "Know Thyself"; when Carradine led his tutee to the Book of Enlightenment, each page was a mirror. Idealistic though it sounds, the saturnine Carradine and his reluctant disciple (Jeff Cooper) made Lee's philosophy seem like an excuse for breaking nonbelievers' bones.

Watching Lee in *Enter the Dragon*, lessons that could be gassy or dangerous become concrete and admirable. When Lee keeps his foes from invading *his* circle of iron, he puts value back into the phrase "creating space." His integrity works like an invisible shield. His presence is so unself-conscious and sure, he's less a beacon of selfhood than a paragon of honesty and wholeness. Jackie Chan may have brought his own unique form of martial arts comedy to movies. But as a heroic ideal, no one has filled Lee's fighting shoes. No one's even invaded his space.

The Entertainer (1960)

by Charles Taylor

"I'M DEAD BEHIND THESE EYES," says Archie Rice, the broken-down music-hall comedian of *The Entertainer.* Night after night, in a light, blase baritone, he sings his theme song, "Why Should I Care?" to the sparse on-holiday crowds who turn out to watch him go through the motions of his tired act. Archie isn't kidding. He doesn't care, and for all the forced energy he puts into mincing around the stage of the cavernous seaside music hall he's booked for the season, he's very nearly a ghost.

But as played by Laurence Olivier in his greatest contemporary performance, Archie's deadness is a living, malignant thing. No character has ever better embodied the hatred and resentment that performers feel toward their audience. Archie doesn't court the crowd as his dad, the old trouper Billy Rice (Roger Livesey), still does when he gets up to lead his club in some old music-hall numbers. Billy takes pleasure in giving of himself; Archie is a knotted ball of frustrated want. Beneath every crummy joke, every sad song and dance, lies his hatred of the audience ("that dumb, shallow lot out there" he calls them) and, even more strongly, his hatred of himself.

Onstage, Archie is the leering captain of a sinking ship, determined to drag everyone else down with him. In his bowler and bow tie, makeup shadowing his popping eyes and turning his mouth into an upward curl, he has the obscene grin of a debauched harlequin. (You see a similar look in another performance of the time, Jason Robards's Hickey in Jose Quintero's legendary revival of *The Iceman Cometh.*)

That sinking ship is, of course, England. It was playwright John Osborne's idea to use the fading world of the English music hall as a metaphor for fading, corrupt England herself. It's a big, obvious, didactic idea, but a potent one. Osborne's play, which premiered at London's Royal Court Theater in 1957—starring Olivier and directed, as is this film, by Tony Richardson—was set during the 1956 Suez Crisis, an event that revealed the fissures between traditional Britain, which saw British resistance as being in the patriotic spirit of the Blitz, and the young, who felt that that earlier courage had calcified into something insular and petty and self-congratulatory. When Archie sings the line "If we all stand for the dear old country, the battle will be won" (in the fittingly named "Thank God We're Normal"), he stands for a tired, wrung-out nation still holding on to its dreams of empire. His youngest son Mick (Albert Finney), a British paratrooper, has been taken prisoner by the Egyptians; Archie listens to the radio hungry for any tidbit of news, but he can't make the connection between the jingoistic slop he's shilling and his own son's fate.

The meaning and impact of *The Entertainer,* its shock and its thrill, is inseparable from the presence of Olivier. He owns Archie Rice the way Brando owns Stanley Kowalski. To the theatrical establishment who derided the Angry Young Man school of theater and fiction (also populated by angry young women like the playwright Shelagh Delaney and the director Joan Littlewood) as vulgar and defeatist, the participation of one of the pillars of the British theatrical tradition must have seemed like collaboration with the enemy. To the writers, actors, directors, and critics who championed the new movement, Olivier's casting as Archie Rice was a victory.

But then, why wouldn't Olivier have been drawn to a role as great as Archie Rice? Even his work in the classical repertoire had been characterized by a contemporary visceral excitement. It would be hard to think of a *less* traditional actor more closely identified with the classics. His film performances as Henry V, Hamlet, and Richard III, and his staggering performance as Othello, which would follow *The Entertainer* five years later, are all marked by immediacy rather than reverence. He understood Shakespearean heroes *physically* instead of just as declaimers of verse. It was even possible to detect in Olivier a willingness to shock (nowhere more so than in the way he made Othello's blackness go deeper than his makeup).

Archie isn't beautiful to watch, the way Olivier's Hamlet is, or redolent of thick sensuality, as is his Othello. Olivier seems physically diminished in the role, a brittle shell of a man ready to crumple inward, exposing his rotten core. Onstage or cajoling his family into a show of forced good cheer, there is a kinetic wiriness to Archie. He often begins sentences with "Hey!" as if he's trying to prod his listeners awake. But when he reaches for an anecdote that won't come, like the story he tells his daughter Jean (Joan Plowright, who would become Olivier's wife after the film) about two nuns, or when he's both sated and empty lying in bed with his young mistress (Shirley Anne Field), the deadness in his eyes seems to have spread to his whole disgusted being. In Archie's most passive and muted moments, Olivier seems to be under the spell of a paralyzing poison that has settled into his bloodstream. Nowhere more so than in the light, almost fey dismissiveness of the hand gesture that accompanies Archie's final words to an audience: "Let me know where you're working tomorrow and I'll come see *you*." So what if they hate him. Why should he care?

Archie Rice, selfish enough to think of abandoning his neurotically dependent wife Phoebe (Brenda De Banzie), craven and desperate enough to send his father to his death by putting the elderly man back on the stage, doesn't allow Olivier the heroics of his Shakespearean roles. But there is something of the same suspense, the fascinated horror of seeing how far down he'll go. And if John Osborne's language isn't poetic, the playwright's genius for poisonous, self-lacerating invective scales its own heights.

Archie's real skills as a performer come out in the scenes with his family crowded together in the close quarters of their shabby digs. There his talent for mocking mimicry, for finely honed putdowns wrapped in the false smile of encouragement, come across with a lethal sharpness that the terrible jokes of his stage act can't match. The scenes of familiar squabbling, of petty annoyances that escalate into torrents of loathing, recall the tears and blood of another family of the theater, the Tyrones of *Long Day's Journey into Night*.

Tony Richardson would go on to win enormous praise for his appropriation of nouvelle vague energy in his adaptation of *Tom Jones*. But that film seems like so much grafted-on trickery now, not nearly as innovative as the work that preceded it. No other director did more to bring the new movement in British drama to the screen, in 1959 filming Osborne's *Look Back in Anger* (starring Richard Burton), which he had also directed onstage, and in 1961 directing the lovely, now nearly forgotten film of Shelagh Delaney's *A Taste of Honey* (starring Rita Tushingham). The innovation apparent in *The Entertainer* isn't simply in the way that Oswald Morris's cinematography picks up the seediness of the seaside resort where the Rices live. Nothing can kill a movie's energy quicker than dreary naturalism. But Richardson didn't settle for just a surface naturalism. He made sure that Osborne's urgency to communicate came through, and in the process he connected with an audience who found it bracing to hear the things they felt in their gut finally being expressed at the theater and in the movies.

Richardson's *The Loneliness of the Long-Distance Runner* is often cited (along with movies like Karel Reisz's *Saturday Night and Sunday Morning* and Lindsay Anderson's *This Sporting Life*) as the beginning of the early-1960s renaissance of

British film. But Richardson's earlier work has never really received the credit it deserves, even though it still retains the excitement of bringing new realities to the screen while later, more praised pieces of British "relevance" like John Schlesinger's *Billy Liar* or Karel Reisz's *Morgan!* now seem fey, self-conscious, and dated. The irony of *The Entertainer* was that a film so devoted to naming what was dead, dishonest, and stultified in England demonstrated what was still vital in the country: a theatrical heritage where the greatest master of its classical tradition could feel at home in its most brutally honest new work. *The Entertainer* proved, as Archie Rice might have said, that there was life in the old girl yet.

The Exorcist (1973)

by Terrence Rafferty

WHEN WILLIAM FRIEDKIN'S *The Exorcist*, based on William Peter Blatty's best-selling theological-horror novel, opened on December 26, 1973, it was not only the movie event of the Christmas season that year; it also became the dominant pop-culture phenomenon of the final days of Richard M. Nixon's presidency. One wouldn't want to make too much of this: to suggest, for example, that Mr. Blatty's tale of the expulsion of a possessing demon from the body of a twelve-year-old girl in any way enhanced the national will to eject rascals from the White House would be stretching a point. You could do that. But it would be wrong.

It was, however, undeniably a fairly hysterical time, and audiences' reactions to *The Exorcist* at the very least reflected something of the era's high-strung personality. There were reports that preview audiences were so upset by the film's blasphemies, obscenities, and graphic physical-shocks that several viewers fled the theater, fainted, and/or vomited. (As it turns out, the scene that evoked the strongest flight response was a long sequence of medical testing.) And although such reactions are perfectly valid critical comments on many movies, in the case of *The Exorcist* audience revulsion became a kind of selling point: people lined up for hours, braving the winter cold, to see little possessed Regan (Linda Blair) swivel her head 360 degrees, hurl her well-meaning mother across the room, belch profanities at anyone within earshot, crush the genitals of a psychiatrist, masturbate with a crucifix, and spew green liquid in the faces of unsuspecting Jesuits.

I have to confess that I did not stand in line for *The Exorcist* that winter but caught up to it later, when the fuss had died down. Because I was at that time living in a university dormitory, I really didn't need to go to the movies to see people vomiting and passing out. And the spectacle of clever priests drinking Scotch and wrestling with their faith had less exotic allure for me than it had for many members of the audience: I'd known Jesuits all my life, because my father taught at Brooklyn Prep, a Jesuit high school of which, as it happens, Mr. Blatty is an alumnus. When I finally saw the picture, the audience was clearly shaken, but the screening was medically uneventful.

The Exorcist has come back, in a new, longer version. Since the advent of home video, more and more films have been turning up on cassette and DVD in altered states designated as "director's cuts." This edition of *The Exorcist,* however, appears to be essentially a writer-producer's cut: many of the additional scenes are those that Mr. Blatty has, over the years, loudly criticized Mr. Friedkin for excising. (The director had banished Mr. Blatty from the editing room because he was being, in his words, "a pain.")

As recently as two years ago, when Mr. Friedkin and Mr. Blatty were interviewed for a BBC documentary (which is included on the twenty-fifth-anniversary "Special Edition" DVD), the director still believed that his cut of *The Exorcist* was "as close to a perfect film as you can make," while the writer continued to argue that the movie's current ending left his story dangerously vulnerable to theological misinterpretation: for all these years, Mr. Blatty has been bugged by the knowledge that some viewers thought the Devil had won.

But Mr. Blatty has apparently worn Mr. Friedkin down. The new *Exorcist* restores the writer's preferred ending (which is also the final scene of the novel), an exchange of excruciating jocularities between a middle-aged police detective and a young Jesuit, in which we are given to understand that the spirit of the story's martyred hero, Father Damien Karras (Jason Miller) lives on. On this issue, Mr. Friedkin was right the first time. The scene was an embarrassment in the book, and it is immeasurably worse on the screen: Lee J. Cobb's grotesque performance as the detective italicizes every inanity. The triumph of the Devil isn't any more depressing than the idea that grown men might actually talk to each other the way this priest and this cop do.

Other changes are trivial. There's a brief shot of Georgetown in Washington—where the heroine, Chris MacNeil (Ellen Burstyn) and her satanically challenged daughter live—inserted before the film's original opening sequence, in which the title character, the elderly archaeologist-priest Lankester Merrin (Max. von Sydow), digs for evil in northern Iraq. The new beginning is inoffensive but useless, as are a handful of superimposed images of scary-monster heads that have been added to later, more horrific scenes in the MacNeil household: they are coals to Newcastle, or, if you will, priests to Georgetown.

The longest restored sequence, an additional (earlier, less grisly) diagnostic scene, slightly improves the structural clarity of the narrative. And for horror-movie aficionados, the main attraction of the expanded *Exorcist* is undoubtedly the inclusion of the legendary (well, to some) "spider walk"—i.e., the scene in which Regan skitters down a staircase on all fours, hands first, and her body facing upward. It's a good, unnerving shock effect: whether the picture needs another of those is, I guess, a matter of taste.

BY FAR THE BEST THING ABOUT this *Exorcist* is that it makes a bit more room for Max von Sydow, arguably the planet's greatest living actor. Father Merrin is just a routinely brilliant supporting turn for him, and in a way this character is to von Sydow what Obi-Wan Kenobi was to Sir Alec Guinness: the role that the general audience would forever identify him most closely with. But the movie wouldn't work at all without his enormous, mysterious authority and grace. Mr. von Sydow's terse readings suggest the let's-get-it-done manner of an old spiritual gunslinger wearily cleaning up one more rotten town: he appears to be the one person involved in the movie who understands that it's not a theological parable but an exceptionally perverse western. The revised *Exorcist* gives him a few more scenes, and though they're brief, anything that increases the amount of Max von Sydow in the world has to be considered a force for good.

Like every powerful horror movie, *The Exorcist* gains from being seen on a big screen, with an audience primed to scream and talk back. No one should expect vomiting and fainting this time, though. Horror is mainstream entertainment now, and our collective tolerance for gore, obscenity, and even invasive medical procedures is exponentially greater than it was in the Trickster era. Our gross-out threshold has risen as fast and as high as the stock market—thanks largely, it should be said, to *The Exorcist* itself. In 1973, moviegoers stood in line to get queasy. We must have acquired a taste for it, because we haven't stopped yet.

Faces (1968)

by Andrew Sarris

I WOULD LIKE TO RECOMMEND *Faces* (at the Little Carnegie) without restructuring the reader's aesthetic expectations, but I know by now that I can't escape the consequences of my criticism. *Faces*, if seen at all, should be seen with a degree of tolerance for its rough edges and raw nerve endings. Indeed the first half-hour strains so hard for its strained conviviality that the movie becomes a bad bet to last two hours without bursting a blood vessel. Writer-director (but here not actor) John Cassavetes begins the proceedings with a framing scene that is recalled in retrospect as a half-baked Brechtian distancing device. It doesn't really belong to the picture, but curiously it works on its own terms. A comically hard-boiled TV producer (John Marley) grumpily sips his early-morning dawn's-ugly-light coffee in a screening room consecrated by his staff to the exhibition of a slice of real life in which Mr. Marley himself is to be reincarnated as one of the pathetic protagonists. Already we are being treated to the ear-shorn, nose-heavy facial distortions of camera-verite, not to mention the serpentine person-to-person and room-to-room camera movements with which we have become so familiar on television's more lunatic spectacles such as the when-is-Mr.-Nixon-coming down-Herb show on election night. Look at me! the camera screams too stridently. Look how honest and real and true I am! This viewer, I must confess, braced himself at this point for a strenuous session of formlessness masquerading as fearlessness. And who are all these strangely worn unknowns? The only familiar face among the players is Gena Rowlands (Mrs. John Cassavetes), and even she has hardly been victimized by overexposure these past few years. The whole project smells so strongly of poverty row that the more cautious critic may beware the thin line between inspired naturalism and nagging indigence. Exterior shots, for example, are rarer in *Faces* than in the raunchiest sexploitation films. Scenes go on and on with Warholian exhaustiveness (though not exhaustion). And Cassavetes lets all the players laugh their heads off to the point that nervousness is transformed into purgation. Strange, different, but is it good? The notion of art as selection and compression gets short shrift in *Faces*. All in all, there are only seven master scenes with three very brief transitions and virtually no parallel editing for contrast or irony. No one seems to be cut off and nothing seems to be cut.

Even at its best, *Faces* cannot be considered a triumph of cinematic form, and the formalist in me has been resisting the sloppy eccentricities of Cassavetes ever since *Shadows* a decade or so ago.

Ultimately, however, *Faces* emerges for me as the revelation of 1968, not the best movie to be sure, but certainly the most surprising. (Luis Buñuel's *Belle de Jour* merely caps a career that has crested many times before.) After its somewhat strained beginning, *Faces* not only works; it soars. The turning point is the first desperately domestic conversation between John Marley and Lynn Carlin, a conversation swept along on its banal course by gales of nervous laughter, a conversation accompanied by physical withdrawal behind the luxurious barriers of space, walls, doors, and furniture, a conversation that in its lacking topical details and symbolic overtones is perhaps closer to aimless soap opera than to deliberate drama. But it works in ways that are mysterious to behold as if for once a soap opera was allowed to unfold out of its own limited logic for two hours without interruptions for commercials or station identification. What we have in *Faces* therefore is not only a failure to communicate but a reluctance to terminate, and this reluctance is one of the reasons *Faces* achieves an otherwise inexplicable intensity of feeling that transcends the too easily satirized milieu of affluently superficial Southern California. Although it is concerned almost exclusively with the lecherous delusions of pickups and pick-me-ups, *Faces* is never sordid or squalid. Cassavetes stays with his tormented, alienated characters until they break through the other side of slice-of-life naturalism into emotional and artistic truth.

Faces works even if we question its creator's original intentions. Who can ever say for sure that *Faces* is not a kind of serendipity cinema, that is, a movie that started out as a dull diatribe against American life and ended up as a heroic saga of emotional survival through an endless night of loneliness and shattered defenses. *Faces* is certainly more interesting in itself than for all the things that can be said about it, a mark of merit more intrinsic than extrinsic. Still, Cassavetes deserves full credit for the inspired idea (possibly intuitive) of developing characters objectively in odd-numbered relationships before exploring them intimately in even-numbered couplings. Hence, the first scene features two men competing in the apartment of the girl they've picked up in a bar. The infernal triangle brings out all the self-hatred of the errant husbands and takes us quite logically into a scene of domestic coupling through which self-hatred takes on new dimensions. The husband tells the wife he wants a divorce, and thus two become one and one, but when he calls the girl he picked up earlier in the evening, it turns out that she is occupied with a double date. No matter. The tormented husband bursts in on the party of four to make an unwelcome fifth, scuffles grotesquely with an equally aging, equally affluent philanderer, but then everyone makes up as a sixth girl is recruited to restore the original double coupling of the evening and leave the husband alone with his original date. The arithmetical progression proceeds four to five by intrusion, five to six by augmentation, and finally two and four by division. Meanwhile the deserted wife and three of her more domestically disaffected girlfriends visit a go-go dance joint where they allow themselves to be picked up by a swaggering but thirties hippie. (The movie was shot at least two years ago, and thus the skirts look curiously long and the dances relatively coherent, a good sic-transit-go-go-gloria argument against ever trying to be too timely.) The circle of five disintegrates into a series of jealous explosions until wife and hippie are left alone in illusory togetherness, a dubious coupling that leads the wife to the medicine cabinet in search of the ultimate number—zero.

All through the movie, people are intimating that they want to be alone with each other even though they have been conditioned to function only in a crowd. They are driven to sex not by desire but by an adolescent bravado that they know instinctively is spiritually futile but still they pay lip service to the ideal of intimacy, the very ideal their society has degraded with its dirty jokes and infantile inhibitions. The characters in *Faces* start off as a lineup of emotional cripples, but somehow they all make it to the finish line with their souls intact. Among the players, I would single out Lynn Carlin, John Marley, Seymour Cassel, and Gena Rowlands for special praise out of a virtually flawless ensemble, and if this be actor's cinema, long may it flourish. At the very least, Cassavetes deserves full credit for staging the spectacle with both conviction and compassion.

Fargo (1996)

by Peter Travers

THE FIRST TIME I SAW FARGO, I thought it was funny in the warped way that makes a laugh stick in your throat. The second time, I was nearly moved to tears. I'm afraid to see it again, which is probably the kind of paranoid reaction those SOBs the Coen brothers would like to provoke. Yes, they are *that* contrary, not to mention untrustworthy. In interviews they pull a Hitchcock and say it's only a movie, there's no deeper meaning, yadda, yadda, yadda. So if you want to read something into *Miller's Crossing* or *Barton Fink,* you look like a jerk. After a well-received 1984 debut with the noirish *Blood Simple* and a 1987 hit with *Raising Arizona,* the Coens were hammered critically for being cold, technical, film-school showoffs, especially for their megabudget 1994 flop, *The Hudsucker Proxy.*

Fargo is meant as a return to their poor but honest roots, cinematic proof that the Coens have a heart. They do. But watch out—these guys are tricky. Joel Coen, the elder brother (he was forty-one at the time *Fargo* was released in 1996), is billed as the writer and director. Ethan, then thirty-eight, is the writer and producer. Talk to any actor who ever worked on a Coen brothers movie and they'll swear up and down that both Joel and Ethan direct. So forget the billing. And pay no attention to the credit: edited by Roderick Jaynes. No such guy. The Coens do their own editing; they made Jaynes up. They also say that *Fargo* is a true story about events that took place in Minnesota in 1987. Conceding that the names have been changed at the request of the survivors, they claim in a title card that the rest has been told "exactly as it occurred . . . out of respect for the dead." Yeah, right. So what's the "no similarity to actual persons" disclaimer doing in the final credits?

Have I mentioned yet that *Fargo*—lies and all—is some kind of classic? Let me do so right now. The damn thing gnaws at your insides the way no Coen brothers film has done before. Just when you think the film is faking you out, it pulls you up short with a jolt of genuine emotion. Remember Mike Yanagita? But that's jumping ahead.

To begin: *Fargo* takes place in Minnesota, which the Coens maintain is their birthplace. So, with typical Coen perversity, the first shot—a car driving through the snow—is set in Fargo, North Dakota. The plot concerns one Jerry Lundegaard (William H. Macy), a Minnesota car salesman who has come to a bar in Fargo to hire two scuzzballs—Carl (Steve Buscemi) and Gaear (Peter Stormare)—to kidnap his wife, Jean (Kristin Rudrud), and collect a ransom from her mean-spirited, tightwad daddy, Wade (Harve Presnell). Jerry means no harm to come to Jean, the mother of his son. He just wants cash to cover a bad business investment. But the kidnap plan goes awry when Jean puts up a fight and bites Gaear so hard he needs to search her house for "unguent." Innocent bystanders start getting killed as the kidnappers botch their escape.

The Coens take their time setting up their characters. But oh how sweet it is to watch them work their deft magic. Take the kidnappers. As they drive to Minnesota, Gaear gives his partner the silent treatment, which drives Carl nuts. "I don't have to talk either, see how you like it," says Carl. "Total fucking silence." Buscemi and Stormare elicit lethal laughs—think Jay and Silent Bob, only homicidal.

Then there's Macy, an actor who can make something vivid of a dull, colorless character. The Coens show us Jerry at work, feigning moral indignation when a customer accuses Jerry of selling him a phony antirust system called "Truecoat" (a great Coen word). At home, Jerry feigns everything, including the manhood his dominating father-in-law has long since clipped from his scrotum. Nobody plays quiet desperation like Macy.

He might have stolen the film outright were it not for Frances McDormand as the pregnant Police Chief Marge Gunderson (a role that would win her the Oscar as best actress). Marge hails from up Brainerd, the town with the huge statue of Paul Bunyan. At first it's hard to get a fix on Marge with her earflaps and flat, "Ya, sure, how ya doin'?" accent and the way she dotes on her husband, Norm (John Carroll Lynch), a wildlife painter. On the way home from a gory crime scene, Marge takes the time to stop and buy Norm nightcrawlers for fishing. He shows up at her office to feed her a burger and fries from Arby's. Then you realize: It's true love.

Marge is a breakthrough role for McDormand (*Mississippi Burning, Short Cuts*), who is sublimely funny and touching without ever pushing for effect. Marge is smart, thorough and unflappable. Investigating a homicide in the snow, she bends over the corpse of a state trooper and looks like she's about to barf. Marge is no wimp. "It's just morning sickness," she tells her dim-bulb partner Lou (Bruce Bohner), who thinks they can catch the culprits if he can trace the rest of the numbers on license plates that begin "DRL" on a vehicle seen fleeing the crime scene. "I'm not sure I agree with you 100 percent on your police work there, Lou," says Marge, who knows "DLR" means dealer plates. Marge is having a giggle at Lou's expense, but McDormand plays her without an ounce of cruelty.

Which brings us to the allegedly irrelevant scene in which Marge meets an old beau, Mike Yanagita (the estimable Steve Park), for a drink at a hotel restaurant. Mike smiles like sunshine—"I saw you on the TV; I always liked you so much"— but through Park's marvel of a performance reveals his character as a delusional stalker, a fact that renders the usually voluble Marge speechless. Mike, who refuses to see Marge's marriage and protruding belly as an impediment to their dating, could have been her life partner. It was that close. Far from being irrelevant, the scene offers character insights that are crucial to our understanding of Marge and her relationship with her husband.

Fargo is a film that demands and rewards close attention. Whether Marge is interrogating a rude Jerry ("Sir, you have no call to get snippy with me") or pulling a gun on a psycho like Gaear, she won't let malfeasance taint her worldview ("There's more to life than a little money, you know?"). The Coens never condescend to this character, even when she discovers a human leg in a wood chipper. But that may be giving too much away. *Fargo* earns its surprises, and the Coens (they won an Oscar for the screenplay) deliver them in all their grotesque glory, ably abetted by the gifted cinematographer Roger Deakins (he's for real).

Joel and Ethan Coen, the sons of college profs, are often criticized as snobs who like to put down peons. They deny the charge. But why believe them? Trust your own instincts, and chances are you'll still find *Fargo* a hypnotic blend of mirth and malice. It's impossible to resist the freaky fun of the actors as Macy, Buscemi, and Stormare perform black-comic riffs in the snow. And McDormand wins your heart, making Marge so endearing that she could spin off into her own TV series (*I Love Margy?*), a possibility that could drive the Coens into despair. Then again, you never know with these princes of perversity. Joel claims that he is married to McDormand, which leads me to suspect that it's really Ethan.

Frankenstein and
The Bride of Frankenstein (1931, 1935)

by Richard T. Jameson

IN 1931, THE DIRECTOR ROBERT FLOREY lived in a Los Angeles apartment with a view of a Dutch-style bakery and its logo, a windmill complete with turning vanes. Florey had just been assigned by Carl Laemmle Jr. to direct a production of *Frankenstein* for Universal, and as he mused on a possible look for the film, he found himself considering a windmill as a key location—perhaps the site of the scientist's secret laboratory. As it happened, it would be James Whale, not Florey, who directed *Frankenstein,* and Henry Frankenstein would set up shop in "an abandoned watchtower." But that windmill got lodged in the collective brain of the filmmaking team (also in one line of dialogue absentmindedly retained from an early script draft) and finally made it onscreen as an opportunistic but aptly crazed-Gothic setting for the film's fiery climax.

It's all very well to talk about aesthetically unified masterpieces and posit them as the definition of film art. But movies are a messy business, and the irksome (glorious?) truth is that some landmark films have become utterly indispensable and culturally pervasive despite being created by committee and riddled with imperfections. In the case of *Frankenstein,* the imperfections include half-baked sequences, tedious subsidiary or comic-relief characters, mannerisms and structural faults all but mandated by the conventions of the day, and abrupt lacunae traceable to censorship or to front-office insistence on a shorter running time. Not that anyone would dispute director James Whale's status as "auteur" and an inimitable stylist whose signature is all over *Frankenstein's* decor, staging, lighting, composition, editing, and characterizations. But there is a sense in which this milestone of the horror genre and indelible fixture in Western culture uncannily took on a life of its own—perhaps even, to an extent, created itself.

Consider the thoroughness with which "Frankenstein" entered popular consciousness as a misapprehension. In the 1931 film, as in the 1818 novel by Mary Godwin Wollstonecraft Shelley, Frankenstein was the aristocratic scientist—"the modern Prometheus"—who stole lightning from the heavens to give life to a creature he'd assembled from parts of dead bodies. Yet almost immediately, audiences (and people who had only heard about the movie) started applying the name to the creature—superhuman in size and strength, effectively unkillable, and murderously insane. This was reinforced by "Frankenstein" becoming all but interchangeable with "Boris Karloff," the harsh, foreign-sounding, slightly ersatz name of the actor who had played the Monster. How did the confusion arise? Perhaps it was only a testament to star quality—Karloff's and the creature's. "Frankenstein" was too ringing a name to squander on an effete gent in a lab smock (the top-billed, but soon eclipsed, Colin Clive). In any event, the conflation of roles was condoned forthwith by Universal. In the prologue to *The Bride of Frankenstein,* the 1935 sequel, Lord Byron (Gavin Gordon) congratulates authoress Mary Shelley (Elsa Lanchester) on her imagining of "Frankenstein, a monster created out of cadavers out of rifled graves." And indeed, the very title *The Bride of Frankenstein* invites multiple readings as to which is who.

Then again, ambiguity was built right into the initial production. Whereas Universal's first 1931 horror hit, Tod Browning's *Dracula,* mostly kept faith with the period and settings of the Bram Stoker novel, *Frankenstein* takes place in a nowhere universe; contemporary fashions rub up against generic peasant wear (Tyrolean-Magyar), while a polyglot cast of stage Brits and flatfooted American movie types try to look as if they belong in a nonspecific Mittel-Europe where hanged felons are left creaking on crossroads gallows in the medieval manner. The village near the Frankenstein estate is an elaborate German town set left over from Universal's Academy Award–winning prestige picture *All Quiet on the Western Front* (1930), but otherwise the prevailing decor marks a problematic—but ultimately fortuitous—accommodation between the budgetary constraints of a marginally major studio and the theatrical expressionism James Whale had already cultivated as a stage director and designer. As realized by Universal's redoubtable art director Charles D. Hall, the film's patently manmade landscape features stark hills and starker trees thrust straight up against stormy skies that crowd close behind the players—who could in fact reach out and touch their canvas splendor. The spatial derangement of the environment achieves apotheosis in the eerie sequence of the Monster invading the Frankenstein manor on the day of Henry's wedding. The bridegroom and his cohorts run first to the top floor, then to the cellarage, drawn by the unseen Monster's eldritch groans. How *is* he getting from one zone to another, as if passing through solid stone? We never know.

That the Monster is a monster is never in doubt, and it's perfectly understandable that the local citizenry should take up arms against him when he starts killing their neighbors. But we also understand that the poor bastard never had a chance. Wrenched into life and then abandoned by a fickle Creator, implanted with a criminal brain, and tormented almost from "birth" by Henry's torch-wielding assistant Fritz (genre mainstay Dwight Frye), the Monster is driven to slaughter even as he yearns foremost to reach for the light. Karloff's miming of this aspiration remains heartbreakingly eloquent despite decades of imitation and parody. And just as King Kong became the most sympathetic figure in the RKO monster movie of that name two years hence, Whale would decisively adjust the vectors and valences of sympathy in *The Bride of Frankenstein,* a sequel as inevitable as its superiority was unexpected.

Following the aforementioned prologue—which introduces a creator of another sort, Mary Shelley, to continue her exemplary tale from a lightning-lit, clifftop castle distinctly reminiscent of Henry Frankenstein's tower—*Bride* casts back to the burning windmill where *Frankenstein* ended. There have been changes in the minutes/years separating the action of the two films. Ignoring the inconvenient postlude that had been hastily added to *Frankenstein* to show Henry recuperating after his fall, *Bride* reverts to Henry apparently dead—but only so that the twitching of his hand can signal survival, as a similar twitching of the creature's hand signaled coming to life in the first film. Tiresome characters (Henry's father the Baron; best friend and romantic rival Victor) have been allowed to disappear without comment. Better actors have replaced dull predecessors: the liquid-eyed Valerie Hobson in for Mae Clarke as Elizabeth, Henry's betrothed; E.E. Clive taking over as the burgomaster; and Una O'Connor drafted from Whale's intervening *The Invisible Man* (1933) to play Minnie the maid, a screech-owl Greek chorus obsessed with whether people are in their proper beds. The righteous outrage of the townsfolk has mutated into sadistic glee over the

Monster's presumed destruction. And to tip the director's hand, when the Monster rises to send two of them to their deaths in the waters under the mill, Whale marks their separate splashes with droll nonreaction shots of an imperturbable owl.

In short, *Bride* replaces the Gothic portentousness of the original with acid black comedy, as well as a heightened, breathlessly sustained pitch of energy (a flamboyant fluidity of camerawork, and an adventurous music score by Franz Waxman instead of, in the case of *Frankenstein,* none at all). However many days or weeks may have passed during the events of *Frankenstein* (there's really no telling), *Bride* crams a third of its running time into one frenzied night, with near-corpse Henry brought back to life and settled in what should have been his marriage bed, only to be enticed out of it and off to yet another secret lair by a fellow scientific heretic. The entrance of this new character, the preternaturally gaunt Dr. Praetorious (Ernest Thesiger, an old theatrical crony of Whale's), is anticipated by Elizabeth's hysterical vision of "a figure like Death" coming to separate her and Henry, and announced by Minnie—in perhaps the most outrageous intro in Hollywood history to date—as "a very queer-looking gentleman." Queer-looking and brazenly queer-sounding, too: as both the dialogue and Thesiger's deliciously fruity delivery make clear, Praetorious regards Elizabeth, the conventional bride of Frankenstein, as a tedious rival and obstacle to his seduction of Henry to come "probe the mysteries of life and death together."

Nor does Whale—a well-regarded and successful Hollywood figure who lived openly as a homosexual—stop at having a little fun with a campy villain. *The Bride of Frankenstein* develops a complex, and still startlingly brave, theme of the Monster as the ultimate outsider, someone feared and rejected by society even more for what and who he is than anything he has done. This covert gay analogue is soon interwoven with another line of iconic reference: Captured by the mob at a hilly place of rocks, the Monster is bound and raised on a pole in a simulacrum of the Crucifixion (which Whale emphasizes with half a dozen separate camera angles and the equivalent of a long gasp in the editing). Escaped, then pursued anew, he literally descends into the underworld, the graveyard (his movement directly lined up with a slanting Christus), to confront Death—Praetorious. Only in this case, the potential Redeemer doesn't conquer Death but rather allows himself to be drawn into a bargain with him. Again there is a peerless Karloff moment: bending over the silken profile of a dead woman in her coffin, the Monster tentatively salutes, "Friend? . . . " And from that point on, the film rushes magisterially toward its climax, and the high-water mark of classical Hollywood horror: the creation of a new Bride of Frankenstein (again, with devastating irony,

Elsa Lanchester). True to her name, she prefers her maker, Henry, and loathes the "man" she was born to love. Inconsolable, the Monster accepts his destiny: "We belong dead." And in an ecstasy of grief and the craziest gleam of triumph the movies ever dreamed, they are.

The General (1927)

by Roger Ebert

BUSTER KEATON WAS NOT THE GREAT STONE FACE so much as a man who kept his composure in the center of chaos. Other silent actors might mug to get a point across, but Keaton remained observant and collected. That's one reason his best movies have aged better than those of his rival, Charlie Chaplin. He seems like a modern visitor to the world of the silent clowns.

Consider an opening sequence in *The General* (1927), his masterpiece about a Southern railway engineer who has "only two loves in his life"—his locomotive and the beautiful Annabelle Lee. Early in the film, Keaton, dressed in his Sunday best, walks to his girl's house. He is unaware that two small boys are following him, marching in lockstep—and that following them is Annabelle Lee herself (Marion Mack).

He arrives at her door. She watches unobserved. He polishes his shoes on the backs of his pants legs, and then knocks, pauses, looks about, and sees her standing right behind him. This moment would have inspired an overacted double-take from many other silent comedians. Keaton plays it with his face registering merely heightened interest.

They go inside. He sits next to her on the sofa. He becomes aware that the boys have followed them in. His face reflects slight unhappiness. He rises, puts on his hat as if to leave, and opens the door, displaying such courtesy you would think the boys were his guests. The boys walk out and he closes the door on them.

He is not a man playing for laughs but a man absorbed in a call on the most important person in his life. That's why it's funny. That's also why the movie's most famous shot works—the one where, rejected by his girl, he sits disconsolately on the drive-rod of the big engine. As it begins to move, it lifts him up and down, but he does not notice, because he thinks only of Annabelle Lee.

This series of shots establishes his character as a man who takes himself seriously, and that is the note he will sound all through the film. We don't laugh at Keaton but identify with him.

The General is an epic of silent comedy, one of the most expensive films of its time, including an accurate historical recreation of a Civil War episode, hundreds of extras, dangerous stunt sequences, and an actual locomotive falling from a burning bridge into a gorge far below. It was inspired by a real event, "The Great Locomotive Chase," and William Pittenger, the engineer who was involved, collaborated on the screenplay.

As the film opens, war has been declared, and Johnny Gray (Keaton) has been turned down by a rebel enlisting officer (he is more valuable as an engineer, although nobody explains that to him). "I don't want you to speak to me again until you are in uniform," Annabelle declares. Time passes. Johnny is the engineer of the *General*, a Southern locomotive. The train is stolen by Union spies, and Johnny chases it on foot, by sidecar, by bicycle, and finally with another locomotive, the *Texas*. Then the two sides switch trains, and the chase continues in reverse. Annabelle was a passenger on the stolen train, becomes a prisoner of the Union troops, is rescued by Johnny, and rides with him during the climactic chase scenes that end with the famous shot of the *Texas* falling into the gorge (where, it is said, its rusted hulk remains to this day).

It would seem logically difficult to have much of a chase involving trains, since they must remain on tracks, and so one must forever be behind the other one—right? Keaton defies logic with one ingenious silent comic sequence after another, and it is important to note that he never used a double and did all of his own stunts, even very dangerous ones, with a calm acrobatic grace.

The train's obvious limitations provide him with ideas. An entire Southern retreat and Northern advance take place unnoticed behind him, while he chops wood. Two sight gags involve his puzzlement when railcars he thought were behind him somehow reappear in front of him. He sets up the locations along the way, so that he can exploit them differently on the way back. One famous sequence involves a cannon on a flat car, which Keaton wants to fire at the other train. He lights the fuse and runs back to the locomotive, only to see that the cannon has slowly reversed itself and is now pointed straight at him.

One inspiration builds into another: To shield himself from the cannonball, he runs forward and sits on the cowcatcher of the speeding *Texas*, with no one at the controls and a big railroad tie in his arms. The Union men throw another tie onto the tracks, and Keaton, with perfect aim and timing, knocks the second off by throwing the first. It's flawless and perfect, but consider how risky it is to sit on the front of a locomotive hoping one tie will knock another out of the way without either one smashing your brains out.

Between chase scenes, he blunders into a house where the Northern generals are planning their strategy, and he rescues Annabelle Lee—but not before Keaton creates a perfect little cinematic joke.

He is hiding under the dining table as the Northerners confer. One of them burns a hole in the tablecloth with his cigar. Annabelle Lee is brought into the room, and we see Keaton's eye peering through the hole—and then there's a reverse shot of the girl, with Keaton using the hole in the cloth to create a "found" iris shot—one of those shots so beloved of Griffith, in which a circle is drawn around a key element on the screen.

The General was voted one of the ten greatest films of all time in the authoritative *Sight & Sound* poll. Who knows if it is even Keaton's greatest? Others might choose *Steamboat Bill, Jr.* (1928). His other classics include *Our Hospitality* (1923), *The Navigator* (1924), *Go West* (1925), and *The Cameraman* (1928), in which he played a would-be newsreel photographer who lucks into his career.

Born in 1897, the same year as the cinema, he grew up in a vaudeville family. As part of the act, he was literally thrown around the stage; like W.C. Fields, he learned his physical skills in a painful childhood apprenticeship. He started in films with Fatty Arbuckle in 1917 and directed his first shorts in 1920. In less than a decade, from 1920 to 1928, he created a body of work that stands beside Chaplin's (some would say above it), and he did it with fewer resources because he was never as popular or well-funded as the Little Tramp.

Then the talkies came in, he made an ill-advised deal with MGM that ended his artistic independence, and the rest of his life was a long second act—so long that in the 1940s he was reduced to doing a live half-hour TV show in Los Angeles. But it was also long enough that his genius was rediscovered, and he made a crucial late work, Samuel Beckett's *Film* (1965), and was hailed with a retrospective at Venice shortly before his death in 1966.

Today I look at Keaton's works more often than any other silent films. They have such a graceful perfection, such a meshing of story, character, and episode, that they unfold like music. Although they're filled with gags, you can rarely catch Keaton writing a scene around a gag; instead, the laughs emerge from the situation; he was "the still, small, suffering center of the hysteria of slapstick," wrote the critic Karen Jaehne. And in an age when special effects were in their infancy, and a "stunt" often meant actually doing on the screen what you appeared to be doing, Keaton was ambitious and fearless. He had a house collapse around him. He swung over a waterfall to rescue a woman he loved. He fell from trains. And always he did it in character, playing a solemn and thoughtful man who trusts in his own ingenuity.

"Charlie's tramp was a bum with a bum's philosophy," he once said. "Lovable as he was, he would steal if he got the chance. My little fellow was a workingman, and honest." That describes his characters, and it reflects their creator.

The Godfather and
The Godfather Part II (1972, 1974)

by Michael Sragow

ALTHOUGH FRANCIS FORD COPPOLA has often been depicted—and loves to depict himself—as primarily an emotional and intuitive director, *The Godfather* is a film filled with correct *choices*, painstakingly thought out and passionately carried through. Part of what made it a breakthrough as a crime movie is that it's about *gangsters* who make choices too and aren't propelled simply by bloodlust and greed. They're battling for position in New York's Five Families, circa 1945–1946. If Don Vito Corleone (Marlon Brando) and his successor Michael (Al Pacino) come off looking better than all the others, it's because they play the power game the cleverest and best—and the game is sordidly exciting.

For all the movie's warmth, you could never confuse the Corleones or their allies and competitors for fun-loving ethnic types. The first scene shows the Don exacting deadly patronage, coercing an undertaker named Bonasera into vows of love and pledges of unmitigated loyalty in exchange for a feudal bond that can't be broken or forgotten. Before Coppola has finished cutting between Don Vito accepting fealty in his office to his daughter celebrating her wedding outside— with the sepia interiors and golden exteriors illustrating the split in the Corleones' lives—we've also heard the Don tell a Sinatralike singer, Johnny Fontane (Al Martino), that "a man who doesn't spend time with his family can never be a real man."

Once Coppola ties the themes of power and family together, he takes off with a story in the grand tragic manner. Its theme is the corruption of once justifiable goals, their altering through histories of struggle and domination. The Corleones are one generation removed from Sicily. They're in the business of staying alive in America, and part of their business requires them to kill.

The growth of Michael Corleone and Pacino's startling physical and emotional alteration in the role give the film its shape. A college grad who is also a World War II hero, he tests his strength and cunning in the streets to avenge his father's near-murder. He states his rationale to his girlfriend (later wife) Kay, played by Diane Keaton: "My father's no different than any other powerful man. Any man who's responsible for other people, like a senator or president." Kay responds: "You know how naive you sound? Senators and presidents don't have men killed." In a line that marked a breakthrough for mainstream political awareness when the film premiered in 1972, Michael wearily answers, "Who's being naive, Kay?"

But when Michael says his father's way of doing things is finished, he *is* being naive. And the way Pacino plays him, you can tell that deep down he knows the vortex of mob violence has sucked him in. Pacino's performance is so intimately felt-out that each milestone (or, in Kay's view, millstone) on his path both catches you by surprise—and registers indelibly. There's the moment he stands guard in front of the hospital and realizes that "his" hands aren't shaking (though the good-hearted baker's helper next to him can scarcely hold on to his cigarette). There's the chilly air of corporate homicide he adopts to prove to his brother, Sonny, that his plan to kill his father's would-be murderer and a crooked cop is "not personal . . . it's strictly business." And there's the volcanic eruption of the actual double homicide.

What makes this both horrifying and seductive is that we're not just seeing the hardening of a killer but the strengthening of a young man who's getting back to his roots. That becomes clear when he hides out in Sicily and marries a local beauty named Apollonia (Simonetta Stefanelli). It's as if blasting the dreams of a straight life and getting scarred in single-warrior combat have reconnected him to the earth. He returns to New York with the authority of someone who's touched psychic bottom.

To this day it's jolting to see Brando as Don Corleone—the receded hairline, the gray pencil moustache, jowls hanging off a twisted mouth, and a voice cracked from years of command. Brando makes the character extraordinarily complex largely through his physical expressiveness. He walks as if his shoulder blades were pinned behind him (which emphasizes an old man's paunch in front). But the sensibility beneath the authority is astonishingly agile: the Don can suddenly break into mimicry, or turn his daughter in a waltz with a slight protective bent that catches sentiment in movement. Brando puts so much substance into his relatively few scenes, blowing hot and cold with equal eclat, that he enables Coppola to draw parallels between his sons and himself through nuances at once fleeting and concrete.

James Caan plays the eldest boy, Sonny, like the Don without his lid on. He feels that when he's indulging his appetites (for action and for sex), he's fueling the fires that protect his family. But his lack of control triggers a gang war that ends in his own death. Caan animates his body with a high-strung, barely controlled rage; when he lets go, kicking and bashing his wife-beating brother-in-law Carlo (Gianni Russo), the effect is scary and exhilarating. He's like a Brando action hero on amphetamines. (Carlo's wife, Connie, played by Talia Shire, gives a vividly unsentimental performance, expertly toeing the line between pathos and hysteria.) John Cazale's Fredo, who'd be next in line were it not for his weak nature, has the disarming nakedness and sensitivity Brando showed in movies like *The Men*. Even Robert Duvall, as Tom Hagen, Don Vito's German-Irish adopted son and consigliere, echoes Brando in his eloquent wariness, his furtive intelligence.

The film begins with a trumpet solo that sets off sad, comic, and heroic vibrations. As the brass flourish turns into a waltz, courtship strolls and wedding bashes, church rituals and ritual murders, merge in an eternal dance of life and death. Part of the black magic of *The Godfather* is the way it depicts how Catholicism operates in the Corleone universe—as salvation *and* cover for evil. When Coppola intercuts a christening with a mass assassination, *The Godfather* brings us into the worldview of the wicked, where there is no God, only godfathers.

With breathtaking confidence, *The Godfather Part II* (released in 1974) expands the tragedy and black comedy of its predecessor. It takes the aging Vito Corleone of the original back to his youth, pointing up the irony of his rise in Little Italy's crime hierarchy after having lost his parents to a vendetta in his native Sicily. Vendettas—"honorable" killings—are often the subjects of romance. But here, to the House of Corleone, vendettas prove as potent an ancestral curse as any suffered by the House of Atreus. Coppola cuts from the younger Vito to his successor, Michael—and whatever glow Michael got when he reached power fades as he sets about consolidating it. The Don's legacy of hypocrisy and crime eats away at Michael's soul.

These two movies together are not really about the deterioration of the American Dream. What they say is that for the immigrant groups that became the country's backbone—Italians, Jews, Irish, and others—the American Dream was limited from the start by the burdens of poverty, unsettled scores, and insular ethnic cultures. As in the Old World, they were prey to powerful economic and political forces. But here those forces took more various, insidious forms. Many Vietnam-era movies told us that America is evil, but the more complex, implicit message of these two films is that in America the evil sleeps with the good. The same Senate committee that exposes the Corleones includes a politician in the family's pocket—one of many who've paved the Corleones' road to criminal ascendancy.

In the original *Godfather*, Michael wanted more than anything to escape the Corleone tradition, to be his own man and an American, but familial love and obligation took charge of his desires. In *Part II* he is as haunted by his father's ghost as Hamlet is. He's learned everything from his old man except the things that can't be learned, and he can't hide his inadequacy. And in many ways, Michael is a victim of history. By the time he becomes Don, there's not much family feeling left in the Five Families; the mob has adopted business practices as impersonal as those of the CIA, and not even lionhearted Vito, had he lived, could have reversed that trend. But if Michael's role is that of an antihero, Pacino's ability to invest it with tension is heroic; he gives a dynamic interpretation of depression and listlessness.

There is still gayety as well as viciousness in the Corleones' subculture—that's what makes the picture shattering. Michael V. Gazzo plays Frankie Pantangeli, a Corleone capo and one of the movie's most amiable characters. He evokes instant nostalgia for Vito's happier times, whether looking at canapés—which he pronounces "can-a-peas"—with distrust, or teaching the tarantella to a Nevada band. He contrasts movingly with Lee Strasberg as Hyman Roth, the mob financial wizard who almost persuades Michael to buy into Batista's Cuba. Strasberg even seems to regulate his character's pulse; he's instinctively calculating.

Robert De Niro's young Vito has the same careful intelligence, focused warmth, and regal bearing as Brando's Don. But he's a lithe young man with a smidgen of naive enthusiasm. When he and his partners take proprietary pride in their olive-oil company front, they look as delighted as any wholesome greenhorns opening shop. Yet Vito is ready to forge a chain of murder that will wrap around his clan for generations—twisted yet unbroken, like an infernal Moebius strip. Although *The Godfather* and *The Godfather Part II* depict an American family's moral defeat, as a mammoth, pioneering work of art it remains a national creative triumph.

Gone with the Wind (1939)

by Eleanor Ringel

THE FIRST TIME I SAW *Gone with the Wind* was in 1967.

My best friend and I went downtown to see it at the Loew's Grand where, as we were well aware, the movie had premiered in 1939.

It was a sunny Sunday afternoon in October. We were sixteen, the same age as Scarlett at the beginning of the movie.

We dressed up. We wore Sunday school clothes, girdles, and stockings and, if memory serves, white gloves.

Going to *GWTW* wasn't just going to the movies. It was an event, a landmark in our young lives, a chance to see the movie that had made our hometown world-famous.

The Loew's was decked out in a subdued version of its 1939 plantation finery. Inside were souvenir programs to further remind us we were treading where the sainted had trod. Through these same doors, into this same lobby, had come Vivien Leigh and Clark Gable, Olivia de Havilland and David O. Selznick. And, of course, Margaret Mitchell.

We'd both read her book; it had been required reading at our school. We knew that Scarlett had a seventeen-inch waist and more beaus than we'd managed to attract in our entire dating careers. We knew Atlanta burned and Bonnie Blue died and Rhett walked out.

We knew what happened. What we didn't know was how magnificently it could happen in the hands of a master showman such as Mr. Selznick. At intermission, we sat stunned, swept away by the epic scope of it all. And if the second half proved less glorious and maybe even a little tedious in its soap-opera convolutions, by the time the last-reel death count started, we were weeping. We began as soon as we saw Mammy's tear-streaked face after Bonnie fell off her pony and didn't stop until the lights came up. We sniffed our way out of the theater and waited on the sidewalk (the same sidewalk. . .) for our parents to pick us up.

Going to *GWTW* as a privileged white Atlanta teenager in 1967 was like paying a respectful visit to something important, something that was a part of our past and, for better or worse, our present. Scarlett's sheltered world, before it was shattered by the war, wasn't all that different from our own comfortable cul-de-sac lives of country clubs and private schools.

What shook us most was Scarlett's loss. Not of slaves and crinolines—we were better than that—but of a sense of safety, of order, of grace. Of knowing how to live by certain rules. That those rules were more beneficial to some than others—well, we knew that, too. But like Scarlett, we'd think about it tomorrow.

For now, we'd put on our best clothes and go to the Loew's to pay our respects to a gracious and quintessentially Southern grande dame.

The second time I saw *Gone with the Wind* was in 1969. It was at the Brown University student union. I wore what I always wore around campus: grungy bell-bottom jeans, a ragged sweater, and my Woodstock Nation attitude.

Still, it was with a certain native Atlantan pride that I watched the auditorium fill up for *GWTW* and settled in for four hours of escapism, Hollywood-style. Sure, I now dismissed the longing for "a patrician world" where "the Age of Chivalry took its last bow" as sentimental, racist bunk. But that didn't diminish my love of the movie.

Then an astonishing thing happened. When Mammy (Hattie McDaniel) stuck her head out the window and yelled at Scarlett to put on her shawl, the audience hissed. And when Gerald O'Hara (Thomas Mitchell) took his daughter high up on that hill overlooking Tara and told her, "Land is the only thing that lasts," they snickered.

I was appalled. It was such a stupid, knee-jerk response. These Northern (or Midwestern or whatever) know-it-alls, with their self-congratulatory anti-Southern bias, didn't understand why we loved and revered Mammy; they didn't even know who Mammy was. And they jeered at our white columns, seeing only the master-slave implications and none of the honor and beauty and grace that often resided there as well.

Eventually, the movie silenced them. It was, after all, Hollywood at the height of its manipulative powers, and it would take a pretty amazing college kid to resist the charms of Miss Leigh and Mr. Gable.

But their initial catcalls lingered, forcing me to face what I'd put off in 1967: namely, that a genteel racism is part and parcel of the movie's romanticism. I could love Mammy and Big Sam all I wanted, admire their wisdom and bravery and humor, but they bought into the slave system as cheerfully as their white owners. The fact was, Mammy had a mind of her own but no name of her own.

So I made a deal with the movie: I would never forget its racist subtext. But I would also keep in mind that watching *GWTW* and worrying about its civil rights and wrongs was useless. It was like evaluating *Lawrence of Arabia* solely in terms of its Arab stereotypes. I could still love it even though it reduced an entire group of people to colorful savages.

And I could still love *GWTW*, though never with the same tunnel vision of my first viewing. I felt this way: In 1939, this country was a long way from resolving its attitudes about blacks. It still is. But *GWTW* isn't the problem. We are.

The third time I saw *Gone with the Wind* was a week ago. On a blustery Wednesday afternoon, I walked down to CNN Center where my fellow Brown alum, Ted Turner, has been showing *GWTW* daily for three years.

There were fourteen of us there: a sprinkling of conventioneers, a young man in a cowboy hat, an older woman in a mink coat, a well-dressed black woman about my age, and two French tourists with a small flotilla of shopping bags. The theater was a long way from the Loew's Grand. Small and boxlike and sterile, it was multiplex-generic. The preshow noise was courtesy of a local rock station; Scarlett and Rhett waited their turn while we heard about an overturned tractor-trailer in Smyrna (now known as the birthplace of Julia Roberts).

Then the theater darkened, and up there on the screen was ... a "Merry Christmas" wish from Sprite.

I shrunk into my seat, prepared for a dispiriting experience, a bittersweet coda on this eve of *GWTW*'s fiftieth. Tara had survived Yankees and knee-jerk college students, but it looked ready to succumb to the shameless hucksterism of the 1980s. It was going to be a long afternoon.

Then Max Steiner's music swelled, those mighty letters streamed across the screen, and, reader, I admit it: I burst into tears. Scarlett flirted with the Tarleton twins, Mammy stuck her head out that window (no hisses now), and Gerald O'Hara bequeathed to his headstrong daughter his undying love for the red clay of Tara.

Ten minutes into the movie and I was transfixed. It didn't matter where I was. It didn't matter that the heads were cut off that tiny screen. It didn't matter that a distracting green squiggle marred the print from the time Charles Hamilton proposed until the reading of the casualty list from Gettysburg.

None of it mattered. I was caught up in that "dream remembered," as city-boy Ben Hecht called it—part Old South, part Old Hollywood, part remembrance of things past ... my past.

Gone with the Wind is now a movie of ghosts for me. The glamorous ghosts of its legendary stars. The ghosts of its unlikely cocreators—David O. Selznick, the Hollywood Jew, and Margaret Mitchell, the daughter of the Confederacy. And the half-remembered ghosts of my past selves, each time I returned to this make-believe world of "Cavaliers and Cotton Fields."

Last week, I wept for Bonnie Blue and for Vivien Leigh. In my mind's eye, I saw the shadow of *King Kong*'s Skull Island through the flames of Atlanta, as well as Hattie McDaniel, clutching her well-deserved Oscar and promising to be "a credit to her race." I heard the whine of Leslie Howard's plane as it crashed into the sea, shot down by the Nazis; I also heard the screams of that poor Confederate soldier as his leg was amputated ("Don't cut—please, don't cut!")

Gerald O'Hara was wrong. Land isn't the only thing that lasts. *Gone with the Wind* has lasted, as magnificent as it is phony, as stereotyped as it is stunning.

It is indeed a monument to "a civilization gone with the wind"—the 1930s as much as the 1860s. Enduring and immutable, it is what movies are all about. Not a grande dame, as I once thought, but a grand illusion.

Perhaps the grandest illusion of them all.

Like highway construction, *Gone with the Wind* revivals always seem to be under way in Atlanta. At least seven premieres have followed the big one in 1939:

—Premiere No. 2, 1940: With the Loew's Grand entrance decorated to resemble a huge birthday cake, Atlanta celebrates the first anniversary of *GWTW*. Alas, sequels usually disappoint; a Hollywood contingent, including Vivien Leigh, tries to attend, but the plane is turned away from Atlanta because of fog.

—Premiere No. 3, 1947: MGM reissues the film with new prints. At 8 A.M. on opening day, a line of ticket buyers already has formed in front of the Loew's.

—Premiere No. 4, 1954: Atlanta observes the fifteenth anniversary with a parade (music by the Brown High Rebel Band, naturally), a screening, and the christening of Margaret Mitchell Elementary School. Clark Gable cables his regrets.

—Premiere No. 5, 1961: To mark the Civil War centennial, what else? Miss Leigh, Olivia de Havilland, and David O. Selznick attend the festivities, which include a Confederate costume ball at the Biltmore. Unbelievably, a reporter at a news conference asks Miss Leigh which character she played.

—Premiere No. 6, 1967: With the release of a widescreen version, Atlanta rolls out the red carpet again. After a visit to the Cyclorama and dinner at Aunt Fanny's Cabin, a dwindling number of celebrities (including Miss de Havilland) return to the Loew's, again dressed up like Twelve Oaks.

—Premiere No. 7, 1976: Atlanta doesn't exactly stage *GWTW*'s TV debut, but it watches like it's perusing family photos. The movie actually premieres on Home Box Office in June, but most people remember NBC's two-night showing in November, days after Jimmy Carter is elected president.

—Premiere No. 8, 1989: Ted Turner orchestrates the golden anniversary of his favorite property.

The Gospel According to St. Matthew (1964)

by Rob Nelson

IF LEONARD MALTIN'S MOVIE & VIDEO GUIDE can be taken as a reliable arbiter of American mainstream taste (how else can it be taken—as a polemic?), its backhanded praise of Pier Paolo Pasolini's *The Gospel According to St. Matthew* indicates some of what the Italian filmmaker would have faced in preaching to the Hollywood faithful circa 1964. "Ironically," ventures Maltin's book, "[the] director of this masterpiece was a Marxist." And what's the irony, exactly? That a Marxist could make a "masterpiece"? That a Marxist could make a film about the life and times of Jesus Christ? It oughtn't to be the latter. I mean, how else to classify a lumpen-loving Savior who literally turned the tables on temple moneychangers if not as a devout anticapitalist? ("Only with difficulty will a rich man enter the kingdom of God" is a key line in both the movie and its source.) For his part, Pasolini was given to describing himself as an atheist, which couldn't have helped discourage the Venice Film Festival crowd from throwing spitballs, tomatoes, and raw eggs during *Gospel's* world-premiere screening. Nevertheless, the maestro's calmly contentious sermon on the mount also managed to win a special jury prize at the fest, as befits a film that worships the dialectic above all else.

A defiantly earthy antiepic, *The Gospel According to St. Matthew* is a period piece in costume only, placing its rather scruffy, contemporary-looking Christ in the steep southern Italian hills of Calabria—a clear signifier of the working class at a time when more fashionable parts of the country were busy living "la dolce vita." Influenced as much by the austere style of Dreyer's *The Passion of Joan of Arc* as by early Italian Renaissance painting, Pasolini composed much of the film using stark close-ups of his nonprofessional actors' blemished faces, unmistakably emphasizing the human element over the divine. No DeMillean miracles here: The debut appearance of the teen angel of the Lord is made mystical merely through the wonders of film editing. (Now you don't see her; now you do.) The Satan who tempts our Redeemer in the desert appears no more otherworldly than the puffy-faced pederast of Fuller's *The Naked Kiss*; God the Father's hallowed p.o.v. is represented by a shaky reverse zoom and a one-line voiceover.

Irreverent even in his fidelity to the Gospel's own antiestablishment spirit, Pasolini briefly considered casting Jack Kerouac as Jesus, until he realized that the photo of the beat icon that had caught his eye was ten or fifteen years old. (The director also pondered messiahs played by Allen Ginsberg, Spanish poet Luis Goytisolo, and Muscovite communist Yevgeny Yevtushenko.) In the end, he hired a baby-faced yet curiously smoldering Spanish economics student named Enrique Irazoqui—a young Pasolini fan who'd never acted before but who earned his keep through the sort of artlessly mesmerizing performance that only an amateur can give. It was essential to Pasolini that his film not appear the least bit elitist. The director's increasing disdain for neorealism, whose conventions he had more or less embraced in his first two features (*Accatone* and *Mamma Roma*), stemmed largely from the movement's dogmatic asceticism and, in turn, its failure to connect with the mass audience. Taking his Jesus to the streets, as it were, Pasolini retained neorealism's pseudodocumentary images but cut them to the beat of everything from Bach and Prokofiev to African music and a Negro spiritual. Thus, *Gospel* suggests a sort of postmodern neorealism rather than the thing itself. (Martin Scorsese would take much the same tack a quarter-century later with *The Last Temptation of Christ*.)

Such stylistic apostasy naturally upset defenders of the aesthetic faith, although this was hardly the gravest of *Gospel*'s sins. Pasolini, as he'd seemed to hope, truly got it from all sides: Many European Marxists were incensed by the movie's literal depiction of the supernatural. Others of the left found fault with the film for appearing to doubt the value of political action, the hero's resurrection ostensibly failing to offset the fatalistic message of his death (shame on Pasolini for sticking to the book). And Parisian rationalist intellectuals found it hopelessly archaic. (Meanwhile, the timely tenure of Pope John XXIII—a radical reformer to whom the film is dedicated—protected Pasolini at least in part from charges of blasphemy.) In another era, perhaps, the world's feminists might have been heard to complain that the Virgin Mary (played in her later years by the filmmaker's own mother) seems little more than a birthing device in Pasolini's vision. As it was, the criticism was sufficient to encourage the director to defer to the source material, claiming that the movie had most surprised and disturbed those who hadn't read the Gospel—a surprising and disturbing text in its own right.

Indeed, there's a sense in which the greatest shock of Pasolini's *Gospel* is how faithful it is to Matthew's. As in the Good Book, the movie's Italian peasant Jesus comes not in peace, but with a sword—metaphorically speaking. Naturally, the director claimed to have been most attracted to Christ's revolutionary rhetoric.

And so, in a film that draws its dialogue directly from the Bible, he selects those passages that emphasize the Redeemer's harsh activist side—the one heard less often in conventional New Testament adaptations (or, for that matter, in church). Gruffly ordering his disciples to surrender their earthly privilege and separate from their families, and expressing his clear preference for the poor and the meek who shall inherit the earth (while scarcely cracking a smile), this is hardly a Jesus of unconditional love. (Pasolini's strategic use of jump-cuts—particularly during the bravura Sermon on the Mount sequence—do little to smooth out the Savior's rough edges.) Of course, even a Christian message as gentle as "Love thy neighbor as thyself" would have had undeniable political resonance in 1964, just two years after the end of France's brutal war with Algeria—not to mention what was happening in Vietnam.

If the essence of the Gospel is the inevitability of human suffering, Pasolini's crucifixion scene follows suit by refusing to let the viewer off the hook. Blatantly unsentimental even in its silent cinema–style shots of Christ's hysterically sobbing mother (who, appropriately, appears even more tortured than the man on the cross), this rather utilitarian denouement isn't so much about the glorious gift of Jesus dying for "our" sins as it is about the stubborn withholding of catharsis. Confrontational to the very end, Pasolini dispenses even more swiftly with the resurrection (no Hollywood magic here, either), leaving the viewer safe only in the knowledge of continued struggle. Such holy frustration calls to mind a critique leveled years ago by Scorsese's own parish priest, who complained of *Taxi Driver*: "Too much Good Friday, not enough Easter Sunday."

The Graduate (1967)

by Jami Bernard

THERE ARE TWO VERSIONS of Mike Nichols's *The Graduate,* and only one of those is a brilliant, scalding portrait of an aimless college graduate adrift in a world he rejects but doesn't have the energy or know-how to escape. The other version, equally funny but nearly as aimless as Benjamin Braddock himself, is the pan-and-scan version made to fit on TV screens. See this movie widescreen or letterboxed, or don't see it at all.

In the opening scene of the landmark 1967 film, Ben (Dustin Hoffman in his first star-making role) arrives at the airport, home from college. While the Simon and Garfunkel soundtrack plays the eerily apt "The Sounds of Silence," the camera begins its tireless depiction of Ben as isolated, mute, choked off from the world. First he is a face in a crowd on the airplane. Then he glides along passively on an escalator, as in life, nudged to the far right of the screen with vast emptiness stretching before him. (Except, of course, in the pan-and-scan version, in which he is oddly front and center in close-up.)

"What are you going to do now?" he is asked at the party his parents throw to show him off to the neighbors. "I'm going to go upstairs," he says, misunderstanding. The neighbor clarifies that the question is about Ben's future, a topic of unending speculation and sly jibes throughout the movie. "I want it to be . . . different," he says in the nearly toneless, ultra-deadpan, sleepwalking style that Hoffman used to such unique comic effect.

Different, indeed. But different, how? All that summer, Ben drifts in his parents' pool. His face is refracted by glass windows and the murky, gurgling depths of his fish tank. Wearing a diving suit and mask in which his father has mummified him for his birthday, he stands submerged in the pool, a deep-sea creature mired in the shallow waters of his upbringing. Better down there than among the chattering idiots by poolside.

The most specific advice Ben gets regarding his future (unsolicited, of course, but offered with the wink-nudge of a hot stock tip) is also the most general, frightening, and soulless—"plastics!"—which became a watchword for dreary conformity.

The late 1960s was a time of great social upheaval in America, a time of drugs, antiwar demonstrations, the sexual revolution, the splitting of society along generational and political lines. Ben is almost untouched by this. He's a virgin when Mrs. Robinson (Anne Bancroft), his father's partner's wife, seduces him in take-no-prisoners style. He espouses no cause and feels nothing as he floats in the amniotic fluid of that summer of indecision between college and "real life." The movie expressed the confusion felt at the time by a population caught between the old school and the heady possibilities of a new one. When Mrs. Robinson tells her daughter, Elaine (Katherine Ross), that it's "too late" for her to run off with Ben and grab life by the throat, Elaine retorts, "Not for me!" Life may have passed by the middle-aged, alcoholic Mrs. Robinson, who gave up art studies to have an unplanned baby and a shotgun wedding, but the Elaines and Bens of the world still had choices, if only their parents would give them enough leash.

The camera continues to describe and comically exaggerate Ben's alienation. He is almost always alone onscreen, to the right of the composition, with a great expanse of emptiness to his left. Only later when he finally has a goal he can believe in, claiming Elaine even though she is about to be married, is Ben finally on the left side of the screen, no longer drifting, now filled with purpose, rushing toward the destiny he has chosen.

At the end of the film, he shares the frame equally with Elaine on the back of the bus as they move ahead into an uncertain future. He has found a kindred spirit with whom to share his isolation. But the ending is unsettling, if not downright pessimistic. What, exactly, are they running to? Probably plastics and a bad marriage. They've been together all of a few minutes, and already there are the sounds of silence between them.

Ben's quest for meaning in his life is the theme of the movie, but the fun of it resides in his initially bumbling affair with Elaine's mother, who Ben continues to refer to as "Mrs. Robinson" even when in bed together. Bancroft was only in her midthirties when she played Mrs. Robinson, which accounts for the shapeliness of her stockinged leg, through the crook of which we can see Ben, typically panicked. Hoffman was close to thirty when he was cast. "Mrs. Robinson, you're trying to seduce me . . . aren't you?" he falters before she sets the ground rules for what will be a wordless, unengaging affair that leaves Ben feeling even more alone than before. "We're gonna do this thing, we're gonna have a conversation!" he insists during one encounter as she keeps trying to turn out the light.

The comedy seems effortless, thanks to several elements, not least of which was director Nichols's longtime comedy association with Elaine May, which honed his timing and his wicked, absurdist, society-skewering sense of humor. With intellectual precision, Nichols rehearsed his actors for three weeks prior to filming in such detail that they could have "taken it on the road," as one of the team later recalled. Notice the well-oiled comic bit when Ben tries to stop the hotel clerk (Buck Henry) from summoning the bellman: Henry hits the bell; Hoffman flattens the bell to silence it; Henry slaps at the bell again but gets Hoffman's hand instead; Hoffman withdraws his hand sheepishly and each gives the other a look. Rat tat tat tat, considering that most of the movie moves like Benjamin underwater in his wetsuit.

The casting was also fortuitous. Coscreenwriter Buck Henry has said that they were initially going after an all-American look, where Ronald Reagan and Doris Day could perhaps play Ben's parents and Robert Redford and Candice Bergen could play Ben and Elaine. They referred to this early dream casting as "the family of surfboards," a very blond, square-jawed bunch of Southern Californians who seemingly had it all. Hoffman, who had thought he was destined to play ethnic actors because of his height, looks, and New York theater base, was inspired casting, like a genetic throwback in the middle of this perfect family, or a baby switched at birth, a cuckoo egg left in a red warbler's nest, someone who just couldn't fit in. He was part of a wave of leading actors of the 1970s with character-actor faces, like Al Pacino and Robert De Niro.

Occasionally, Nichols would leave in something improvised by the actors. When Ben startles Mrs. Robinson by putting his hand on her breast, he walks off and sets to banging his head against the hotel room's wall. Nichols thought that was just so Ben, consternated and reprimanding himself, but Hoffman had started cracking up at Bancroft's stunned response and he was actually trying to get a hold of himself without breaking character. It stayed in the film. And that little squeak of anxiety Ben occasionally emits is something Hoffman observed in his older brother.

Nichols sometimes gets credit for things that were beyond his control—the Christ imagery, for example, as Ben spreads his arms to tap against the church window as he bellows for Elaine. That was simply, according to Hoffman, the only way to reassure the people who had agreed to the location shoot that he wouldn't break the glass. The filmmakers thought it a cheesy compromise at the time, but Nichols whispered to Hoffman, "Make it work!" He did.

Greed (1924)

by Todd McCarthy

THIS REVELATORY FOUR-HOUR VERSION of Erich von Stroheim's *Greed* represents a triumph of film restoration. An enormously successful attempt to rehabilitate one of the two or three most celebrated and mourned mutilated masterpieces in cinema history, Rick Schmidlin's loving work of scholarly craftsmanship can't perform the impossible feat of bringing the 1924 adaptation of Frank Norris's *McTeague* fully back to life. But it does the next best thing by vividly clarifying the film's true dimensions and the staggering depth of its detail.

Von Stroheim's original *Greed* ran at a length generally reported as $9\frac{1}{2}$ hours, a version that was shown only once, on January 12, 1924. The extravagant filmmaker personally cut the picture down by about half, proposing that MGM, the new company that had inherited the film from its original producer, Goldwyn Studios, release it in two parts. When Louis B. Mayer rejected this idea, von Stroheim privately asked his director friend, Rex Ingram, to edit it down to three hours, whereupon Metro executive Irving Thalberg, who had been von Stroheim's nemesis previously at Universal, took the film away from him and assigned editor Joe Farnham to cut it to conventional length; the 140-minute version was a flop upon its release at Christmas 1924, and Thalberg had the silver nitrate film on which it was made burned, thereby preventing the picture from ever being reassembled.

Even in its severely truncated form, *Greed* was sufficiently impressive to take its place among the great cinema classics; in the *Sight & Sound* poll of the best films of all time, it ranked No. 4, higher than any other silent film. The quixotic dream of one day somehow finding or conjuring up the picture's original version has always represented a Holy Grail for buffs, a dream that Schmidlin was able to pursue in the wake of the recent success of his "director's cut" of Orson Welles's *Touch of Evil*.

Schmidlin and editor Glenn Morgan have managed their task through the use of hundreds of scene stills from the picture, obtained from a number of collections. Following the original script by von Stroheim and June Mathis and injecting the original intertitles to provide dialogue and describe action, the restoration team has fleshed out scenes familiar from the 140-minute version and provided visual and narrative samplings of other sequences unseen since 1924. Beyond this invaluable carpentry, there's color tinting per the director's instructions, a hitherto unknown full-color sequence, and a new score by Robert Israel that is superior in every respect.

A story that illustrates in the most extraordinary detail how the everyday strivings of ordinary people can be inexorably undermined by their basest instincts, *Greed* charts the life of McTeague (Gibson Gowland), an ill-educated mining-town man—part hulking ruffian, part sentimental fool—who struggles to become a dentist in early-twentieth-century San Francisco and marries his best friend's girl, Trina (ZaSu Pitts), only to watch his fortunes decline. His wife becomes an obsessive miser after winning a lottery, and he loses his livelihood upon being betrayed by his jealous former friend, Marcus (Jean Hersholt). Famously, it all ends under the scalding sun of Death Valley, McTeague handcuffed to the man he has just killed, doomed to perish because of the pervasive poison of greed.

In addition to seeing actual gold colors strewn through the ore during the early mining sequences, the new version offers plenty of additional exposition:

McTeague's dissolute father's boozing, whoring, and death; McTeague's apprenticeship with an itinerant dentist; and his being informed of his mother's death.

Once the action moves to San Francisco (von Stroheim shot as much as possible on location, including Polk Street and environs, the ferry, the undeveloped East Bay waterfront), stills reveal extensive scenes at the dog hospital where McTeague's close friend Marcus works, much greater delineation of the denizens of the boarding house where McTeague lives, the nearly Renoiresque evocation of Sunday outings and picnics with the largely German supporting characters, McTeague's courtship of Trina, the romance that slowly develops between two neighboring old-timers that culminates in the color scenes representing true happiness, Trina's giving McTeague an enormous (tinted) gold tooth, and much greater detailing of the couple's wedding and dinner celebration. Part one of the restoration runs 110 minutes.

Part two, which lasts 129 minutes, picks up five years later and elaborates a subplot involving the demented marriage between boarding-house manager Maria and junkman Zerlov, an auction of the impoverished McTeague and Trina's belongings, and, most significant, the life of McTeague as a penniless hobo living on the streets. An element of the film that comes across far more strongly now is von Stroheim's portrait of the lower classes, society's bottom strata consisting of saloon dwellers, riffraff, the dispossessed, and the forgotten. Also more visible is the scale of some of the city scenes, in which hundreds of extras were employed to give teeming life to the streets of San Francisco. As good as the first half is, the additions the restoration makes to the second half are even more crucial and enlightening.

Coverage of the many photographs is done in diverse ways, sometimes using them as stationary stills and at other times panning within them to create a certain dynamic. In general, this is so well done that any carping about individual choices would amount to ludicrous nit-picking. Visual quality is outstanding. Topping it all off is Israel's melodious score that is churning and brooding by turns and has flavors of Chopin, Wagner, and Bernard Herrmann, just for starters.

Like most of the films von Stroheim made during his directorial career, which scarcely lasted a decade, *Greed* is a triumph of ultrarealism. Philosophically, it is witheringly wise in its view of humanity's capacity for folly; thematically, it represents a still-relevant cautionary tale about the fragility of the American dream.

Happy Together (1997)

by Armond White

WONG KAR-WAI'S *Chungking Express* and *In the Mood for Love* are his expected masterpieces—romantic and social studies in the tradition of Godard's heterosexual classics *Masculine-Feminine, Contempt,* and *Pierrot le Fou. Happy Together* may be film culture's first gay masterpiece since Jean Genet's *Un Chant d'Amour.* Like that film, it is an unexpected masterpiece—but for a variety of reasons.

Cultures merge in *Happy Together*—China and Argentina, love and cinema: Wong Kar-Wai essays each as romantic yearning and visual intoxication, then blends them. He turns standard melodramatic story (breakup, makeup, moving on) into a sensual representation of the tortures one lover experiences every time a shallow, cheating mate entices him with the suggestion, "Let's start over." These love-drunk cycles reverb at high pitch through Wong's hyperkinetic style, matching media overload to his characters' emotional exhaustion. Through Lai Yui-Fat's (Tony Leung) and Ho Po-Wing's (Leslie Cheung) bickering and bound-together relationship, he discerns 1990s individuals' solipsistic retreat into quixotic obsession. Wong sees these two men from Taipei (plus a third) as stranded in postmodern alienation repped by Buenos Aires exile.

Filming outside Asia for the first time, Wong finds existential drama everywhere his camera points. He emphasizes sharp, blunt portraits: erotic fascination (pouring water down a back and kissing it); irrational anger (tearing apart a lover's neatly kept room); and contemplative solitude (floating on a barge through a blue-shadowed dawn). These are not random camera studies but a rapturous, select investigation of ardor and longing done with home-movie immediacy.

An unmistakable work of pop instinct, *Happy Together* suggests the music video Pet Shop Boys deserved for [their] subtle, elegant (and ignored) multiculti album *Bilingual.* PSB's use of Brazilian-style drumming (the percussion of sex underscored each song) has its equivalent in Wong's restless visual inquisition. Astor Piazolla's tango rhythms are its forlorn, romantic pulse, a sound somehow evocatively French. Actually PSB's drums were in fact European—a clever, crosscultural simulation. And although Wong parades his awareness of pop themes for this personal story (including the Turtles tune "Happy Together," even a Frank

Zappa cut), where PSB got politically explicit ("To Step Aside," "Before," "Single"), Wong uses formal artifice to reveal timeless circumstances of lovers abandoned to themselves, trapped in a foreign/familiar idyll.

Starting with a frankly erotic coupling and a remembered dispute (in black and white), Wong creates a new template of adult difficulties. Argentina's real life *cantinas,* restaurants, dancehalls, and flophouses express mocking liveliness, distant community in terse, antiexotic images. They fit Wong's instinct for the textures of cultures, media, and consciousness mixed together. *Evita* should have looked this vibrant. As shot by Christopher Doyle (*Temptress Moon*), Buenos Aires is the world given the refreshed outline that comes from the irony of being displaced yet appreciating life. Wong's rapacious appetite for beauty pulls at his story's terrified suggestion of disconnections and fractured lives.

These kinetic experiments make Wong the first feature filmmaker since Godard to give serious avant garde tropes a common, romantic touch. It's apparent in his exploratory attention to details, keeping voluptuous observation fleet and disjunctive. Wong draws one's love of cinema into the erotic suspense. One image—a rotating lamp with a shade depicting the Iguazu Falls the couple longs to visit—is constantly returned to, a totem of their shared passion, curiosity, and distance. (Like the real thing seen in two hypnotic sequences, it conveys emotional tumult.) A close-up of that lamp is followed by a shot of Lai alone, staring out a window, contrasting the lamp's white burn-out with the window's sun-yellow glow. Wong turns cinema's technological extremes back on themselves, comparing new flash to the look of silent-movie tinting. Putting rough and slick styles together, Wong sparks a viewer's sophistication. He uses color not for realism but—surprise!—*for color.* Whether or not casual filmgoers care, Wong has reimagined the very nature of cinema's emotional presentation. His editors Wong Ming-Lam and William Chang Suk-Ping (who is also his production designer) often sustain the breadth of action—complete camera trajectories—then cut to an angled still shot. Movement and rest, flow and punctuation, make these rigorous fragments *mean.*

Concentrating on the drama's primary site (a bedroom), Wong uses it as a fulcrum conveying the lovers' emotional seesaw. The space in the room is wide as alienation, as tight as intimacy. The importance of its objects and structure are accentuated by assorted lighting schemes and geometric compositions. A shot recalling Wong's *Ashes of Time* features a red bedcover glowing in the background but, foreshortened in space, abutting a luminous green hanging lantern—it's sheer psychedelic audacity. In *Prick Up Your Ears,* two lovers occupying a British bed-sit was merely claustrophobic, but Wong trounces that simplification by making changeable temperaments aesthetic. You not only feel the pressure that leads to a jittery fight montage, but further amazement comes when Wong cuts from that crucible to the aftermath outside. This last shot stabilizes the scene, showing his control and understanding. On a visionary tear, Wong follows it with Lai's escape to a barge where soothing, royal-blue water floats by—a mood shift as assured as a great dancer slowing down to strut.

Every shot is a postmodern statement and poetry: dejected Lai hosing away blood at an abattoir, immigrant workers playing soccer in sapphire evening light. Wong's cognitive fancies grapple with the same frustrations drawn out in Ingmar Bergman's marriage films, but he's refreshingly nonponderous; his insistence on speed and perception intensify response. He knows modern audiences already know this turf (even when its walked by gays), so his quickened sophistication cuts to the quick of love: in anger or horniness, Lai and Ho shift cots across the cramped room or Lai gets out of his sick bed to cook for the demanding Ho. Wong's time-shuffling style combines memories like he mixes black-and-white and color footage; obsessively examining the paradox of Lai's and Ho's erotic sync and emotional incompatibility.

"Is this the final edit or is the subject now a bore?" Neil Tennent sang on *Bilingual*. His dry declamation, keeping dance time as he prayed for a new way to love, also describes Wong's achievement. The only difference here is pace, not wit. (Lai's query "All I hear is my heart beating, can he hear it too?" gets drowned out by the roar of a stadium crowd.) *Happy Together's* poignance isn't in Lai's obvious confessional voice-over, but in Wong's impassioned imagery which take this *Of Human Bondage* tale past masochism and the facile uncertainties of most alienation stories.

Chang, a satirical character who begins a second narration late in the film, brings a new spirit to the melancholy combination of love and movies, feeling and perception. When he complains "movies give me a headache," Wong is appropriately teasing pomo consciousness. Chang's childhood eye problems increased his sensitivity, so he listens to everything around him, annoyingly eavesdrops on lovers' phone calls and yet his empathy pulls Lai to life. "Have we become close?" Lai wonders when they hug goodbye. Awakened from despair, he eventually goes to the Iguazu Falls alone then, when he realizes Chang's a soul mate, visits Chang's family *back in Taipei*. And Wong's visual cues for Lai's new insight tip the film toward ecstasy: Before leaving Argentina, Lai imagines Hong Kong on the other side of the world upside down—he sees crisscrossed freeways upturned, neon signs about to drop, and overcast skies like reflective lakes. It's nostalgia made staggering—and a bravura reminder that Wong's presentation of romantic sacrifice and friendship has high irony, mysterious depth. *Happy Together* combines images, emotion and cultural disparity into the movies' sweetest, most aching tune of regret.

High Noon (1952)

by Emanuel Levy

CONTEXT AND SUBTEXT ARE FAR MORE IMPORTANT than text in Fred Zinnemann's *High Noon,* a western that over the years has assumed a mythical meaning and overrated status in American film history. At present, *High Noon* is better known as the movie directly responsible for the making of *Rio Bravo:* Howard Hawks found *High Noon* so repulsive and offensive that he made *Rio Bravo* as a counterresponse.

Though heralded at the time as a classic in the western genre, *High Noon* looks today more schematic and self-conscious than such vintage westerns as *Stagecoach, The Searchers,* or *Rio Bravo.* With the McCarthy era over, the tensions and vital undercurrents in the movie are diminished. Indeed, *High Noon* used its hero as a mouthpiece for liberal pieties and civic sermons, which reflected the politics of its filmmakers: producer Stanley Kramer, screenwriter Carl Foreman, and director Zinnemann. Known for his Republican leanings, the film's star, Gary Cooper, was probably unaware at the time of the film's political message.

Nominated for seven Oscars, including best picture, *High Noon* won four awards. In one of Oscar's shameful, unfair chapters, the 1952 best picture, Cecil B. DeMille's circus melodrama *The Greatest Show on Earth,* unaccountably won over the far superior *High Noon* and John Ford's picturesque romance *The Quiet Man.* Evidence suggests that *High Noon* lost the top prize for political rather than artistic reasons. Even so, *High Noon* features one of Cooper's best performances—it's hard to imagine the film without him—for which he won a second best actor Oscar; the first was for *Sergeant York.*

Aging marshal Will Kane (note the symbolic name) is about to leave town after marrying a Quaker (Grace Kelly) when he learns that Frank Miller, whom he had sent to prison, has been released and plans to come back to Hadleyville to get even with him. Burdened with fear of fighting alone, after his plea for help is rejected by every member of the community, Kane must choose between running out of town and saving his neck, as his wife Amy wishes, or facing the villains by himself. Amy, whose brother and father were killed by the Indians, holds that "there's got to be a better way to live." Needless to say, Kane meets the challenge single-handedly, ultimately winning the understanding and even help of his wife.

Bosley Crowther, then dean of the New York film critics, was so excited when the movie opened that he wrote:

> Every five years or so someone with an appreciation for legend and poetry scoops up clichés from the Western and turns them into an inspiring work. Meaningful in its implication, as well as loaded with interest and suspense, *High Noon* is a Western to challenge *Stagecoach* for the all-time championship. Though made out of ordinary materials of the Western formula, *High Noon* achieves the shape of a democratic allegory, reaching people in the same way, and for the same reasons, as *The Best Years of Our Lives*.

However, Pauline Kael and other astute critics dismissed the film's insights as primer sociology.

Over the years, *High Noon* has been subjected to various ideological interpretations. Some critics see the film as a symbolic allegory about American foreign policy during the Korean war, propagating the idea that war, under certain circumstances, is both moral and inevitable. Marshal Kane wants to maintain peace, after cleaning up the town five years before (World War II), but, reluctantly, he has to face a new aggression (the Korean War). According to this reading, the Quaker wife stands in for American pacifists and isolationists, though she, too, later realizes the importance of supporting her husband.

Critic Philip French regards the film as a liberal statement, the archetypal Kennedy western, standing in contrast to *Rio Bravo,* which is the archetypal Barry Goldwater western. *High Noon* is thus seen as a parable about a marshal, who stands alone to defend his moral principles in the McCarthy era. The townsfolk, who refuse to help Kane and desert him, are viewed as powerless members of mass society, afraid to stand for their civil rights. The only members willing to help Kane are an old crippled man, wearing an eye patch, and an excitable teenager.

No matter what perspective one takes, there's no doubt that *High Noon* deals with such issues as civic responsibility, active involvement in social causes, and heroic behavior during crises—all problems loaded with political overtones in the early 1950s. Its cynical commentary on the masses' fear of involvement in controversial issues proved to be prophetic during McCarthy's political witchhunting.

Arguing that responsive citizens should have nothing but contempt for the cowardice of ordinary folks, the film also spoke for the necessity of joint action, if enemies are to be defeated.

As mentioned, *Rio Bravo* originated in opposition to *High Noon,* which neither John Wayne nor Hawks liked, feeling that its spirit deviated from the "Real West" and the simplicity of the western format. Hawks didn't think "a good sheriff was going to run around town like a chicken with his head off asking for help." Instead, "a good sheriff would turn around and say, 'How good are you? Are you good enough to take the best they've got?'"

Wayne's objections to the film were even stronger, describing its plot as "defeatist" and "the most un-American thing." According to the star, the rugged men of the frontier, who had battled the Indians and nature, would not be afraid of four villains. Instead, they would unite "to make the land habitable." Wayne was particularly offended by the last scene, which shows Cooper putting the marshal's badge under his foot and stepping on it, an image later borrowed by Don Siegel for the ending of *Dirty Harry.* Wayne never regretted having forced Foreman into exile in England, where he worked underground using a pseudonym. Asked what gave him the right to do so, Wayne said, "I thought he'd hurt Coop's reputation a great deal."

Wayne's motto—"I am not a man of words or nuances"—summed up his objection to *High Noon,* which stressed "psychological insights" and "introverted and sensitive" heroes. "Real cowboys," claimed Wayne, "didn't have mental problems, and didn't have time for this couch-work." In the older westerns, sheriffs were men of action and few words: They didn't ponder or subject their tortured souls to self-examination the way Kane did.

But in the 1950s, the heroic, idealized John Ford/John Wayne western was gradually displaced by "adult" ("mature" is the word then used) westerns. *High Noon* followed in the footsteps of Henry King's *The Gunfighter,* promoting a subgenre that was concerned with the psychology of characters, their inner conflicts and moral dilemmas. And *High Noon* itself led to a cycle of socially conscious westerns and contemporary dramas, such as *Bad Day at Black Rock,* a modern yarn that was actually a western in disguise, subordinating the traditional action elements to the development of "serious" themes, specifically, the tension between strong individual protagonists and the mass-oriented and impersonal American society. All of a sudden westerns discovered Freudian psychology, quickly adopting such concepts as libido, superego, and social conscience.

High Noon also indicated the vast changes in Hollywood's conception of the law and its representatives. In the 1950s and 1960s, marshals and sheriffs underwent a transformation that both humanized and weakened them. Psychological, issue-oriented movies such as *High Noon* slowed down westerns not only in their plot but also in their pacing.

Auteurist critics still debate who's fully responsible for *High Noon*'s final shape and overall impact: producer Kramer, whose liberal politics were also evident in other pictures; left-wing scripter Carl Foreman; or Zinnemann, who had previously shown a penchant for taut suspenseful dramas. Others claim that perhaps Cooper, who was in top form after years of mediocre work, should receive more credit for the picture's emotional resonance—after all, Cooper was the screen embodiment of the honor-bound yet humble noble man.

Much has been made of the western's structural novelty: The actual story runs from 10:40 A.M. to high noon, almost matching the film's running time, 84 minutes. Visually, too, Floyd Crosby's stark, black-and-white cinematography and long shadows, specifically of Kane marching in an empty street, were impressively realistic. Ironically, from the first day, the front office complained about the poor photography. Zinnemann recalled in a 1973 interview: "Floyd and I thought that *High Noon* should look like a newsreel would have looked if they had newsreels in those days, and we also studied Matthew Brady's photographs of the Civil War." Up to that time, there was almost a religious ritual about the way westerns were made: There was always a lovely gray sky with pretty clouds in the background. Instead, Crosby used no filters, granting the sky a white, cloudless, burnt-out look, and his flat lighting gave the film a grainy quality.

Sharp editing, credited to Elmo Williams and Harry Gerstad, contributed to the tightly controlled tension. In one scene, Zinnemann shows over Kane's shoulder a white paper on which a slowly moving pen scrawls, "last will and testament." He then cuts to the pendulum of the clock—the movie's recurrent visual motif—and to a shot of the prairie from the empty railroad tracks. Applying striking montage, the viewers see in quick succession of shots, the faces of people waiting in the church and saloon, the quiet street outside, the thugs waiting at the station, and the tracks again. Suddenly, there's a whistle of the train and, looking down the tracks again, a wisp of smoke is seen from the approaching train.

Finally, many viewers remember *High Noon* for its music: Dmitri Tiomkin won an Oscar for best score in a nonmusical film, and Tiomkin and Ned Washington won the best song Oscar for the highly melodic ballad, "Do Not Forsake Me, Oh My Darling."

Invasion of the Body Snatchers (1956)

by Robert Sklar

AMONG ITS DISTINGUISHED COMPANIONS in this volume, Don Siegel's 1956 science-fiction thriller *Invasion of the Body Snatchers* stands alone in representing the significance and occasional splendor of the Hollywood B-picture.

Glorified in recent years for their legendarily cheap, off-the-cuff style of film-making, B-pictures were first designated in the 1930s when the studios set up separate units to produce inexpensive films to run as the second half of double features (a two-for-the-price-of-one exhibition practice of that era). Although the B-units closed down in the 1940s, the name stuck for later low-budget genre flicks like *Invasion of the Body Snatchers.* Lacking stars and first-run theater distribution, the film barely got reviewed outside the Hollywood trade papers. But it soon took on a second life on television and within a few years achieved secure stature as a cult classic.

Considering its lowly status and budgetary constraint (the distributor and financial backer, Allied Artists, formerly the Poverty Row studio Monogram, set a $300,000 ceiling), *Body Snatchers* had a first-class pedigree. The producer was the distinguished independent Walter Wanger, struggling to restore his name after serving a prison sentence for shooting and wounding the lover of his wife, actress Joan Bennett. Siegel was building a reputation as an action director and had teamed with Wanger on a moneymaking and critically acclaimed prison drama, *Riot in Cell Block 11* (1954). The source was a serialized novel by Jack Finney in *Collier's* magazine, with Daniel Mainwaring, scriptwriter on the quintessential film noir *Out of the Past* (1947) among many other works, writing the screenplay.

Invasion of the Body Snatchers arrived as part of an explosion of science fantasy and science horror in mainstream popular culture, fueled by the atomic age, the advent of space rocketry, and Cold War anxieties. "So much has been discovered these past few years that anything is possible," says Dr. Miles Bennell (Kevin McCarthy) after he discovers that mysterious seed pods grow into human forms and take over actual persons, retaining their former physical characteristics but completely transforming their personalities. "It may be the results of atomic radiation on plant life, or animal life . . . some weird, alien organism . . . a mutation of some kind." Once a pod is ready to become you, the moment you fall asleep you're a goner.

The pods launch their silent revolution in the fictional Southern California town of Santa Mira (location shooting took place in the town of Sierra Madre). The basic story begins with the doctor returning to town by train, having been called back from a medical convention because his appointment schedule has unexpectedly become crowded. People want to talk about their loved ones who suddenly don't seem like their old selves any more, but the problem is solved when they too succumb to the pods. It ends with Miles Bennell as the town's last remaining human and the pod people growing more pods in huge greenhouses and shipping them by truck to take over Earth. Escaping to a highway, Miles stands in the middle of traffic and cries, "You're next! You're next!"

This is a considerably darker scenario than the source novel, which ended with the pods flying off to find a more propitious planet and the remaining pod people surrendering to federal agents. In postproduction, the filmmakers mulled adding more explanatory structure—for example, a prominent journalist introducing the story—as a way of tempering its disquieting implications, turning a horror fantasy into a metafiction. They postponed release for nearly half a year while developing an opening and closing frame that, as in films like *The Cabinet of Dr. Caligari,* asks spectators to consider whether what they're watching is a madman's tale. At the beginning Miles is delivered to a hospital by a police car, where he begins to narrate what happened in Santa Mira. At the end, "You're next!" dissolves back to the hospital, where doctors are convinced he's insane, until a report of a crashed truck filled with seed pods sends them to the telephone to alert authorities.

Like many genre films in Hollywood's blacklist era, *Invasion of the Body Snatchers* functions as an allegory, raising questions about contemporary society that could not be confronted as directly in a realist manner. But the question is, an allegory of what? Such works scatter clues as much as they take stands, and within the film's fundamental opposition between endangered individuality and insidious conformism lies considerable room for multiple interpretation.

Was it a warning, in familiar Cold War style, against communistic ideology that turns friends and neighbors into squadrons of malevolent drones? No doubt. Yet was it not also, more subtly, critical of postwar America and the strains of an acquisitive, competitive society from which individuals might welcome relief? Miles remarks that humanity had already slowly been draining away through human indifference rather than extraterrestrial intervention. And even as the heroic holdout he's not immune from the film's implied critique. He refers to a failed marriage that he attributes to the demands of a doctor's life. A liberal dispenser of pills for any and all conditions, he's also quick to refer his patients for psychiatric consultation ("you don't have to be losing your mind to need psychiatric help").

Under its bucolic surface Santa Mira seems to have had a simmering mental health crisis. Once the psychiatrist becomes a pod person, he explains to Miles, "Santa Mira was like any other town. People with nothing but problems." But the pods drifted down from outer space and offered solutions. "Love. Desire. Ambition. Faith. Without them life's so simple, believe me." Miles's woman friend Becky (Dan Wynter) protests, "I don't want a world without love or grief or beauty." Of course the film unequivocally sides with the party of humanity. It gives the spectator little room for ambiguity as the pod peoples' calmly voiced rationales turn toward anger, violence, and aggressive expansion. Yet the sense remains of a troubled community even in the best of times, sustaining itself through medication and psychotherapy.

Invasion of the Body Snatchers was originally released in a SuperScope widescreen format. Cinematographer Ellsworth Fredericks and art director Edward "Ted" Haworth designed a dark, claustrophic noir ambiance for the film, breaking up the wide image with partitions, walls, doors, corridors, and enclosed spaces. It was remade under the same title in 1978 by director Philip Kaufman and again in 1993 by Abel Ferrara, with the title *Body Snatchers*.

Jailhouse Rock (1957)

by Carrie Rickey

WHEN THE HEAVY-LIDDED ELVIS PRESLEY swaggered onto the screen in *Jailhouse Rock* (1957), his third picture, he shook the music and movie industries to their bedrock. Elvis quaked the landscape so profoundly that he was uplifted and crowned rock's King, dethroning pop royalty Frank Sinatra, who himself had dethroned popster Bing Crosby a decade earlier.

Understand that Elvis was not the first rock-film star. That had been another hillbilly with a beat: Bill Haley, frontman of *Rock Around the Clock* (1956) and

Don't Knock the Rock (1957). A cheery apostle of the new sound, Haley possessed a doughy sex appeal but lacked the rebel shadings, contours, and attitude that made Elvis first a Goliath-slayer and, soon after, King of Kings.

At one matinee of *Jailhouse Rock* adults (namely, my parents) thought he resembled Michelangelo's marbled David with a jet-black pompadour, suggestive lips, and gyrating hips. Teenagers (namely, my sisters) thought he resembled James Dean with a guitar. Watching *Jailhouse Rock* in 2001 I would add that he furthermore resembled a surly choirboy who couldn't suppress his orgasmic grunts. To tally the Elvis attributes is to realize how he was the fleshly embodiment of every imaginable contradiction of classicism and romanticism.

In the Elvis canon, *Jailhouse Rock* is the origin story, explaining how he might have come by his snarling, surly attitude, and proceeding to rehabilitate him and repackage him for popular consumption. Heaven knows, *Jailhouse Rock* is not the best Elvis movie (that would probably be *Flaming Star* or *Viva Las Vegas*). And heaven knows, it's not a particularly good movie. But *Jailhouse Rock* remains the most eloquent record of two seismic events that rocked 1950s America: The Rise of the Teenager and The Elvis Phenom.

Elvis gave voice to that eternal teenage imperative, "Treat Me Nice" (as he demands musically here). His very presence made him the link in the rebel chain that connects James Dean in *Rebel Without a Cause* to Warren Beatty in *Splendor in the Grass* to John Travolta in *Saturday Night Fever* to Brad Pitt in *Legends of the Fall*.

When first we meet Elvis's Vince Everett, he is riding a forklift on a construction site, smiling about payday, and joking that he plans to use his salary "to buy a line of chorus girls and have 'em dance on my bed." Immediately he is established as a working-class kid (as opposed to the middle-class youth played by James Dean in *Rebel Without a Cause*) who believes that money buys him sex. (He's oblivious to the fact that women of all ages, and men too, are drawn to him as bees to nectar.)

In a subsequent scene, he buys drinks for the house in a downscale tavern, attracting the attention of a slatternly blonde whose (protector? pimp? boyfriend?) roughs her up. In defending her honor, Vince beats up the woman-beater and kills him, landing himself a jail sentence for involuntary manslaughter.

In the slammer, Vince bunks with that slab of country ham Hunk Houghton (Mickey Shaughnessy), who's so impressed with the way the kid strums a guitar that he offers to help him on the outside—for a price. And when Vince gets sprung, he works Hunk's connections and catches the ear of music huckster

Peggy van Alden (Judy Tyler), who professes to be all business but excites Vince's pleasure instincts.

At a time when Brando astride a motorcycle and Dean behind the wheel of a hot rod were the dominant images of misunderstood youth, *Jailhouse Rock* framed the misunderstanding musically. When perky Peggy introduces Vince to her parents, both academics, their intellectual friends pontificate about jazz tonalities. Vince, who hears only rock's primal rhythms, finds this beside the point.

And at a time when teens—that emerging demographic—felt put upon, *Jailhouse Rock* framed the adult/teen struggle in power terms. Adults—like the record exec who gives Vince's song to a more established artist to record—are the exploiters who take from the powerless and give to the powerful.

It's enough to justify Vince's bad attitude. And when he hits it big, he hits back, manhandling women and minions the way the judges and wardens and execs have manhandled him. In perhaps the most attenuated Act Three in movie history, he realizes the error of his ways. In a confrontation where he is physically struck, Vince controls his anger and does not strike back. Hey, even a teenage caveman can evolve.

Cinematically, *Jailhouse Rock* is that curiosity, a widescreen Metro-Goldwyn-Mayer musical shot in black and white. Director Richard Thorpe, best known for costume musicals such as *The Student Prince,* exploits the panoramic format only in one sequence, the title number. It features Vince—now filming a TV variety show—before a male chorus line of adoring inmates—in prison uniform, snaking down a firepole. Even in 1957 this number was more Metro than Memphis, choreographed like the Gene Kelly spoof of *The Wild One* in *Les Girls,* rather than something a rock idol might have imagined. (In hindsight, it portends Elvis's future Vegas productions.)

As a seismic event, *Jailhouse Rock's* reverberations are still felt. For the Elvis who emerges in this movie modeled how teenagers might style defiance. And it showed their parents that a bad boy could be rehabbed into a good citizen.

Ju Dou, Raise the Red Lantern,
Red Sorghum (1990, 1991, 1987)

by Andy Klein

EVEN IN HOLLYWOOD—that bastion of free-enterprise, capitalist filmmaking, where money talks loud and ideology barely whispers—there is an inevitable intertwining of cinema and politics. How much more tightly woven then are cinema and politics in communist countries, where the means of (film) production are controlled by explicitly political entities?

All of which is to set up the notion that it is impossible to fully appreciate the *historical* importance of Zhang Yimou's *Red Sorghum* (1987) and his other early films without some sense of the environment from which they arose; and extraordinarily difficult for foreigners to understand the convoluted political pressures confronted by Zhang and other so-called Fifth-Generation filmmakers.

What do we mean by "Fifth Generation"?

Rather than take new students each year, the state-run Beijing Film Academy waits for a single class to finish the multiyear program before admitting the next group of students—hence, the numbered "generations." The Fifth Generation, who studied from 1978 to 1982, includes Zhang Yimou, Chen Kaige (*Farewell My Concubine*), Tian Zhuangzhuang (*The Blue Kite*), and Huang Jianxin (*The Wooden Man's Bride*). Most significantly, this was the first class to go through the program after the massive social disruptions of the Cultural Revolution, during which the Film Academy was shut down for more than a decade.

The class graduated and made their initial films during a period filled with the hopes of expanding liberalism—hopes that would take a staggering blow in 1989 at Tiananmen Square. *Red Sorghum* was not the first film to emerge from this group, though Zhang was involved in the making of its most notable predecessors: he was cinematographer on Zhang Junzhao's *One and Eight* (1983) and Chen Kaige's *Yellow Earth* (1984) and *The Big Parade* (1985), and was both cinematographer and star of *The Old Well* (1986), directed by Wu Tianming, the Fourth Generation graduate who acted as mentor to his younger colleagues. (At the Tokyo International Film Festival, Zhang won the best actor award for *The Old Well*; in addition to occasionally appearing in his own films, he also gave a memorable performance as an ancient warrior who wakes up in modern times, in

Ching Siu-Tung's first-rate 1989 Hong Kong comedy/romance/action film, *The Terra Cotta Warrior*.)

For his own first feature, Zhang chose to adapt Mo Yan's novella *Red Sorghum*. The film is framed almost as a fairytale: a never-seen narrator explains that this is the story of his grandparents—a possibly romanticized legend whose accuracy he can't attest to. His grandmother, Nine (Gong Li, in her screen debut), while still a teenager, is forced into an arranged marriage with the wealthy but leprous owner of a local winery. On her way to the winery, her party is attacked by a bandit; she is rescued by the head litter-bearer (Jiang Wen). It is unclear whether the miserable Nine ever consummates her marriage with her diseased husband. But, on her way to her parents' home a few days after the wedding, she and the litter-bearer make passionate love in the midst of the sorghum fields.

On her return, she discovers that her elderly husband has disappeared mysteriously, presumably the victim of foul play—quite possibly at the hands of the litter-bearer, with whom she now takes up permanently. Together with the winery's foreman (Teng Ru-Jun), they collectivize the operation and achieve new prosperity that is interrupted years later by the invading Japanese.

For Westerners, the arrival of the invaders is a shocking and fascinating moment. The story elements up to that point—as well as the notion that the narrator is repeating a tale learned in childhood—suggest a fairytale land or some very distant past: arranged marriages, reclusive lepers, highwaymen, even some possibly magical occurrences. But when the Japanese roll up in trucks, with their familiar World War II costumes, we realize that this Chinese mythical era is actually the 1930s—not so very long ago at all.

The plot is melodramatic, but not as silly as it may sound in such condensed form. And even the most extreme melodramatic elements are made believable both through Gong's performance and through the film's sharp and evocative visual style. Zhang and cinematographer Gu Changwei, working with rich colors on a CinemaScope canvas, carefully present the action against sweeping rural panoramas. Many of the visual conventions suggest that Zhang absorbed not only Western movies but even (in the more specific sense) "western" movies—Ford, Peckinpah, and Leone, in particular.

Both the subject matter and style of *Red Sorghum* represent a remarkable balancing act on Zhang's part. As someone whose late teens and early twenties were spent amid the dangerously shifting sands of China's political structure during the Cultural Revolution, Zhang was surely concerned about finding subject matter that would interest him and yet still pass muster with whatever authorities might be in power by the time the film was released. Starting with *Red Sorghum* and continuing throughout the rest of his career to date, he has clearly evinced a sympathy for female troubles; nearly all of his protagonists are women. Hence, the horribly oppressed position of women in prerevolutionary society was the perfect focus for his debut (and two of his next three films, as well).

Still, by the standards of mainland cinema in the 1970s and 1980s, *Red Sorghum* was impolite, lurid, even sensationalist. The heroine welcomes sex, even in a form that borders on rape; the main male character, the litter-bearer who becomes the narrator's grandfather, is, much of the time, a drunken, pathetic boor, who, doglike, asserts his "rights" to the woman by urinating in the wine; its scene of the Japanese invaders ordering a Chinese butcher to skin his own friend is played for maximum horror.

At the same time, the film (in what is perhaps its weakest element to Western eyes) pays homage to communist Chinese ideals: not merely in its historically understandable demonization of the Japanese army but in the ham-fisted association of capitalist ownership with an aging, leprous lecher and of joyful, successful collectivization with the beautiful, vital young Nine. One can imagine party officials nodding approvingly at the symbolism within the script, even if they were shocked by the final product.

In fact, despite some aesthetic and political criticism, *Red Sorghum* was a success on almost all fronts: it was a controversial commercial hit in China; and it became the first film from the People's Republic to win the top prize at a major international festival when it took the Berlin Film Festival's Golden Bear. This led to distribution around the world, including the United States.

Since then, Zhang has gone through an interesting stylistic development. After attempting a purely commercial feature with *Code Name Cougar* (1989), an apparently negligible action film never released in the United States, he refined his visual style further in *Ju Dou* (1990), another tale of adultery and arranged marriage in the old days, whose plot is similar to James M. Cain's oft-filmed *The Postman Always Rings Twice*. Here his camerawork was even more controlled than in *Red Sorghum*, moving much of the action inside (where *Red Sorghum* was composed almost entirely of exterior shots).

He brought this claustrophobic, tightly determined look to its ultimate in his fourth feature, *Raise the Red Lantern* (1991), which, like *Ju Dou*, was nominated for a best foreign film Oscar. In this film, Gong plays yet again a young woman forced into marriage with an older man—in this case, a wealthy landowner who already has three wives. She finds herself engaged in a never-ending struggle with the other wives for the master's attentions—with ever-shifting alliances, double-crosses, and deceptive ploys that would make the canniest politician look like an innocent.

After the opening few shots, the camera never leaves the husband's sprawling mansion. If that weren't claustrophobic enough, Zhang favors symmetrical compositions, generally shot straight-on; and, except when absolutely necessary, he avoids camera movement. If Gong's character is trapped in a social prison, we are trapped with her; and every visual choice reinforces this. For all its fascinating intrigues, *Raise the Red Lantern* is one of the most oppressive great movies ever made.

Despite yet another brilliant performance from Gong, this visual style leaves almost no room for life or spontaneity; and, having taken it as far as he could, Zhang seems to have done a stylistic 180 after *Raise the Red Lantern*. With the exception of *Shanghai Triad* (1995), he has wisely embraced a rougher, less "perfect" style in all his films from *The Story of Qui Ju* (1992) up through his 2000 production *The Road Home*; at its most extreme, in 1997's *Keep Cool!*, he brings us a ragged, disjointed narrative told with handheld camera and jump cuts. That he has proved equally adept at this mode of working has only confirmed his position as the most versatile of the Fifth Generation directors.

Killer of Sheep (1977)

by Armond White

AMONG THE MOST RESPECTED American movies of the past quarter century, *Killer of Sheep* is, ironically, one of the least written about. It has a cultural reputation (being one of the first films named to the National Film Registry in 1992) without yet garnering an actual critical defense. Only in a 2001 number of the literary magazine *First of the Month* has *Killer of Sheep* received a worthy, serious, concentrated consideration. There, social-literary critic Ben DeMott analyzed the way Charles Burnett "seeks simply to do justice to the ordinary events that suck the most marginalized of his people into will-lessness and contempt for the fairy tale of 'personal identity.'"

For audiences who now come to *Killer of Sheep* in one of the increasingly rare museum or repertory house showings (as yet unavailable on DVD or video), the film is so distinct from the kinds of movies we're accustomed to being made about Americans of Color that it almost always needs some kind of introduction—to its poetry, to its daring, to its unfashionable way of looking at modern urban experience. In the years since its 1977 premiere *Killer of Sheep* stands to convict both the facile stereotypes and meaningless flatteries of most urban-themed (read: black-themed) movies. The best way to approach *Killer of Sheep* is to appreciate that there is enormity in its simple vision. It gives witness to a specific African American hellishness, a tour that is also a gateway to understanding an unease common to all Americans.

During Burnett's survey of life in the Watts section of Los Angeles, boys are seen from below leaping against the sky, across a void. The black-and-white imagery seems fabled, like a Morris Engel or Helen Levitt documentary. It's not a passing observation, the camera fixes on the feat, looking up like a circus spectator, an incredulous citywalker focused on a potential suicide, like an appalled parent or social worker. This sight of vaulting youthful (both carefree and careless) becomes, well, dreadful. So goes one of the film's key ambivalent moments. An essential poetic image of trepidation and potential tragedy, it proves a relation to urban life that is different from Engel's or Levitt's. In fact, Burnett's inspiration was a continent away. As a UCLA film student, Burnett had two major influences: First, he had discovered the Italian neorealist films of Vittorio DeSica. Second, this discovery happened at a precarious moment when mainstream Hollywood cinema was initiating the crude depictions of black urban life in Blaxploitation movies. *Killer of Sheep* shows Burnett's awareness of a different reality and, even more remarkably, his determination to express a different kind of American cinema. (His colleague in this cinematic challenge was Melvin Van Peebles, whose groundbreaking *Sweet Sweetback's Baadasss Song* got Hollywood's attention but is actually a more serious and experimental film than any of the Blaxploitation entertainments.)

Killer of Sheep respects the mundane aspects of black American life, even when it isn't flattering or superficially exciting. Burnett trusts that circumstances that define an impoverished American existence can be the source of drama. He's richly aware like the playwrights of the Negro Ensemble Company and the 1960s black arts movement but is committed to a realist, rather than theatrical, aesthetic. He knows that by showing the disappointment of men and women who attempt to sustain their relationships in the midst of social despair doesn't simply portray them as miserable but presents the flipside—their intense, humane desiring. This imperative makes *Killer of Sheep* a landmark achievement. Burnett updated Italian Neorealism's special style of humanism from the midcentury and found the ambition and failures particular to the century's end. That's why, seen today, *Killer of Sheep* strikes one as a still-relevant, primal expression of American experience.

Stan (played by Henry G. Sanders), the young head-of-household with a wife and two children, represents the American struggle that most domestic filmmakers avoid. Burnett focuses on the family's anxieties as more than simply topical, they are inherited from both society and blood. The opening scene (sometimes disorienting to viewers) depicts a moment from Stan's childhood, when he received angry instruction from his own father to fight for himself (and for his family) because self-reliance is life's only certainty. This scene's stark wisdom announces the film's texture—personal, commonsensical, bluesy. Burnett's use of music to underscore and contrast the blighted lives of Stan's family instructively demonstrates the kind of creativity and sustenance that *could* come of the experience. Whether it does or not depends upon a person's temperament and tenacity. Knowing that difference also depends upon the vision and seriousness of the artist. From Robeson's "That's America to Me" to Dinah Washington's "This Bitter Earth" or even Little Walter's "It's a Mean Old World," unsentimental blues wisdom forms the foundation of Burnett's drama. That's something no other American movie had ever accomplished.

When Stan and a friend attempt to sell a used car motor, Burnett observes the sheer destitution of poor American life when disadvantage feeds into haplessness and the casual nihilism of a nearly defeated people. *Killer of Sheep* captures the mean way tired people fight back against futility, even when it's only to fight against themselves. Such complex human motivation is what glib Hollywood and prejudiced social journalism never attempts to understand but choose cheap moralizing to avoid. The mean fight is there among the children shown in *Killer of Sheep*, the boys who dirty a girl standing next to clean linen. There's a recognition of violent anger in the vignette of the G.I. being thrown out of a woman's home; she rants while—shockingly—her children sit huddled on a sofa, observing the adult hostility. Burnett studies both the worn-down adult and newly aggrieved youthful sides of this national crisis. He captures the tension that ghettoizes—belittles and immiserates—peoples' experience. Perhaps this is one reason for the film's lack of popularity, it's face-to-face with misery in scenes that make it intimate and authentic. Self-recognition is a scary thing in American movie culture.

There is no more powerful depiction of physical and spiritual impotence than the scene between Stan and his wife (Kaycee Moore). Sometimes enigmatic, Stan is the most elemental black male screen figure until Harry Belafonte's aptly named Seldom Seen in Altman's *Kansas City*. It's his simplest moods that affect us: moments of his miscommunication with his wife, or the barely understood longing he expresses to a friend. (Holding a cup of hot coffee to his forehead, Stan says, "Doesn't this remind you of a woman when you're making love?") These primal modern-male frustrations go beyond the meaningless romantic pleasantries of most movies to the blues-bedrock of human need.

Burnett also has a longing. He makes a precarious leap across a communications void in *Killer of Sheep*, boldly attempting to connect with the popular audience on terms that that audience (black or white) is unused to. The proof of Burnett's risk—his insistence on serious, credible filmmaking—is that he has had hardly any followers. The closest he's gotten to a disciple came unexpectedly in the work of twenty-five-year-old white Texan David Gordon Green (director of *George Washington*), who at a New York Film Festival Q-and-A admitted *Killer of Sheep's* influence, particularly "Burnett's small humors"). It is precisely the small and humorous aspects of *Killer of Sheep* that have weighed against its more popular acceptance. Such knowledge, rarely solicited by American films, derives from a source of experience and art that puts most other—generally escapist—cinema to shame. And it also shames a viewer to recognize these characters, the world they inhabit, the behavior they reflect back onto the audience. What else can explain Burnett's remarkable portrait never finding favor with either the Blaxploitation audience, the 1980s buppie/independent audience, or the 1990s hip-hop movie audience? *Killer of Sheep's* American truth allows no franchise of sensational blandishments.

You can be stunned by the accuracy of Burnett's allegory when Stan's job in a meatpacking plant affords an essaylike digression on slaughterhouse activity—including the ritual betrayals of a Judas Goat. A perception that extraordinarily precise places *Killer of Sheep* above the ken of most contemporary filmmaking. (It was "independent" before that label lost its meaning.) Burnett's conscious of pain, but he's also capable of beauty. Quiet, domestic scenes of Stan's wife and two kids so torn apart by exhaustion, frustration, envy that they cannot yell or lash out (only look at each other) have an unusual emotional and political potency. To see what's true in these scenes is to recognize their beauty in the most painful sense. American critics have never cited a domestic genre equal to Italian Neorealism because they never had to. That *Shoeshine, Bicycle Thieves, La Terra Trema* standard of harshness and beauty has only been achieved with one homegrown film. And *Killer of Sheep* is it.

L.A. Confidential (1997)

by Peter Rainer

THE 1950S-ERA LOS ANGELES of *L.A. Confidential* is Noir Central. Its denizens are tattooed in shadow; the play of light and dark in the streets, the police stations, the morgues, is fetishistic. The postwar L.A. touted in the travelogues and billboards is a boomtown, but what we actually see is unsettling: a city of the future infested by people with only a past.

Like the best noir crime thrillers, *L.A. Confidential,* directed by Curtis Hanson and very loosely based on the 1990 James Ellroy novel, suggests a menace even greater than the one we are presented with. It's been a long time since we've had sordidness this ripe in the movies. Hanson and his cinematographer, Dante Spinotti, understand why we allow ourselves to be taken in by noir—it sexes up our own worst suspicions about how the world works.

With a cast of more than 100 characters, Ellroy's novel is a sprawling overload of plots and subplots. The overabundance has an obsessive, almost punitive quality, as if the L.A. horror could no longer be contained within the confines of a single narrative. Pulp noir is, almost by definition, a slick genre, but Ellroy's book is a rare thing—a noir *epic.* If you stand back from its jumbled panorama, it comes together like one of those compressed 3-D images that suddenly snap into focus if you stare at them long enough.

Hanson and his coscreenwriter, Brian Helgeland, have hooked into Ellroy's depraved, moody-blues mind-set and tricked out a story line from his welter of happenings. The movie is still a dense thicket of subterfuges and wrong-way turns, but at least it's negotiable.

Besides, confusions are a part of noir. We don't look to these movies for handy resolutions, and the films that wrap things up for us are often the least resonant. Hanson makes this mistake at the end of *L.A. Confidential,* but otherwise he demonstrates that every safe exit is really a trap door. The result is perhaps the best noir crime movie since *Chinatown*—not that, aside from *Devil in a Blue Dress,* there has been much competition.

The assumption in noir has always been that appearances are *not* deceiving. If you're fat, you're gross; if you're a woman, you're no good; if you're rich, you're sleazy. It's a reactionary genre—or it would be except for the strain of sentimentality that runs through it. (Think of Raymond Chandler's Philip Marlowe—the white knight of the dark streets.)

The key to *L.A. Confidential*—what makes it different—is that just about everybody in it *isn't* what he or she seems. Sometimes the characters are even *worse* than you imagined; sometimes they show off a valor and a rue that spin you around. The mysteries to be solved in *L.A. Confidential* aren't only whodunits. The flip-flops of character are mysteries, too. We never are sure how people will act in this film, and that unease is part of its texture. It keeps us off kilter until the end.

Ed Exley (Guy Pearce), when we first see him, is a Los Angeles police officer on the make for a higher rank. College educated, the son of a decorated cop killed on the job, Exley, with his wire-rim glasses and pursed, polished features, is almost comically straight-arrow. But there's connivance built into his uprightness, which he uses as leverage to get what he wants. In a police force rife with corruption, Exley accommodates himself to his image-conscious higher-ups as a do-gooder—a poster boy. When a number of his fellow cops brutalize some Mexicans brought to the police station on Christmas Eve, Exley alone rats on his comrades—and wangles a promotion for it. He's not wrong to rat. The cops—spearheaded by Dick Stensland (Graham Beckel), along with his partner, Bud White (Russell Crowe), and Jack Vincennes (Kevin Spacey)—behaved like racist thugs. But Exley uses the ugly incident as an *opportunity,* knowing full well he'll be shunned, or worse, by his fellow officers. He doesn't care; he doesn't really want to be liked by them anyway.

It's to the film's credit that Exley's apple-polishing is given its due. So is the cynicism and sense of betrayal from the other cops. We don't see much more of Stensland except his corpse, but White the bully-boy turns soulful and becomes Exley's antagonist. Taken by Capt. Dudley Smith (the marvelous James Cromwell) as a strong arm on crime raids, White inevitably is drawn into a collision course with the golden boy. It's as if he and Exley were fated to square off.

Vincennes is the most jaded of the cops. Dressed nattily—he wears his finery the way a lizard wears its skin—he makes side money setting up Hollywood busts for Sid Hudgeons (Danny DeVito), the yowly editor of a tabloid magazine called *Hush-Hush.* Vincennes also works as an adviser to the television series *Badge of Honor,* which portrays the LAPD as shining warriors. He values his sleekness because it camouflages the scumminess of his operation. But he also values the scumminess; it confirms his wisdom about how rotten things are. Vincennes fancies himself a connoisseur of the vile.

What gives Spacey's performance its edge—its greatness—is that finally we can see how little this connoisseurship means to him. Inside the sleek cynicism is a weariness with what he has become. When Vincennes is given an opportunity by Exley to right a wrong he perpetrated—a Hollywood bust turned murder—he jumps at it. His chance for redemption transforms him. It's as if the real person—guileless and decent—has melted away the mask.

Perhaps the reason Vincennes comes across as the most layered of the film's characters is because his take on things—detached yet impassioned—matches Curtis Hanson's. When Vincennes is at his sleekest, it's as if everything he speaks issues from an echo chamber of irony; he's supremely facetious. And Hanson directs the action in the same double-edged way. Underneath the cool-cucumber flipness, he's terribly engaged.

He realizes you can't direct a 1950s crime noir as if we were still living in the 1950s. When the police chief (John Mahnon) talks up the LAPD as a "great force in a great city," it's balanced by his directive to the cops regarding some black suspects in a brutal mass murder. For their apprehension he urges "all available force," and, to his credit, Exley gags at the euphemism. He mutters to himself, "Why not just put a bounty on them?"

Noir, for all its up-from-the-streets atmosphere, is situated in a pulpy never-neverland where everything we see and hear seems encoded yet explicit. The emphasis in L.A. Confidential on the racism and corruption of the LAPD grounds it. It's as if we were witnessing the origins of an outrage that is still with us. When White, the self-styled avenger of battered women, shoots a rapist and then makes the shooting look like self-defense, we feel unclean watching the fix—even though our outrage matches White's. We're privy to an obscenity, and Hanson makes us feel our own complicity in it.

In fact, throughout L.A. Confidential we feel implicated in the luridness of what we're watching. That's one of the dirty pleasures of noir. Hanson has shuffled through these shadows before. His script for the almost unknown 1979 Elliott Gould thriller, The Silent Partner, was a marvel of malice. Despite some questionable casting involving the likes of Steve Guttenberg and James Spader, Hanson's early features as a director, The Bedroom Window and Bad Influence, were expertly creepy neo-noirs.

The casting in L.A. Confidential is mostly first-rate—though a little of DeVito's smirky bombast goes a long way—and the creepiness is more masterfully stage-managed than ever. Hanson has finally come into his own. A former movie critic, he seems to be playing out in this film his own fantasia on the noirs that formed him. When we follow the trail of blood in the Nite Owl Coffee Shop—the murder trail that leads to the black suspects—Hanson intensifies our dread drop by drop. It's as if an Edward Hopper all-night diner had blurred into a charnel house.

At the same time, Hanson is reaching for a more sentimental and valorous conception of the noir thriller than we are accustomed to in the movies. It's his way of recasting the genre by making it less reactionary. And so, in place of the standard-issue noir vamp who drives men to their doom, we get Kim Basinger's Lynn Bracken—the whore with the heart of gold. Lynn is a prize filly in the stable of pimp-financier Pierce Patchett (David Strathairn), who runs a house of prostitution featuring women surgically altered to look like movie stars. (Such a ring actually existed in Hollywood.) Lynn is the Veronica Lake stand-in, and Bud White falls for her. He lets her know she's *better* looking than Veronica Lake— that's how we first know he loves her.

In his squad car, in the rain, he watches her from afar. Much later on, feeling jilted, he slaps her in the rain. (What would noir be without rain?) Lynn is the bright angel of noir who replaces the vamp, and it doesn't quite work. She's such an ethereal goddess that you crave some poison in the mix—something slutty and indefensible. Basinger has the right vanilla parfait look—she's certainly a pulp-master's wet dream—but she's given things to say like, "Bud can't hide the good inside of him." And we're meant to agree with her.

Transforming a noir vamp into a touchy-feely angel of mercy isn't much of a bonus; noir shouldn't be this soggy and righteous. When someone like Jack Vincennes fights to reclaim his goodness, we can at least recognize the smarm it came out of. Lynn, though, is untainted from the get-go.

What this all means, I suspect, is that Hanson is much better at malice than virtue. He can't make the scenes with Lynn come alive because they're cream-filled with good intentions. It's the same creaminess that mars the film's ending. (The book's fadeout is vaguely similar but far less smug.) In a way, Hanson is a victim of his own success here: He's so good at nastiness that the counterbalancing sweetness pales in comparison.

He's not always at his best on the dark side either: A scene involving the strong-arming of the D.A. (Ron Rifkin) is poorly staged, and there are a few too many cutesy-ironic touches, like the shot of Vincennes under a movie marquee for *The Bad and the Beautiful.*

But Hanson understands in his bones what draws us to this netherworld: We want to know where the bodies are buried. In one particularly startling sequence we actually find out—White crawls under a house and pulls up a decaying corpse. It's as if in this scene White becomes the Ulysses of noir. He's reached the rot that noir tries to slick up and glamorize.

The three lead cops in *L.A. Confidential* react to depravity; they have a conscience. Hanson wants to give us a richer sense of character than the standard noirs, and, by the end, his cops have earned their chops. The blood on Exley's face no longer looks decorative and out of place, as it did in the beginning. It looks like it belongs there—it's a part of his story. *L.A. Confidential* is about a war within the police ranks, and it's also a film at war with itself. Hanson craves the lurid shock of pulp, but he also wants to go beyond pulp. With his smarts and his almost tragic sense of the consequences of vice, he just about gets there.

Landscape in the Mist (1988)

by Michael Wilmington

FEAR, EXHILARATION, HARROWING ISOLATION. . . . These are among the elements of Theo Angelopoulos's piercingly sad masterpiece, *Landscape in the Mist (Topio Stin Omichli)*. It's a movie wondrously wrought, heart-breakingly beautiful, and it conveys, with stunning impact, part of the alienation of the whole postwar era: the death of the past, the steady erosion of optimism, the loss of the consolations of family, religion, tradition, and political idealism.

Working at the peak of his inspiration and gifts, Angelopoulos crystallizes that disquiet in a pared-down plot: the odyssey of two illegitimate Greek children, wandering over the highways and railroad lines of their country. Searching for a "father" who proves to be an illusion, they move toward a dream within a dream, a film within a film, a landscape dissolving in strange and inexplicable mists.

Like many great poets, Angelopoulos lets images, feelings, and ideas overwhelm his story. Here Voula, 14 (Tania Palaiologou), and Alexander, 5 (Michalis Zeke), have been deceived by their mother into believing their absent father is "away" in Germany. When they flee for the border to "join" him—taking illicit rides on trains, hitchhiking on vans and lorries, and suffering poverty, rape, and exploitation—they are taking a dangerous leap of faith, an eerie plunge toward liberation and danger. In a way, it's a search for order in a chaotic world, a search for a God the world tells them is nonexistent, for an affirmation masking their own sad or sordid origins.

Throughout *Landscape,* we are always aware of life on the edge, of the uncertainty and fragility of most human endeavor. The children, outside a boisterous nocturnal wedding celebration, tearfully watching the last flailing agonies of a dying horse, become quintessential victims, prey to all they meet. Their only benefactor is a buoyant young motorcyclist, just about to be drafted: Orestes (Stratos Tzortzoglou), a van driver for a failing, itinerant theater troupe—the "Travelling Players" from Angelopoulos's 1975 classic of the same name, returning for an encore.

A joyous but tormenting scene of repressed love is enacted to rock 'n' roll on a windy beach; border guards sweep murky grounds with a searchlight and fire into the darkness. A hair-raising rape scene takes place offscreen as cars whiz past an ominous parked truck. A huge stone hand, remnant of past Greek glories, is lifted from the ocean and vanishes, helicopter-borne, into the distant sky.

Angelopoulos can be variously opaque, languorous, cryptic, and seemingly maddeningly mannered, but *Landscape* is a film that seems, by contrast, luminously simple. A lyrical road movie about a journey across a dreamy and desolate modern pornography, *Landscape* may remind us at times of filmmakers as various as Antonioni, Mizoguchi, Dreyer, Murnau, or Bresson, but this shattering work quickly generates its own pure and powerful note. The realm it opens up is both real and surreal. The petrol stations, cafes, the brutal rape—all these evoke the here and now. A bizarre snowfall appearing as by magic in a seaside street, the vision of the helicopter carrying the giant hand—these suggest fantasy, memory, the past.

Angelopoulos's cowriter on *Landscape in the Mist* and his four other most recent films is Tonino Guerra, Antonioni's most frequent collaborator. And though we see some of the chillingly gorgeous austerity of Antonioni in *Landscape in the Mist*—as well as in *The Beekeeper* (1986), *The Suspended Step of the Stork* (1991), and *Eternity and a Day* (1997)—*Landscape*'s vision suggests another era of Italian film as well, the child's-eye approach of the great early neorealist films: Rossellini's *Rome: Open City* and *Paisa* and De Sica's *Shoeshine* and *The Bicycle Thief*. More in subject though, than in style: the child's view here is replaced by a vaster perspective, the eye, perhaps, of a lonely god. Much of *Landscape* seems shot under a sky impenetrably overcast, gray, autumnally chill, sometimes thick with driving rain—or filled with that sudden, ecstatic snowfall—and it unwinds on vast plains that stretch around the tiny figures of the children, as they make their hard and lonely way.

Since Angelopoulos, as always, tends to shoot in extremely long takes—staggeringly well choreographed and executed, translucently lit by cinematographer Giorgos Arvanitis—all the characters begin to seem mere figures in the landscape, stripped of freedom. (In *Travelling Players*, a four-hour film, there are only eighty separate shots.) Many of Angelopoulos's severest critics complain that his extreme visual style and sparse dialogue renders his characters lifeless, puppetlike—lacking the sensual reality of the children in *Shoeshine* or *Open City* and their ability to generate love from the audience. But our distance from Angelopoulos's children and the way the landscapes dwarf them is crucial to the film's effect. We must see them lost in their world, trapped in their time.

Angelopoulos has directed three of the most beautiful and profound films of our time, *Landscape in the Mist, The Travelling Players,* and *Eternity and a Day,* yet they're still remarkably little known and little seen—and often little appreciated when they are seen. Perhaps it's because we've lost our taste and appreciation for, or even our comprehension of, the kind of cinematic poetry Angelopoulos distills. Caught between high-tech gloss on the one hand and rougher-hewn iconoclasm on the other, we may be blind, in many ways, to works that don't pretend to have all the answers: films like *Landscape,* which reveal their own pure sense of the overpowering beauty, terror, and mystery of life.

In a better time and place, at least for foreign-language films on American screens—Theo Angelopoulos might not have gone so grotesquely unrecognized here for the three decades of his filmmaking career. A victim of bad international timing, Angelopoulos may also be a victim of his own intransigent perfectionism, his stubbornly personal vision and style. His three greatest films give us the world crystallized in a single perfect image: the hand rising from the sea (*Landscape*), the performance always cut short (*Players*), the last dance before the past and its sunlit sea (*Eternity*). But *Landscape in the Mist,* especially, is a sublime poetic summation of his feelings, memories, and insights at a particular place and time.

Greece is a country of poets, and Angelopoulos finds his own poetry in his land's beauty and corruption, in betrayal and witness, and in loss and pain; in children estranged from their father, in a country estranged from its heritage, in love's paralysis, art's frustrations, the mists of death—and above all, in the rich and resonant silence around him—the silence of history, of the landscapes, of the mountains, ocean and sky, all caught in the fixed or travelling gaze through which (like Joseph Conrad) he finally makes us see.

Most great films contain two or three memorable set-pieces; *Landscape in the Mist* contains almost nothing else. And though many movies gain their significance from an immediate social context, or compared with other work around them, *Landscape in the Mist* is a film for the ages. If it is not a classic, then the word has no meaning.

Lawrence of Arabia (1962)

by Michael Wilmington

DAVID LEAN'S LAWRENCE OF ARABIA is an aesthete's epic: a battle film where the carnage is waged on immaculate sands against high skies, where the heroes are improbably handsome and the desert a golden, dazzling backdrop for their adventures. Based on the exploits of T.E. Lawrence of Arabia during World War I, this much-prized classic can be faulted at times for its history or psychology, but never for its looks.

Few adventure films ever have had such astonishing physical beauty. As shot by Freddie Young (and his great second unit cinematographer Nicolas Roeg), there's a scintillating clarity in the city and village scenes (done mostly in Seville, Spain, and Morocco) and the vast Saudi Arabian landscapes: movielands as haunting as John Ford's Monument Valley: a Xanadu of boys' adventure, dune after dune sliding off toward the blinding sky.

Though the movie is full of sand and heat, we don't always feel them. Lean's chilly precision cools the desert off, kisses some of the blood off Lawrence's hands. I saw *Lawrence* for the first time at the age of fifteen, and for years afterward I could recall much of it at will—especially the long sequence where Lawrence (Peter O'Toole) sees Sharif Ali Ibn El Kharish (Omar Sharif) for the first time riding toward him through the desert in shimmering heat waves that seem to break Sharif Ali's camel mount into black abstract fragments: the vision an eerie harbinger of disasters to come. (Lean held this truly hypnotic shot, in his first cut, for almost twice the length we see here. Later, he lost his nerve and shortened it). The whole movie is a vast objet d'art, full of grand tableaus, sweeping action, and polished, epigrammatic speeches. The dialogues (written by playwright Robert Bolt and, uncredited, Michael Wilson) drip with irony and foreshadowing. *Lawrence* has been attacked for the way O'Toole's magnetic performance and limpid blue eyes turn the title character into a mask and a cipher. But, if we want the history, we can always read Lawrence's *Seven Pillars of Wisdom* or the rest of the source material. Lean's film gives us something different: high adventure wedded to stunning visual beauty, esthetic excitement married to bloody danger, suave irony coupled with chaos and futility.

O'Toole's Lawrence is an adventurer who flirts with disaster, wants to be consumed by another culture. The huge close-up early on where he holds his finger in the lighter flame—which immediately dissolves into the desert landscape—suggests a desire to annihilate part of himself, become something purer, harder: "playing with fire" in a deep and dangerous way. We remember afterward the quiet delight with which he first travels through the Arabian desolation, the blanched anguish on his face at his leave-taking, his intoxicated glee in battle, and the way his face crumbles when he flirts with death once too often.

If I were a more sophisticated fifteen-year-old, I might have guessed that Sharif Ali's memorable entrance presaged something far more intense. Like many of Lean's other films, especially *Brief Encounter* and *Doctor Zhivago, Lawrence of Arabia* is a tale of impossible love. But here the lovers (subconscious, of course) are Ali and "El Arens," who consummate their passion only in bloody warlike deeds. Something may have happened between Lawrence and his desert comrades in real life, but never here. The sense of frustration becomes a shiver under the film's hot vistas, and when Lawrence is finally raped and sodomized in the film, by the oily Turkish bey played by Jose Ferrer (one of the "lost" scenes restored for the 1989 re-release), it plays like a twisted fulfillment of these teasing undercurrents. He's captured by the bey's men right after sporting with Ali on a spy mission—playing madman, god, and tease. All throughout the film, Ali is both sidekick and simmering presence—but, more important, he comes to stand for the impossible union with Arab culture Lawrence wants.

O'Toole was twenty-five when he made *Lawrence* (so was Sharif). He'd acted mostly at the Bristol Old Vic and done a handful of films (including *The Savage Innocents* with *Lawrence* costar Anthony Quinn, where director Nick Ray had another actor redub O'Toole's dialogue). But *Lawrence* remains his greatest role and performance, an incredibly effective piece of anti–typecasting. If Lawrence had been cast correctly as a smaller man (like John Mills in Terence Rattigan's *Lawrence* stageplay *Ross*), the movie would have lost much of its impact. It might not even have worked as well with Lean's first choice, Marlon Brando—who would probably have been wilier and more sensual. Instead, this is Lawrence as he might have imagined himself: aesthete-adventurer, blond god.

In O'Toole's burned hands, Lawrence swings between exhilaration and despair, madness and glory, the poles on which the movie pivots. The pragmatic newsman who follows his exploits, Bentley (Arthur Kennedy, as a fictionalized Lowell Thomas), calls Lawrence a "shameless exhibitionist"—but by the end he's a shameful exhibitionist, an intensely private man who has somehow willed himself into extroversion, toppled over into giddy excess, before his inevitable entombment in legend.

We remember O'Toole's face, but the film is really a portrait of its maker, David Lean. Lean shot for two years, spending and shooting prodigally. (Sharif Ali's entrance alone took more than a month.) And that reckless perfectionism is reflected in the movie's form: the glassily beautiful surfaces, the turbulent interior. Lean is a maker of huge, ravishing, uneasy films, and this is an epic—his highest achievement—that thrills and disturbs as you watch it; so taut and fine it seems at any moment, like O'Toole's Lawrence, ready to snap.

Reconstructing it in 1989 was a vast, complex, uneasy effort too. Over the years, the picture had lost more than an hour, from an original running time of three hours and two minutes. The missing footage had to be located (in the Columbia vault) and then painstakingly refurbished. O'Toole, Kennedy, Quinn, and Alec Guinness (as the imperturbable Prince Feisal) all redubbed part of their original dialogue, and Martin Scorsese supervised the initial phases of the editing, with Lean himself taking over at the end.

Lean began as an editor for Michael Powell and others. In the 1930s, in fact, he was known as the best cutter in England, and his structural brilliance is obvious though the whole film. Its two-part construction of rise and fall, glory and decline, is crucial to the final effect. The complete *Lawrence of Arabia* is a symphony of war, and its very amplitude is part of its power: poetry and bloodbaths, battles and reverie, genius and madness.

In *Lawrence*, the idea of male bonding, that action movie staple, is raised to a sublime and scary level—as if all the politics of the region hinged on one man's bruised psyche, as if the earth turned on his burned heart. The movie is a stirring portrait of a genuine hero, but Lean's *Lawrence of Arabia* also critiques what it celebrates. And in part, it undermines what it exalts. That's one reason why it's still one of the great movie epics: an archetypal daydream of bravery and disaster.

See it once—as I did in my teens—and it stays with you: the dunes, the sky, the search for the lost man; "It is written . . . "; Anthony Quinn as the hawk-faced Auda Abu Tayi crying, "I am a river to my people!"; the screaming desert raid on the train (shot by Andre De Toth); El Arens's white robes gleaming in the sun, then stained with blood and betrayal; the taking of Aqaba—and, at the very beginning, those shots of the green English countryside and Lawrence's wild ride on his Vincent Black Shadow motorcycle, a burst of boyish exhilaration that ends in twisted wreckage on a quiet country English road.

M (1931)

by Morris Dickstein

FRITZ LANG MADE HIS REPUTATION in the 1920s with films that were bold, brooding, mythical, and fantastic: the allegorical *Destiny* (or *The Weary Death*, 1921); the story of a master criminal and man of disguises, *Dr. Mabuse, the Gambler* (1922); a visually stunning epic, *The Nibelungs* (1924); a lavishly produced science-fiction fable about a divided society, *Metropolis* (1927); and the pulpy tale of a clandestine spy network, *Spies* (1928). Usually written with his wife, Thea von Harbou, and starring his favorite actor (and her ex-husband), the demonic Rudolf Klein-Rogge, these dreamlike films are shadowed by fatalism and paranoia, a dark sense of powerful subterranean forces that lurk behind the world of appearances. In *M*, their first sound film, made in 1931, Lang and von Harbou took a leap into contemporary life, tracking these irrational energies through the individual psyche and the modern city.

German Expressionist films were stylized, obsessive, and artificial. *M*, on the other hand, presents itself innocently as a crime documentary or police procedural drama. Originally called *Murderers Among Us*, it was loosely based on the case of a notorious serial killer in Dusseldorf. Lang explores how an epidemic of child murders, played up by sensational journalism, disrupts the life of a city of four and a half million (obviously Berlin), sowing fear everywhere, setting neighbors and strangers against one another, putting even the most harmless behavior under suspicion. As the police sift thousands of tips and clues, the criminal underworld is itself disturbed and organizes its own manhunt to find the killer. But as played by Peter Lorre in his first major screen role, the culprit, Hans Beckert, is as much victim as villain; like the city as a whole, he is swept up by a surge of violence he cannot control. And when ordinary criminals, with the help of a network of beggars watching every street, capture him and put him on trial in an abandoned brewery, Lorre makes a blood-curdling speech about the horrendous urges that periodically drive him to kill. When his "defense attorney" calls for him to be turned over to the police, a jury of criminals, hardly distinguishable from plain citizens, turns into a furious lynch mob that cries out for his blood, unwittingly demonstrating the agonizing point Lorre has made.

Lang's movie exposes the savagery that slumbers lightly beneath the soft skin of civilization. He intercuts the rational methods of the police investigation, such as fingerprinting and graphology, with the more intuitive attack of organized crime, for both are desperate to uncover the murderer in their midst. The police employ map and compass to parcel up and search out the dark corners of the city, but Lorre is finally fingered by a blind beggar who recognizes the tune he whistled (Grieg's "In the Hall of the Mountain King") as he bought a balloon for one of his young victims. Where the police use painstaking legwork and pore through the files of old mental cases, the criminals and beggars track Lorre from block to block, branding him in chalk with a large M as he nervously dispenses paternal kindness to his next target. When he flees in alarm, Lang films the empty streets from above, so that he looks like a rat in a maze; and after he hides in the dark storage rooms of an office building, an army of crack burglars descends to ferret him out. As the haunted becomes the hunted, Lang perversely makes us sympathize with him. M portrays the police and the underworld as mirror images of each other, comfortable and familiar partners in a time-honored social dance. The killer, seemingly harmless and respectable, trapped as much by his own impulses as by those who hunt him down, is the wildcard that neither of these forces can control.

Much of the movie turns on Peter Lorre's amazing performance as he emerges slowly into view, with his epicene body, sluggish movements, startled looks, and, finally, his pleading, hysterical voice. In many ways this is silent film acting— physical, gestural, exaggerated—since Lorre speaks very little until his final trial. We "see" him first as a dark shadow across a Wanted poster, making the acquaintance of his newest victim. At other times we observe him making grotesque faces in a mirror, or gazing into his own reflection in store windows, or half-concealed behind an ivy-covered trellis in a cafe, or almost lost in dim clutter where he is hiding from his pursuers. He writes to the newspapers because he wants to be caught, to be stopped, and each time the urge overcomes him he begins incongruously to whistle, like a man trying hysterically to calm himself down. With his bulging eyes, porcine face and fingers, slack, sensual lips, clawlike hand movements, and hunched, haunted gait, Lorre's slack appearance is at once gross and elusive, unthreatening and nightmarishly strange. He is a man of shadows and concealments, a hidden darkness. We confront him directly only at the end, in his appeal to the "jury," when he finally confronts himself, suddenly articulate as the psychopathic element no society can fully repress. Like Dostoevsky, Lang takes lurid thriller material to a higher level.

The genius of M is less in the story, which is routine, than in the technique Lang brings to it. Like Hitchcock in *Blackmail* and von Sternberg in *The Blue*

Angel, their first sound films, Lang combines the visual storytelling of silent cinema with an exceptionally creative use of sound. The movie begins with children playing an elimination game in a bare courtyard, as one of them sings of "the nasty man in black" who will come to "chop you up." This is seen in a high-angle shot from the viewpoint of their anxious, overworked mothers. Soon, when one girl actually disappears, the violence remains offscreen: her death comes home to us, as it does to her mother, through images of an empty courtyard and stairwell, an untouched dinner setting, the sight and sound of a cuckoo clock, her mother's plaintive cry. Finally, her ball rolls to a stop and her child-shaped balloon, caught in some overhead wires, floats free, like a spirit escaping the body. The blind beggar will bring along the same balloon when he identifies her killer.

Lang counterpoints sight and sound, letting us visualize patches of dialogue through visual tableaux. We have seen Lorre's trackers ransacking the office building, but as the police finally hear the story, Lang's camera, in a series of separate shots, gives us a complete inventory of their thorough work. When the police inspector craftily implies that a night watchman was killed, to force a suspect to confess, we see the watchman devouring a hearty meal. As the shaken captive tells all, tipping off the police to the location of the impending "trial," the camera takes us to the scene in a seamless transition from sound to image. Through parallel cutting Lang draws an analogy between the pompous Inspector Lohmann (Otto Wernicke), convening the forces of law and order, and the violently determined chief criminal Schränker (Gustaf Gründgens), marshaling the powers of the underworld. Both give vehement, marginally comic performances that suggest their pretensions and shortcomings. From the movie's Freudian viewpoint, their methodical, self-important tactics have limited power, since, like Lorre himself, we are all at the mercy of forces we can scarcely understand. To convey this, Lang often shows his actors controlled by something outside the frame: the gang of thieves recoiling from the arrival of the police, or Lorre reacting in guilty horror to the blind witness, who taps him on the shoulder to tell his accusers they have their man. Sound amplifies these moments but they would work just as well if they were silent scenes, as some of them nearly are.

Despite its stylized touches—its mirror-effects and shadows, its visual metaphors—*M* naturalizes the fantastic elements of Lang's earlier films, turning myth into modern psychology and pulp into social documentary while deepening Lang's pursuit of the bizarre and the irrational. The murderer among us also becomes the murderer inside us, the gruesome power of instinct, obsession, and aggression against which we have little real defense. For years *M* circulated in muddy prints, badly cut and poorly subtitled, but a restored version in the late

1990s enabled us to see it as again Lang made it, not as a creaky antique. Working in the last troubled years of the Weimar republic, with Hitler's storm troopers on the horizon, Lang in M gives his paranoid vision its most realistic framework, providing a transition to the fraught and effective crime stories he would later make in his twenty years of filmmaking in Hollywood.

The Maltese Falcon (1941)

by Richard T. Jameson

> *In 1539, the Knight Templars of Malta, paid tribute to Charles V of Spain, by sending him a Golden Falcon encrusted from beak to claw with rarest jewels––but pirates seized the galley carrying the priceless token and the fate of the Maltese Falcon remains a mystery to this day.*

THAT CRAWL APPEARS FOLLOWING the opening credits of *The Maltese Falcon*, set to dreamy-sinister music and laid over a dark image of the peregrine statuary seemingly poised in some undiscovered tomb. The grammar is regrettable (surely it should be Knights-Templar?) and suggestive of some haste. Was the foreword perhaps added at the last minute, in an act of desperation, after preview audiences had grown fidgety with reel upon reel of baroque conversations and ornately peculiar comings and goings in a collection of offices and hotel rooms purporting to be modern-day (1941) San Francisco? More than half the film elapses before anyone even mentions the titular bird, let alone accounts for its immense value and lurid history. Yet strike the keynote with that one-sentence prelude and the mantle of legend settles over the entire proceedings.

Of course, *The Maltese Falcon* has become positively encrusted with legend in the six decades since its release. It's *the* classic hardboiled private-eye movie; the nervy maiden offering of its celebrated director, John Huston; the first glamorous star vehicle for Humphrey Bogart, an icon of American cinema and the twentieth century's definition of existential cool; and still the most triumphantly well-cast movie from Hollywood's golden age (rivaled only by *Casablanca*). Watching *The Maltese Falcon* now, everybody and his brother know they're in the presence of something extraordinary. But it's tantalizing to contemplate how easily the brass ring might have been missed—how close the picture might have come to being just another detective thriller, like the two previous screen versions of Dashiell Hammett's groundbreaking novel (respectively so-so, in 1931, and ludicrous, in 1936).

Private eye Samuel Spade (Bogart) is lolling in his swivel chair and rolling a Bull Durham cigarette when his secretary announces "a Miss Wonderly to see you." The lady in question (Mary Astor)—initially a soft fog behind opaque glass—is an aggressively demure creature all aflutter because her sister Corinne has run off with a shady man named Thursby. Could Mr. Spade do something about it? Mr. Spade's partner Miles Archer (Jerome Cowan), a leering sleaze, shows up just in time to usurp the assignment—and within hours/minutes gets abruptly dead. With the police sniffing after Sam as prime suspect (he had, after all, been sleeping with his partner's wife), the detective starts improvising. He's not the only one: The dainty Miss Wonderly (there is no sister Corinne, by the way) becomes the evasive Miss LeBlanc and soon owns up to the scullery-maid moniker Brigid O'Shaughnessy; she and Spade will become allies, after a fashion, and lovers. A lisping Levantine named Joel Cairo (Peter Lorre) also retains Spade's services, then keeps pulling a gun on him. There are two guns in the trenchcoat pockets of a sullen hoodlum (Elisha Cook Jr.) who always seems to be haunting nearby doorways, and just as the pot is really starting to boil, everything and everyone becomes very still at the mention of "the fat man."

John Huston had been laboring as a Warner Bros. screenwriter for several years, after a genially miscellaneous and gadabout early manhood. A couple of particularly successful assignments (Howard Hawks's *Sergeant York* and Raoul Walsh's *High Sierra*) won him a shot at directing as well as writing something that Warners briefly planned to call *The Gent from Frisco*. The writing came easy: Huston asked a secretary to type out a scene-by-scene breakdown of Hammett's novel; studio boss Jack L. Warner happened to see the "script," congratulated Huston on licking the adaptation, and told him to start shooting next week. Virtually all the film's flavorsome dialogue is Hammett's, and so, of course, is the plot about a slippery private detective and a fractious cabal of outré characters willing to sacrifice anyone, including one another, to possess an ancient artifact beyond price. As it happened, Huston not only had the good sense to be faithful to Hammett's original and capitalize on its myriad strengths; he also found in it a theme and worldview that would define his own body of work.

For Huston, the Maltese Falcon is only the first instance of an unholy grail in pursuit of which a collection of strangers make temporary common cause. Whether prospecting for *The Treasure of the Sierra Madre,* plotting to steal a fortune in diamonds in *The Asphalt Jungle,* aiming to sink a German battleship with

The African Queen, chasing God and vengeance and *Moby Dick,* hunting wild mustangs in *The Misfits,* getting battered to win a purse in *Fat City,* or dreaming of a kingdom in Kafiristan as *The Man Who Would Be King,* Huston's motley crew of questers never really find anything but themselves. Aspiration makes a beeline for absurdity; defeat and victory alike are mostly a matter of dumb or bitterly ironic luck. It's the journey, not the destination, that counts, and almost always the only achievable triumph is the weary serenity of self-knowledge.

Still, *The Maltese Falcon* is an exemplary first film, and its dominant tone is a sassy smartness, not despair. Indeed, the narrative personality of the film and the personality of its protagonist are one and the same from the moment Spade is introduced. He will dominate every action and interaction and serve as our point-of-view reference for everything that happens. With only a couple of exceptions—the abrupt, abstract depiction of the film's first murder and the fadeouts of two later scenes—we see nothing that Spade does not see himself (a cardinal principle of the private-eye genre). Even more important, we see him seeing it. Sam's ongoing, moment-to-moment assessment of the shifting vectors of allegiance and advantage, the trade-off of truth and hastily adapted fiction on the part of his fellow denizens of the *Falcon's* night-world, is the most privileged spectacle the film has to offer.

The Maltese Falcon, like its elusive namesake, is eternally in motion, despite the fact that it transpires in a fiercely interior environment (even the few street scenes feel like interiors) and an inordinate amount of it consists of people talking about things (or the possibility of things) that occur offscreen. Now, "talky" is usually a bad word when it comes to movies. But Hammett's talk is tensile and exotic, and the way Huston films it, talk is dynamic action. The camera is ever ready to adapt, adjust, to satisfy a lively curiosity about an ever-surprising world. Producer Henry Blanke advised his tyro director to "shoot each scene as if it was the most important one in the picture; make every shot count." Huston did, with the result that nothing, not even the incidental behavior of anonymous passersby or the riffling of fake I.D. plucked from a suspect's wallet, fails to crackle with energy and insinuation. The dialogue scenes play like relief maps of mined terrain. Looming close-ups are juxtaposed against tiny figures tucked away in the distant corners of the same frame. When two police detectives come to brace Spade in his apartment, just their postures, their positions in the frame and the difference in how they're lit, testify to the bulldog antagonism of Lieutenant Dundy (Barton MacLane) and the reluctance and discomfort of Sergeant Polhaus (Ward Bond), who regards Sam as a friend. Among the Falconers, visible tensions are still more fraught, even when the illusion of affability and rapport is being assiduously courted.

Affability and rapport run nowhere higher than in Spade's (and by all means Humphrey Bogart's) scenes with Kasper Gutman, the most obsessive votary of the Black Bird. Gutman, "the fat man," does not make his appearance until midfilm—and Sydney Greenstreet, the sixty-one-year-old stage veteran tapped for the role, was making his own first appearance on a motion picture screen. It's a moment beyond price. Glimpsed in the distant background as his gunsel Wilmer (Cook) opens the door of their hotel suite, he emerges from behind a vase of roses, his bulbous trunk floating on twinkletoes, his arm capturing Spade's own to draw him into his parlor and his enchantment, snorting companionably.

Gutman is quite mad, but his madness is instinct with grandeur. It is he who, finally, speaks of the Falcon and elevates its pursuit to a cosmic principle. Long after the film has ended, and the sundry on-screen and off-screen corpses have all been accounted for and morality has been satisfied, the viewer realizes that, by the time he does so, Gutman has no practical reason to tell Spade about the Falcon and its fabulous history. It's just that, as he remarks elsewhere, "I must have my little joke now and then." In his heart, Spade deplores him, but John Huston loves him. So do we, and we'll never shake the secret wish that in an alternative universe Sam Spade might yet take him up on his invitation to "join us on the Quest." The Maltese Falcon remains a mystery to this day.

The Man with a Movie Camera (1929)

by J. Hoberman

WHEN PEOPLE, LIKE THE NEOPHYTE Houston film critic whose letter arrived yesterday, ask me my "all-time favorite movie" or "the greatest movie ever made," I brace myself for a look of blank incomprehension and say, "Dziga Vertov's *The Man with a Movie Camera*."

Say what? If Vertov (1896–1954) is the least recognized of major filmmakers, it is only partly because film history has yet to sort itself out. Vertov's oeuvre confounds film history as it is generally conceived. To recognize his centrality is to open oneself to the possibility that the most passionate and inventive movies of the past century may not have been narrative features at all but rather the documentaries and the experimental films, the seven-minute animations and four-minute music videos, which, along with Hollywood B movies and the entire production of Third World behemoths, have been resolutely marched to the medium's margins.

If Vertov had never made anything other than *The Man with a Movie Camera*, he would still be among the cinema's greatest masters. Released in 1929, at the end of the silent era, *The Man With a Movie Camera* is the epitome of machine art, the grand summa of the Soviet futurist-constructivist-communist avant-garde. This kaleidoscopic city symphony—conjoining Moscow, Kiev, and Odessa in one dizzying metametropolis—may be the most densely edited movie ever made. Vertov matches the rhythm of a single day to the cycle of life (birth, death, marriage, divorce) and the mechanisms of moviemaking to the logic of industrial production.

Made without titles, employing strategies of visual analogy and associative montage so intricate they have yet to be named, *The Man with a Movie Camera* is both a Whitmanesque documentary portrait of the Soviet people and an ecstatic ode to human labor as a process of transformation. It is also unceasingly self-reflexive—a primer, in fact, for film viewing. Vertov considered this heroic piece to be the movie that finally broke free from "the tutelage of literature and the theater and brings us face to face with 100 percent cinematography." More than any movie I know, *The Man with a Movie Camera* celebrates the sensory bombardment of twentieth-century urban life. You can never step into the same river twice; nor, given its exhilarating tempo, can you see the same *Man with a Movie Camera*. The split screens and superimpositions, shock cuts and variable-speed motion aside, the editing is so dense that there are never less than a half-dozen things going on. The visual rhymes and perceptual jokes are so intricately cross-referenced that the placement of each shot involves multiple chains of meaning.

Not until the mid-1960s, with Jean-Luc Godard's *Two or Three Things I Know about Her* and Stan Brakhage's *Scenes from under Childhood*, would anyone attempt a film of such audacious complexity. A sort of cinematic *Ulysses*, or cubist documentary, *The Man with a Movie Camera* was so far ahead of its time that one can almost forgive the usually generous Eisenstein for labeling it a work of "formalist jackstraws and unmotivated camera mischief." Even in 1971, Jean Rouch (who took his notion of cinema verite directly from Vertov's "kino pravda") called it "a film which we have not completely understood."

A film that need only be seen once to be understood and enjoyed but demands to be studied on an editing table to be fully appreciated, *The Man with a Movie Camera* has the remarkable effect of encouraging the viewer to identify with the filmmaking process. Perhaps this is what Vertov had in mind when he later wrote, "The method in which I work is the most unexplored in the cinema. My methods demand superhuman efforts of organization, technique, way of life and so on. It is the most thankless way to work. Believe me, it is really hard: yet I hope that one day I shall achieve the victory of realism over formalism and naturalism, and become a poet who can be understood not by a few people but by millions."

The Marriage of Maria Braun (1978)

by Kevin Thomas

THE MARRIAGE OF MARIA BRAUN is the first real commercial success in his native land for R.W. Fassbinder after a prodigious and prolific decade of filmmaking that has established him as a primary force in the new German cinema. (Fassbinder would go on to make three more features plus the superb, monumental fifteen-hour, thirteen-part *Berlin Alexanderplatz* for TV before his death from a drug overdose in 1982, but *Maria Braun* would be the commercial high point of his career as a film director.)

While it's easy enough to see why this film, about a woman struggling to survive in World War II and its grim aftermath, would have far wider appeal than many of his taxing experiments, it is actually one of his most ambitious and complex works, revealing above all a mastery of tone.

Fassbinder's admiration for Douglas Sirk, the German-born Hollywood director of such stylish melodramas as *Written on the Wind* and *The Tarnished Angels*, is well known and would seem to have influenced *Maria Braun* strongly. Like Sirk, Fassbinder is able to express compassion for stormed-tossed heroines with much wit and flair.

In *Maria Braun*, Fassbinder in essence takes the conventions of the woman's pictures of the 1940s to their delirious limits as a way of commenting on the absurd nature of war, the German character, the plight of women, life itself, and especially love. On its most accessible level, the film is a soap opera with Maria clawing her way to the top of the business world with the determination and self-destructiveness of a Joan Crawford heroine.

Fassbinder begins on a comic note as his heroine Maria (Hanna Schygulla), her wedding interrupted by a bombing, doggedly insists that the vows be completed as she, her bridegroom (Klaus Loewitsch), and their minister stretch out flat on a rubble-strewn street, fearing for their lives. A half-day and a whole night with her husband before he goes off to the Russian front, where he is soon reported missing in action, is enough for Maria to develop an obsessive love for him that sustains her as she turns to her considerable sex appeal in order to survive after Germany's defeat.

Hanna Schygulla has the audacity to make Maria come vibrantly alive and to carry off with ease her every (and often melodramatic) act and gesture so that they reverberate with Fassbinder's serious implications. Schygulla heads a potent cast, a number of them Fassbinder regulars like herself. Veteran European leading man Ivan Desny has much dignity as the older man vamped by Schygulla but who falls in love with her all too deeply.

Maria Braun is a superb period piece richly lit by cinematographer Michael Ballhaus, a Fassbinder regular. In every sequence there are those touches of tenderness and outrageous irony that are distinctly Fassbinder's. Best of all is this remarkable, challenging, and satisfying film's final and ambiguous action, which may be debated for a long time to come. But there's no question that Fassbinder means to identify the fate of Maria Braun with that of Germany itself.

Metropolis (1927)

by Armond White

OUTSIZED IN ITS VISUAL CONCEPTION, wild in its political and psychological imaginings, Fritz Lang's *Metropolis* remains one of the great science fiction films along with Kubrick's *2001: A Space Odyssey,* Tarkovsky's *Stalker,* Godard's *Alphaville,* and Ridley Scott's *Blade Runner*, and it is the primary influence on them all. *Metropolis* is, certainly, more than "science fiction," but that label provides a convenient way to understand a film that, among its most staggering qualities, has proven to be many things for many viewers.

At the peak of the German-silents phase of his career, Lang explored the kinetic and chimerical potential of the film medium with daring equal to Griffith and Eisenstein. He took national subjects from ancient mythology to contemporary social intrigue and gave them his personal idiosyncrasy, additionally endowing them with the particular epic grandeur for which the still newly impressive art form was especially admired. After the success of his Niebelungend series, Lang in 1926 was in a position to fulfill the popular audience's increased appetite for the otherworldly. In *Metropolis,* he cast his imagination forward, into a future where mankind still struggled with its contradictory brutal nature and utopian hope. Despite the particular Germanic political aspects of this effort (critiqued in Siegfried Kracauer's *From Caligari to Hitler*), Lang revealed that much of *Metropolis's* futuristic, dream-city look was inspired by his first view of the New York City skyline. Through this inevitable European and New World amalgam, the film combines traditional mythic prognostication with a modern sensibility. It is just such paradoxical elements (a love-hate critique of new technology, admiration-repulsion with social ideology) that form a basis for the film's vitality and endless fascination. (From subject to style, *Metropolis's* impact could be felt as immediately as in Chaplin's 1935 comedy of industrialization *Modern Times* and can be seen as recently as in the crowded skies of Luc Besson's *The Fifth Element* and George Lucas's *The Phantom Menace.*)

H. G. Wells famously remarked that *Metropolis* was "quite the silliest film." And certainly the 1936 film *Things to Come,* a William Cameron Menzies production based on Wells's novel, takes a more conventional approach toward futuristic fiction, almost as if deliberately countering *Metropolis.* But generations of viewers have taken Lang's "silliness" to heart (*Metropolis* has aged better) and, in turn, found inspiration in Lang's folly. *Metropolis* is not esteemed for its credibility so much as for the beauty and intensity in Lang's evocation of dreams and nightmares to come—as well as the artist's own eloquently expressed trepidation and excitement. The story, from a script by Lang's wife, Thea von Harbou, imagines two social classes: the wealthy elite living in above-ground skyscrapers, and downtrodden workers who toil underground. Freder, son of the Industrialist who controls Metropolis, rebels and helps the workers—led by saintly Maria—in their revolt against tyranny. The Industrialist enlists an evil inventor Rotwang to create a robot replica of Maria to confuse the workers and sabotage their revolution. This nearly destroys the city in a flood that occurs when laborers abandon their tasks until workers and the Industrialist, led by Freder and sanctioned by the radiant Maria, come together in an alliance of capital and labor.

All that enhances this lunatic scenario is Lang's gift for composition and rhythm; he uses von Harbou's story for a series of unforgettable, energized tableaux. No matter that the film's concept combines biblical allegory, Wagnerian grandiloquence, and jumbled (Marxist, protofascist, Spenglerian) social theories. What might seem an awkward mix plays with remarkable smoothness and eye-popping surprises. Lang, known for his facility with sinister atmosphere, exults in editing, patterned compositions, wonderment. He confirms his standing (along with Murnau) as a master of big-screen German Expressionism. *Metropolis* inflates paranoia and awe through imagery that has long had powerful psychological fascination. Maria's sermon to the workers leads to a flashback representation of the Tower of Babel legend (and her apocalyptic projection of civilization's fall) that no straight biblical epic has matched. In such instances, *Metropolis* is both fairytale and cautionary tale. Lang's uncanny epic anticipates the mixture of tones and moods that—almost prophetically—later generations would theorize and accept without laughing as Pop Art ironies.

Consider Rotwang's creation of the false Maria. It is depicted in a dazzling carnivalesque blend of technology and wizardry, the infernal and the fantastic. The sequence derives from *The Cabinet of Dr. Caligari* (a production on which Lang assisted), but it also influenced the diabolical creation sequences of the later *Frankenstein* movies—a sign that Lang's tonal shift from art-film sobriety to popular enchantment was true to the medium and its cultural appeal. An unexpected symbol for such bizarre virtuosity can be seen in Rotwang's creation—the robot Maria winks at the camera as if divulging Lang's humorous complicity with the burgeoning audience for cinema, the mechanical fantastic. Lang's imaginative visual wit propels *Metropolis*; that's what gives the film visual energy and integrity apart from whatever thematic readings can be cobbled together from its religious and political story elements. One can respond viscerally—and even deeper—to scenes that depict man's domination by machines and industry (the sequence of Freder attempting to keep up with the swinging arms on a man-sized, clocklike apparatus definitively visualizes capitalist enslavement). But such effects are just one in Lang's fluent pageant of extraordinary impressions. Like the sequence when Rotwang traps the real Maria in a catacombs, tracing her frantic movements with a pitiless spotlight, or the great flood in which a Boschian crowd of bodies desperately surge toward either safety or damnation, Lang's images stir the subconscious. *Metropolis* may be a projection on the future but it plays on feelings and recognitions that feel deeply familiar. Lang achieves magnificence.

In 1984 music producer Giorgio Moroder commissioned a color-tinted version of *Metropolis*, replete with a pop-and-disco score. It had the effect of increasing the film's popularity—making it seem as much a part of the 1980s cultural moment as the Madonna "Express Yourself" video that director David Fincher conceived as a full-color copy of Lang's folly. And surprisingly, Mororder's painstaking, imaginative alteration did not diminish Lang's visionary impact. All the more reason that technology should be viewed with awe—as Lang knew (and Maria winked).

Modern Times (1936)

by David Denby

WHEN I WAS A GRADUATE STUDENT at Stanford a few years ago, I saw *Modern Times* with a group of students involved in a long, difficult protest against university complicity in the Vietnam War. Like so many striking students in America during the late 1960s, we were using a film series to keep up morale. It's a rotten way to use movies, and that night's experience with *Modern Times* showed why. Before the movie started one student stood up and said that Chaplin was a great modern radical and that *Modern Times* was his most explicit attack on capitalism. I felt this was nonsense but nonetheless kept silent and waited for the reaction. It was all fairly predictable: vast amusement during the factory satire; ironic cheers when the Tramp picks up a red flag and inadvertently leads a left-wing parade; surprise and outrage when he thwarts a jailbreak; bafflement when he tries to get back into a jail as a refuge from life outside; general apathy when it became clear that Chaplin was somewhat less committed to social revolution than, say, Che Guevara. The disappointment was acute, and after the film some of the students solemnly decided that Chaplin "hadn't really gotten it together."

It's impossible, of course, to find anything more than a very coy flirtation with radical politics in *Modern Times*. The film derives its power from its rejection of twentieth-century urban life, but that rejection is largely aesthetic and moral, and we are hard put to deduce any specific political line from it. For Chaplin, modern times are hard times, and like Dickens's great novel, the movie is in part an attack on the killing rationality of industrialism—the mechanical rationality that, humanly, is so deeply irrational. But it's the production line that Chaplin satirizes, not capitalism per se, and I hope I am not naïve in assuming that, despite his occasional fellow-traveling, Chaplin would feel the same way about the working day in a steel mill on the Volga.

The movie expresses the greatest possible revulsion from the public, external side of modern life—the anxious, demeaning, exhausting business of factories, strikes, riots, police, etc. The Tramp's natural fastidiousness has never expressed a stronger judgment of things as they are; but when his existence becomes unbearable he doesn't turn to protests or organizing his fellow workers (how could the Tramp organize anything?) but to purely anarchic escape—madness and disruption and fantasy—and to a private world of loyalty and companionship. Still, when the Tramp and "the gamin" walk down the road at the end, it is not for want of trying to enter society. In *Modern Times*, the Tramp makes his most determined attempt to lead an ordinary life; we remember the film, among many reasons, because it suggests that even the most conventional desires—for a home and a job—can be problematic, even hopeless, in a world no longer suited for human accommodation.

Like *The Gold Rush* and so many other Chaplin movies, *Modern Times* wrests its comedy from a background of starvation and disaster. Chaplin has said that his humor depends on getting the Tramp in and out of the maximum amount of trouble, and perhaps we continue to honor him as the greatest of modern comedians because the Tramp's difficulties are always so much more extreme than anyone else's and his resistance so much more heroic. Certainly, for those of us who grew up on the paltry suburban discomforts of film and television comedy in the 1950s and 1960s, the poverty and dereliction in the Chaplin comedies will always provide an occasion for awe.

The Gold Rush, with its hunger and greed and its great images of freezing whiteness, is one of the high points of American cinematic naturalism, whereas in *Modern Times* the terrible threats to life and sanity are conveyed through heavy stylization. The factory set—with its clean "impersonal" facades, immense dials and levers, and two-way television communication—has a definite science-fiction, futuristic look, and at first we may be a bit puzzled since Chaplin makes no attempt to set the rest of the movie in the future ("New Ford V-8 for 1935," a billboard teasingly proclaims behind the starving hero and heroine). Afterward, we realize that Chaplin has used futurism as the most accessible metaphor for the inhumanity of technology. He doesn't need the grime of a real factory because it's the essential character of mass production that he's getting at. Henry Ford had introduced the assembly line roughly twenty years before *Modern Times* was made, but the shock of that invention—it's implication of man's final, utter subordination to the machine—must still have been strong enough to make people wonder if the future had not invaded the present and robbed it of its human grace.

With his genius for seizing on the leading characteristic of a situation and extending and exaggerating it into satire, Chaplin emphasizes the almost obscene physical intimacy in the new relationship between man and machine. The feeding machine is undoubtedly the most hilarious contraption in the American cinema, but this is truly a case of hilarity releasing dread. The machine reminds us of an electric chair or some other torture device, and its physical violation of Chaplin's body is as frightening as it is funny. In a counterpart to the feeding machine, Chaplin is fed into the machine, swallowed whole like a modern Jonah. The Henry Ford type of factory may have been the immediate inspiration for *Modern Times*, but this particular fantasy of being eaten by a machine—with its disturbing mixture of horror and voluptuousness—had apparently obsessed Chaplin since boyhood.

In his autobiography he describes an encounter with a printing press at the age of ten:

It started to roll, grind, and grunt; I thought it was going to devour me. The sheets were enormous; you could have wrapped me in one. With an ivory scraper I fanned the paper sheets, picking them up by the corners and placing them meticulously against the teeth in time for the monster to clutch them, devour them and regurgitate until they rolled out at the rear end. The first day I was a nervous wreck from the hungry brute wanting to get ahead of me.

Obsessed with their own intentions and uninterested in Chaplin's, the students I mentioned before missed out on the true radicalism, the true bitterness, of *Modern Times*. One of the greatest of American comedies is also one of the most pessimistic. Given the stress of modern work and society, the movie only holds out three choices: jail, insanity, escape. The Tramp had often been called a representative of common humanity, but after *Modern Times* it became painful to think of him that way; for if the Tramp embodies us all and there is literally no place for him except on the outside, then we are not at home either.

Mr. Smith Goes to Washington (1939)

by Robert Sklar

IN THE LATE 1930S, more securely atop the pinnacle of American cinema than the Hollywoodland sign, Frank Capra could afford to be bold. Over a five-year span he had won three Academy Awards as best director, for *It Happened One Night* (1934), *Mr. Deeds Goes to Town* (1936), and *You Can't Take It with You* (1938). The first and last of these titles also had been picked as best picture. In 1939 he ended a four-year term as Academy president and assumed leadership of the new Screen Directors Guild. Ambitious and apparently unassailable, he was able to launch a project that others had tried but failed to get off the ground: a controversial story involving corruption in the United States Senate, released in 1939 as *Mr. Smith Goes to Washington.*

Years later, in his 1971 autobiography *The Name Above the Title,* Capra related a tale about a visit he supposedly received, when he had fallen ill following his first Academy Award, from a mysterious "little man . . . completely bald, wearing thick glasses" who admonished him to use his artistry for higher purposes than screwball comedy. *Mr. Deeds* was the first of the more serious endeavors that followed. Then came, among others, *Mr. Smith, Meet John Doe* (1941), and *It's a Wonderful Life* (1946). These are among the most honored and cherished works in America's film heritage. Yet they also strike many viewers as ambiguous and troubling.

Among Hollywood's most significant filmmakers, Capra's reputation is surely the most contested. His four major titles on political and social themes—*Deeds, Smith, Doe,* and *It's a Wonderful Life*—are instantly recognizable for similarities of style, story, and character that, taken together, add up to a unique signature. What some call "Capraesque," however, others not so flatteringly label "Capracorn." The films feature naive, small-town idealists fighting against the ruthless power of political machines, media barons, capitalist predators, and urban elites. Defeated and humiliated, these overmatched innocents are rescued by the moral might of an aroused community, by the otherwise powerless little people whose united support acclaims the downcast heroes as natural leaders. Uplifting and sentimental, Capra's political films seem to offer a consoling myth of national character that has captivated audiences over generations. At the same time, they've been attacked as conformist, demagogic, manipulative, phony.

In recent years Capra's critics have interpreted this divided opinion about the director as stemming, in part, from previously unacknowledged divisions within the films themselves. It's as if, following his mythical visitation from the hairless stranger, Capra consciously decided that his serious films had to be inspirational, while at the same time he was unable to suppress a more fundamental instinct for tragedy. The result is that an uneasy dualism between cheerfulness and dread pervades these films. Their resolutely upbeat last-minute victories and vindications can't erase the deeply disquieting effects of earlier defeats and heartbreaks. *Mr. Smith Goes to Washington* is a clear case in point.

Mr. Smith stemmed from an original short story, "The Gentleman from Montana," by Lewis R. Foster (which won the film's only Academy Award, out of eleven nominations, including best picture and best director). It was loosely based on the early career of U.S. Senator Burton K. Wheeler, who was attacked and falsely indicted when, as a freshman senator in the 1920s, he fought corruption in the presidential administration of Warren G. Harding. The Hays Office, mindful of pending Senate bills that would have adversely affected the movie industry, discouraged other studios from going ahead with the story. But once it fell into Capra's hands, his clout prevailed.

In Capra's version, from a screenplay by Sidney Buchman, an idealistic scoutmaster, Jefferson Smith (James Stewart), is improbably chosen to fill an interim Senate vacancy from a graft-ridden western state. In Washington, D.C., the gawky young legislator gazes with awe on the monuments and symbols of the nation's democratic heritage, while he becomes an object of ridicule from his worldly Senate colleagues and a cynical press corps.

Gradually, however, Smith's dedication and vision win over his initially caustic secretary, Saunders (Jean Arthur, whose character in *Mr. Deeds,* a reporter, went through a similar transformation toward that naive hero). Smith's plan to build a national boys' camp on wilderness land in his home state comes into conflict with the political boss who runs the state and schemes to build a dam on the same site. Smith is devastated when he learns that his senior colleague, Senator Joseph Paine (Claude Rains), whom he idolizes, is in on the crooked deal. Slandered by Paine, ruined, and about to be tossed from the Senate, Smith finds solace and strength (and Saunders's support) at the Lincoln Memorial and launches a one-man Senate filibuster.

Here, leaving behind the Wheeler story and 1920s scandals, Capra's larger themes come strongly into play. For the filmmaker was clearly shaping his depiction of American political institutions for the contemporary moment, and it was no coincidence that the film's October 1939 premiere took place several weeks after Germany invaded Poland, starting World War II in Europe. Capra enlisted the then well-known radio commentator H.V. Kaltenborn for an on-screen appearance as a live radio reporter on Smith's filibuster. Noting the presence of diplomats from foreign dictatorships in the Senate gallery, Kaltenborn comments that Smith's action represents "democracy's finest show."

But is it anything more than a show? It turns out that Smith's home state bears a striking relationship to those foreign dictatorships. The political boss controls the local press and twists the news against Smith, while employing brutal thugs to keep opposing viewpoints from reaching the public. Thousands of telegrams pour into the Senate—nearly all of them against Smith. Despairing, exhausted, Smith collapses. But he has rekindled his senior senator's sense of rectitude. Shamed, Paine tries to commit suicide. He recants his role in the boss's nefarious schemes. Amid pandemonium, Smith belatedly triumphs.

When the film premiered in Washington, the congressional response was decidedly negative: How dare Hollywood paint senators as corrupt and the Senate susceptible to demagogic manipulation? But in the longer haul, Capra's apparent intentions prevailed among critics and spectators. *Mr. Smith* was recognized as a film that dramatized the fragility of democracy at a time of world crisis, as well as the necessity for citizens individually and collectively to stand up for their beliefs and their nation's democratic traditions. Despite the final plot reversals and Smith's ultimate validation, the political boss's capacity to unleash ruthless violence and blatantly slant the news has not yet been confronted.

Mr. Smith is at base a somber film, laced both with uplift and unease. Yet a stark recounting of its narrative trajectory risks overlooking how much its seriousness rests on a comic foundation. With roots both in silent comedy and the 1930s screwball genre, Capra deployed a superb cast of character actors to lighten the heavy political going through pace, wit, and human warmth. Thomas Mitchell as a reporter and Guy Kibbee as the state governor are two among many supporting players worthy of mention, and Harry Carey, a cowboy star of John Ford's silent westerns, was an inspired choice as president of the Senate. To a dramatic tale concerned with the values of a modern western state and, more broadly, a perilous moment for western civilization, Carey conveyed the craggy integrity of Hollywood's legendary Old West.

Nashville (1975)

by David Sterritt

IT WAS CLEAR IN 1975, and it's still clear decades later, that *Nashville* is the film Robert Altman was born to make.

Altman has directed other films of distinction, to be sure. He was a slow starter—years of TV episodes and a few minor movies preceded the 1970 comedy *M*A*S*H,* which introduced his personal style and launched the major phase of his career—and his (occasional) peaks of popularity have been separated by (frequent) spells of relative obscurity, the most lengthy of which extended clear through the 1980s. Still, he has directed a larger number of momentous movies than most filmmakers manage to do, from *McCabe and Mrs. Miller* and *Thieves Like Us* to *The Player* and *Short Cuts,* and he is regarded by most right-thinking cinephiles as an original and influential artist. To say *Nashville* is his masterpiece is to say it's a central work from a central figure of modern American cinema.

It's also a real sweet honey of a number, to borrow the language of its country-tinged screenplay. With a whopping twenty-four characters, a cluster of social and political themes, and more than two and a half hours at its disposal, it turns America's country-music capital into a colossal *Grand Hotel* bubbling with life, lunacy, and the pursuit of hipness. Altman moseys through this humming Babylon the way self-reflexive filmmakers have long meandered through Hollywood—peering curiously behind its billboards and facades, glancing wryly at the glitter but gazing intently at the humanity lurking beneath it. Altman gives similar treatment to other milieus in later films, most notably the film industry in *The Player* and the art world in *Vincent & Theo,* but he's never outdone *Nashville* for wit, insight, or audiovisual audacity. It brims with the bad and the beautiful, careening among comedy, drama, public spectacle, private angst, sociocultural commentary, and magic tricks—and all without dropping the beat of music, music, music that's ultimately the movie's heart and soul.

The current that carries all this along is a political campaign—surprising at the time from a filmmaker more interested in personalities than ideologies, but revealing of the direction he'd take in future projects like the stageplay adaptation *Secret Honor* and the *Tanner '88* television series. Hal Phillip Walker is the candidate's name, and the Replacement Party is his cause. We never see him onscreen, but we do hear a lot of his rhetoric, and some of it has an almost-makes-sense loopiness that recalls the goofy (il)logic of a Preston Sturges advertising parody (*Christmas in July*: "If you can't sleep at night, it's not the coffee, it's the bunk!"). It also anticipates the real-life silliness of H. Ross Perot and his Reform Party campaign. "When you pay more for an automobile than it cost for Columbus to make his first voyage to America," says Walker with blithe disregard for the notion that words might actually mean something, "that's politics."

But in *Nashville* as in life, most people pay only fleeting attention to the man who'd like to run their country. Their own joys and sorrows interest them more, so that's where the movie's real action is. Its two dozen characters comprise an eclectic catalogue of loves, hates, hopes, fears, ambitions, and desires, turning Altman's epic into one of cinema's very few meaningful microcosms of the American scene. The scarlet thread that ties the movie together is the gradually unfolding tale of a young man who's edging his way toward assassinating a public figure. But the subsidiary stories are at least as effective, centering on everything from the mental instability of a singing star to the stream-of consciousness musings of a BBC reporter who doesn't quite realize what a stranger she is in this strange, strange land.

Nashville touches on moral issues but does little moralizing, preferring to let us draw our own conclusions. While its style is sometimes theatrical, it more often has a sense of documentary authenticity and improvisational spontaneity. Loose ends dangle from its fabric realistically, evocatively, mysteriously. The violent climax seems as inexplicable as it is startling and sad. Yet the movie's final vision is at once wistful, hopeful, and—above all—affirmative of the pulsing social rhythms that hold individuals together in a media-drenched modern society.

Amid the multilayered bustle of the film's plots and subplots, Altman pans, tilts, zooms, tracks, and cranes his cameras with boiling energy, plus a sense of purpose and proportion that stands out in his oeuvre to this day. The soundtrack is assembled with equal virtuosity, marking a high point in Altman's pioneering use of multiple recorded tracks. The narrative structure gets scattered at times, and Joan Tewkesbury's screenplay (clearly just a blueprint for the finished film) dips now and then toward the sentimental and unsubtle. Altman keeps everything under firm control, however, by measuring all the hubbub against the bedrock expressiveness of the human face and form. The faces and forms he shows us have the look of regular people rather than movie stars, and some of them have never been in a film before. Newcomers fill certain major roles, such as Ronee Blakley as Barbara Jean, a country singer with severe emotional problems. In other cases they hover in the background, their unschooled mannerisms lending *Nashville* an extra charge of genuineness. More genuineness comes from Altman's decision to have the actors write their own songs for the movie's many musical interludes. This angered some in the pop music industry—what makes these mere actors think they can compose real tunes?—but it adds immeasurably to the authentic populism that informs both the subject and style of the film.

There are stars in *Nashville* as well as just plain folks. Lily Tomlin and Henry Gibson, both instantly recognizable in the mid-1970s from TV's hugely popular *Laugh-In* show, are perfectly cast as a gospel performer with a difficult home life and an egotistical singer thrilled with his own importance. Karen Black gives one of her best performances as the second-best rising star in the city. Keenan Wynn does the same as an aging man who can't quite figure out what he's doing in this out-of-control environment. Several of Altman's regular collaborators are also on hand, from Shelley Duvall and Bert Remsen to Keith Carradine and Gwen Welles.

It took a few years for Altman to follow up the promise of *Nashville* with a similarly ingenious offering. His next movie, the 1976 western *Buffalo Bill and the Indians, or, Sitting Bull's History Lesson,* failed with critics and audiences, partly because of tensions between his wish to make a "very historical" film while maintaining his artistic prerogative to "present history on an emotional level" with results that are "correct philosophically, if not actually," as he unhelpfully said at the time. The hallucinatory *3 Women* fared even worse, confusing all but his most perceptive admirers with its deliberately diffuse narrative and oneiric visual style.

Only with the 1978 comedy *A Wedding* did Altman further refine and expand the large-canvas ingenuity that *Nashville* brought to such impressive heights. Not that most reviewers or moviegoers saw it this way. *A Wedding* was greeted with disappointment even by Altman admirers, many of whom found it a botched effort to reproduce the *Nashville* magic rather than the adventurous step beyond *Nashville* it really attempted by doubling the number of characters, restricting the place and time to a single home on a single day, and telling its loosely structured story through a bold visual style that proceeds from dignified, almost ritualized order toward an increasing unpredictability that reflects the social and spiritual chaos lurking just beneath the all-too-human surface of the nuptial event it chronicles.

Altman's career as a theatrical filmmaker grew even shakier with *Quintet* and *A Perfect Couple* in 1979 and didn't start to improve until *Vincent & Theo* struck a positive critical chord in 1990, a full fifteen years after *Nashville* seemed to confirm him as a directorial genius. For most Altman loyalists, *Nashville* remains his greatest achievement, enhanced and enriched by its extraordinarily textured soundtrack, restlessly roving cameras, allusive images, and offbeat performances. Not to mention its canny blend of cynicism, sentimentality, tuneful songs, colorful clothes, and underlying affection (not the misanthropy some carping critics claim to find) for the odd mix of people it so imaginatively portrays. All this and lotsa laughs, too. *Nashville* is one sweet honey of a number.

The Night of the Hunter (1955)

by Peter Rainer

AS A TEENAGER IN THE LATE SIXTIES, I first saw *The Night of the Hunter* not inside the hushed precincts of a New York revival house but, instead, on commercial-interrupted television. Wedged between the hawking of wares, the film was still flabbergasting. Not only had I never seen another film like it; I had never *imagined* anything like it. Subsequently, in art houses and film societies, I gave myself an education in the great movies of the past; the film's visual influences—especially, and quite consciously, D. W. Griffith, silent German Expressionism, and *The Magnificent Ambersons*—became increasingly obvious. But one of the great paradoxes of *The Night of the Hunter,* which is about a deranged preacher's pursuit of two young runaways in the Depression-era Ohio River back country, is that it recalls so many other movies and yet is one-of-a-kind. Charles Laughton, whose only directorial effort this was, tapped into the feeling tone of Griffith's pastoralism; he slipped inside the sinister, chiaroscuroed lubricity of the early Lang and Murnau movies. He gave the aestheticism of those movies a new lease on life and a new appalling comic tone, too: Perhaps the most disturbing and original aspect of *The Night of the Hunter* is how deeply *funny*, in all senses of the word, this frightening story truly is. The movie can be seen not only as a kind of summation of what came before but also as a forerunner of what would come later, in the yin-yang tonal shifts and slapstick horror of such films as *The Manchurian Candidate* and *Lolita* and *Bonnie and Clyde* (which is also set in the Depression) and *Blue Velvet*. And so we have another paradox: The movie is both recipient of a tradition and precursor of a new one.

A big reason *The Night of the Hunter* seems so fresh—even though it was shunned by the public upon its release in 1955—is because it lacks the well-oiled sameness of mood that even the most notable Hollywood movies of its time had. Its crazy-quilt emotionalism is much closer to how we experience the world now. Still, the extreme mood swings in *The Night of the Hunter* have always disrupted audiences, even its most fervid appreciators. The movie is amazingly soulful and yet, unless you get the hang of it, it can be baffling. When I saw the film at an evening tribute for its star, Robert Mitchum, not long before he died, some in the audience howled in all the "wrong" places, convinced that the preacher's high dudgeon and Laughton's storybook symbolism were flubs or, even worse, put-ons. But the howls, if I'm not reading too much into them, also carried an undercurrent of discomfort and perplexity. In the air that evening was at least the grudging realization that *The Night of the Hunter* was no ordinary movie, bad or otherwise. Those members of the audience who think they're smarter than this film always end up outsmarting themselves.

If you were to show *The Night of the Hunter* to an audience of children, I suspect it might be more easily grasped by them than by adults. It mixes the horrid and the peculiar in a way that kids intuitively understand. The Davis Grubb novel on which the film is based is highflown hillbilly Gothic, but Laughton recognized at its core the glowing radium of a resonant tale. (The script is credited to James Agee, and certainly the film is an emanation of his lifelong obsessions with myth and poverty and Christianity and childhood abandonment, as well as his love for artists such as Griffith; nevertheless, Laughton reportedly pared down or discarded much of what Agee gave him and went back to the book, where most of the film's dialogue, and even some of its imagery, comes from, though virtually none of its gallows humor). No other American movie has so intimately resembled an elaborate children's fable *as imagined by a child*. The look of the film—shot by *Amberson's* Stanley Cortez—leaves the impression of something newly imprinted, as if everything were being seen through the eyes of a rapt cherub for the first time. There's an exaggerated purity to the imagery. The film's terrors are epically black, the enchantments are transcendant, starlit.

Mitchum's roving preacher Harry Powell is a false prophet whose falseness is instinctively sensed by children. (Most adults are taken in by him.) With L-O-V-E tattooed across his right fingers, and H-A-T-E tattooed across the left, Powell is a flagrant demon; his pocket switchblade slices through his trousers when he's aroused. (If there is such a thing as Old Testament Freudian, Harry Powell personifies it.) His nemesis is Miss Rachel, played by Lillian Gish, a mother hen who gathers up foundlings and runaways and brings them into her home. Rachel is as immaculate as Harry is depraved; she lives by the Scriptures and knows them well enough to recognize when they are being fouled.

And yet nothing is as simple as it seems in *The Night of the Hunter*. The visuals are conceived in tones of jet black and pearl, but the film is far from schematic: The darkness and the light are always bleeding into each other. Rachel abhors Harry, but hearing him in the night intoning "Leaning on the Everlasting Arms," she joins in the singing even though she sits inside her house with a rifle in her lap to defend her brood against him. Harry is a trickster who seems to have entered into the story in order to test the spiritual mettle of the pure-in-heart, and those not so pure-in-heart, too. If the film has any literary antecedent, it would not be Davis Grubb's book, but rather Melville's *The Confidence Man* or Twain's *The Man Who Corrupted Hadleyburg*, comic-horror texts with a sly, enraged comprehension of man's weakness and duplicity.

Serving time in a penitentiary at the start of the film, Harry finds himself sharing a cell with Ben Harper (Peter Graves), condemned to be executed for a robbery in which someone was killed. The stolen cash, as Ben tells it, was meant to feed his wife Willa (Shelley Winters) and their two children, Pearl (Sally Bruce), who is perhaps four or five, and John (Billy Chapin), who is around ten. Try as he might, Harry can't extract the hiding place of the money from Ben before he dies; but he makes it his business, when he's released from prison, to woo and marry Ben's widow. He loathes her wedding night advances and she loathes herself for having made them. The shy, dutiful Willa vows to become the chaste woman Harry wants her to be, but her face at the torch-lit revival meeting where she proclaims her sins has a hideous carnal ferocity to it. (Perhaps *this* is the woman Harry wants.) Harry mesmerizes Willa into a brief life of terrible piety before finally dispatching her. *The Night of the Hunter* expresses the sheer terror that men can hold for women, and women for men. Willa and Harry are riven by more than the secret of where the money is hidden; they're separated from each other by something insuperably elemental between the sexes, a difference, in the movie's terms, almost of species. Harry's murder of Willa occurs off camera, but we see its aftermath: her submerged body resting in a rusted open convertible at the bottom of the lake, her long hair streaming out in an undercurrent thick with delicate water grass. It's an image to place beside Shakespeare's description of the drowned Ophelia.

Harry loves the orotundity he gives his syllables; there's fire and brimstone in the breath. When John and Pearl, stolen cash in tow, break away from him and race for the river, the low, strangly yowl he lets out is both shockingly funny and hair-raising—a bogeyman's aria. The children's flight from Harry, which ends with their rescue by Rachel, is one of the most supernally eerie sequences ever filmed. (Walter Schumann's buoyant, infernal score sets the movie's mood throughout.) The toylike boat that carries them along the moonlit Ohio is framed in the foreground by a succession of immense, looming close-ups of frogs and caged birds and spider webs and a pair of shivering rabbits. This is the extended sequence that makes some audiences groan, perhaps because it is so grandiloquently *obvious;* but I think its greatness lies precisely in its obviousness. Who, except curdled cynics, would reject the grandeur that comes from such an enhanced symbolism, which is no different in kind or in depth of lyric feeling from a fearful Bible story or a Grimm's fairy tale?

Mitchum had his greatest role in *The Night of the Hunter,* and it's his finest performance. His cunning and his torpor, which always carried a sadistic, sensual edge, achieve here a kind of apotheosis. He's more malevolently erotic in this film, with its storybook homilies and bejeweled night skies, than in any of his hothouse melodramas. Sex—the awareness of the temptations it can bring—etches through the imagery; it's what is held back and denied and still corrodes the screen. But it is the hatred of sex—Harry's hatred—that is the true corrosive in this film. He's twisted by his own abhorrence, and yet his writhings are a form of self-stimulation. Harry's consmanship works so well (for a time) with Willa and her townspeople because, in their own way, they are just as aghast as Harry is at the pleasures of the flesh—and just as drawn to them, too. The reason Harry has made such a success of himself is because he shows up in a community ready-made for his handiwork.

Thus, the pastoralism of the Griffith films, which this town evokes, is undercut by Laughton even as it is being commemorated. He draws out the hysteria that was always present just below the surface of these sanctified rural tableaux. (The hysteria comes from fearing the loss of innocence.) It makes poetic sense that Laughton would cast Lillian Gish in *The Night of the Hunter,* not only because she was Griffith's greatest actress but also because, in such films as *Way Down East* and *Broken Blossoms* and *Orphans of the Storm,* she expressed both the luminescence of her virginal heroines and also their affrighted souls. In *The Night of the Hunter,* Rachel may be the savior of these orphans of the storm, but there is also the suggestion of a life once lived apart from the goodness she engenders. (She speaks cryptically of her estrangement from her son.) Rachel is a worthy adversary for Harry because, one feels, her purity has already been tested. She has seen enough of life to account for the Harry Powells of the world, while Harry has no real conception of purity except as something he must annihilate. And so, in a sense, the preacher is the true innocent in *The Night of the Hunter;* the L-O-V-E and H-A-T-E spelled out across his fingers represent the breadth of his existence. He's untainted by complexity. Rachel, for all her motherly chipperiness, sees things whole. The waifs she raises are her bulwark against wickedness; she herself is a kind of idealized waif, gifted with worldly wisdom. (Has any actress ever looked more youthfully beautiful in old age than Lillian Gish?) Rachel proclaims that children are man at his strongest, that they will abide and endure. It's an affirmation that is also a plea. She's soliciting the fates for a reprieve from horror. *The Night of the Hunter* is a fable that passes from darkness to light, but we are left in no doubt that the wolf is forever at the door.

Night of the Living Dead (1968)

by Kevin Thomas

AFTER NEARLY FOUR DECADES of reviewing films for the *Los Angeles Times*, I still regard George Romero's original version of *Night of the Living Dead* as the scariest movie I have ever seen. Romero made two nifty sequels, a not-bad *Living Dead* remake and the overly long but imaginative *Knightriders,* treating bikers as medieval knights and starring Ed Harris, but nothing he has ever done has had the impact of his first feature.

I saw it under ideal conditions: without any idea at all of what I would be seeing, and in my favorite theater of all time.

Back in the 1960s double features were still in fashion, and our downtown movie palaces on South Broadway, their grandeur admittedly fading, were nonetheless all operating, as were some smaller theaters dating back to the teens. It was a time when exploitation pictures were in full swing, most of them opening without previews. Many movies were still opening on Wednesday, which meant reviews would run Friday; soon studios and distributors would realize that if they opened on Friday they could avoid negative reviews for unpreviewed films on the very day when people would be deciding what movie they want to see over the weekend.

I have been going to the Los Angeles Theater, an elegant faux Versailles pile now closed except for special events, as far back as I can remember, and that's where I went to catch *Night of the Living Dead,* booked with *Dr. Who and the Dalaks,* a mere four blocks from the paper. As it turns out I was one of the first to see what became a near-instant horror classic. This is what I wrote for the Friday, January 10, 1969, edition of the *Los Angeles Times:*

> *Night of the Living Dead* and *Dr. Who and the Daleks* prove you can no more judge movies by their titles and ad campaigns than you can books by their covers.
>
> The first is a genuinely scary little horror picture for adults and the second, a diverting science fiction fantasy for all ages. Both were made with far more imagination than money. For once an exploitation double bill gives the customer his money's worth.
>
> The initial venture of Pittsburgh's Image Ten Productions, *Night of the Living Dead* wrings maximum effects from an absolute minimum of means.
>
> Virtually the whole film takes place in a Western Pennsylvania farmhouse in which a group of people have sought refuge from the rapidly-multiplying legions of the "living dead," those who have recently died only to come alive minutes later as remorseless flesh-eating ghouls. Apparently they have been revived by radiation from a satellite that exploded during a probe of the planet Venus. They can be stopped only by a bullet through the brain or by being consumed by fire.
>
> Inside the farmhouse are an assortment of seven people, organized by a comparatively calm and resourceful Negro (Duane Jones). From TV and radio they learn the eastern third of the United States is overrun by the living dead. Civil defense units are mobilizing, however. Will help arrive in time? Will these seven pull together or let themselves be defeated by internal dissent?

From this classically simple situation director George A. Romero and writer John A. Russo build an amazing amount of suspense. Romero keeps things constantly happening and directs with limitless energy. Indeed, countless far more ambitious movies could benefit from such drive and vitality. Although too gruesome for the kiddies, Night of the Living Dead is taut and uncompromising, ending on a note of bitter irony. Performances are adequate and often better, especially in the case of Jones, who clearly has what it takes to go on to bigger things.

Nosferatu (1922)

by Andy Klein

F. W. MURNAU'S 1922 *Nosferatu: A Symphony of Horrors* is not only a glorious film; it also stands as a cinema "first" on several counts, not all of them so glorious. It was arguably the first great monster film and the first film to see the power in blending the expressionistic style of *The Cabinet of Dr. Caligari* with more naturalistic exteriors; it was—despite some evidence of a slightly earlier, now lost Hungarian version—probably the first film adaptation of Bram Stoker's *Dracula*; and, as a result, it was also the center of the first significant copyright infringement case in the history of cinema.

The facts are simple: Murnau and his collaborators—screenwriter Henrik Galeen and producer-designer Albin Grau—were making a low-budget independent film and could scarcely afford to negotiate for the rights to one of the most popular novels of the time. Since international copyright law—which, even today, is a source of contention among politically disparate countries—was in its infancy, the filmmakers simply changed the names of Stoker's characters and abridged and altered the book's story.

Nonetheless, the similarities are so numerous and undeniable that Stoker's widow, Florence, was able to have the film suppressed and spent most of the 1920s trying to ensure that the negative and all prints were destroyed. While Mrs. Stoker obviously had a legitimate moral case, film historians can only be grateful that her zeal was only partly rewarded: she nearly managed to eradicate a film that is both a masterpiece and a key film in the career of one of the medium's greatest artists . . . *and* that had huge importance in the development of modern film style. (Sadly, she was successful enough that even the best prints of *Nosferatu* leave much to be desired.)

In Murnau's version, Dracula is renamed Orlok, Jonathan Harker is Thomas Hutter, Van Helsing becomes Bulwer, and Renfield (the most changed major character) is reincarnated as Knock, whom we first see as Hutter's employer, before his thrall to Orlok causes him to be locked up in a madhouse. The London setting is changed to Wisborg, Germany; and the time is moved back nearly fifty years, to 1838, the year of a great plague in Germany.

Unlike *Caligari*—which took place in a wholly distorted, artificial milieu—*Nosferatu* starts out full of sweetness and light, with only hints of some subterranean evil. Murnau begins with a daytime shot of prosperous Wisborg, then shows us a few moments in and around the Hutter home, where Thomas (Gustav von Wangenheim) picks a few flowers for his wife, Ellen (Greta Schröder).

Ellen's reaction is the first hint of something amiss in their marriage: "Why did you have to kill all those poor flowers?" she asks. Without ever rubbing our noses in it, Murnau drops more hints that this seemingly sweet, idyllic marriage is deeply flawed: Thomas is a naive, grinning goofball, while Ellen seems brooding and troubled. It is implied much later in the film that their marriage is sexless and that Ellen's discontent may be related to her husband being essentially an overgrown preadolescent.

Thomas works for a realtor, Knock (Alexander Granach), who sends him to Carpathia—"the land of thieves and phantoms," as Thomas excitedly tells his wife—to sell a neighboring house to the mysterious Count Orlok (Max Schreck). Again there are hints of something ugly brewing: Murnau shoots Knock as devious, with some ulterior objective; the realtor reads a letter from Orlok that is written in no identifiable human language but rather in some combination of codes and diagrams.

As Thomas proceeds toward Orlok's castle, he heads from the natural world into the supernatural—and Murnau takes us from open air through sinister woods and then into the darkness of Orlok's lair. With the first appearance of the vampire, this stylistic shift toward expressionism becomes complete.

Much has been said about Schreck's performance and makeup, all of it deserved. Both in looks and manner, he was simply the most horrifying figure to have appeared on the screen to that time. Murnau creates revulsion not merely through Schreck's makeup, but the inhuman stiffness of his movements and the sexual implications of his approaches to Thomas and, by proxy, to Ellen.

As soon as the vampire appears on screen, Murnau changes the film's editing style, as well as his visual style: during the middle third, he crosscuts between Ellen, back in Wisborg, and Orlok and Thomas in Carpathia. Cleverly, the crosscutting suggests that Ellen has a stronger fateful bond with Orlok than with her husband. As Thomas and Orlok both race toward Wisborg, she keeps talking about "his" approach: her friends assume she means Thomas, but we know she is speaking at least as much of Orlok.

Indeed, Orlok and Thomas are exact opposites or, in Freudian terms, two halves of the same being. Orlok, immediately upon getting to Wisborg, manages to do what Thomas apparently never has during his marriage: he spends the night in bed with Ellen, in an embrace that is sexual on every level but the surface. Had Thomas had any sort of mature sexual component to his personality, perhaps Ellen wouldn't have been so susceptible to Orlok's power; but his infantile nature means that Ellen's discovery of sexuality is with a creature who represents unmediated id, so out of balance that the encounter is lethal.

Like most expressionist films, *Nosferatu* begs for a Freudian analysis, which, given the period and the culture, is not at all surprising. But there are other levels on which the film works—at least one of which leaves a bad taste in the mouth.

While I am not vaguely suggesting conscious anti-Semitism on Murnau's part, it is hard to watch the film today, through the lens of subsequent events, without making the connection to the next two decades of German history: the culture within which Murnau was working was the same culture that was about to grow mad with long-brewing racial hatred. As Orlok, Schreck is fitted with the same huge hooked nose and grasping talons that have traditionally been associated with Shylock and Fagin. He lives off the blood of others, much as Jews were believed to drink the blood of Christian babies. He and Knock communicate in a strange secret written language that is impossible for the rest of the citizenry to understand.

Worse yet, Knock and Orlok both seem to be part of some secret, monied cabal, whose purpose is to pollute, corrupt, and control the sleepy, unsuspecting populace. Orlok's arrival is accompanied by the plague; and he himself is associated visually with vermin.

It would not take much—no more than the rewriting of a few title cards, substituting the word "Jew" for "vampire"—to turn *Nosferatu* into a perfect Nazi-era propaganda drama. (The stereotypes are specific enough that the same exercise will not work with any other group.) In Fritz Hippler's notorious 1940 Nazi "documentary" *The Eternal Jew*, the shots that link Jews to swarming rats could easily have been lifted straight from *Nosferatu*.

Again, this doesn't mean that Murnau was making an anti-Semitic film any more than all Hollywood filmmakers throughout the 1930s and 1940s, working within a culture filled with now-rejected racist stereotypes, were making explicitly racist films. There is no trace of anti-Semitism elsewhere in Murnau's work; it is reasonable to assume that he was simply using the dominant cultural language of his time and place. Indeed, while Murnau himself is known to have been gay, he nonetheless uses the vampire's ambiguous sexuality—the distaste that is invoked by his approach to Thomas—to creep out his audience.

Still, *Nosferatu* works on some much more universal level than all this suggests. There is a rather large cultural gap between Germany in the 1920s and the United States eighty years later; yet *Nosferatu* has maintained much of its power to shock and repulse us. While modern audiences may laugh at the "state-of-the-art" special effects—Murnau used negative images, stop-motion, double exposures, and every other trick technically available to him—many of them still work, despite our years of seeing them imitated. Together with Schreck's performance, the sinister visual style, and the disorientingly distorted time scheme, they have enabled *Nosferatu* to remain "undead" after all this time.

Los Olvidados (1950)

by Rob Nelson

THE MEAN OLDER SIBLING OF EVERY HELL-is-for-children shocker from *Pixote* to *Kids* and *Ratcatcher*, Luis Buñuel's *Los Olvidados* came into the world in 1950 bullying its own elders—the liberal-humanist batch of Italian neorealist weepers such as *Shoeshine* and *Bicycle Thief.* "I tried to expose the wretched condition of the poor in real terms," claimed Buñuel, "because I loathe the films that make the poor romantic and sweet." So where De Sica's put-upon street urchins were at least allowed to look adorable (or adoptable) while staring out from behind bars or trudging through the rain, the pitiless Mexico City gutter punks of *Los Olvidados* (a.k.a. *The Young and the Damned*)—who delight in literally pulling the ground out from under a legless man and robbing the blind—would hardly have seemed of the same species to most viewers of the time.

Pressing the point, Buñuel introduces his gang of little terrors playing bullfight in a vacant lot, his camera assuming the p.o.v. of a snorting young "bull" as it charges past the matador's cape—an early hint that this film "solely based in real life" (per the printed prologue) will be not only more bestial than its predecessors, but a bit more subjective. "Neorealist reality is incomplete, conventional, and above all rational," Buñuel declared during a lecture at the University of Mexico in 1953. "The poetry, the mystery, all that completes and enlarges tangible reality, is utterly lacking." Suffice it to say that *Los Olvidados* rediscovers those elements with a vengeance, particularly in the "Grand Guignol" dream sequence that ruptures the film's ostensible objectivity at the half-hour mark, as thirteen-year-old Pedro imagines his mother offering him a glistening slab of raw meat, which is subsequently snatched away by the gang leader Jaibo. Mocking neorealism's bourgeois appeal, Buñuel had hoped to lend a certain "mystery" even to the characters' waking hours, at one point planning to place an incongruous top hat in the poor mother's kitchen and a 100-piece orchestra on the scaffolding of a building under construction.

Alas, there was only so much the surrealist maker of *Un chien andalou* and *L'age d'or* could get away with here. Shot on the cheap for 450,000 pesos (about $50,000) in a mere twenty-one days, *Los Olvidados* was Buñuel's third Mexican film for European producer Oscar Dancigers, who'd revived the Spanish director's career after a fifteen-year hiatus with a pair of frivolous mainstream comedies, the second of which had apparently made enough money to justify an impossibly bleak film inspired by newspaper reports of Mexico City slum kids. Earning 18,000 pesos for the effort (which sounds like a pittance until you consider that it's 350 times more than his young and damned hold at their wealthiest moment), Buñuel wore his shabbiest clothes while touring the city's *barrios bajos* for several months prior to shooting, talking to psychiatrists about the horrors of juvenile poverty and observing them first hand.

"All [the] characters are real," boasts the movie's prologue. And so they may be, although, in deference to censors, the director was obliged to suggest that they weren't only Mexican. Whether it was Buñuel's subtly satiric idea or Dancigers's last-minute attempt at diluting a very bitter pill (reports vary), the documentary opener, comprising stock footage of New York, Paris, and London skylines, makes the point that Mexico City's "pits of misery" are part of a "universal truth"—lest anyone mistake the movie's searing vision for a specific one. And yet, in other ways, *Los Olvidados* offers itself as a distinctly Mexican allegory. Buñuel scholar Peter William Evans has interpreted the character of Li'l Eyes, a teary Indian orphan in a poncho and sombrero, as symbolizing the defeat of socialism under president Lazaro Cárdenas, whose plan to distribute land to Mexican Indians was reversed in the 1940s. And the movie's blind street musician Don Carmelo—whom the initially gentle Li'l Eyes briefly considers bashing on the head with a boulder-sized block of rubble—is a clear stand-in for right-wing dictator Porfirio Díaz, whose merciless views of law enforcement the blind man can't see clearly but espouses nonetheless.

Indeed, there's a sense in which the musician plays to the sort of crowd who'd prefer to see Buñuel's critique of status quo complacency as just another social-problem melodrama. "Laugh," Don Carmelo instructs his audience, "but in [Diaz's] times, there was more respect, and a good woman stayed at home . . . ."

That such sexism is voiced by an increasingly ignoble figure (this "poor blind man," per Buñuelian subversion, turns out to be a pedophilic lecher) helps distance the director from his film's own questionable characterization of women. The preponderance of milk imagery accentuates the need of *los olvidados* for both nourishment and human kindness, while Pedro, the movie's good-boy-gone-bad-by-association, is burdened with a mother who mostly refuses to supply either. Even in a film of overwhelming cynicism (or "realism," as you prefer), Mom doesn't come off well: Buñuel's nasty cut from the mother's sexual propositioning of her son's friend to a shot of dress-wearing dogs dancing a jig for spare change seems to equate one bitch's carnival act with another's. And yet the mother is no less a victim than her son: Turns out the reason she finds it so hard to love Pedro is that he was the product of rape.

No wonder the film's documentary prelude vows to leave "the solutions to these problems in the hands of the progressive forces of our times." Within the movie itself, every "progressive" effort fails grotesquely, including that of the smug authoritarian who presides over the "school"—more like a youth slave-labor camp, in fact—where Pedro is sent by the juvenile court. Although the film's radical pessimism was acclaimed at Cannes, where Buñuel took both the best director prize and the International Critics' Award (and where the poet Octavio Paz stood outside the Palais des Festivals distributing copies of his admiring essay), it earned a more backhanded compliment in the movie's native land. *Los Olvidados* opened on a Thursday in Mexico City and closed just two days later in the wake of protests from national labor union officials who demanded the filmmaker's expulsion from the country. Cowriter Pedro de Urdemalas, who supplied some of the boys' colorful slang, refused to have his name appear in the credits. In his autobiography, *My Last Sigh*, Buñuel recalls poet Léon Felipe's wife Berta attacking him "nails first" after a private screening in Mexico, exclaiming that his movie was a crime against the state.

At the other extreme, the legendary French critic André Bazin called *Los Olvidados* "a film of love." Indeed, what more gracious gift could Buñuel give to his villain Jaibo than the movie's final shot of subjective surreality? As the gang leader lies dying from a policeman's bullet (while the Diaz surrogate crows, "One less! One less!"), his fevered hallucination of being chased by a rabid dog into a black hole—the image of a child at play in hell—conjures instant sympathy for the devil. Nevertheless, even Buñuel's friend, the Marxist critic Georges Sadoul, found the film to be overly pessimistic. "People will be disgusted with their own humanity" is how Sadoul summarized his initial reaction in the preface to the director's published script of *Viridiana*. "They'll see atomic annihilation as a blessing." Buñuel not only objected to his friend's interpretation but offered that, if Sadoul could prove his point, the filmmaker would sever the part of his anatomy that "separates a bull from an ox." *Los Olvidados* may be a film of love, yes, but it's also the work of a grown tough guy.

On the Waterfront (1954)

by Robert Sklar

MORE THAN MOST MOVIES, *On the Waterfront* carries the almost unbearable weight of its era's struggles and the personal histories of its makers. The 1954 Academy Award best picture has had as many detractors as admirers over the years. Someday the film may be appreciated apart from painful memories and bitter recriminations, but that moment has not yet arrived.

The film clearly offers a great deal to appreciate. Its exposé of the gangster-ridden longshoremen's unions on the New York–New Jersey docks was a rare instance of social problem cinema in a safe, conformist decade. With performers trained in the intense, psychologically based style of New York's Actors Studio, it stands as perhaps the single most powerful expression of ensemble Method acting in Hollywood movies. And it's a striking example of motion picture artistry achieved through the collaborative talents of many hands.

Hollywood immediately recognized all these attributes. The movie community gave *On the Waterfront* an unprecedented twelve Academy Award nominations and voted the film eight Oscars. Elia Kazan won as best director, Marlon Brando as best actor, and Eva Marie Saint as best supporting actress. Budd Schulberg took the award for his story and screenplay, and additional Oscars were claimed for cinematography, art direction, and editing. The nonwinning nominees were just as distinguished—Leonard Bernstein for musical score and a remarkable trio of players nominated in the supporting actor category, Lee J. Cobb, Karl Malden, and Rod Steiger.

But nearly everyone recognized at the time that these awards were political as well as artistic. Hollywood had been suffering the traumas caused by years of hearings by the House Committee on Un-American Activities (HUAC) investigating "communist infiltration" of the movie industry. Witnesses had been forced to "name names"—to inform on others—or face blacklisting. Informers saved their careers but lost lifelong friendships, even marriages. The hearings were a humiliating charade, since HUAC and the FBI already knew every name the informers gave up.

Then came *On the Waterfront,* with its bold assertion that informing was an act of moral heroism. When he finally agrees to testify against corrupt union boss Johnny Friendly, Brando's character Terry Malloy can feel that he is no ratfink squealer but a vital cog in the defense of democracy against tyranny. By cheering *On the Waterfront* Hollywood persuaded itself for a brief moment that the destructive debacle of the hearings marked a triumph of patriotic service.

Few were unaware of what was also personally at stake in the film. Director Kazan, son of Greek immigrants, had testified before HUAC and named names. So too had screenwriter Schulberg, son of one of early Hollywood's Jewish moguls. A third informer among the film's principals was the actor who played Johnny Friendly, Lee J. Cobb.

Cobb later regretted his testimony, saying he gave in because he was ill and broke. But Schulberg and Kazan have never wavered in defending their stance. In his 1988 autobiography, *Elia Kazan: A Life,* the director wrote, "When Brando, at the end, yells at Lee Cobb, the mob boss, 'I'm glad what I done—you hear me?— glad what I done!' that was me saying, with identical heat, that I was glad I'd testified as I had."

Development on a waterfront film began long before it turned into a justification for HUAC informers. The original collaboration was between Kazan and playwright Arthur Miller, who wrote a screenplay, *The Hook,* based on the murder of a union reformer on Brooklyn's Red Hook docks. The Columbia studio was interested in the project but, in the early 1950s political climate, wanted a stronger anticommunist slant. Miller withdrew his script; Kazan later felt that his HUAC subpoena may have come as retaliation. Their friendship ended for a decade. (When Miller was called to testify in 1956 he refused to inform on others and was cited for contempt of Congress, but he got off with a small fine and a suspended sentence.)

Schulberg had also been working on a script based on a series of newspaper articles on waterfront corruption. After he and Kazan had gone through their HUAC ordeals, the two men got together. Walking the docks for further research, Schulberg discovered a "waterfront priest" who became the character Father Barry (portrayed by Karl Malden) and gave the narrative its aura of religious redemption and righteousness. Producer Sam Spiegel backed the project, Brando joined in, and *On the Waterfront* was on the way to its ambiguous place in movie history.

While it's impossible to separate the film from its own conflicted past, *On the Waterfront* still provides many cinematic pleasures. The three least well known of the Oscar winners made indispensable contributions. Art Director Richard Day created the atmosphere of the docks and their working-class urban neighborhoods with evocative realism. Boris Kaufman, a Russian Jewish émigré and younger brother of famed Soviet documentarian Dziga Vertov (whose original name was Denis Kaufman), photographed these settings in stark black-and-white deep-focus cinematography. Editor Gene Milford shaped a classic mix of close-ups and long shots.

Above all the film is a triumph of performance. Few scenes in American film history are more famous than the sequence in the back of a taxi with Brando's Terry and Rod Steiger as his older brother Charlie. Charlie, who works for the corrupt union, has been sent to dissuade Terry from informing. During their conversation Terry, a former boxer, realizes that Charlie had made him throw a fight that destroyed his career. "I could've been a contender," Terry cries in anguish. He rejects the demand, an act that leads directly to Charlie's murder by the mob. This cruel retribution cancels out the brothers' mutual betrayals and turns Terry's informing into an act of private revenge as much as of civic duty.

Critics continue to debate whether *On the Waterfront* conveys democratic values or an image of dockworkers who are passive followers of whoever leads them—the tyrannical boss or the informer. Is it a true exposé or one that leaves the actual holders of corrupt power (briefly glimpsed in a quick shot of "Mr. Upstairs" during Terry's testimony) untouched? If nothing else, *On the Waterfront* is a monument to the artistic aspirations and the political compromises of its time.

Open City (1945)

by Peter Brunette

WHILE CERTAINLY ROBERTO ROSSELLINI'S best-known film, and the film that brought him and the Italian industry international fame in 1945, *Open City* is in many ways his least typical. This film that was quickly to be seen as a direct challenge to the conventional cinema of the time—read, Hollywood cinema—is, in fact, one of the often highly experimental director's most conventional efforts, at least in terms of its narrative and dramatic structures.

The most probable explanation for this is that, for the first time, Rossellini's story, the just-ended German occupation of Rome, was so powerful, and so demanded to be told, that a driving narrative impulse pushed aside all other aesthetic considerations. Reality itself had become so dramatic that the director realized, perhaps, that the best course was simply to try to get it all down on film, and in the most straightforward and traditional manner possible.

The shooting of *Open City* was carried out in terrible conditions, when the occupying German troops had barely left Rome; the producers were all gone, the studios at Cinecittà were devastated, and in a country that was on the verge of social and economic collapse, there was little money available for something as frivolous and nonessential as a movie. It was these very hardships, of course, that forced Rossellini to break the rules by filming in the war-torn streets, thus giving the film its unique, still powerfully gritty look. And the fact that the director had to cadge bits of 35mm films from street photographers is precisely what gave the images the startling authenticity of a newsreel.

The film's focus is on Don Pietro (Aldo Fabrizi), a priest who works with the anti-Nazi underground. One of his parishioners, Pina (Anna Magnani, in the greatest role of her life), thinks only of protecting her young son and of her forthcoming marriage to Francesco, another partisan, who, with the aid of Don Pietro, is trying to hide Manfredi (Marcello Pagliero), an important figure in the Resistance. By the end of the film, all but one of these figures will be dead, innocent victims of the Nazis.

Conventional narrative elements abound, such as the rather obvious slapstick involved when an Austrian deserter frightens us and Don Pietro by pulling out his gun, when he means only to deliver a message rolled up in an ammunition cartridge. A partisan attack to liberate a truck full of prisoners resides clearly in the action-film category, though it is accomplished with a paucity of means that paradoxically causes it to be more convincing than a well-bankrolled Hollywood version would have been. Similarly, the script also manages to stay on the easy level of heroism and cowardice, and these simple notions, the staple of Hollywood westerns, are never for a moment seriously interrogated.

But however we might want to chastise Rossellini for his embrace of conventional narrative in this film—if we do—it is clear that he does it very well indeed. There is no slack, no narrative fat. All of the characters are tightly intertwined for maximum efficiency, and the result is a complex and thickly populated fresco of history and desire. Exposition is accomplished instantly, in bold, swift strokes, and we are plunged into the narrative at a gallop from the first minute of the film, when Nazi troops come looking for Manfredi. Comic and tragic moods alternate throughout in an invigorating and emotionally involving way, each providing a counterpoint to the other. Individual scenes are also exquisitely accomplished.

Thus, the sequence in which Pina is shot down as she runs after the Nazi truck carrying her fiancé Francesco is one of the most brilliantly affecting moments in all film. Pushed up against the wall with the other women, she seems out of harm's way, so her suicidal outburst is even more shocking when it comes.

One of the most historically interesting themes of *Open City* is its exploration of Nazism as corruption. To us in the twenty-first century, it may seem self-evident, but in 1944 humanists like Rossellini were still trying to come to grips with the meaning of the Nazi phenomenon. The evil Major Bergmann tortures and murders in the name of the destiny of the Third Reich. His cohort, Ingrid, is a lesbian; for Rossellini, sexual inversion is the sign par excellence for decadence, as in his portrait of the homosexual Nazi teacher from *Germany, Year Zero,* made two years later.

Despite Rossellini's earlier anticommunist, nationalistic films, the vehemence of his outrage against the Nazis in *Open City* is genuine, and it causes him to portray the struggle between good and evil in clear, uncomplicated, black-and-white terms—for the last time in his career. But this vehemence also serves to underline the fact that the film takes it very easy indeed on the Italian fascists. One of the difficulties for a non-Italian audience in watching *Open City* is visually distinguishing the fascists from the Nazis, and thus Rossellini's subtle exculpation may be missed. Throughout the film, in fact, the Nazis are seen as the evil ones, the actively malevolent force; the fascists and other Italian collaborators are portrayed in the humiliating, but decidedly less culpable, role of lackey. The Nazis' obvious hatred of the feckless Italians is itself thematized and conveniently serves as one more example of Nazi evil. At the end of the film, when Don Pietro is to be executed, the Italian firing squad, respecting the cloth—unlike the barbarous Nazis—wavers and ends up shooting harmlessly into the ground and it is the Nazi officer who finally has to kill the priest with his pistol. Throughout the film the Italian collaborators, portrayed as having managed to retain their deepest human values in spite of everything, themselves come to be seen as much the Nazis' victims as any other group, therefore enjoying our sympathy.

But clearly, the most important—and most complicated—theme of *Open City* concerns the nature of the partnership formed to combat Nazi corruption (if not in historical actuality, at least in Rossellinian wish-fulfillment), that between the communists and the Catholic Church. This was no mean trick for the director, considering that his previous picture, *L'uomo dalla croce* (1943), had posed them as natural, bitter enemies. But he does manage, in a remarkable balancing act, to portray them both favorably, primarily because of the handy presence of a common enemy whose horribleness everyone could agree on. For one thing,

Rossellini is acknowledging the historical fact that no matter what one personally felt concerning its politics, in effect, the Communist Party *was* the Resistance, while other political groups preferred to sit it out.

Bergmann's obsessive questioning of priest at the end of the film provides the chance to offer a new rationale for accepting the communists. Bergmann shouts that Manfredi is "a subversive, an atheist, an enemy of yours!" and Don Pietro calmly, if rather vaguely, replies: "I am a Catholic priest and I believe that a man who fights for justice and liberty walks in the pathways of the Lord—and the pathways of the Lord are infinite." Hardly a ringing endorsement, as not a few Marxist critics have pointed out, but in terms of the emotion projected at that moment on the screen, it is certainly convincing. Further connections between the communists and Catholics are given a visual palpability. For example, many of the shots of Manfredi being tortured strongly suggest the bruised and battered Savior of Christian iconography. In one shot, his arms are even pinned up against the wall, in an obvious reference to Christ's crucifixion..

Nevertheless, while the Catholic and communist are, ostensibly, on the same footing, at least in terms of their moral rectitude, the entire film is seen in Catholic, or Christian, terms. Don Pietro is the moral lens through which we are meant to regard the various forms of iniquity on display. The communist partisan Manfredi, in other words, is not really given any thematically important dialogue, and the heavily dramatic form of the story insists that his encounter with his Nazi tormentor, Bergmann, takes place not on the level of ideas but rather on the level of action-film machismo—not is he right, but can be withstand torture? The only character who does get to express the presumably communist version of things is Pina's fiancé Francesco, in his wistful and captivating talk about the future as he sits with Pina on the stairs in front of his apartment. Here again, however, his desire for freedom and hope in the future are expressed in lovely but vague and, historically and politically speaking, utterly unrealizable terms.

Most conflicting interpretations of the film's ultimate meaning center visually around its final images. As Don Pietro is about to be executed, he hears the young boys whistling as a signal of their support. He is shot, and the last image of the film shows the boys, weary but supporting each other, trudging down a hill back toward the center of town. The Roman skyline, dominated by the dome of St. Peter's, forms the background of the shot as the film ends. The sequence is clearly symbolic, but of what? Some Italian critics have chosen to emphasize the dome, insisting that only in the church is there hope for the future of Italy. But the dome is seen firmly in its context of the entire city of Rome, just as the church is an important part of Italian society, but hardly everything. Some have chosen to see the ending as utterly pessimistic, full of nothing but death and destruction, while others have emphasized the fact that the boys, symbols of Italy's future even though crippled and depressed, are at least supporting one another down the hill. One mark of the film's richness is that this question will never be definitively answered.

When *Open City* was first screened for prospective domestic distributors there was general dismay over what was perceived, in the context of the dominant Hollywood production values of the time, as the utter amateurishness of the film-making. Only after being received triumphantly the following year in France and the United States (when the American critic James Agee first saw it, he wrote in *The Nation* that he was so moved by the experience that he wouldn't be able to review the film for another three or four weeks!) that it was given a second chance in Italy. Since that time, of course, it has come to be seen by most Italian critics as the most important film ever made in that country and, by critics around the world, as one of the greatest films in the history of the medium. Its power remains undiminished to this day.

The Palm Beach Story (1942)

by David Ansen

SMASHING SUCCESS AND ABJECT FAILURE—these are the poles of Preston Sturges's mile-a-minute comedies. (And the poles, it later turned out, of his own riches-to-rags career). A penniless bum can rise to be the governor of Illinois (*The Great McGinty*). A hapless 4F reject becomes a war hero (*Hail the Conquering Hero*). A disgraced small-town girl and her nerdy boyfriend become international celebrities when she gives birth to sextuplets (*The Miracle of Morgan's Creek*). And what goes up can just as easily come down in flames: In *Sullivan's Travels,* a rich and famous movie director is arrested and forced into hard labor. In *The Sin of Harold Dibblebock,* a college football hero ends up a troll in a dusty, dead-end office. Sturges's satirical stomping ground is All or Nothing America, whose God is the Dollar, whose conscience (when it has one) is Puritan, whose favorite myth is Horatio Alger.

Sturges had an acute comic sense of the fluidity of American society, which bestows fortune and fame in a fickled frenzy. Nowhere is this more apparent than in *The Palm Beach Story,* as screwy a screwball romantic comedy as Hollywood ever produced. Its protagonists, Tom (Joel McCrea) and Gerry (Claudette Cobert) are a Park Avenue couple fallen on hard times. The rent is overdue, their marriage is on the rocks . . . and salvation comes in the form of the funniest and most unlikely *deus ex machina* a screenwriter has dared devise. He's a deaf, cantankerous old millionaire who calls himself The Weenie King (he's made his fortune in sausages), and he's sniffing around Tom and Gerry's apartment, considering whether to rent it, when he bumps into Gerry in the bathroom, takes a shine to her, listens to her woes, and on the spur of the fairytale moment bestows upon her $700, solving the couple's immediate economic problems and setting Sturges's plot into nonstop motion.

The gesture is so blithely arbitrary you can't help but think Sturges is making fun of the very concept of the plot device. He is letting us know from the get-go that *The Palm Beach Story* is constructed out of pure artifice. His genius is in transforming that artificiality into delirious fun. I wouldn't necessarily say that this farce is Sturges's greatest film—*The Lady Eve* touches deeper, more elegant chords; *Morgan's Creek* is more ferociously audacious; *Sullivan's Travels* is the more heartfelt—but no Sturges comedy makes me laugh harder. This movie, written on the eve of America's entry into World War II and released in the dark hours of 1942, is solely dedicated to the pleasure principle. All rules of logic and verisimilitude are cheerfully disrespected. He didn't name his couple Tom and Gerry for nothing: the reality of this tale is as elastic as a cartoon.

Its subject, however, is primal American stuff—sex (which Sturges calls "Topic A") and money. Indeed, money informs just about every scene in the movie. Colbert's heroine, who instigates the breakup, is fed up with living on the edge. She thinks she's holding her inventor husband back, a "milestone" around his neck ("millstone" he corrects her). She wants to use her feminine wiles to raise money for his visionary project—an airport suspended by steel cables that floats atop a city—but Tom's male pride won't let her. So she takes matters into her own extremely competent hands, rushing off to Palm Beach to get a divorce and, in that playground of the rich, to meet a millionaire who can both finance Tom's dream project and her own future. "You have no idea what a long-legged gal can do without doing anything," Gerry tells the chagrined Tom.

Arriving at Penn Station with no money, no ticket, and no luggage (having wrangled a free taxi ride from an admiring cabdriver), Gerry immediately proves her point when she is taken under wing by the eleven members of the Ale and Quail Club, who invite her aboard the train as their "mascot." Ah, the Ale and Quail Club! These dissolute and disorderly millionaires, who drunkenly turn the train ride into a chaotic hunting party complete with howling dogs and blazing shotguns, are invariably the first thing anyone thinks of when *The Palm Beach Story* is mentioned. Anarchic, overgrown boys, they are portrayed by members of the Sturges stock company of brilliantly eccentric character actors, including William Demarest, Robert Warwick, Chester Conklin, Rosco Ates, Jimmy Conlin, and Arthur Stuart Hull as the club's president, a man with a surreal hiccup. Undoubtedly one of the slapstick summits of 1930s and 1940s comedy, this immortal sequence also contains what has become the movie's one mark of shame—its utterly stereotypical treatment of the terrorized black porter as a pop-eyed, servile comic foil. Sturges may have been the most unconventional Hollywood humorist of his day, but in racial matters he was a very conventional white man of the 1940s.

Pursued by hunting dogs and drunken old men, Gerry flees into a sleeping car and her fateful encounter with the film's thirteenth millionaire—actually billionaire John D. Hackensacker III. (Any resemblance to another rich John D. entirely intentional.) He is played, unforgettably, by Rudy Vallee, gamely sending up his own already archaic Whiffenpoofer self-image. This courtly tycoon, who keeps a detailed list of all his expenditures (but never bothers to add them up) is quickly smitten by Gerry's charms, but any notion that her virtue is imperiled is rendered mute by Hackensacker's old-maidish affect. Topic A is clearly far down on his list, as his sister, the sexually voracious and oft-married Princess Centimillia (Mary Astor) is quick to point out. In her 1990 book on 1930s romantic comedy, *The Runaway Bride*, Elizabeth Kendall argues that Sturges is intent on demonstrating "that rich people are really so ridiculous, so maimed, so unnatural and so tiresome that with all their money they still can't be endured." Sure, Gerry will eventually shun Hackensacker's loot to reunite with her struggling but sexy husband, but Kendall misreads the tone of this fantasy. Sturges portrays the rich as supremely silly, but it takes a pretty didactic mind to miss the affection that underlies his satire. Hackensacker may be a stingy tipper (he thinks tipping is "undemocratic"), but he's the ultimate good sport, agreeing to turn over $99,000 to Tom even when he discovers he's not Gerry's brother—as he was pretending to be—but her once and future husband. Far from being Sturges's repudiation of the wealthy classes, *The Palm Beach Story* is his fond sendup of a world he knew all too well. It was on a train trip to Palm Beach in 1930 that he met his own second wife, the cereal heiress Eleanor Post Hutton.

It's of course inevitable that Tom and Gerry get back together again. We've seen from the start that the spark of sexual attraction still ignites them. In this, *The Palm Beach Story* fits snugly into the "comedy of remarriage" tradition exemplified by such films as *The Awful Truth* and *The Philadelphia Story*. But the truth is we are never urgently invested in their romantic dilemma. There's an odd ambiguity about Tom and Gerry's marriage; the audience isn't sure how seriously to take Gerry's insistence that she wants a divorce—the original title of the movie was *Is Marriage Necessary?*—and the emotional payoff of their reconciliation pales next to the reunion of Cary Grant and Irene Dunne and Katherine Hepburn in those earlier films. Yet for all the times I've seen *The Palm Beach Story* I've never perceived this as a flaw, just a fact. McCrea's character runs to Palm Beach to win his wife back, but he doesn't really *do* much to earn his way back into her heart (or ours). It's the would-be adventuress Gerry's story, if it is anyone's, and even her quest is overshadowed by the comic mayhem Sturges choreographs around her. *The Palm Beach Story* is above all a triumph of ensemble comedy. It's the whole cockeyed, never-never land Sturges conjures up—populated by such one-of-a-kind creatures as The Weenie King, the members of the Ale and Quail Club, and the Princess's lapdoglike gigolo Toto (Sig Arno), who speaks in a language known only to him—that sets this movie apart from any other. It's a screwball vision of high-society America as a romper room where anything goes and all troubles can be swept away by the writing of a check. Only one other picture calls it to mind—and that was made seventeen years later. It's hard not to think that memories of that sleeping car scene and John D. Hackensacker in his speedboat seeped into Billy Wilder's mind when he dreamed up *Some Like It Hot*. Who is that dotty millionaire in a sailor's cap played by Joe E. Brown but Rudy Vallee two decades and too many cocktails later? It's nice to imagine that the funniest film of the 1950s learned a few tricks from the funniest film of the 1940s.

Pandora's Box (1928)

by Charles Taylor

YOU CAN ALWAYS BE CERTAIN they'll be an uproar when a foreign actress is chosen to play a character who has come to be regarded as a national heroine. We laugh now at the way Margaret Mitchell fans were appalled that a British actress, Vivien Leigh, had won the role of Scarlett O'Hara, although the same thing happened in Britain when it was announced that American Renée Zellweger had been chosen to play Bridget Jones.

But if those performances (and a far greater one, the Corsican actress Falconetti's in Carl Dreyer's *The Passion of Joan of Arc*) are any indication, then national heroines should always be played by foreigners.

One of these periodic nationalist brouhahas occurred in the late 1920s when the great German director G.W. Pabst announced that a relatively obscure American actress, Louise Brooks, had been chosen to play that incarnation of Weimar decadence, Lulu, in his adaptation of two plays by Frank Wedekind, *Erdgeist* and *Die büchse der Pandora*. Brooks, who walked out of her contract with Paramount to work with Pabst, had been featured in American silents like the Philo Vance mystery *The Canary Murder Case* and William Wellman's melodrama *Beggars of Life*, but she had never become a big star. In a sense, she was already playing her greatest role: herself.

Years after Brooks had stopped making movies (her last picture was the 1938 John Wayne horse-opera *Overland Stage Raiders*), the wildly passionate pronouncements of her admirers, the terse bitterness (and self-pity masquerading as hardness) of her periodic writings (collected in the 1982 book *Lulu in Hollywood*), the list of men she had been involved with (Charlie Chaplin, Buster Keaton, and W.C. Fields, among them, and also CBS Chairman William Paley, who kept her for years after their affair ended), and the mystery surrounding her reclusive existence in Rochester, New York, all combined to create the myth of Louise Brooks. It was the myth of the artist too pure for Hollywood chicanery, whose genius was recognized by Europe while she went unheralded in her own country. It took Kenneth Tynan's 1979 *New Yorker* profile to kick start the vogue for Louise Brooks in America. Europe had succumbed years before. In 1959, Henri Langlois, the founder of the Cinematechque Française, flew Brooks across the Atlantic for a showing of *Pandora's Box*. The Italian cartoonist Guido Creoax used her image for his strip *Valentina* (as it had been used for the 1920s American strip *Dixie Dugan*). And movies had been paying homage to Brooks for years. Cyd Charisse in the "Broadway Melody" number from *Singin' in the Rain,* and Anna Karina as the prostitute Nana in Jean-Luc Godard's *Vivre Sa Vie* were just two of the girls who had sported shiny black bobs and straight bangs—"the black helmet," as Tynan called it.

It's very likely that what kept Brooks from being a star in Hollywood was a combination of smarts, an unwillingness to show obedience to the studios, self-destructiveness, and laziness (qualities that all come through in Barry Paris's biography of Brooks). Reading her writings, you're aware of how carefully she has crafted her failure to seem like a triumph: the refusal to play the Hollywood game. And you can balk at that self-mythologization, or at the enthusiastic declarations of her partisans—Henri Langlois: "There is no Garbo! There is no Dietrich! There is only Louise Brooks!"; Kenneth Tynan: "The only star actress I can imagine either being enslaved by or wanting to enslave"—and still be struck dumb by her presence in *Pandora's Box*. More than seventy years later, Louise Brooks as Lulu remains the most potent and disturbing erotic presence ever captured on film.

It's no diminishment of Brooks to say that it is as a presence, rather than as an actress, that she makes such an impact. She herself once said, "When I acted, I hadn't the slightest idea of what I was doing. I was simply playing myself, which is the hardest thing in the world to do—if you *know* that it's hard. I didn't, so it seemed easy. I had nothing to unlearn. When I first worked with Pabst, he was furious, because he approached people intellectually and you couldn't approach me intellectually, because there was nothing to approach." Tynan quotes one Berlin critic of the time as saying "Louise Brooks cannot act. She does not suffer. *She does nothing.*" It's not true, of course. But what Brooks does in *Pandora's Box* is the exact opposite of what you'd expect from how the part had traditionally been conceived in both Wedekind's plays and in Alban Berg's opera.

The men who become involved with Lulu all meet their doom, but it was Pabst's inspiration not to have his heroine (and she is a heroine) lead them to it. As conceived by Pabst and played by Brooks, Lulu is an innocent with all the amorality that implies. Part of it is Brooks's build. No voluptuous temptress she, Brooks, diminutive and small-breasted, her face clear and open beneath her dark bangs and darker eyes, has the lissome, carefree movements of a dancer. (In fact, she had briefly been a member of the legendary Denishawn dance troupe.) It's no accident that, especially in the opening scenes, Pabst portrays Lulu as a child. She cuddles on the lap of Schigolch (the peerlessly corrupt Carl Goetz), the shabby old lecher who was her first lover (and, it's implied, her pimp), as if he were a caring granddaddy. Introduced to Schigolch's friend, the variety show strongman Rodrigo (Krafft-Raschig), she swings from his muscular arm as if it were a jungle gym. In the midst of a quarrel with Schoen (Fritz Kortner, who looks and moves as if he's just eaten a heavy meal that hasn't agreed with him), the rich publisher who is keeping her, she kicks her feet and pouts like a child who hasn't gotten her way.

Living from moment to moment, Lulu responds solely to pleasure. And having been favored with a ray of her thoughtless sensual freedom, the men who fall for her willingly follow a path to their own destruction. She succeeds in getting Schoen to break off his engagement to a sensible, dull girl, and his response is, "This is my execution." It proves to be a self-fulfilling prophecy. On their wedding night, convinced that Lulu will be his ruin, he tries to persuade her to kill herself. The gun goes off, leaving Schoen dead. At her trial, even his ineffectual son Alwa (Franz Lederer) testifies on her behalf. But she's found guilty, and a cordon of admirers effects her escape. What follows is a scene that distills the heedless essence of the character. Returning to Schoen's flat, Lulu enjoys a smoke, fluffs up some pillows to relax with a fashion magazine, and runs a bath. Her murder conviction has become no more than a tiresome appointment from which she's extricated herself, something already forgotten.

The rest of the film follows her flight, with the help of Alwa, Schigolch, and Rodrigo, to a floating casino/bordello in Marseilles and finally to shabby, freezing digs in London. The climax of the film has been best described by Brooks: "It is Christmas Eve and she is about to receive the gift which has been her dream since childhood. Death by a sexual maniac." Jack the Ripper, to be exact, who appears out of the London fog. Even he is not immune to Lulu's charms.

The critic James Harvey once admiringly characterized the performances in Howard Hawks's *Rio Bravo* as "pure behaving." And that's what we see in Louise Brooks, something so natural and unaffected that we can believe, according to Brooks, that she once answered a clergyman who asked how she felt playing such a girl, "Feel! I felt fine! It all seemed perfectly normal to me."

The performance resonates because of the context Pabst provided his star. *Pandora's Box* is not so much a reversal of conventional morality as it is another world in which convention and morality do not exist. (The same cannot be said of Pabst and Brooks's follow-up, 1929's *Diary of a Lost Girl,* traditional material that would have been more suited to Griffith and Gish.) It's a world of sexual usury. "Everyone wants my blood—my life," Lulu cries to Schigolch at one desperate point. Nothing has changed; it's just that she's no longer getting anything in the bargain. Perhaps the greatest example of Pabst's complete reversal of expectations occurs in the Christmas Eve scene with Gustav Diesel as Jack the Ripper, which is the tenderest in the movie. It's riven with tension, as we wait for the Ripper to revert to his homicidal ways. But the moments before, as they huddle in Lulu's squalid, ice-cold flat and kiss as he holds a sprig of mistletoe above her head, is the only sexual exchange in the movie where the characters are not trying to get something from their partner.

Lit with a knife-blade precision, the film is told episodically in a stark, jarring Expressionist style, whether we are in the art deco lair of Schoen or the foggy, near-Gothic nighttime exteriors of London. When Pabst is really cooking, as he is in the backstage scenes before Lulu makes her debut in the variety show Schoen is producing, or in the wedding celebration leading up to Schoen's death, the rapid, escalating pace fuses contemporary neurotic anxiety and eroticism. Watch the violence with which Kortner grabs and shakes Brooks (she claimed his fingers left ten bruises on her arms), or the way he appears to be breaking her fingers as he opens her hand to place in it the gun he is offering for her suicide.

For all the fascination with psychology that the film betrays (like the Oedipal conflicts between Schoen and Alwa, and the father-daughter relationship between Lulu and her older patrons), it is, in some basic way, post-Freudian. As with *Last Tango in Paris* (a far lusher and romantic film, yet one of the descendants of *Pandora* nonetheless) it is not, as Freud would have it, that everything comes down to sex, but that sex comes down to everything else. So few films have dealt bluntly with the psychology of sex—apart from *Pandora* and *Tango,* a short list would include Marco Ferreri's *The Last Woman* and Catherine Breillat's *Romance*—that Pabst's still feels contemporary. Using a melodrama of a sexual destruction, he made the radical step of eradicating from it all sense of guilt and sin. What Louise Brooks's Lulu still represents of her source is the title of one of Wedekind's plays, *erdgeist,* earth spirit. When she leaves the film, with a simple shot of her hand going limp, you feel as if the life force itself has evaporated in a wisp of London fog.

The Passion of Joan of Arc (1928)

by Roger Ebert

YOU CANNOT KNOW THE HISTORY of silent film unless you know the face of Renee Maria Falconetti. In a medium without words, where the filmmakers believed that the camera captured the essence of characters through their faces, to see Falconetti in Dreyer's *The Passion of Joan of Arc* (1928) is to look into eyes that will never leave you.

Falconetti (as she is always called) made only this single movie. "It may be the finest performance ever recorded on film," wrote Pauline Kael. She was an actress in Paris when she was seen on the stage of a little boulevard theater by Carl Theodor Dreyer (1889–1968), the Dane who was one of the greatest early directors. It was a light comedy, he recalled, but there was something in her face that struck him: "There was a soul behind that facade." He did screen tests without makeup and found what he sought, a woman who embodied simplicity, character, and suffering.

Dreyer had been given a large budget and a screenplay by his French producers, but he threw out the screenplay and turned instead to the transcripts of Joan's trial. They told the story that has become a legend: of how a simple country maid from Orleans, dressed as a boy, led the French troops in their defeat of the British occupation forces. How she was captured by French loyal to the British and brought before a church court, where her belief that she had been inspired by heavenly visions led to charges of heresy. There were twenty-nine cross-examinations, combined with torture, before Joan was burned at the stake in 1431. Dreyer combined them into one inquisition, in which the judges, their faces twisted with their fear of her courage, loomed over her with shouts and accusations.

If you go to the Danish Film Museum in Copenhagen you can see Dreyer's model for the extraordinary set he built for the film. He wanted it all in one piece (with movable walls for the cameras), and he began with towers at four corners, linked with concrete walls so thick they could support the actors and equipment. Inside the enclosure were chapels, houses, and the ecclesiastical court, built according to a weird geometry that put windows and doors out of plumb with one another and created discordant visual harmonies (the film was made at the height of German Expressionism and the French avant-garde movement in art).

It is helpful to see the model in Copenhagen, because you will never see the whole set in the movie. There is not one single establishing shot in all of *The Passion of Joan of Arc,* which is filmed entirely in close-ups and medium shots, creating fearful intimacy between Joan and her tormentors. Nor are there easily read visual links between shots. In his brilliant shot-by-shot analysis of the film, David Bordwell of the University of Wisconsin concludes: "Of the film's over 1,500 cuts, fewer than 30 carry a figure or object over from one shot to another; and fewer than 15 constitute genuine matches on action."

What does this mean to the viewer? There is a language of shooting and editing that we subconsciously expect at the movies. We assume that if two people are talking, the cuts will make it seem that they are looking at one another. We assume that if a judge is questioning a defendant, the camera placement and editing will make it clear where they stand in relation to one another. If we see three people in a room, we expect to be able to say how they are arranged and which is closest to the camera. Almost all such visual cues are missing from *The Passion of Joan of Arc.*

Instead Dreyer cuts the film into a series of startling images. The prison guards and the ecclesiastics on the court are seen in high contrast, often from a low angle, and although there are often sharp architectural angles behind them, we are not sure exactly what the scale is (are the windows and walls near or far?).

Bordwell's book reproduces a shot of three priests, presumably lined up from front to back, but shot in such a way that their heads seem stacked on top of one another. All of the faces of the inquisitors are shot in bright light, without makeup, so that the crevices and flaws of the skin seem to reflect a diseased inner life.

Falconetti, by contrast, is shot in softer grays, rather than blacks and whites. Also without makeup, she seems solemn and consumed by inner conviction. Consider an exchange where a judge asks her whether St. Michael actually spoke to her. Her impassive face seems to suggest that whatever happened between Michael and herself was so far beyond the scope of the question that no answer is conceivable.

Why did Dreyer fragment his space, disorient the visual sense, and shoot in close-up? I think he wanted to avoid the picturesque temptations of a historical drama. There is no scenery here, aside from walls and arches. Nothing was put in to look pretty. You do not leave discussing the costumes (although they are all authentic). The emphasis on the faces insists that these very people did what they did. Dreyer strips the church court of its ritual and righteousness and betrays its members as fleshy hypocrites in the pay of the British; their narrow eyes and mean mouths assault Joan's sanctity.

For Falconetti, the performance was an ordeal. Legends from the set tell of Dreyer forcing her to kneel painfully on stone and then wipe all expression from her face—so that the viewer would read suppressed or inner pain. He filmed the same shots again and again, hoping that in the editing room he could find exactly the right nuance in her facial expression. There is an echo in the famous methods of the French director Robert Bresson, who in his own 1962 *The Trial of Joan of Arc* put actors through the same shots again and again, until all apparent emotion was stripped from their performances. In his book on Dreyer, Tom Milne quotes the director: "When a child suddenly sees an onrushing train in front of him, the expression on his face is spontaneous. By this I don't mean the feeling in it (which in this case is sudden fear), but the fact that the face is completely uninhibited." That is the impression he wanted from Falconetti.

That he got it is generally agreed. Perhaps it helps that Falconetti never made another movie (she died in Buenos Aires, Argentina, in 1946). We do not have her face in other roles to compare with her face here, and the movie seems to exist outside time (the French director Jean Cocteau famously said it played like a "historical document from an era in which the cinema didn't exist").

To modern audiences, raised on films where emotion is conveyed by dialogue and action more than by faces, a film like *The Passion of Joan of Arc* is an unsettling experience—so intimate we fear we will discover more secrets than we desire. Our sympathy is engaged so powerfully with Joan that Dreyer's visual methods—his angles, his cutting, his close-ups—don't play like stylistic choices but like the fragments of Joan's experience. Exhausted, starving, cold, in constant fear, only nineteen when she died, she lives in a nightmare where the faces of her tormentors rise up like spectral demons.

Perhaps the secret of Dreyer's success is that he asked himself, "What is this story really about?" And after he answered that question he made a movie about absolutely nothing else.

Pather Panchali, Aparajito, The World of Apu (1956, 1958, 1960)

by Gary Arnold

BY A CURIOUS AND PORTENTOUS COINCIDENCE, the Academy of Motion Picture Arts and Sciences presented honorary awards to Satyajit Ray and Federico Fellini at consecutive Oscar ceremonies, in 1992 and 1993. Both recipients died shortly afterward. Indeed, Ray was gravely ill and bedridden at the time he accepted his award.

Within a few years of these somewhat belated career tributes, fortieth-anniversary revivals of Fellini's *La Strada* and *Nights of Cabiria,* the respective Academy Award winners as best foreign language film in 1956 and 1957, were in art-house circulation in the United States. So was an imposing, nine-part retrospective series, *The Masterworks of Satyajit Ray,* which began with his revelatory debut feature, *Pather Panchali,* and its sequels, *Aparajito* and *The World of Apu.* Never Oscar contenders in any category, these installments in the esteemed Apu Trilogy first reached American moviegoers in 1956, 1958, and 1960.

The timing was bound to stir nostalgic partiality in Those of a Certain Age. My initial curiosity about movies beyond the Hollywood orbit was aroused by the San Francisco Film Festival, which selected *La Strada* and *Pather Panchali* as grand-prize winners in consecutive years. Looking back, it's gratifying to reflect that the curiosity was amply justified. The juries showed admirable foresight, drawing attention to movies of enduring emotional and aesthetic importance.

Ray revivals are an invaluable exercise in cinematic housekeeping and spiritual regeneration. They tend to purge your system of the most depraved and stupefying impressions that accumulate during any given movie season. There is a substantial humanist tradition in filmmaking, although it's no longer a tradition that commands reliable critical loyalty. A heap of prurience, malice, delusion, and sheer unprofessionalism cloud the screen these days. The *Masterworks* cycle was patiently nurtured through almost three years of restoration work by Sony Classics, AMPAS, and the team of director James Ivory and producer Ismail Merchant, repaying a debt of gratitude for Ray's advice and assistance when they were novice filmmakers.

Ray had an effective commercial champion for several years, the importer Edward Harrison, whose death in 1967 cut Ray's movies adrift from dependable American distribution. But Ray also created something of a monster with the Trilogy itself. Although he remained active and exemplary for three decades, subsequent projects found it difficult to escape the shadow of the Trilogy. Several movies deserved to. For example, it's a little shameful that the ominous *Devi* and elegant *Charulata* have failed to rally new generations of admirers. Victorian period stories, they should be familiar to movie-savvy feminists who pride themselves on historical and psychological sophistication.

Why does Satyajit Ray's greatness still impose itself? The short answer is abiding human interest. The Apu Trilogy remains a distinctive and formidable set of heartbreakers, three masterpieces of pathos that revolve around primal family relationships. They span the years 1910–1940 (a framework that might be clarified more concretely by an occasional date in the subtitles) and emerge as a portrait-of-the-artist chronicle.

Pather Panchali depicts the birth of the precocious Apu into a small, impoverished Brahmin family residing in a crumbling ancestral home in a Bengal village, somewhere within rail distance of Benares. The father, Hari, is an aspiring playwright and occasional priest, obliged to abandon his wife and two children for extended periods in order to pursue work. The mother, Sarbojaya, is keenly aware of their want and vulnerability. She likens their ramshackle domesticity to "living in the forest." The cries of jackals and other animals alarm her. Eventually, this flimsy shelter is abandoned to the forest, symbolized by an admirably directed serpent that slithers across the threshold.

There are wrenching family losses in each chapter. Mortal loss tends to inspire Ray pictorially, beginning with a nocturnal vigil in *Pather Panchali* that becomes a marvel of resourceful staging, editing, and sound effects recording. There are incisive, stunning echoes of this sustained death watch in *Aparajito* and then a tragedy-by-messenger twist in *The World of Apu,* prompting one of the rare out-bursts of physical violence in a Ray movie. It's amazing how effective such moments can be when a filmmaker resorts to them sparingly.

The scene shifts to Benares in the first part of *Aparajito,* which is preoccupied with the emotional distance that begins to separate the adolescent, introspective Apu from his mother, superbly embodied by Karuna Banerjee, whose maternal image remains profoundly moving and inconsolable. The gulf between mother and son is never emphatically illustrated. We apprehend it vividly enough in the domestic interplay and feel heartsick at the realization that there's nothing that can remedy such insidious and intimate pain. It's a natural process. Resisting it would be as futile as trying to prevent the rotation of the earth. In part the estrangement is the result of a passionately shared desire—for Apu's education and social improvement. Scorning such advancement would seem unthinkable to both characters, but accepting it also makes them strangers as Apu grows up.

Matured into a young man with promising literary aspirations, Apu is found in Calcutta in the third film and portrayed by Soumitra Chatterjee. A genteel and rather complacent state of bohemian poverty is transformed overnight when Apu is promoted from wedding guest to emergency bridegroom. This turn of events inspires one of the most beguiling passages in the Ray inventory: the romantic idyll of Apu and his bride Aparna, a genuine vision of loveliness in the person of Sharmila Tagore, a teenage beauty comparable in allure and fascination to the young Elizabeth Taylor at the time Ray cast her as consorts to Chatterjee in *Apu* and *Devi.* Returning from the near-catastrophic wedding party to Apu's rooftop abode in Calcutta, the newlyweds become acquainted and devoted, sharing a Seventh Heaven rapture until tragedy intrudes again. Apu must weather one final loss before reconciling himself to life.

Ironically, the hero has articulated a desirable outlook that fails him when tragedy strikes. In an early episode Apu summarizes his prospective novel for a friend. The description serves as an admirable argument for the achievement of Satyajit Ray. "His education, his hardships," Apu remarks, "broaden his mind and sharpen his wits. Although things are always difficult for him, he doesn't turn his back on life. He doesn't try to escape reality. He has learned that the whole point of life is in facing reality."

Ray didn't need to grope for essential meanings when he filmed the Trilogy, which derived from a pair of popular autobiographical novels, published in the 1930s, by the Bengali writer Bibhuti Bhushan Banerji. The first two films borrow the original titles: *Pather Panchali* is translated as "The song of the road" and *Aparajito* as "The unvanquished." Ray had nurtured a desire to film the books for years before he could initiate the project. Born in Calcutta in 1921, Ray belonged to a distinguished literary and publishing family. He had illustrated a children's edition of *Pather Panchali* in 1945 while employed as art director for a British advertising agency. Ray helped found a film society in Calcutta and wrote articles about the cinema in the late 1940s. An encouraging encounter with Jean Renoir, who was in India in 1949 to shoot exteriors for *The River,* and a six-month stay in London in 1950, which accommodated an orgy of moviegoing, fueled Ray's own filmmaking aspirations. By the time he commenced sporadic shooting on *Pather Panchali* in 1952, with roughly $2,000, raised through borrowing on his insurance and selling some of his wife's jewelry, Ray had refined his vision of the Banerji novels in graphic as well as dramatic terms. Marie Seton's 1971 book, *Portrait of a Director,* included examples of Ray's sketches and engravings. The finished film appears to burnish and refine those earlier illustrations.

In retrospect it seems obvious that Ray had *Pather Panchali* exquisitely visualized and distilled long before he exposed a foot of film. At the time of the movie's release in the United States, his achievement was occasionally misconstrued as a worthy fluke—the work of a documentary amateur from a primitive outpost of the cinematic world. On the contrary, it was a highly sophisticated feat of shoestring adaptation from book to screen. The scenarios of all three movies rest on bare-boned, episodic frameworks that would probably shatter if Ray lacked expressive command of the medium. Since his prowess is consistently manifest in the imagery and characterizations, the bedrock family conflicts prove intensely authentic and stirring.

Despite the graphic advances made in the depiction of movie violence over the years, Ray orchestrates moments of sudden, irrational domestic violence that humble pyrotechnic flare-ups. The scariest example in *Pather Panchali:* the mother lashing out in shame and frustration at her daughter, who has been accused of theft by a prosperous neighbor. The accusation itself returns to haunt a fabulous closing interlude. In *The World of Apu* the protagonist assaults a messenger bearing dreadful tidings. Our sympathies are so effectively grafted to these characters that it seems a grievous emotional blow when they surrender to rage or despair.

The Trilogy is concentrated on the most intimate and vulnerable relationships: the tangled affections and resentments of five members of a peasant family; a child's loss of one parent and alienation from another; the bliss of a happy, providential marriage followed by a devastating and demoralizing loss; a slow, agonizing process of reconciliation to loss. Supremely basic stuff. Satyajit Ray entered the film medium with an eloquent and stirring appreciation of human essentials, secured by a no-frills mastery of the means necessary to authenticate his material in imagery and nuanced acting. He was a classic humanist from the outset.

Ray's admirable concentration and gravity were also enhanced by a singular lack of condescension toward his characters. For example, there's an extraordinary absence of squalor or sentimental special pleading in the way poverty is depicted in the Apu Trilogy. It's always evident, and we can observe how it scars the characters. The mother's wrathful outburst in *Pather Panchali* is a harrowing example.

However, these impressions don't surrender a particle of human dignity or moral responsibility to the intimidation of hard social conditions. The characters inhabit an impoverished setting that always teems with life and volition. Degradation and despair do not get a free ride. Straightforward and clear-sighted, Satyajit Ray observed human struggles and aspirations without resorting to expediency or idealization. Never quite fashionable, he continues to justify enormous respect and gratitude. Whenever cinematic taste seems to require a back-to-basics correction, Ray is a splendid filmmaker to rediscover.

The Piano (1993)

by Judy Gerstel

"THE HUMAN HEART HAS HIDDEN TREASURES, in secret kept, in silence sealed. . ."

A dozen words by Emily Bronte, one extraordinary movie by Jane Campion.

The Piano swept us away when it was released in 1993. Holly Hunter and Anna Paquin, who played the pivotal mother and daughter roles, won Academy Awards for best actress and best supporting actress.

Relentlessly, compellingly, rhythmically, mythically, like the tide itself or a melody in a minor key inexorably yearning for resolution, *The Piano* immersed us in the joy and danger and reckless abandon of romantic love and carried us to a safe and distant shore.

Curiously, it's a film that some if not many people disdain in retrospect. At a distance of some years, the unabashed intensity and fierce romanticism can seem too rich, too facile, too melodramatic. The picture never did appeal much to men in the first place. Holly Hunter's spare cuckolding heroine, the potent mother-daughter bond, the engulfing female point of view, and the themes of female discovery and liberation do not add up to what's generally thought of as a guy's movie.

But even some women may be embarrassed now at how easily they fell into Campion's manipulative vision of a world sharply divided between nature and negation, between love and duty, imprisonment and liberation, between music and silence.

The New Zealand filmmaker first captivated audiences and critics with the memorable and poetic images in *Sweetie* and *Angel at My Table*—both illuminating unconventional, disturbed female protagonists.

In *The Piano*, Campion marries her images with a story that embraces the Victorian sensibility and Gothic romanticism of the Bronte sisters.

Like poets and composers—and like the heroine of this movie—Campion's meaning and wonder is encoded, more felt and observed than explicitly articulated.

The Piano is the story of an enigmatic woman who marries a man she doesn't love and who can never know her. And while married, she comes to love another man who makes her known finally to herself.

The movie opens with Hunter's voice. She is speaking over scenes of her character, Ada, and Ada's nine-year-old daughter. The period is the mid-1850s and the place is a Scottish household.

With a credible Scottish accent, Hunter explains that she stopped speaking as a child. She says she and her daughter will soon travel to another country where she'll marry a man she has never seen.

"And hark this," she says. "He says God loves dumb creatures so why shouldn't he?"

Clearly this is her mind's voice, but why is she addressing us? And who is the father of her daughter? These are only two of many questions never answered; in exchange, Campion offers answers to questions never asked.

The journey to New Zealand is conveyed in a single symbolic image from below water, of the bottom of a boat passing vertically through the frame. It's an odd though typically arresting choice by Campion, and the full significance of it becomes clear only near the very end of the film.

Soon after the traveling party washes ashore, several things do become clear. The child is the interpreter for the mother, who speaks in sign language; the mother and the daughter are a world unto themselves, allies and protectors of each other; and Ada's piano, beached in a huge wooden crate like a coffin, is not just a musical instrument but the voice of her soul and the embodiment of her sexuality.

When her husband, Stewart (Sam Neill), repressed, bewildered, and foolish, trades the piano for land to his illiterate overseer, Baines (Harvey Keitel), the stage is set for passions as wild as the landscape.

The Victorian conflict of unfettered primitive nature and civilized, mannered society is the context for the story.

Lusty, frankly sexual Maori natives, the rugged, muddy stark countryside, and the pounding surf on the coast are fitted against the strict conventions and dutiful respectability of nineteenth-century colonialism: corsets, teacups, and tight-lipped but comical women in crinolines.

Bridging nature and society are music, sexual love, and childhood. And Baines, too, as someone who has gone native, adorning himself with Maori tattoos and speaking their language. Around Baines's cabin there are always exotic bird songs, strange magical notes of nature.

The staging and details throughout are remarkable, beginning with scenes on the beach. Refusing to leave her piano, Ada and her child remain on the beach through the night. Their makeshift tent glows like a lantern in the dark. Later, Ada plays her piano after waiting what must have been months at sea, and her daughter dances in her petticoats on the sand. Liberation is palpable.

The new owner of the piano, Baines, uses it to lure Ada to his cabin. While she plays, he watches her hungrily, lovingly, understanding what the music does for her and wanting to do it, too. He strikes a bargain, trading the piano back to her, one black key at a time, for each visit, a touch, a flash of flesh, an intimacy.

There's an intensely erotic moment when Baines, on the floor at Ada's feet while she plays, fixes upon a hole in her stocking and strokes the small patch of tender white flesh with one rough finger.

Later, as Ada's husband peers through a window watching his wife's joyful abandon with her lover, as Stewart stands taciturn and unrevealing, a dog licks slobber on his fingers. This is sly and audacious moviemaking.

And the scene of retribution, for Ada does not go unpunished, will make you hold your breath. It is both shocking and inevitable, the price exacted by patriarchy. But it is no less shocking nor inevitable than the betrayal that brings it about—an eye for an eye, a silencing for a cry of freedom, a castration for a cuckolding.

Hunter deservedly is the focus of the critical praise for performances in this movie. She is a force moving through it, fierce and heroic in her will to survive and to love.

But Neill and Keitel are superb, too, as is little Anna Paquin, who plays the conflicted daughter to perfection, in every way her mother's daughter.

Neill's finely tuned villain provokes compassion for his limitations and incomprehension. And Keitel transforms his typically compelling fire in the belly into a tender romantic hero.

In pairing Hunter and Keitel as the lovers, Campion proved herself to be as inspired in casting as in storytelling and picture-making.

If there is a weakness in this movie, it's the coda. Though we probably wouldn't want it any other way, it's a bit too tidy, not of a piece with what went before.

The Piano was on most critics' list of the best movies of the year and deservedly won the Palme d'Or at Cannes. It was nominated for an Academy Award for best picture and Campion was nominated for best director, but the big winner that year was *Schindler's List* and Steven Spielberg. Still, Campion is the only female director recognized with nominations for best director and best picture. And she did win the Oscar for best original screenplay.

Oddly, the score by Michael Nyman, which became a best-selling soundtrack, was not nominated for an Academy Award. More than any other film score, Nyman's music is no mere accompaniment nor even an aural translation of the narrative, themes, and characters. It is the essence of the film titled *The Piano*. The composer deftly incorporates Scottish phrases, playfulness, recklessness, and passion in music that, like Ada and the movie itself, is insistent and throbbing with urgency.

It's Campion's unique achievement that she has made a brave, beautiful, and archetypal film that is also accessible and entertaining. If it is somewhat less stunning in retrospect, it is probably we who have changed, and perhaps even a little by this film.

Psycho (1960)

by Charles Taylor

THE IMPACT OF ALFRED HITCHCOCK'S *Psycho* owes so much to its two big surprises that when the film opened in 1960 Hitchcock not only refused to allow press screenings but had theaters hire Pinkerton security guards to prevent latecomers from entering the theater once the picture had started. He wanted to keep the people who hadn't bought tickets from finding out that Janet Leigh's

Marion Crane is stabbed to death in the shower only forty-five minutes into the movie and that the murderer is Anthony Perkins's Norman Bates, who has succumbed to the personality of the mother he murdered years before.

In many ways, *Psycho* seems like a death knell for the studio system that would lumber on for a few more years before collapsing later in the decade under the weight of filmmakers and audiences sick of the old stultified formulas. It isn't just that Hitchcock made the film fast and on the cheap (it cost only $800,000), using the crew from his television anthology series *Alfred Hitchcock Presents*. And it's not just the shock of the shower murder, its brilliant and savage elisions heralding and in many cases surpassing the screen violence to come. The entire movie is predicated on the conscious violation of the reassuring Hollywood conventions that were so common audiences took them for granted. In the manner of a star taking on a small character part, Janet Leigh is billed last in the credits. But to audiences trained in reading Hollywood convention, Leigh, who's in every scene until her death, who is the only character we are encouraged to identify with in the first half of the movie, *is* the star. It was Anthony Perkins who received top billing, and when he enters the movie he is so sympathetic, so obviously a nice person in a horrible position—a good son who has sacrificed himself to the care of his mad, domineering mother—that he is the natural character to switch our allegiance to after Marion's abrupt death.

Hitchcock establishes our complicity brilliantly. After putting Marion's body and belongings into the trunk of her car, he pushes the vehicle to a swamp and waits for it to sink. When it stops just shy of disappearing beneath the surface, Norman holds his breath and so do we. From identifying with Marion and being shocked by her murder we have already, in the space of a few minutes, become an accessory to erasing the final traces of her existence. We are as anxious for Norman not to be found out covering up "mother's" crime as we were for Marion not to get caught stealing the $40,000 that started her on the journey that ends at the Bates Motel. That's why the final revelation that Norman isn't hiding his mother's guilt but his own made some moviegoers feel as if they were the victims of a cruel prank. A friend of mine was nine years old when the film was released and saw it at the drive-in with his mother. She was shocked by the overall candor, particularly the sight of Janet Leigh in a bra (this was an era when Hollywood stars were typically seen in nothing more revealing than a slip). He was shocked by the revelation of Norman's madness. How, he wondered, could he be tricked into feeling such sympathy for this madman? How could a madman seem so like us?

But secrets only keep so long. Now, more than forty years after its release, *Psycho* is so famous that even people who've never seen it know that Marion is murdered and Norman is the killer. And as with all things that upset or shock or frighten us, *Psycho* has become something a joke, an excuse for quips about showers or mothers. For Perkins, who had been a sensitive, affecting juvenile lead in pictures like *Friendly Persuasion,* it was a joke that never wore off. He *became* Norman Bates to the public (even when playing a very different disturbed young man in 1968's *Pretty Poison,* one of his very best performances), and his increasingly mannered and eccentric acting played into the perception. His participation in several sequels seemed to be the final surrender.

So how is it possible to still watch *Psycho* long after its secrets have been spilled? The answer is that beneath the shocker is a profoundly despairing film, a work as redolent of contemporary desolation and isolation as Eliot's *Preludes.* (It can't be chance that the movie takes place in the weeks leading up to Christmas and no one alludes to or even seems aware of the coming holiday.) Beginning in a desert and ending in a swamp, *Psycho* is a film in which the aridity of sex, work, family, and routine strands its two main characters in the quagmire of their private traps.

That's the phrase Norman uses to Marion during the scene that precedes her murder, a long sequence in his private parlor, a sort of spiritual interrogation that establishes both what links them (their surrender to their own brands of madness—"I think we all go a little mad sometimes, haven't you?" Norman asks Marion) and what separates them (Marion's ability to recognize a way back to sanity—she answers his question, "Sometimes just once is enough"). In the movie's central piece of dialogue, Norman says, "I think we're all in our private traps, clamped in them, and none of us can ever get out. We scratch and claw, but only at the air, only at each other. And for all of it, we never budge an inch."

Watch *Psycho* with those lines in mind and what you'll see is Marion and Norman in a succession of their own traps. For Marion it begins with the cheap Phoenix hotel room where she meets her lover Sam (John Gavin) for a midday tryst, the shabbiness of the place defining the money problems that keep them apart. Then we see the office where she works, and the money that offers the seeming solution to her problem dangled temptingly in front of her. Then the bedroom of the home she shares with her sister, its clean, modest conventionality, the family pictures watching her from the wall (the movie's first example of what Norman will call "the cruel eyes studying you") feeling like a respectable death-in-life. Then the car in which she'll make her futile getaway, all the while unable to stop imagining the worries of the people she's left behind. Then the shower of her cabin at the Bates Motel, where she will be senselessly murdered after deciding to go back to Phoenix and make amends. And finally, the trunk of the car that holds her body and the swamp that swallows it up.

For Norman, the traps are fewer but profound. "I was born in mine," he says, meaning not just the Bates home with its morbid, nearly gothic Victoriana (furnishings from which the stale, dead air of the movie seems to emanate), but his very being, his body in which he will be subsumed by "mother." In our final glimpse of him, a subliminal cut superimposes the face of his mother's grinning ten-years-dead corpse on his own. Earlier, when Norman is apprehended by Sam as he attempts to kill Marion's sister Lila (Vera Miles), Perkins's face twitches in the manner of a man whose personality is coming apart at the seams (just as the titles in Saul Bass's credit sequence pull apart, degenerating from words into meaningless visual patterns). That struggle has ended when we last see Norman: The distance between him and "mother" has collapsed just as the distance between Norman and ourselves has suddenly become too wide to traverse. *Psycho* is his tragedy no less than Marion's. Marion (whose last name is Crane) winds up like the stuffed birds in Norman's parlor, staring accusingly from dead eyes. It's a measure of the bleak empathy of *Psycho* that, caught in their private traps, both hunter and prey can be described by Eliot's line as "some infinitely gentle/Infinitely suffering thing."

The Public Enemy (1931)

by John Anderson

> *"Perhaps the toughest of the gangster films, 'Public Enemy' and 'Little Caesar' had a great effect on public opinion. They brought home violently the evils associated with Prohibition and suggested the necessity of a nation-wide housecleaning.*
>
> *"Tom Powers in 'Public Enemy' and Rico in 'Little Caesar' are not two men, nor are they merely characters—they are a problem that sooner or later we, the public, must solve."*

STENTORIAN IN THEIR RIGHTEOUSNESS and a bit forgetful about rival UA's *Scarface*, these titles were added by Warner Brothers for its late-1930s re-release of *The Public Enemy* in order to meet the niceties of the Hollywood Production Code—which hadn't been around when the film was originally released in 1931 and which *The Public Enemy* helped bring about.

The titles are still there on most circulating prints and on the rentable version and are an indication of the various influences of William Wellman's seminal gangster thriller—the movie that made James Cagney a star, introduced the Grapefruit Facial, and cemented the reputation of Warner as the once and future home of the hardboiled gangster film.

Inadvertently, perhaps ironically, the film's popular success, combined with its blisteringly frank portrayal of the criminal Tom Powers, had also helped lead to the 1934 formation of the Legion of Decency, a watchdog group created in response to films that were usually far less adult in theme than *Public Enemy*—and which, thereafter, made films as uncompromising, or sordid, as Wellman's nearly impossible to make.

Imitation was inevitable, of course—likewise, the failure of almost every subsequent gangster film to recapture the potency of *The Public Enemy,* which charts the rise of Powers from unlovely street urchin to homicidal maniac to avenging angel to hospitalized headshot victim to swaddled corpse. For all the film's creaky hinges, antique acting, and clumsy setups, its ending remains one of the most powerful in movies, a triptych of terror: the sweetly dopey Ma Powers (Beryl Mercer), upstairs in her house, singing, making beds, anticipating Tom's long-hoped-for homecoming. Brother Mike (Donald Cook) getting the ambiguous phone call about Tom's imminent arrival, the doorbell ringing, Mike opening the door—and Tom, sheetwrapped and staring, falling into the house stone dead, as a phonograph needle grinds on with dreadful monotony.

To say a movie is a relic is to suggest it is no longer relevant, no longer possessed of anything to tell us. While *The Public Enemy* is full of stiff, stagey performances and techniques characteristic of the then-three-year-old talking picture (*The Public Enemy* is, and ever shall be, a "Vitaphone" film) it's still a loaded pistol.

For one thing, Tom Powers is an unequivocal statement that sociopaths are born, not made: His brother is a war hero, his mother sweetness and light, his father never spared the rod. Tom, the bad seed, was born, not made. And as a purely sociological document, what it takes for granted is telling: The offhand abuse of a black valet; Cagney's mincing imitation of an effeminate tailor; the understated shame of Tom's shacking up with Mae Clarke (originally to be played by Louise Brooks, who shows up in the credits as the unseen Bess). Similarly, there's the movie's oblivious attitude toward the Faginesque, sexually suspect Putty Nose (Murray Kinnell), whose "clubhouse" serves as an incubator for slum delinquents and who himself, through betrayal, sets Tom and his best friend Matt (Edward Woods) on their criminal path.

In fact, outside of *Public Enemy's* celebrated final scene, its most chilling moment is when Putty Nose, feebly trying to convince Tom not to kill him, sings "Hesitation Blues" at the piano, the camera wanders away, and gunshots provide the coda. The distinct sense is that Tom is avenging his own lost life, one he himself has done nothing to change—making the intellectual vacuum at the heart of Tom Powers as pathetic as Putty Nose himself.

The staging of that particular murder is a bellwether for the rest of the film. Although Wellman set out—and succeeded—in making the toughest, most uncompromising gangster film he could, there are only eight killings in the movie, all of which take place offscreen. The power of the movie, and the lingering sense of having been ringside at a slaughter, lies in the irredeemable quality of Tom, who except for one famous moment of clarity after taking a bullet in the head ("I ain't so tough . . . ") is a character who revels in his own badness.

Wellman's take on the suffocating swarm of humanity jamming early-1930s urban America was likely influenced by King Vidor in *The Crowd* and Paul Fejos in *Lonesome,* two 1928 films that in their very different ways portrayed the worrisome anonymity and spiritual isolation that seemed inherent to cities like New York—places where a kid like Tom could cultivate his pathology virtually unimpeded (although dad didn't help). Wellman makes great, judgmental pans that are gorgeously fluid and that telescope into the meat of the town, where we get a series of scenes featuring young Tom and Matt more or less running amok, flipping men's top hats, and implying a whole life's story to come. Again, Tom was born to be the man he became.

So was James Cagney. The child of a tormented alcoholic father from Manhattan's celebratedly squalid Five Points and a mother tough enough to have scared him out of a prizefighting career, the actor had started in vaudeville and was appearing in *Penny Arcade* with regular costar-to-be Joan Blondell when Warner's bought the show (to make John Adolfi's *Sinner's Holiday* in 1930). Signed to the studio, Cagney appeared in Archie Mayo's *Doorway to Hell* and Wellman's *Other Men's Women* when opportunity—in the form of Tom Powers—came knocking in 1931.

In his first great role, you can already certainly see his fabled physical grace, as well as what would become some trademark Cagneyisms—the way Tom throws a punch, for instance, high and straight from the shoulder, something the relatively diminutive actor probably learned growing up on the then-unfashionable Upper East Side neighborhood of Yorkville. There's also that smile, of course, which might just as easily have come equipped with wit or lead. The hot temper of his character, and the revenge motif of the film, would mark Cagney's characters for years to come.

During the course of Tom's rise and fall among the gangster class from pre–World War I through Prohibition-era New York (Wellman's shot of people using baby carriages to drag home bootleg hootch is a beautiful portrait of desperate thirst), he finds love with men, sex with women. Nails Nathan (Leslie Fenton) develops from Cagney's rival into his pal as they work toward consolidating the city's illicit liquor market; their guilt is compounded by the often sanctimonious presence of Donald Cook, whose Brother Mike returns from war a ghastly broken man, no longer the hard worker and student he once was ("He's learnin' to be poor," is one of Cagney's better lines in the film). The none-too-subtle judgment of *The Public Enemy* is that such veterans were cast off by their government at the same time the impossible Volstead Act made criminals rich.

The women? Somehow, Jean Harlow, who plays the self-admittedly promiscuous Gwen Allen, has consistently been misidentified as the moll who gets the grapefruit in the face (as the story goes, Wellman told Cagney offscreen to do the scene that way, catching Clarke off guard). But Harlow's performance is fascinating, albeit in its own weird way.

First seen walking along a street, where Tom propositions her from an open car, Gwen Allen could be a lot of things—she smiles cryptically, could be ill, is possibly bestial, certainly corrupt. In her later scenes, she's got more of the Harlow glamour, but when she first hits the screen she looks like the poster girl for an Army anti-VD campaign. As a symbol of Tom Powers's moral decline, she couldn't be more apt.

But she doesn't, after all, have a great deal to do with the story. Her significance is she has the upper hand in her relationship with Tom, who lets almost no one have the upper hand with him. Until, of course, that doorbell rings.

For those too young to have seen *The Public Enemy* as a first-run feature—most of us, in other words—its existence has a curious side effect. It's likely that most filmgoers today, and for the last forty years or so, have become acquainted with Cagney through TV—*The Late Show* through Turner Classics—and that *The Public Enemy* is not the first Cagney film they've seen. They've met him, instead, through *Yankee Doodle Dandy* or *Footlight Parade* or via the relatively benign gangsters of *The Roaring Twenties* and *Angels with Dirty Faces*.

Tom Powers, therefore, poses a kind of dilemma, as well as a window into the power of stardom and the power of good acting. Can we see Tom Powers as the homicidal sociopath he is? Or does Cagney's stardom blind us to the real power of Wellman's film? It's a testament to the director, the movie, and, of course, the star that *The Public Enemy* retains the ability to shock us, seventy years and a million gangsters later.

Pulp Fiction (1994)

by Jami Bernard

WHEN QUENTIN TARANTINO TRAVELED for the first time to Amsterdam and Paris, flush with the critical success of *Reservoir Dogs* and still piecing together the quilt of *Pulp Fiction,* he was tickled by the absence of any Quarter Pounders with Cheese on the European culinary scene, a casualty of the metric system. It was just the kind of thing that comes up among friends who are stoned or killing time. Later, when every nook and cranny of *Pulp Fiction* had become quoted and quantified, this minor burger observation entered pop culture with a flourish as part of what fans call the "Tarantinoverse."

With its interlocking story structure, looping time frame, and electric jolts, *Pulp Fiction* uses the grammar of film to explore the amusement park of the Tarantinoverse, a stylized merging of the mundane with the unthinkable, all set in a 1970s time warp. Tarantino is the first of a slacker generation to be idolized and deconstructed as much for his attitude, quirks, and knowledge of pop-culture arcana as for his output, which as of this writing has been Jack-Rabbit slim.

Each segment rises to a giddy crescendo. The hitmen played by John Travolta and Samuel L. Jackson retrieve their boss's valuable suitcase but accidentally shoot their informant in the face, leaving a horrible mess in the car that needs to be cleaned up ASAP. Vincent Vega (Travolta) takes the boss's wife (Uma Thurman) out for an evening, at the end of which she ODs and is brought back from the dead like something out of a low-budget horror movie. A boxer (Bruce Willis) refuses to take a dive but can't leave town until he retrieves the watch his father took great pains to leave him (he hid it in his rectum in a POW camp), and which was inadvertently left in his now heavily guarded apartment. The boxer and the crime boss he stiffed (Ving Rhames) stumble into the hell of a redneck S&M dungeon. And two young lovers (Amanda Plummer and Tim Roth) try to rob a diner but come up against what just might be divine intervention.

These escalations also amount to pissing contests, with the winner advancing up the toughness ladder (something a new generation certainly related to through video games, which are similarly structured). Travolta gets to stare down Willis (whom he dismisses as "Punchy"), something that could only happen in a movie directed by an ardent fan of *Welcome Back Kotter.* In each grouping, the alpha male is soon determined, and the scene involves appeasing him. (In the segment called "The Bonnie Situation," for example, even the big crime boss is so inexplicably afraid of upsetting Bonnie, a night nurse, that he sends in his top guy, played by Harvey Keitel, to keep from getting on her bad side.)

All of this takes place in the course of twenty-four hours, although the stories are shuffled so that one character who has recently been shot to hell on a toilet seat is back in business, unaware of his fate, in a subsequent scene.

On Internet newsgroups, debates rage over such minutiae as what was inside the glowing briefcase, but like many Internet debates, it misses the point. The briefcase was a homage to *Kiss Me Deadly*. Fans are correct in assuming there's a reason for everything in the Tarantinoverse, but they persist in focusing on the literal (the director's fondness for certain breakfast cereals, for example) instead of the broader inspiration of directors such as Godard, whose work Tarantino soaked up as a high-school dropout toiling for minimum wage at a Southern California video store. The dance scene at Jack Rabbit Slim's, for example, is an homage to Godard's *Bande à part*, which is also the inspiration for the name of Tarantino's production company (A Band Apart).

Godard aside, it's true that much of the movie's accessibility is due to how much of himself and his fast-food reveries Tarantino injected into the mix. He really does think a five-dollar shake had better be damn good to justify the price. He has himself been known to lounge all day in his bathrobe, eating Cap'n Crunch and watching cartoons like the drug dealer played by Eric Stoltz. Tarantino was able to tap into the zeitgeist at just the right moment in part because he was living it. Hordes of minimum-wage earners with dreams of overnight fame that would leave them free to continue eating cereal in their bathrobes embraced Tarantino as their White Knight, conveniently ignoring that it is not Tarantino's slackerhood but his knowledge and appreciation of film that makes *Pulp Fiction* so effortlessly entertaining and which got the critical response rolling from the moment of its debut at Cannes.

Along with the hero worship came a different kind of legacy, the evil spawn of *Pulp Fiction* (and of *Reservoir Dogs*). For the remainder of the 1990s, film-school brats churned out dark, jokey, hard-hearted movies where characters babbled on about insignifica and arterial blood sprayed with abandon. Without Tarantino's style, good humor, and firmly rooted love of all things cinematic, these clones were squeezed from the same pastry bag, leaving a nasty smear. Other filmmakers have inspired misguided adoration, but the Tarantino effect was particularly pernicious, perhaps because of the sheer buoyancy of *Pulp Fiction,* its characters, its soundtrack, its *joie de vivre.*

Above all, *Pulp Fiction* is fun, a celebration of the possibilities and inconsistencies of cinema. It puts you on familiar movie ground—the boxer who refuses to go down, the lovers who goad each other into pulling a robbery they can't handle. And yet there is a touching concern with what's happening behind the scenes. How do you remove a blood stain, and how do you do it in a hurry? The hitman is on a long stakeout, so when exactly does he get to go to the bathroom? It is a movie for people who love movies, who believe the movies belong to everyone, who talk endlessly into the night about movies, whereupon they digress to why there are no Quarter Pounders with Cheese in Europe, then realize the sun has come up and they could really go for a breakfast of blueberry pie.

Raging Bull (1980)

by Jami Bernard

IT IS UNFATHOMABLE, particularly with the benefit of hindsight, that in 1980 *Ordinary People* won the best picture Oscar over *Raging Bull*. At the time, both pictures were considered shocking, although certainly not equally so. *Ordinary People* seems today like a TV movie with its easy psychology and barely disguised sentimentality, whereas *Raging Bull* has never ceased to deliver that punch to the gut of foul recognition. It splattered the screen with variations on the word "fuck" like the blood that spewed from Jake La Motta's pulped face onto the ringside judges. *Ordinary People* had Judd Hirsch's comforting wool cardigan to clutch like a baby blanket, but there is nothing warm and fuzzy in *Raging Bull,* no pat explanations, no miraculous redemption. Jake's self-destruction is an unrelieved plunge, and we ache for him not because we like him but because we recognize him, thanks to Robert De Niro's awesome performance and Martin Scorsese's visceral direction. *Ordinary People* was also in its way about sibling rivalry, but if you want the real deal, you go to *Raging Bull,* a movie that also serves as a lesson for biographers that the surest way to the heart of a character, at least on film, is from around the edges and not by the book.

In fact, the movie is very little like the self-serving autobiography on which it's based. The relationship between Jake (De Niro) and his coulda-been-a-contender brother Joey (an amalgam of two characters from the book, played by Joe Pesci) is the heart of the movie. The boxer's actual triumphs in the ring are of little moment save to flesh out a portrait of a man caught in the undertow of his own nature. The ring was the only place where such thanatos could be appreciated and rewarded, even enshrined with the jewel-encrusted middleweight championship belt. Outside the ring he was a mess, unsuited for polite company, in thrall to his inner demons, fearful of the women in his life, suspicious, bad-tempered, unable to make moral choices or weigh consequences. (That he has no idea what in his life is of value is nicely brought home when he smashes up his belt to pawn the jewels, which turn out to be worthless without the belt itself.)

Scorsese may have been robbed of a directing Oscar that year, but De Niro wiped the mat with award upon award. As the Energizer-bunny champ whose inarticulateness is a poetry of frustration and despair, De Niro famously put on an extra 50 pounds (on pasta and milkshakes in Italy) for two months while production shut down. Then he returned to shoot the scenes of Jake in his later years, his belly blocking his brother's view of the broken TV or hanging out from his pants and undershirt like the ignored black sheep of the family. The extra weight was the capper to the man's disintegration from boxing phenomenon to the last tender of his own myth, long after he had driven away everyone who loved him, most particularly the brother who managed him and served as his actual and metaphorical punching bag.

It was De Niro who brought La Motta's book to Scorsese's attention while the latter was making *Alice Doesn't Live Here Anymore*. But it was hardly a straight shot to the screen. De Niro had to pressure and harangue his mentor. Scorsese frankly wasn't all that interested, couldn't relate to the world of boxing, didn't care for the endless script revisions (he eventually brought in Paul Schrader for a script overhaul), and was having a hard time in his personal life. Depressed, overworked, and overmedicated, he made his first emotional connection with the project from a hospital bed after a collapse, where he realized that, like Jake, he was circling the drain and spending every ounce of good will he had banked over the years. The idea of the boxer's (or filmmaker's) inchoate howl of despair held a fascination for him that turned *Raging Bull* into a personal odyssey, which he nevertheless thought would put the kibosh on his career. After all, *Raging Bull* was an evil twin to such competing boxing movies of the day as *Rocky 2*. Further, it was filmed in elegiac black and white, which added to its beauty but which Scorsese, who was just getting heavily involved in the preservation of color film stock, feared would be mistaken for pretentious. (His decision on black and white may have been hastened when Michael Powell, to whom he deferred, commented on early rushes that Jake's boxing gloves were "too red.")

The script was still too dark for the studios, and no one could understand putting a guy like Jake at the center of a movie. An early draft of the script had Jake wondering where to dump the body of his wife, who he thinks he has hit too hard and killed. Scorsese and De Niro holed up on St. Martin (of all places) to work on the script, and when they came back, it was presentable enough for a nervous green light.

It's the movie's inner violence that's tougher to take, the way Jake steels himself for punishment both as a matter of pride and ongoing self-torture. He browbeats Joey into punching him in the face to prove a point. He goads Vicky (Cathy Moriarty), the blonde teenage treasure he picks up at a neighborhood pool and marries (and tortures with his jealousy), into getting him aroused before a fight when they both know he won't follow through. (He plunges himself into ice water to preserve his juices.) The self-immolation is spectacular. "Did you fuck my wife?" he asks Joey, the ultimate accusation for the ultimate transgression. To capture Pesci's reaction so perfectly, that combination of disbelief and revulsion, De Niro surprised Pesci during one take with, "Did you fuck your mother?" That take was a keeper, and the fraternal symbiosis is finally, irrevocably destroyed.

During the 1970s, the new crop of American directors like Scorsese were truly making the films they wanted, and there was both a public appetite for them and a studio checkbook to fund them. The way Jake bawled like a baby after purposely taking a fall was probably how any of the bright lights of the 1970s directing fraternity felt about doing a movie simply for commercial considerations rather than artistic ones. But director power was like yesterday's bell-bottoms as the 1980s ushered in an era of the producer, the beancounter, the movie packager. Even distribution was changing so that movies could no longer take their time cultivating an audience. As Peter Biskind put it in his book *Easy Riders, Raging Bulls, Raging Bull* was a whale from the 1970s beached on the shoals of the 1980s. The time for such daring, personal movies was over. The new taste was for the slick, bland, and predictable, when *Ordinary People* would be as safely daring as things got.

Raging Bull was recognized as a masterpiece by a number of critics, but it buckled at the box office and was not acknowledged until years later as being one of the great movies, possibly Scorsese's best. It could probably not be made now. For all the violence, it is excessively talky by today's standards and totally eschews dime-store psychology. We know Jake and Joey are alike, acorns that must not have fallen far from the tree. They are shown against the backdrop of a rough-and-tumble borough neighborhood where brawls spill out of bars and couples scream at each other, more acorns, similar trees. The implication is that

Jake was not fundamentally different from anyone in the 'hood, he just had more of whatever it was they had and he found a way, at least for a while, to make that work for him.

Rashomon (1950)

by Andy Klein

> *From* The Simpsons:
> *Marge: "You liked* Rashomon*!"*
> *Homer: "That's not how I remember it."*

IT'S RARE FOR ANY FILM'S TITLE to become permanently ensconced in English language usage, let alone a foreign film: yet, describe something as "one of those *Rashomon* situations," and a fair number of Americans (only a fraction of whom will have ever seen the movie) will know exactly what you mean— "he says one thing, she says another, the third guy says something else, and who knows what reality is anyway?" That the concept has been invoked more than once on TV shows like *The Simpsons* and *The X-Files* says something about how deeply it's infiltrated the culture.

Akira Kurosawa's 1950 classic has become the standard shorthand to characterize such situations, even though it was not the first film to present conflicting, multiple accounts of the same events. In 1929, at Fox, John G. Blystone made *Thru Different Eyes*, a now utterly forgotten film that apparently used a similar device in the context of a courtroom setting.

Other films had shown us repeated differing perspectives on single events, the most obvious example being *Citizen Kane*, though in *Kane* the accounts supplement each other without contradiction. And in *Stage Fright*, produced almost simultaneously with *Rashomon*, Hitchcock infuriated some viewers by doing a sort of semi-*Rashomon*—presenting a crucial flashback sequence (from the point of view of the male lead) that is later proved to be either a fabrication or (at best) a self-serving distortion of the truth.

But none of these films, not even *Kane*, had the nerve to leave us at the end unsure about What Really Happened. *Rashomon* deliberately, even aggressively, seems to avoid "solving" the mystery for us.

Technically, Kurosawa based the film on two stories by Ryunosuke Akutagawa: confusingly, he took almost nothing but the title and the one of the settings from Akutagawa's "Rashomon"; all of the "story" and most of the thematic concerns come straight from the author's "In a Grove." I've put "story" in quotes because *Rashomon* is a film where, more than most, "story" and "narrative" have to be kept distinct.

That is, the "story" is short and extremely simple: some time around the eleventh or twelfth century, a samurai named Takehiro (Masayuki Mori) and his pretty wife Masago (Machiko Kyo) are riding through the woods. A notorious thief named Tajomaru (Toshiro Mifune) gets a glimpse of Masago and decides he must possess her. Claiming to have a stash of cheap weapons for sale, he lures Takehiro to another part of the forest and, getting the jump on him, ties him up. He then brings Masago to the same spot and rapes her in front of her husband. None of this is disputed, though little of it can be confirmed, either.

What happens next is less clear, however. All we know is that, shortly thereafter, Takehiro has been stabbed to death; Masago has disappeared; and Tajomaru has been arrested with Takehiro's horse and weapons in his possession.

Who killed Takehiro? Why did Masago run away? What went on among the three after the rape?

A trial is held, at which testimony is heard from a woodcutter (Takashi Shimura), who reported finding the body to the police; a priest (Minoru Chiaki), who had seen the couple earlier; the policeman (Daisuke Kato) who caught the thief; Tajomaru; Masago; and even the ghost of the victim, who testifies through a female medium (Fumiko Honma). The first three witnesses speak rather briefly; Tajomaru is the only who tells the whole story; both Masago and Takehiro only tell what happened after the rape, and their accounts flatly contradict Tajomaru and each other. Akutagawa's "In a Grove" is nothing more than a transcription of the testimony at the trial; Kurosawa reproduces it very closely, omitting one witness and presenting some of the material sheerly visually.

That may be the "story" in *Rashomon*, but it's definitely "not" *Rashomon*. Kurosawa starts the film *after* all these events have taken place: in the midst of a downpour, the woodcutter and the priest are taking refuge within the ruins of the once-impressive Rashomon Gate. They seem depressed and confused. "It's the worst thing ever," the priest says, "worse than fire or famine." A third man (Kichijiro Ueda) arrives and asks what's wrong; when told there's been a murder, he laughs. Happens all the time. What's the big deal?

The priest and the woodcutter begin to tell the story of the trial, at which, as witnesses, they were both present. We see the trial in flashback, but, within that, we see each person's testimony as a second layer of flashback. As we hear (and see) the stories, we realize that it is not the fact of the murder that the priest is distressed by, so much as the implications of the various accounts contradicting each other.

The film is rigorously organized around groupings of three. There are three distinctive locales, each representing different time frames and different levels of narrative, each with its own visual style. There are three characters in the "action" part of the story, and three characters at the Gate. In the middle level, at the trial, there are three trivial witnesses and three major witnesses.

The top level is the dark, dreary Rashomon Gate, which is the "present" and is the only level of narrative we can trust; we, the audience, are actually seeing the scenes of the priest, the woodcutter, and the third man, discussing the "story."

The middle level is the stark, sunny courtyard where the trial takes place; everything is rectangular and orderly; the camera is in the position of a judge or board of inquiry; the witnesses are mostly shot straight-on, with no camera movement. Now this may unfold visually, but we can't be sure we're *seeing* anything real: we are seeing what the priest and the woodcutter are reporting about the trial, and they may well have ulterior motives or character flaws that have corrupted the story. Still, this is not as unreliable as. . . .

The third level: the actions that occur in the woods, the "story." Here, out in nature, Kurosawa shoots everything lyrically. These are chronologically the earliest events and, of course, the least reliable. We aren't seeing what *really* happened; we're seeing what the first-level characters are reporting that the second-level characters claim happened. It doesn't take a degree in communications theory to know that, even with the best of intentions, each additional layer of narration makes the signal-to-noise ratio that much worse; anyone who's played "Whisper Down the Lane" can attest to it. (And you, poor reader, are only getting my characterization of all this, with details selected and organized according to my prejudices about what is and isn't important in *Rashomon*. Have I truly described *Rashomon*? Or merely *my* version of *Rashomon*?)

On a simple factual level, the three major testimonies are largely contradictory; in terms of nuance, they are almost completely contradictory. Of course, there are good reasons to assume that, in this case, the three central characters have material reasons to lie—there is a murder rap at stake—as well as psychological reasons to either misremember events or to have interpreted them in a highly biased fashion, even as they were unfolding.

And in fact, just when we have accepted that we will never know the truth, we get a surprise *fourth* eyewitness account, which contradicts them further—an account from someone who *seems* not to have a personal ax to grind. It should settle the issue, but, no, that person is quickly revealed to have his own reasons to falsify the facts, as well.

In the standard mystery film, we'd find out at the end what really happened. Because even the apparent "solution" (offered in the fourth version) is debunked within the film, *Rashomon* is most often interpreted as suggesting that the absolute truth can never be determined and may not even exist. But Kurosawa, according to his own description of his intentions, was not primarily concerned with the *fact* that it is difficult or even impossible to establish objective truth, but with the reason for that difficulty: "Human beings are unable to be honest with themselves about themselves," he wrote in his 1982 *Something Like an Autobiography*. "They cannot talk about themselves without embellishing. This script portrays such human beings—the kind who cannot survive without lies to make them feel they are better people than they really are."

If we take the director at his word, then it was not necessary for the mystery within *Rashomon* to remain unsolved in order for the film to make its point. And Donald Richie, in the introduction to his indispensable sourcebook on the film (Rutgers University Press, 1987), suggests, with some reservations, that a very, very close reading of the film yields up a likely "true" version. Indeed, it is quite possible that Kurosawa ever so subtly left a trail from which we can identify the killer. For him to have done so wouldn't in any way have detracted from the central ideas he was concerned with in the film.

Rashomon was the first Japanese film to become an international sensation after World War II. Despite the reluctance of its distributor, it was submitted as Japan's entry at the Venice Film Festival, where it won the grand prize; its subsequent release in the United States and elsewhere established Mifune as an international star and Kurosawa as the Japanese director best known to the rest of the world—positions that both men held until their deaths.

It is a tribute to *Rashomon's* lasting power that, after fifty years, it continues to stimulate fresh, lively argument. It is also a tribute that it has spawned so many imitators. Whereas one can only look at the two "official" remakes—the 1964 Martin Ritt western version, *The Outrage* (with Paul Newman, Laurence Harvey, Claire Bloom, Edward G. Robinson, and—gulp!—William Shatner), and Hiroaki Yoshida's 1991 contemporary update, *Iron Maze*—with embarrassment, numerous more notable films have shown its clear influence: from Stanley Kubrick's 1956 *The Killing* and Bernardo Bertolucci's first film, *La Commare Secca* (1962), through Aki Kaurismaki's *Hamlet Goes Business* (1987) and Robert Zemeckis's

Back to the Future 2 (1990), to Bryan Singer's *The Usual Suspects* (1995) and Christopher Nolan's *Memento* (2001).

At least, that's the way *I* see it.

Rebel Without a Cause (1955)

by Jay Carr

WHEN NICHOLAS RAY GATHERED the stars of *Rebel Without a Cause* around him in 1954, he thought he was making a black-and-white juvenile delinquent–themed B movie. Columbia had *The Wild One*. MGM had *The Blackboard Jungle*. Warner Brothers had owned the rights to Dr. Robert M. Lindner's *Rebel Without a Cause* since 1946, tested Marlon Brando in 1947, then tabled it when they couldn't sign him. It was revived for a young actor named James Dean. More than revived. During the shoot, when *East of Eden* was released and Dean became an overnight star, studio head Jack Warner ordered the black-and-white filming to cease and told Ray to start all over again, using color. Dean exchanged his black leather jacket for a red nylon windbreaker and never looked back as *Rebel Without a Cause* was promoted to the A-list. What nobody foresaw was that this modestly begun film would define a new genre, tap the zeitgeist, and be instrumental in opening the floodgates of the 1960s.

Rebel Without a Cause opened on October 3, 1955. Dean died four days before. On September 30, he was driving his Porsche Spyder to a race in Salinas, California (site of *East of Eden*), when it collided with a Ford sedan. Dean, twenty-four, died in his seat of a broken neck. His costars, Natalie Wood and Sal Mineo, would also die young. She drowned, he was stabbed. Over the years this has added to the film's mystique. But it was Dean around whom the film revolves and who launched a new American film archetype—the sensitive teenager as betrayed outsider, struggling to live with integrity in a world that surrounded him with adult delinquency.

Brando was the wild one. Dean was the introspective, poetic one. His Jim Stark is anything but a rebel. In a world of momism and crumbling facades of adult authority figures, he longs for old-fashioned honor, writhes with shame and disgust at the sight of his emasculated father, Jim Backus, wearing a frilly apron over his business suit. His sensitivity to the emotional values to which his parents have dulled themselves and his wistful attempt to impose order on the skewed adult world give him enduring appeal. He's not wild, he's aching because he can't see how to make his life honorable, even when he risks it to save Sal Mineo's doomed young disciple and not so latently homosexual adorer, Plato.

The film, which spans twenty-four hours in the life of seventeen-year-old Jim Stark on his first day at a new school, reaches its first climax in a switchblade fight at the Griffith Park Observatory (although wearing a chest protector, Dean got nicked behind the ear and bled). It ends at the Griffith Park planetarium at night, when Mineo's spooked Plato is shot down by police who think he's armed and dangerous as Dean's Jim Stark stands by helplessly, unable to make the police see that he had emptied the bullets from the pistol that Plato had previously handed him in friendship.

Unlike most so-called juvenile delinquency films, *Rebel Without a Cause* spends almost no time in high school. Its framing planetarium scenes seem intended to impart a cosmic dimension to the film. Certain there's ironic intent in the high schoolers early on being forced to sit through an astronomer's lecture on the order of the universe. What transpires on the planetarium steps at the end speaks of a fundamental disorder of the universe. It was no accident that a trenchcoated planetarium staffer entering the scene as everybody else is leaving is Ray, putting his seal on the moral chaos that makes a mockery of any idea of an ordered universe.

Although *Rebel Without a Cause* takes its name from Lindner's serious book about a psychiatric case study, it took nothing else from Lindner. To a postwar America shook up by the fact that things didn't return to a complacent acceptance of traditional societal roles, jolted instead by an attack on the very legitimacy of adult authority, *Rebel Without a Cause* was rightly perceived as a threat to an already shaky structure. Father didn't know best. Father wasn't even up to behaving as a father, protecting his son and leading him into adulthood. The message Jim Stark was receiving up from the hypocritical, anaesthetized adult world was that Jim and those like him were on their own. *Rebel Without a Cause* is an indictment of adult abdication. The film's only adult capable of showing understanding (a juvenile cop also significantly named Ray) isn't there when Jim needs him and goes looking for him at the precinct house.

The films' tacked-on optimistic ending is just that—tacked on, lacking the vigor and conviction of what precedes it. The film's real message is that the instincts of alienated teens are right, and that if they are to live lives worth living, they must break away from the adult world trying to steamroll, desensitize, and compromise them and create their own world. That's the message of the famous scene when Jim, Plato, and Natalie Wood's Judy play house late at night in a deserted mansion (actually a former Getty mansion, also used for *Sunset Boulevard*). Jim and Judy are the surrogate parents, Plato (ironic embodiment of the Greek philosopher's dictum that the unexamined life is not worth living) their child, although the homoerotic subtext is unmistakable. When Jim and Judy drift off by themselves, leaving Plato at the mercy of gang members hunting them down, Plato relives the abandonment scenario played out by his own father in the film and reacts with terror, fear, and self-destructive rage.

Although everyone in the film apart from Jim is a satellite character, Wood's Judy is the least satisfactory. Initial references to her promiscuity, arising from her conflicted relationship with her own emotionally closed-off father, were toned down, although her unstable nature is indicated by the ease and rapidity with which she switches allegiance from the gang leader (Corey Allen's Buzz, who dies in the chicken race with Jim in stolen cars) to Jim, as if any alpha male will do. Their love-fantasy scene, while surprisingly delicate and even charming, lacks emotional poignance because of the shallowness in the writing of her character. The gang members, on the other hand, are comic-strip caricatures with comic-strip names: Buzz (Allen), Goon (Dennis Hopper), Moose (Jack Simmons), and Crunch (Frank Mazzola). Mazzola, a real gang member, contributed to the research, right down to making everybody connected with the shoot realize that so-called juvenile delinquency wasn't simply the wrong-side-of-the-tracks phenomenon that pop culture had put forth ever since Sidney Kingsley's landmark play *Dead End*—that it involved middle-class kids whose families had their own cars in their own garages, a fact that made the delinquency even more frightening.

Dean's generation—and succeeding ones—identified with Jim's alienated chase after honor. *Rebel Without a Cause* launched not only the James Dean phenomenon but the reputation of Ray as an unruly individualist who nevertheless pioneered on a communal approach with his young cast in order to nail actual teen feelings on film. His often rawly executed work was regarded as proof of his integrity. Just as Dean came to *Rebel Without a Cause* from the acclaim he generated in *East of Eden*, Ray came to the film off what perhaps was the wildest western ever made, *Johnny Guitar,* in which he flamboyantly let the psychosexual chips fall where they may. There was more than a touch of misogyny in Ray's view of postwar American life as stifling and confining. Only Douglas Sirk maintained a more consistent and sustained similar vision.

Ray realized that Dean was the motor and heart of *Rebel Without a Cause*. He not only allowed but encouraged Dean to participate in script rewrites. He even let Dean direct (the scene where Jim confronts his eunuch father in pain and anger and agonized love) and improvise. Jim's opening scene, in which he's seen drunk, cradling a toy monkey, in an obvious reversion to an infantile state, was improvised. It's one end of the arc described by the film. At the end, following Jim's futile attempt to save Plato's life, Jim's father tells him: "You did everything a man could." Without any help from his own father, or any of the other dysfunctional mentor and authority figures in his world, Jim has undergone a rite of passage, growing in one night from frightened child to authentic adult. *Rebel Without a Cause,* an allegory of growth and the painfulness of growth, transcends its own lurid excesses and now-dated topicality to stand as the kind of big pop myth that defines the Hollywood studio movie at its most potent.

The Rules of the Game (1939)

by Jay Carr

THE FILMS OF JEAN RENOIR never land heavy on the eye or the spirit. There are no conquering heroes in them. Identifying profoundly with uncertainty and frailty, Renoir became the poet of chaos theory. He humanized it long before existentialism and physics got their hands on it. Physically ungainly—and keenly aware of it—he costumed himself as a galumphing bear for his ringmaster's role in his masterpiece, *The Rules of the Game* (1939). In that film, he uses bumptiousness and forced garrulousness to conceal feelings he can scarcely contain at the spectacle of a chateauful of people he loves all looking for love in the wrong places. The sensibility—in contrast to the lumpish envelope that contains it—is delicate, observant, embracing, never unaware of the problematic nature of life.

So gently affirmative are Renoir's films that one is taken aback to read that he once described life as a tissue of disappointments. There's always a heartful of pain in Renoir, but it never weights his films down. It's as if they have tempo markings—*allegro, vivace, prestissimo. The Rules of the Game* is like Feydeau (Renoir used one of his sex farces for his first sound film, *On Purge Bébé*), but less vulgar, more cultivated, more ironic, more improvisatory, more deeply felt. The country house party scamperings are anything but a game. They're played for keeps. And the only rule is that there are no rules. Yet *The Rules of the Game* never succumbs to cynicism; it's filled with a respect, bordering on humility, for the desperation and emotional nakedness of people whipsawed by their needs—the exquisitely considerate *arriviste* or a marquis, his combative mistress, his heedlessly romantic wife, and aviator who loves her, a charming drone of a friend, a stern steward, a pert chambermaid, a foxlike poacher who works his way inside the henhouse, all the modish types spilling from the bedrooms.

It's this regard for the integrity of emotion that forbids Renoir form ever feeling contempt for any of his characters. Renoir is film's answer to Mozart—the slow movements of the great piano concertos, the haunting minor-key tonalities of his next-to-last symphony, the smiling tolerance of *Cosi fan tutte,* the piercing wistfulness of *The Marriage of Figaro.* Like Mozart, Renoir was inspired by Beaumarchais, linked to a culture where elegance was held in esteem. Unlike Mozart, he was not a creature of the court and the coffeehouse. Like his famous painter father, Pierre Auguste, Jean Renoir was of the atelier, a craftsman. "Art is making," his father told him, and he listened. He didn't have to be told that the heart has its reasons, or that to understand is to forgive. What he understood best of all was what the world called weakness.

Human relations became the real subject of Renoir's films, even though that wasn't his intention at the start. He married his father's last model, who took the stage name Catherine Hessling. He saw himself as a potter, only leaving his kiln to make his wife a star. His first film was *Une Vie sans Joie,* made in 1924, later retitled and re-released as *Catherine.* Neither that nor his second vehicle for her, *La Fille de l'Eau* (1924), were successes. Renoir's films stemmed literally, if not figuratively, from his father's paintings, many of which he sold to finance the films. "Every sale seemed a betrayal," he wrote, possibly recalling almost going broke to finance his biggest Hessling spectacular, *Nana* (1926).

That encounter with Zola—*Nana* was the most opulent of Renoir's silents—was heavily influenced by Erich Von Stroheim's *Foolish Wives* and in it Hessling's doll-like ferocity made its biggest impression. Her *Charleston* (1927) and *The Little Match Girl* (1928) amount to little more than curios. Still, material and motifs that Renoir later refined show up in these early efforts. The impressionistic water imagery in *La Fille de l'Eau* reached its apotheosis in *The River* (1950), in which Renoir's serenity matched that of India, where the film was shot. And the voyeuristic way in which Hessling's shivering match girl rubs frost off a restaurant window to watch the well-to-do dine presages Renoir's affecting way of avoiding cliché in the seminal *La Chienne* (1931), where he has duped clerk Michel Simon watch numbed through a rain-streaked window as his mistress pulls the man she really loves into bed.

La Chienne, France's first sound film shot on location and Renoir's first hit, was a milestone film—as well as remaining a surprisingly entertaining one, wearing its years lightly. Renoir entered filmmaking to please his wife, then became hooked by it. When he was offered the chance to direct *La Chienne,* he took it and directed another woman (Janie Marese) in its leading role, even though his wife had threatened to leave him because of it—and did. The breakup squared with his essentially pessimistic view of life. For Renoir, the story of the henpecked clerk and Sunday painter who naively falls in love with a prostitute named Lulu and is victimized by her and her pimp resonated provocatively on several levels.

Opening with the kind of puppet show prologue he was to return to in his last film, *Le Petit Théâtre de Jean Renoir* (1971), he proclaims that he's giving us neither a social drama nor a comedy of manners. "It has no moral whatever," he says, "and proves nothing at all. The characters are neither heroes nor villains, but plain people like you and me." In its compassionate detachment, the film seems to foreshadow *Rules of the Game.* But Renoir has a few psychic scores to settle, and the film has bits. Finding in the shambling Michel Simon a surrogate self, he presents the clerk as too cultivated for his milieu and proceeds to depict with tart comedy every tone of his bad marriage—first with a shrewish wife, then with a grabby streetwalker.

Clearly, Renoir also entered this film with strong—and in some ways conflicted—feelings about the role of art (his father's and his own) and about his own role in relation to his father's art and his guilt in selling it. It's impossible not to speculate upon the sources of the timid clerk's rage when he discovers that Lulu, in order to support her pimp, has uncaringly sold the paintings he gave her. Much as Renoir was to move toward serenity and nostalgia in later years, he remained open to degrees of pain and feeling that were alien to his father's canvases, which were filled with freshness and vigor, but never the hesitations and ambivalences in his son's films.

Both women who wrong the Renoir surrogate die in *La Chienne,* but Renoir emerges purged, with a more lightly sophisticated view of the fate of art. In an airy epilogue in which Simon-Renoir, turned *clochard,* blithely exchanges art for money, he says goodbye to a painting being driven off in a millionaire's roadster and hello to day-to-day expediency. What he's really saying hello to is the world of film. *La Chienne*—remade by Fritz Lang as *Scarlet Street* with Edward. G. Robinson—marks Renoir's commitment to an art form that was to enable him to emerge from his father's shadow.

After filming Renoir's *Night at the Crossroads* with his brother, Pierre Renoir, as Inspector Maigret, Renoir made *Boudu Saved from Drowning* (1932), with Simon as the tramp fished from the Seine and threatened with civilization (this film, too, inspired a Hollywood remake, Paul Mazursky's *Down and Out in Beverly Hills*).

Even more warmly steeped in everyday Parisian atmosphere than *La Chienne* with its Montmartre scenes—and all the stronger for it—*Boudu* ends with a burst of pure anarchist impulse close to Renoir's pacifist heart. In it, Boudu escapes the encumbrances of the bourgeois life heaped upon him, faking his drowning, then pulling himself out of the Seine yet again, relishing his freedom. That full-circle pan, in which we share Boudu's sense of reliberation, was to return in *French Can-Can* (1955), with impresario Jean Gabin this time serving as the figure escaping that tied-down feeling.

Although Renoir made two overt Popular Front films, the best of them was covert, *La Crime de Monsieur Lange* (1935), in which his benign impulses toward his actors proved to be the factor that carried the film past the pitfalls of agitprop. Like the best Renoir films, it's a great milieu piece—with a male-run print shop and female-run laundry sitting across a cramped courtyard in affectionate solidarity that ripens into something more when the laundry's proprietress becomes the protector of the man who unwittingly sets in motion a seizure of the print shop by its workers after its evil capitalist boss goes too far in exploiting him. Will the printer, who becomes a hit author with his escapist fantasies about a character named Arizona Jim, get away with murder? The film ends with the audience serving as jury. And Renoir's warmth and humanity extend to the villainous capitalist, Batala, played by Jules Berry with the disarming charm of a boulevardier.

It was Renoir's seizing upon the chance to employ Erich Von Stroheim, his *Foolish Wives* mentor, that made *La Grande Illusion* (1937) the great film it became. Hailed as an antiwar film, with its story of French soldiers escaping a German prison camp during World War I, it became much more than a simple square-off of social classes. When Marcel Dalio also signed on, joining Jean Gabin's vital working-class type as a Jewish banker's son also fleeing the crumbling old aristocratic milieu represented by the prison and breaking away to new beginnings, further richness was added to the social tapestry. But mostly the film belongs to Von Stroheim and Pierre Fresnay, linked by their roots in the aristocracy and finding those links stronger than the national boundaries that came much later in the history of their respective families.

The melancholy nobility of the imminently extinct similarly informs *The Rules of the Game* (1939), which predictably flopped and wasn't recognized as the masterpiece it is until after the war. Renoir's refusal to moralize—or to designate a star and bring his restless camera to rest on him or her—wasn't what the mass audience craved. Working as much from intuition as from programmatic intent, Renoir's country house party all too successfully captures the ephemeral life of a generous and gracious but decadent society dancing on the brink of war. The film's whiff of war is conveyed in a now classic scene in which the aristocrats slaughter birds and rabbits during a shoot—presaging the film's climactic incident of poignantly absurd human sacrifice.

Renoir later said he wanted a certain disorder, wanted to tell a light story about a world dancing on a volcano. His indirection, his refusal to become explicit, is the reason the film remains so hauntingly resonant. Most other directors would simply have satirized characters a bit too given to the heartless mechanics of social games. Renoir went further. Years later, in a documentary filmed by Jacques Rivette, Renoir congratulated Marcel Dalio for his play of emotions during the scene where the Marquis de la Chesnaye, an eccentric collector, unveils an elaborate mechanical orchestra to amuse his guests. "The combination of humility and pride, success and doubt, on the edge of so many things, nothing definite—it was my best shot," Renoir says.

Later, using color film, Renoir the apostle of contemporary lyric realism turned to artifice, reduced his scale, turned backward in time. In *The Golden Coach* (1953) and *French Can-Can* (1955), with their remarkably similar stories of women turning their backs on love for careers as artists, Renoir seemed determined to re-create his father's sunlit visual world—but with greater detachment. It's as if he took his early thirties disappointment in his first wife—and his renewed belief in art—one step too far. In the fablelike *Golden Coach,* set in an imagined Peru, actress Anna Magnani rejects suitors representing domesticity, passion, and power. Ditto for dancer Françoise Arnoul in *French Can-Can,* with its idealized Moulin Rouge milieu. *Elena and Her Men* (1956), starring Ingrid Bergman as a Belle Epoque Juno who also wreaks amatory havoc, allows her to succumb to love, but otherwise is just as sumptuous—and Olympian—as *The Golden Coach* and *French Can-Can.* Like Orson Welles, furtively longing for a bygone world in *Citizen Kane,* and then not so furtively longing for it in *The Magnificent Ambersons,* Renoir unmistakably genuflects to the world of his youth in this trilogy.

But in all Renoir's films, you find at the core the spirit of his warm, sympathetic, melancholy Octave in *Rules of the Game.* He wanted to be an orchestral conductor, but the world never warmed to him, says Renoir-Octave, who affably falls in with the world's perception of him as a failure. Yet Octave, the outwardly clumsy, inwardly suave seducer, is—like the man inhabiting him—the figure most sensitive to the feelings of the others and their mercurial mood shifts. Although Renoir's touch is always gentle, he won't let Octave off the hook, yanks him from diversionary buffoonery to sobering self-awareness. Subtle, prismatic, acute, infinitely embracing, *Rules of the Game* is one of the century's undisputed masterworks. Renoir thought he was reworking Beaumarchais and de Musset, but *Rules of the Game*—right down to its figure of the little poacher bringing mischievous nature indoors—seems kin to Shakespeare's *Midsummer Night's Dream*. It's a sublime comedy of the mutability of human feelings that manages, without ever becoming sentimental, to turn into a celebration of humankind.

Schindler's List (1993)

by Jay Carr

NOTHING IN STEVEN SPIELBERG'S previous work prepares us for *Schindler's List* or for its mythical central figure, an unlikely angel dancing on the rim of hell, snatching Jews from death. It's a stunning achievement, a film that re-creates the Holocaust not as something abstract but as felt knowledge. Its impact is mostly visceral. This is pretty much the way it must have been, you tell yourself as you sit tensely watching German troops listen silently in the stairwell of a ransacked apartment for telltale noises of Jews in hiding, or as a bored Nazi commandant with a beer gut sits on a balcony with a rifle, shooting Jews at random. Or even as you realize that an improvised road is paved with pieces of Jewish gravestones, that even in death the Nazis won't leave the Jews alone.

The usual terms of praise for a film must be jettisoned because *Schindler's List* goes beyond the usual boundaries of film. It's as much a stunning avoidance of pitfalls as it is a triumph of existential immediacy. There isn't an aesthetic choice in it that didn't amount to a moral choice for Spielberg as well, and he acquits himself magnificently, bringing his prodigious image-making gifts from the arena of lonely childhood yearnings to the area of global history. After several compromised tries at making a serious film, he finally emerges here as a mature filmmaker doing justice to the most serious subject of the century.

Schindler's List, filmed in Poland at the invitation of the Polish government, a minister of which cited his country's need for closure, is informed by the fact that unlike Warsaw, which was mostly leveled, Krakow remained pretty much intact. Schindler's actual factory still stands, used today by a manufacturer of radio parts. This all-or-nothing project, steeped in atmospheric rightness provided by Krakow locales, required Spielberg to measure up to his intimidating subject ethically as well as technically, and he has. A triumphant merger of craft and commitment,

Schindler's List reminds us that there's no substitute for a virtuosic image-maker taking on a subject close to his heart and soul.

Most of the right moves were made before Spielberg moved a single camera to Poland, starting with the decision to film in black and white, mostly at eye level, close-up, with a lot of handheld camerawork. Often, the handheld camera has tended to seem a jittery self-indulgence, but here it works, an analogue for the chaos and arbitrariness into which Europe's Jews were flung. The black-and-white textures aren't gritty, like the old newsreels they evoke. They're velvety, hard-edged, which at once reinforces the precision and detail that are twin strengths, promoting the only-yesterday urgency Spielberg means to capture, and does.

He's right to let the details—most transposed from Thomas Keneally's historical novel drawn from accounts of survivors—carry the film. To have punched the film up with histrionics would have ruined it, and Spielberg carefully avoids any italicizing that would seem redundant and puny, given the larger story. He's also right to leave the character of Oskar Schindler a bit of a mystery. Explaining him would have been fatal. Indeed, the film's only move that seems a misstep comes at the end, when Schindler momentarily expresses regret that he didn't save more than the 1,100 Jews he managed to shelter by a deft combination of bribery and manipulation. Ambiguity—apart from hewing closer to the truth—makes Schindler more dramatically interesting. We don't know what precisely turned him from an untroubled profiteer, getting rich off Jewish slave labor, to a savior, using his profits to buy the lives of Jews and to buy exorbitant black-market food to keep them alive.

In the film, as in the book, the turning point comes when he's seated on horseback alongside his mistress on a hill, watching as the Nazis march into the ghetto and slaughter the Jews they had just herded into it, they said, for safety. Spielberg takes a chance here, as the coat of a little girl who miraculously toddles away unobserved is highlighted in—symbolically—red. But it works, and the sight of Schindler looking on, yet apart, is an analogue for Spielberg's own aesthetic distancing. To heap drama, much less melodrama, on top of such intrinsically shattering events would have caused the film to self-destruct. Which is why Spielberg has, if anything, underplayed the dramatic events related in the book, some of which are too theatrical to be believed. For example, when Schindler plays blackjack with a Nazi for the life of a Jewish cook—an event that really occurred—we see only the setting up of the game and the dealing of the cards before Spielberg wisely cuts away.

Liam Neeson was an inspired choice as Schindler. With his slightly predatory stoop, he moves with the confidence of a worldly bluffer, eyes glistening like a born gambler's, letting us know without a word that part of the appeal of his dangerous game lies in its high stakes. Although the film downplays the real Schindler's womanizing, Neeson is convincing as well when it comes to Schindler's hedonistic side. And while it might seem difficult to believe, there's humor as well in *Schindler's List,* most stemming from Schindler's shrewdness at knowing how to get things done by pushing German bureaucratic buttons. He argues his right-hand man off a death-camp train not by making moral points but by questioning the correctness of the paperwork, a knack he later escalates to bring a trainful of Jews out of Auschwitz on the grounds that he needs them for war production in his enamelware factory, which manufactures field-kitchen equipment.

Not that the Holocaust's larger horrors are in any way neglected. They're all the more chillingly brought home by entering our field of vision matter-of-factly: Jews saying that things could be worse and denying death-camp rumors; a truckload of children singing as they're being driven off to the ovens; Schindler himself reminding us what a relative thing mercy is as he hoses down a packed car of stifling prisoners as the Germans laugh. As with Neeson, the others move beyond usual levels of acting, not just impersonating their characters, but seeming to embody them with totally conviction and commitment. Chief among them are Ben Kingsley as the brains of Schindler's operation and—his piercing gaze never lets us forget—its conscience, and Ralph Fiennes as the nightmarish commandant, Amon Goeth.

The latter's absolute life-and-death power transformed him into a god of death, killing arbitrarily, capriciously, wantonly. Bloated on blood as well as on beer, he's brutal and stupid and at times mesmerizingly eerie in his disconnection from inhibition, a riveting portrait of corruption. Would-be neo-Nazis, not so incidentally, will be forced to face up to the fact that, beneath those cool SS uniforms, the German war machine ran on lies, psychosis, thievery, and monstrous mediocrity. *Schindler's List* took a long time to gestate, but once it started happening, it came together with astonishing speed, purposefulness, and rightness. *Schindler's List* really got to me. Its haunting, potent, jolting images turn it into another kinetic—and inextinguishable—Holocaust museum.

The Searchers (1956)

by Peter Travers

DIRECTED BY JOHN FORD AT THE PEAK of his introspective powers, *The Searchers* is arguably the best and most emotionally devastating western ever crafted. Working with simpatico cinematographer Winton C. Hoch, Ford came closest in *The Searchers* to edging the poetic majesty of his beloved Monument Valley with a despairing sense of shame. Ford, who died in 1973 after making 125 features that included *Stagecoach, My Darling Clementine, She Wore a Yellow Ribbon*, and other westerns of lasting stature, would have never admitted to such pretensions. As he once said, "It's no good asking me to talk about art." No need either. *The Searchers* does it for him. From the first long shot of John Wayne on horseback—observed riding home by a woman silhouetted in a doorway—the film is awash in the beauty of open spaces and the terror of trapped psyches. The image of Wayne standing apart from the family that greets him serves as a springboard for Ford's harshest view of the West, which is seen as a hotbed of racist attitudes in the script Frank S. Nugent adapted from the novel by Alan LeMay.

Wayne plays Ethan Edwards, a former Confederate soldier. The war has been over for three years, but the mysterious Ethan is just now returning to the Texas farm of his brother Aaron (Walter Coy). Bitterness weighs heavily on Ethan, despite the warmth of Aaron, his wife Martha (Dorothy Jordan), and their three children, Ben, Lucy, and ten-year-old Debbie (Lana Wood). Even Old Mose, the kindly eccentric memorably played by Hank Worden, feels the chill. Aaron's grown adopted son, Martin (Jeffrey Hunter), has it worse. Martin is part Cherokee, and Ethan's racism runs deep.

Ford's start in silent films made him a master of expressive action without dialogue. In one scene, Texas Ranger Samuel Clayton (Ward Bond) accidentally observes Martha caressing a coat that belongs to Ethan. Clayton observes the gesture and takes in its meaning—Martha is in love with her brother-in-law—but quickly averts his eyes. Critic Andrew Sarris, an early champion of *The Searchers* when the best picture Oscar was going to the inane *Around the World in 80 Days*, wrote that "nothing on earth would ever force this man to reveal what he had seen." It's a code of ethics much admired by Ford. Later, after most of Ethan's family is slaughtered by Comanches, he turns on those who ask what he saw: "Don't ever ask me. As long as you live, don't ever ask me more."

The core of the film is taken up with Ethan's search for Debbie, who has been kidnapped by the Comanche Chief Scar (Henry Brandon). Martin leaves behind his fiancée, Laurie (Vera Miles), to join Ethan on his search, which lasts for seven years and intensifies Ethan's rancor. He shoots an Indian in the eyes because he knows Indians believe that will condemn their spirits to wander. To Martin's horror, Ethan even threatens to kill the grown Debbie, played with touching confusion by Natalie Wood (Lana's older sister), because she's become the wife of Scar: "She ain't white anymore," Ethan roars. "She's Comanche." Listen again to the way Wayne bites off the last syllable of that word. It's a distillation of hatred.

Wayne gives a towering performance that seems to grow in bruising power with the years. Ethan's obsession with racial, sexual, and cultural purity is ingrained, part of an American mind-set that has lasted for generations and finds modern parallels in intolerance toward everything from mixed marriage to AIDS. Ethan's incalculable influence on other screen characters extends to Darth Vader (dark father) in George Lucas's *Star Wars,* and the strict Calvinist, played by George C. Scott, who can't forgive his porn-star daughter in Paul Schrader's *Hardcore,* and the cabby (Robert DeNiro) determined to rid of the world of the scum who turned a child (Jodie Foster) into a prostitute in Martin Scorsese's *Taxi Driver.* The male rage that follows a perceived violation of women also informs such works as Mike Hodges's *Get Carter* and Steven Soderbergh's *The Limey.* Like Ethan, the tormented avengers who prowl these films seek an elusive inner piece.

One scene in *The Searchers* burns deepest in the memory. Ethan, riding hard to catch his terrified niece, pulls her into his arms and then, just at the second when she thinks he is about to kill her, says: "Let's go home, Debbie." For Ethan, it's a moment of reconciliation, but hardly one of resolution. Like the Indian he shot in the eyes, Ethan will never find peace. He brings Debbie home to live with Martin and Laurie, but Ethan knows there is no place for him there. Ford knows it, too, in his bones. In the last shot, Ford again frames Ethan in a doorway, still a restless figure who has let spite bury love.

The Searchers ends as the door closes on this genuinely tragic figure, plunging him into a darkness that seems eternal. No door in film history has ever closed more emphatically or left an audience more open to search its heart for answers.

The Seven Samurai (1954)

by John Anderson

IN A RECENT CUSTOMER "REVIEW" logged in at the unavoidable Amazon.com, we learned that Akira Kurosawa's *The Seven Samurai* was, like, okay. But hardly as cool as the movie it so obviously ripped off, *The Magnificent Seven.*

As hard as it is to believe sometimes, the Internet was not invented *solely* to give vent to unedited ignorance; Amazon.com is under no legal obligation to correct any of the misinformation it and other such sites casually ejaculate into the electronic ether every day. Besides: The writer didn't notice that *Seven Samurai* was released in 1954 and John Sturges's star-studded (and studly) Hollywood western four years later? Forgivable. The real issue is lack of judgment, poverty of taste.

The Magnificent Seven is a fun movie, action-packed, larded with such provenders of 1960s beefcake as Steve McQueen, James Coburn, and Yul Brynner, with the bonus of Horst Buchholtz totally unchained. There's no better movie with which to spend a rainy Sunday afternoon, providing one has access to salsa, chips, beer, and Barcalounger.

But *Samurai*—also known as *The Magnificent Seven* in its earliest manifestation—is a fully coherent work of art, an epic in every respect, including its length (which this fan refuses to concede is even slightly protracted). To merely call it a classic is glib—but it *is* a classic, because it continues to provoke, to impassion. Yes, it spawned western interest in Japanese cinema precisely because it appealed to other-than-Japanese taste—it's the great example of Kurosawa's absorption and reimagining of Western entertainment (and, of course, the western) into a Japanese context, of recycling in a way that Hong Kong directors would do with John Ford a couple of decades later.

But it is also a film that, coming as it did less than ten years after the country was nuked and defeated, reimagines Japan.

Even Amazon reviewers know the basic story: A village of farmers, under siege by brigands, sets out to contract a band of mercenaries to fight their battle. The village has little to offer; the men who take the job it will do it, as one amused samurai says, "For food . . . and the fun of it." The villagers fear the samurai—less than they do the brigands, but not by much. The distrust people have for their own saviors is one of story's sharpest points and consistent themes.

In the script—by Kurosawa, his *Rashomon* collaborator Shinobu Hashimoto, and Hideo Oguni—the hero warriors are actually *ronin,* or samurai without masters, soldiers of various shogun defeated in the civil wars of sixteenth-century Japan. Left to wander, they are fugitives, pursued by rival samurai, sometimes victimized even by village farmers. The first one we meet—the eldest, the leader, and the chief strategist-to-be—is Shimada (Takashi Shimura), who is shown having his head shaved. A ritual of shame? Possibly—Shimura, who bears a rather ironic resemblance to Ward Bond, can strike a look of solemnity bordering on the funereal. But not, what he's thinking about is the task at hand: A thief has taken a small boy hostage in a nearby barn. Disguised as a monk, Shimada will get close enough to save the boy and butcher the kidnapper, who collapses in the first of what will be several balletic, slo-mo descents by the dead into the mud and dust.

That dust, that mud, are part of what separates *Seven Samurai* from all its imitators (even Sturges's *The Great Escape,* which is also cut on the *Samurai* template of hero "specialists" and honor among the few). The natural world is always part of the film, and the characters inseparable from nature. Whether through furious action or the starkly eloquent close-ups that reveal so much of the inner life of his characters, Kurosawa places them in a world that's windy, dirty, and wild.

Wildest of the samurai—not a samurai at all, at first—is Kikuchiyo, the farmer's son-turned-warrior portrayed by Toshiro Mifune, perhaps the greatest of all Japanese film stars (international film stars, certainly). Mifune had made an indelible impression in Kurosawa's *Rashomon,* but in *Seven Samurai* his Kikuchiyo is sheer exuberance, buffoonery, bravery, strutting like a cock, shrinking in shame or acting with unquestionable courage. Kikuchiyo is the heart of the movie; Mifune is magnetic.

In *The Magnificent Seven* the Buchholtz character, Chico, is an amalgam of Kikuchiyo and Katsushiro (Isao Kimura), the young, highborn romantic who witnesses Shimada's rescue of the young hostage and immediately enlists in the war with the brigands (although he has no training). Shimada treats him as a son, protecting him from danger virtually throughout the film, treating him with as much kindness as he shows Kikuchiyo contempt. It is Katsushiro who falls for the local girl and who ultimately joins the farmers after their defeat of the brigands. It is Katsushiro who also hero-worships Kyuzo (Seiji Miyaguchi), the master swordsman who is Kurosawa's coolest creation.

Kyuzo is the ultimate samurai; devoted to his art, single-minded in its perfection, and unconquerable. In one of those close-ups that Kurosawa makes so overwhelmingly poignant, partly because they are so infrequent and intense, Kyuzo looks at the gushing Katsushiro ("You are . . . great") with a face that, in its lantern-jawed stoicism, says all the film has to say about the sacrifice of warfare. Or of art. Katsushiro is the eternal observer, Kyuzo the artist, even if his medium is death.

Kyuzo is also the personification of honor and it is honor, in several incarnations, that's the overriding theme of *Samurai*. Kurosawa was no Mishima, but in *Samurai* we see a longing for a world that validates skill and integrity, a return to a time when these things mattered more than might and technology—a time that may never have existed but has forever been part of the heroic mythology of Japan. And America too. It's no coincidence that in *The Seven Samurai,* the samurai who are killed are killed by bullets. (That three guns are in the hands of the brigands is as semiotically significant as the fact there are forty brigands.) Although its practitioners are masters of the bow, the spear, the sword, the way of the samurai is no defense against the impersonal (or cowardly) methods of modern weaponry. It's hardly an allegorical leap to see A-bombs vs. Imperial Japan.

The Seven Samurai is film about honor, male honor, and maleness—Kurosawa's most persistent symbol of the last are the bamboo staffs carried by the peasants trained by the samurai. Wobbly and misaligned at first, they grow straighter and sharper as the movie progresses, finally taking up particularly potent residence as the lethal-looking spikes implanted in the moat dug by the villagers, aimed at the advancing horde.

And yet, the most affecting scenes in the film involve women. Sex is a constant subtext of the film; the male villagers fear their women being raped by the brigands or seduced by the samurai. When the jolliest samurai, Gorobei (Yoshio Inaba) expresses a wish that villager Rikichi (Yoshio Tsuchiya) get married soon, Rikichi turns away in a rage. Shortly, we find out why.

A small patrol of samurai and farmers is dispatched to thin out the band of forty expected to attack the town at dawn and find a kind of brigand's brothel where men and women lie in postcoital comas. The samurai set fire to the house, planning to slaughter the men as they run through the doors. As they watch through the wall as the fire takes hold, one woman, looking both stupified and disgusted, awakes, is initially alarmed by the smoke, but then assumes a look of satisfaction: She'll happily let them all burn.

But when she comes through the doors of the flaming building she takes one look at Rikichi, runs back into the fire, and is consumed. It is, of course, his wife. As the house falls around her in an image of total holocaust, a samurai's effort to save Rikichi ends in the samurai's being shot by an unseen hand. The universe is in chaos.

This scene, and one that follows—in which an old village woman whose son has been killed by brigands is allowed to hack a prisoner to death—marks another of the less heroic but nonetheless important themes of *Seven Samurai*: What war means. To the samurai it is their life, but also a kind of pastime, a means of proving their honor. To the villagers it means torment and oppression. The samurai may be disgusted by the breach of the warrior's code when the villagers kill a supine prisoner, but the rage displayed by the farmers toward one of their tormentors shows how distanced the soldiers can be from the realities of war. The echoes can be felt all the way to one of Kurosawa's last films—*Rhapsody in August*, about the legacy of Nagasaki. It certainly provides the element of intellectual potency that separates *The Seven Samurai* from any and all of its shallow imitations.

The Seventh Seal (1957)

by Peter Keough

WHAT WOULD INGMAR BERGMAN'S *The Seventh Seal*—his first and finest masterpiece and one of the great works of art of the twentieth century— be like without Death? No, not death per se. No movie would survive without death; certainly no film by Bergman. I'm talking about Death the pasty-faced personification of our mortality as played by the actor Bengt Ekerot, later featured in the Swedish TV movie *Bombi, Bitt, and Me* in 1968, and who himself would be checkmated by the Grim Reaper on November 26, 1971. Rather than being a figure of terror, Death in *The Seventh Seal* is comic relief, a figure of fun. Cheating at chess, cutting down trees to topple victims, this Death is not far removed from that of William Sadler's wraith playing Twister, Clue, and Battleships in *Bill & Ted's Bogus Journey*.

Okay, I exaggerate. Let's not forget that the film is set in the thirteenth century, when the Black Death razed Sweden and the rest of Europe (for my money, Bergman is the greatest director of disaster movies; I'll take *Shame* over *Armageddon* any day). Nonetheless, even among the horror and hopelessness, people were still looking for good entertainment. Dispirited Crusaders like errant knight Antonius Block (Max von Sydow) return home after years of carnage and disillusionment in the Holy Land to ask what was the meaning of it all. And what do they find? The music videos and tabloid TV of their time: morality plays, processions of flagellants, and witch burnings. And, of course, the Big Game, the chess match with Death.

Life is a game, and Death is a player. Whether seated at a board or walking the boards, Death appears as the ultimate diversion. No doubt *The Seventh Seal* confronts the terror of the void and the absurdity of mortality, the 1950s being the glum heyday of existentialism, but lately I've come to believe it's more about the power of illusion and artifice. Everybody quakes before the reality of death, but who can resist taking a peek when he takes a bow onstage? As the cynical fresco painter comments when asked about his morbid subject matter, "A skull is more fascinating than a naked woman." And the artist who renders that skull is more powerful than the dread verity it represents.

Sometimes the face that veils the skull fascinates too. Photographed by Gunnar Fischer, Bergman's cinematographer of choice prior to his long collaboration with Sven Nykvist, faces and landscapes shimmer like visions in *The Seventh Seal*. There's Block's, of course, which looks like a luminous, tormented, Easter Island effigy. There's the face of the reclining stranger near the beginning of the film whom Block's faithful, if faithless, squire Jöns (the redoubtable Gunnar Björnstrand) asks for directions ("Was he dumb?" "No, he was most eloquent"). There's the face of the witch, the teenage girl about to be hoisted onto a scaffold and burned for consorting with the Devil. Cradled in Von Sydow's massive hands, this doomed face lingers as one of cinema's most wrenching images; she insists he can see Satan in her eyes, but in them he can see only terror.

And then, of course, there is the face of Death. Bulbous, pale, inscrutable— add some smoke and mirrors and you've got no less than the bogus poobah from *The Wizard of Oz*. "I have no secrets," indeed. Not to beat the comparison to death, but *The Seventh Seal* is yet another variation on that sacred Hollywood ur-text with Max von Sydow in the Judy Garland role. Here, too, the home-seeking hero gathers a party of fellow misfits and stragglers to join him in his seemingly impossible mission. Along the way they encounter a witch and a scary forest and find out that there is indeed no place like home.

Not Block's castle, certainly, where the knight finally reconnects with his wife ages after he left her a young bride to waste his youth fighting for the faith. Their reunion is less than heartwarming (Honey, I'm home! Let's read passages from the Book of Revelations!). Rather, the home there is like no place at all. It's a state of mind, perhaps, the instant of beauty and peace that transcends analysis and anguish.

Block gets a glimpse of this when he drops in on a troupe of traveling players. Let's face it; Bergman can be a little heavy-handed. After depicting a circus family grotesquely debased in *Sawdust and Tinsel* (1953) a few years earlier, here he transforms it into the Holy Family. Joseph (Nils Poppe) and Mia (Bibi Andersson) and their little baby not only mirror the biblical trio, but Jof even has visions of the Virgin and baby Jesus cavorting by their campsite. Jof has big ambitions for his own infant, Mikael, whom he dreams will one day accomplish juggling's ultimate trick—making one ball stand still.

That might be Bergman's dream, as well; if not one ball, then one moment of beauty that will resist transience and mortality and abide forever. Such a moment can pass like the dust that blows over the road crossed by the parade of flagellants, but it can also open into what might be eternity itself.

The moment sneaks up on Block as he dines al fresco with Jof and Mia in a traditional Bergman bucolic interlude reminiscent of films such as *Smiles of a Summer Night* (1955). They offer him a rustic communion of fresh milk and wild strawberries (the fruit that will provide the title and the talisman of memory in Bergman's next film) and Block takes in the birdsong, lute playing, and romping infant and reflects, "I shall carry this memory carefully in my hands as if it were a bowl brimful of fresh milk. It will be a sign to me, and a great sufficiency."

And what of Death? Well, he's in the scene too, sort of—an actor's mask hanging prominently in the background. In the midst of such an affirmation of life, death is reduced to a hollow artifice, a player's false face with which to titillate an audience. Shortly after this epiphany, Block concocts what proves to be a winning strategy against his terrible opponent. He can't win the game itself, but he can use the game to distract Death long enough to allow Jof, Mia, and Mikael, the embodiment not only of the family but of art itself, to slip away. Far from being a morbid exercise in despair and dread, *The Seventh Seal* is a vindication of life and make-believe, the closest Bergman gets to a musical comedy, climaxing with that rousing showstopper, "The Dance of Death."

Singin' in the Rain (1952)

by Judy Gerstel

ONLY A CURMUDGEONLY wet blanket couldn't love *Singin' in the Rain.*

Often and accurately described as America's most beloved musical, the 1952 picture was set twenty-five years earlier, followed the filmic conventions of its time, and still managed to be presciently postmodern—as well as slyly subversive and deliciously entertaining for all time.

What makes *Singin'* so seductive and pleasurable?

As with *Casablanca* and other classics, it wasn't immediately recognized as a movie that would make its way onto critics' and moviegoers' short lists of best and favorite films some fifty years later.

Singin' is the cream that rose to the top when MGM milked the creative forces of the Freed unit, the collaboration of Arthur Freed, Vincente Minnelli, Stanley Donen, and Gene Kelly. The Freed unit started out with *The Wizard of Oz,* then produced *Meet Me in St. Louis* (1944), *On The Town* (1949), and *An American in Paris* (1951).

Seven Brides for Seven Brothers (1954) and *Gigi* (1958) followed *Singin'*, considered the pinnacle of the American movie musical. It's a glorious, exuberant, witty picture with memorable songs and choreography elegantly integrated with the story and with a title song and dance that has come to represent the movie musical and the optimism and innocence of postwar America.

At one level, *Singin'* is a pastiche of songs, narrative, and choreography borrowed from other productions (and characters borrowed from real life): a "catalogue" musical in Hollywood terms.

The title song, in fact, was written by Freed and composer Nacio Herb Brown for a Follies-like stage show in 1927, the year in which the *Singin'* story takes place. Most of the songs in the movie were written by the duo for productions in the late 1920s.

But *Singin'* is not just any pastiche. It's infused with the genius of Gene Kelly, who codirected, choreographed, and starred. It was Kelly who insisted that dancer Donald O'Connor costar as sidekick Cosmo, just as Kelly's leading man character in the movie, Don Lockwood, insists on sharing his fame with Cosmo. O'Connor performs with such verve and over-the-top impudence that he practically steals the picture. The character was modeled after Freed, who worked as a studio musician in the silent era.

The casting is also notable for the introduction of nineteen-year-old Debbie Reynolds in her first leading role. She's the perky chorine Kathy Selden. She and Lockwood meet cute when he leaps into her open convertible while trying to escape his ravenous fans. Selden smartly refuses to fall for the swaggering Lockwood's reputation and slick charm, taunting him with being a mere movie actor instead of being a "real" actor on stage. The banter establishes the requisite tension that's only heightened when Selden is the girl in the cake at the studio party later that same evening celebrating Lockwood's new movie.

Selden's girl-next-door earnest wholesomeness is the foil for the spoiled, demanding platinum blonde bimbo Lina Lamont, Lockwood's partner onscreen and his would-be partner offscreen. Lamont doesn't speak in the earliest scenes. When she does, the plot is set in motion by the simultaneous realization of the other characters and the movie audience that this superstar's exaggerated Brooklyn accent and shrill, braying voice could instantly torpedo a talking picture. Jean Hagen plays Lamont as Judy Holliday with PMS and won an Oscar nomination for best supporting actress—the only nomination bestowed on the picture.

Lamont sees Selden as competition—both personally and professionally. In a reverse of *All About Eve,* the over-the-hill star is the manipulative shrew and the up-and-coming ingenue is the trusting and deserving innocent.

Just as the latest Lockwood/Lamont blockbuster, *The Dueling Cavalier,* is about to be released, *The Jazz Singer* takes the country by storm as the first successful talking picture. What to do except turn *The Dueling Cavalier* into a talkie? The attempts are hilarious, and disaster looms. But before the rainy night is over, the trio of Lockwood, Selden, and Cosmo come up with the idea of turning *The Dueling Cavalier* into a musical, *The Dancing Cavalier* (though at one point Cosmo suggests *The Dueling Mammy*) with Selden dubbing the voice of Lamont.

The witty, wry, behind-the-scenes screenplay by Betty Comden and Adolph Green is loosely based on a 1932 movie, *Once in a Lifetime,* that was itself an adaptation of a play by Moss Hart and George S. Kaufman about Hollywood's traumatic transition in the late 1920s to talking pictures.

Singin' in the Rain revels in tweaking the Hollywood sensibility, inviting the moviegoer into the knowing joke that in Hollywood, illusion is everything. The disconnect between what Hollywood projects onscreen and what happens backstage is played out from beginning to end, from the opening sequence to the final sequence. One scene after another dramatizes not simply deception but illustrates the actual rending of reality and pretense.

In the opening sequence, outside the Chinese Theater where their latest silent film is premiering, Hollywood's shining couple, Lockwood and Lamont, join sidekick Cosmo at the microphone of a Louella Parsons–like gossip maven (Madge Blake).

Both Lockwood and Lamont are clad in white, the hue that is all colors and no color and that throughout the film represents dissembling and falseness. Lamont's platinum white hair is part of this, as are the contorted white wigs and extravagant white costumes Lockwood and Lamont wear in their silent film costume dramas. The chilly, vapid whiteness is a stark contrast to the vivid blue and golden yellow of the opening credits, the colors that throughout the movie connote high spirits, imagination, and sincerity triumphing over fakery, cunning, and gloom.

When the gossip maven insists that Lockwood relate his story of how he came to be Hollywood's great leading man, he launches into a patently high-falutin' account of his rise to fame. But while Lockwood talks about art, drama, and dignity, a lively flashback musical number ("Fit as a Fiddle") featuring Lockwood and Cosmo as vaudevillians shows the truth about their hardscrabble background and lowly beginning.

It's only the first of several incidents that contrast the revelation of truth with the lies manufactured for public consumption.

It's also the first of a glorious collection of musical numbers that are seamlessly integrated with the narrative. With one or two exceptions—the fantasy dance with Cyd Charisse ("Broadway Rhythm") that's an imagined scene from *The Dancing Cavalier,* the movie within the movie, and an awkward love song sung on an empty stage ("Would You?"), song and dance in *Singin'* are emotional exclamations and flourishes evolving naturally from exuberance, tenderness, desire, and sheer joie de vivre. Or they are signature notes of character—for example, the antics of Donald O'Connor's Cosmo.

So clever and enchanting is *Singin' in the Rain* that it can smartly send up the artifice of Hollywood and still seduce us with that very artifice.

Star Wars (1977)

by Matthew Seitz

OF ALL THE FILMS OF THE 1970s, none was more influential that *Star Wars*. Other landmark works from that era could rightly claim to be more complex, more challenging, more adult, but none could claim to be more widely seen and enjoyed. (Many saw it more than once.) This mythic adventure about a gee-whiz farmboy rescuing a princess and saving the galaxy proved that a primitive fairy tale with high-tech effects could thrill moviegoers the world over, regardless of language, cultural difference, even age. It made stars of its unknown leads—Mark Hamill, Carrie Fisher, Harrison Ford—and spawned a spinoff industry peddling tie-in merchandise, from toys and T-shirts to comic books and trading cards. It introduced new visual effects and sound technology that would change how films were produced. Its unprecedented financial success—the top grossing film of all time with $250 million in box office and $1 billion in merchandising—convinced the studios to abandon their old financial model, wherein lots of money was earned by lots of films, and embrace a new model, wherein ever-increasing amounts of money and effort were devoted to developing more movies like *Star Wars*.

The film's detractors (they are numerous) often forget that on paper *Star Wars* seemed weird and uncommercial. Lucas, an intense, detail-oriented film-school grad, wanted to make *Star Wars* for years, but the major studios kept turning him away, fearing audiences still shaken by Vietnam, Woodstock, and Watergate would laugh an earnest space fantasy right off the screen. Lucas finally got financing from 20th Century Fox thanks to the success of his nostalgic, critically acclaimed youth drama *American Graffiti*.

The result, the first installment in a hoped-for trilogy, opened with a printed introduction backed by a trumpet blast and got cornier from there. A sci-fi reworking of Japanese filmmaker Akira Kurosawa's 1959 samurai folktale *Hidden Fortress*, about a group of mismatched heroes trying to rescue a kidnapped princess, *Star Wars* felt at once contemporary and primitive, knowing and innocent—a pop-culture polyglot swashbuckler, with bad guy in shiny black armor (body by David Prowse, voice by James Earl Jones); an earnest hero (Hamill) who learned from a wizened mentor, Obi-Wan "Ben" Kenobi (Alec Guinness); Princess

Leia (Fisher), a tough-talking, straight-shooting diplomat-spy who knew the whereabouts of plans that could defeat the empire; Han Solo (Ford), a cocky space smuggler with a seven-foot-tall nonhuman sidekick named Chewbacca (Peter Mayhew), who looked like a cross between Bigfoot and Benji; and two androids, R2-D2 and C3PO (Kenny Baker and Anthony Daniels), who bickered the way Laurel and Hardy might bicker if Hardy wore a gold tinfoil body suit and Laurel delivered his lines in Esperanto while locked inside a trash can.

Although *Star Wars*'s panoramic dreamscapes were created with processes more complex than the ones devised for Stanley Kubrick's landmark *2001: A Space Odyssey* (1968)—including computer-controlled cameras and some of the most sophisticated makeup yet created—the film's rescue-a-princess-and-save-the-universe storyline was far simpler. Lucas told the tale with a calculated naivete that baffled art-house hipsters and thrilled kids of all ages. Released two years after the end of the Vietnam War and three years after Richard Nixon resigned his presidency in disgrace, Lucas's space opera avoided politics, psychology, social commentary, and every other fashionable movie subject and got back to the basics: good guys vs. bad guys.

But if *Star Wars*'s story and mood were willfully primitive, its conception was sophisticated. Lucas designed the film to push subconscious buttons. Lucas's jargon-filled screenplay was full of mythic notions shoplifted from the works of bestselling myth-explainer Joseph Campbell. The movie's orchestral score (by John Williams, who scored Steven Spielberg's 1975 shark tale *Jaws* and many other blockbusters) was romantic, propulsive, and relentless. Cinematographer Gilbert Taylor's eye-popping CinemaScope compositions—nearly every one storyboarded in advance—were packed with references to Lucas's favorite genres: westerns, war flicks, pirate pictures, creature features, samurai epics, and Saturday morning serials, which advanced their pulpy plots in hammer-blow chapters that typically ended with the hero getting tossed into a shark tank or spiraling to earth in a burning plane.

It was, in the words of *Time* magazine critic Richard Schickel, "a subliminal history of movies." There were nods to *The Wizard of Oz*, *The Searchers*, and even Nazi propagandist Leni Riefenstahl's *Triumph of the Will*. References to one genre opened up into references to another genre like doors in a house of dreams. Luke's desert homeworld, Tattooine (actually Tunisia) was photographed like a Technicolor western from the 1950s; it was a place where farmboys screamed across the horizon in battered hovercars, bandaged-up Sandpeople scavenged like mutant Comancheros, and beasts of every shape and species drank together in dingy spaceport pubs. (Live jazz nightly; bring your own blaster.) The bad guys zipped from solar system to solar system inside a space station the size of a small moon, pulverizing planets with a death ray. Darth Vader, the empire's most powerful general, was a wheezing biomechanical dark knight who could strangle disrespectful underlings with a gesture of his black-gloved hand. Vader's former teacher and sworn foe, Kenobi, was a tender-voiced hermit who lopped off enemies' limbs with his lightsaber and spoke in crypto-Zen riddles about "the Force"—a living energy field that bound the galaxy together. It was the kind of movie where the hero and heroine escaped enemy soldiers by swinging across a ravine with a grappling hook, and the cocky smuggler who deserted the rebels in their hour of need because he didn't believe in causes reappeared during the final battle to help the hero save the day.

Star Wars drew rave reviews from a few influential critics (including Roger Ebert, who gave it four stars). It earned several Oscar nominations, including best picture and director. It made more money (adjusted for inflation) than any film since 1939's Gone with the Wind). It was followed by two sequels: 1980's The Empire Strikes Back, widely considered the best of the series, a darkly elegant fable that introduced the tiny green Jedi master Yoda and revealed the true nature of Luke's relationship to Vader; and 1983's Return of the Jedi, a dull, clunky finale full of slobbering reptiles and pudgy teddy bears that fans saw twice anyway. Twenty-two years later, Lucas wrote and directed a prequel, The Phantom Menace, the first volume of a new trilogy explaining how Vader succumbed to the dark side of the Force. As of this writing, all four chapters occupy slots on the list of the top grossing movies ever made.

Yet Lucas's triumph was viewed by some critics and historians as a step backward for movies and for American popular culture in general. ("Heartless fireworks ignited by a permanently retarded director with too much clout and cash," groused Time Out.) Star Wars was blamed for dispelling the adventurous, artistic mood that had built up in Hollywood since the late 1960s, emboldening young, film-literate directors to make such grownup blockbusters as Bonnie and Clyde, The Graduate, and The Godfather (directed by Lucas's mentor, college chum, and sometime coproducer Francis Coppola). Sure enough, major studios fell all over themselves to produce movies with similarly broad, simple appeal—everything from science-fiction epics (including the Alien and Star Trek franchises) to comic-book adaptations (Superman, Batman, Spider-Man). Lucas gave his foes ammunition by retiring from film direction for two decades while producing a string of preadolescent fantasies—including Howard the Duck, Willow, and the cliffhanger-derived Indiana Jones movies, which starred Ford and were directed by Lucas's friend Steven Spielberg, a more adventurous pop storyteller with an equally boyish sense of spectacle.

By the mid-1980s, some media critics said Lucas's pre-Vietnam attitudes toward morality and war helped pave the way for the return of archconservative politics in America (president Ronald Reagan named his proposed missile defense system "Star Wars"). By 1997—the year a digitally revised *Star Wars* was re-released, grossing another $200 million worldwide—*Esquire* film columnist David Thomson wrote a piece titled "Who Killed the Movies?" His answer: Spielberg and Lucas.

Such charges wounded Lucas, a devotee of postwar European art films who modeled his debut feature, the bleak science fiction parable *THX-1138*, on Jean-Luc Godard's *Alphaville*, and its followup, *American Graffiti*, on Federico Fellini's *I Vitelloni*. He considered himself a freethinking visionary—a can-do maverick who built his own self-contained, privately owned dream factory, Marin County–based Lucasfilm, to stop the suits from standing between him and his dreams. He seems torn between saying he shouldn't be held responsible for the dumbing-down of a whole medium and insisting that there was no dumbing down to begin with. During the publicity tour for *The Phantom Menace*, Lucas's PR reps offered reporters documents that purported to prove that more independent films had been made since *Star Wars* than in the years leading up to it.

No matter: The debate over the film's influence has not eclipsed its appeal. With the re-release of the original trilogy, the arrival of the prequel, and an accompanying tsunami of media coverage, a generation of moviegoers not yet born in the 1970s embraced Lucas's vision of good and evil squaring off a long time ago, in a galaxy far, far away.

La Strada and
Nights of Cabiria (1955, 1957)

by Gary Arnold

MOVIEGOERS ATTRACTED TO THE FILMS of Federico Fellini in the early 1960s, during the vogues for *La Dolce Vita* and *8 1/2,* invariably mistook Marcello Mastroianni for the director's preeminent acting instrument. Fellini had encouraged the misconception, of course, casting Mastroianni as a glamorpuss alter-ego in both pictures. Years went by before Fellini contrived a mocking alter-ego, in the 1980 sex farce *City of Women*, that also suited Mastroianni's underrated comic flair.

Mastroianni had been in about forty Italian movies before Fellini recruited him. The Federico-Marcello idolatry that began to proliferate after *La Dolce Vita* was always a bit insufferable to people who had discovered Fellini's work a few years earlier. As a rule this group had been profoundly touched by the performer who dominated the initial Fellini art-house vogue in the 1950s and remained his supreme acting instrument: his wife Giulietta Masina, an indispensable focus of pathos in two extraordinary heartbreakers, *La Strada* and *Nights of Cabiria*. Born within a month of each other in 1920, Masina and Fellini were married in 1943. Wartime careers as a reporter, cartoonist, and humorist had drawn Fellini into the entourage of the comic actor Aldo Fabrizi and director Roberto Rossellini. All ended up collaborators on the breakthrough sensation of the immediate postwar period, Rossellini's *Open City*. Fellini contributed to the screenplays of about two dozen films before making a codirecting debut with Alberto Lattuada on the 1951 show-business comedy *Variety Lights*. Something of a family affair, it accommodated roles for Giulietta Masina and Lattuada's spouse, Carla del Poggio. Fellini made his solo directing debut the following year with the delightful marital farce *The White Sheik*. It anticipated one of the great Masina roles: she makes a fleeting appearance as a cheerful, friendly streetwalker named Cabiria. His fourth feature, made in 1954, was *La Strada*, a haunting, tragic fable about a brute named Zampano (Anthony Quinn), his slave-mistress Gelsomina (Masina), and a puckish circus performer known as the Fool (Richard Basehart). A formidable hit wherever it played, the movie remained a first-run fixture in Manhattan for three and a half years after opening in 1955.

So Giulietta Masina was indispensable to the Fellini career from the outset. She endeared herself phenomenally as Gelsomina, the waif who embodies instinctive affection and abused innocence. The character was immediately recognized and cherished as a Chaplinesque figure of comic impishness and vulnerability. Gelsomina dolls and trinkets were marketed in Europe. Having invented a character that expressed fundamental yearning and goodness to the moviegoing portion of his species, Fellini ruefully observed that he could have made anything with "Gelsomina" in the title. He resisted that temptation. Three years later husband and wife surpassed themselves in certain respects by breaking hearts all over again in *Nights of Cabiria*, immortalizing a resilient heroine who might be described as Gelsomina's fallen sister.

La Strada may be the most brilliantly schematic parable of human longing and sorrow since D.W. Griffith's Broken Blossoms in 1920. Many aspects of the story would seem more comfortable within the lyric conventions of silent moviemaking or the opera stage. Fellini succeeded in a feat of poetic reduction that one tends to resist intellectually. In La Strada he distills human nature into three symbolic, ultimately estranged characters. An indication of the movie's greatness is that resistance to its simplifications is nearly impossible to maintain while the fable itself is unfolding on the screen. It sabotages skeptical defenses even as you question the Master Plan.

The warmhearted, naïve Gelsomina is sold into servitude by an impoverished mother. The deal makes her the chattel of Zampano, a sullen and brutish strongman. He travels a village and small-town carnival circuit on a motorcycle. A small van is hitched behind. We would now think of Gelsomina and Zampano as a homeless couple. They camp out, and all their belongings are in that rickety van.

Gelsomina reconciles herself to Zampano despite his morose and occasionally abusive behavior. She even relishes the performing side of her chores as his "assistant." The act brings out the hammy, hopeful aspects of her personality. Though far from enviable, this marriage of convenience seems workable until a blithe troublemaker crosses their path: Basehart as a tightrope walker, Il Matto.

A personification of instinctive mirth—and an "elite" performer in this milieu—the Fool considers both Gelsomina and Zampano irresistibly ridiculous. She grows fond of him despite his jibes at her expense. Ominously, Zampano has no sense of humor. When the Fool subjects him to ridicule, the pranks backfire tragically. Despite the woeful consequences of this eccentric show-biz triangle (never a romantic triangle, since Gelsomina feels bound to Zampano and the Fool is a loner), the movie feels emotionally satisfying and conclusive. A myth of human need and estrangement has been enacted with a distinctive quality of believability. In addition to breaking down conceptual resistance, La Strada also makes you feel a curious cathartic exaltation about witnessing the ultimate loneliness of human beings.

Fellini doesn't conceal his aims. The theme is even explicitly articulated: everyone, no matter how mean his condition, has a purpose in life. Whatever happens has meaning, even the appalling things. The contradictory convincer: this overly optimistic outlook is subjected to a grave, rigorous artistic demonstration. It's presented as a desperately necessary consolation for hard usage and disappointment. Without this lifeline, despairing humans would find it difficult to justify existence. Moreover, certain kinds of loss are downright inconsolable. The last image of the film lingers on a desolate survivor.

Fellini had written pivotal roles for Anna Magnani in the aftermath of World War II. Nights of Cabiria evolved from a pretext she had rejected: a Roman prostitute is picked up by a famous actor after a fight with his peevish girlfriend. This situation became the first of three extended episodes when Fellini realized Cabiria with Giulietta Masina, reaching back for the minor character she had portrayed in The White Sheik. There was a collaborative project for the Fellinis between La Strada and Cabiria: the neglected but powerful Il Bidone, a curiously poignant character study of petty thieves. An ominous party sequence anticipates the more elaborate exploitation of festive tension and despair in the subsequent Fellini features, Cabiria and La Dolce Vita.

Farce and pathos are balanced more adroitly in *Cabiria* than in any other Fellini movie. An appropriate alternate title would be *Cabiria Saved from Drowning*. The heroine takes one fall after another, beginning with a shove into the Tiber by a faithless boyfriend named Giorgio, who runs off with her handbag. Bystanders must pull Cabiria from the drink and administer artificial respiration. Returning to consciousness, she proves a drenched ingrate, concealing her humiliation by acting furious with her rescuers.

This note of pint-sized asperity differentiates Cabiria from the lovable but passive Gelsomina from the outset. Simultaneously short and short-tempered, Cabiria prides herself on being a tart who can manage without a pimp and afford a house of her own, a cinderblock bungalow located in an indelibly stark yet livable stretch of unincorporated countryside about twenty miles from Rome. At once cursed and blessed with a short emotional fuse, Cabiria is instantly demonstrative, unguarded, and explosive when expressing any emotion. The funniest thing about her wised-up facade while on the job soliciting customers is the sheer goofiness of the pretense that she has seen it all and can't be surprised.

On the contrary, we discover that she is habitually vulnerable to betrayal and disillusion. The scenario pulls the rug out from under Cabiria methodically, promising better things that can't be secured. An evening of serendipitous luxury in the company of a film star, Alberto Lazzari (Amedeo Nazzari), is short-circuited when his girlfriend Jessie (the laughably named Dorian Gray) reappears. An afternoon of religious ecstasy during an excursion to a shrine is sabotaged by Cabiria's hungover realization that no one in her party has been spiritually transformed by the experience. Finally, the courtship of a shy, solicitous clerk (Francois Perier), met outside a variety theater, sets up Cabiria for a devastating romantic betrayal. Summarizing the character in 1957, Fellini described Cabiria as "fragile, tender, and unfortunate." He envisioned her as an exemplary blend of victim and survivor. The saving grace is that "after all that has happened to her, after the collapse of her naive dream of love, she still believes in love and in life. . . . In spite of everything Cabiria still carries in her heart a touch of grace."

Considerably more than a touch. Although the sentiments sound fondly plat-itudinous, the ornery streaks in Cabiria help to keep audience empathy on the vigilant, hard-earned side. The movie achieves a stunning, exceptionally tough-minded note of consolation at the fadeout, only moments after Cabiria has suf-fered her greatest setback. Fellini acknowledged Chaplin's *City Lights* as an inspiration. This influence is initially apparent in Nino Rota's musical themes dur-ing the opening credits. The affinity is brilliantly evoked in the fadeout, which depends on Masina's ability to reawaken signs of emotional recovery and suscep-tibility on Cabiria's face without overdoing the glimmers of optimism. She pretty much nailed it for eternity. Her head slowly rotates from side to side, acknowl-edging a group of friendly strangers in the setting. At the same time her eyes almost but not quite make direct contact with the camera lens, acknowledging all the sympathetic strangers in the movie audience.

The fortieth anniversary revival of *Cabiria* restores the print to an untattered condition and adds a fresh, expanded set of subtitles, probably more accurate and colloquial than the original batch in 1957. This version also restores a haunting sequence that was eliminated after the Cannes Festival premiere showing. It was discovered in a French print that became one of five basic sources for restoration supervisor Brigitte Dutray.

It's easy to see how the sequence might have been discarded. It comes out bod-ily without doing any harm to the plot. Nevertheless, some expendable things may give you intangible benefits. The missing piece from *Nights of Cabiria* fits this description. Called the "man in the sack" sequence, it is positioned right after a transitional episode that follows the Lazzari encounter and anticipates the pil-grimage to the shrine. Picked up and then stranded on the outskirts of Rome by a truck driver, Cabiria is trying to find her way back to a public thoroughfare when a car appears out of the morning fog. She gets a ride back to civilization from the driver, a good Samaritan on his rounds of visiting craters and caves that turn out to house some of the destitute of Rome. He carries a heavy sack and dis-tributes food and blankets to this needful, subterranean population. His most conspicuous client is a stout and aging former prostitute known as Bomba, who once commanded top dollar for her illicit favors. Arguably, the episode adds an effective note of apprehension about Cabiria herself while also making an imme-diate social point about Roman poverty and homelessness. However, these prac-tical considerations are overwhelmed by a curiously sinister, desolate undercurrent. Despite his charitable behavior, the man with the sack bears a disconcerting resemblance to the Grim Reaper.

Federico Fellini, Giulietta Masina, and Marcello Mastroianni failed to survive the 1990s, alas. Fellini and his wife died within a few months of each other. Those departures made it impossible for them to participate in the fortieth anniversary encores of either *La Strada* or *Nights of Cabiria*. But the films continue to speak eloquently for their collaboration, which elevated the medium's finest traditions of lyrical humanism and compassionate allegory.

Sunrise (1927)

by Jonathan Rosenbaum

ALTHOUGH, LIKE MANY OTHERS, I was first introduced to the possibility of movies as an art form when I first saw Orson Welles's *Citizen Kane*, the film that confirmed that possibility and started me writing film criticism was F.W. Murnau's *Sunrise*. I discovered *Kane* as a high school junior, circa 1960, and first encountered *Sunrise* as a college sophomore three years later; if the former experience was something like an assault, the latter was a good deal closer to a seduction.

The few books of film criticism I could find in that period tended to disparage *Kane* as "uncinematic," but it was a sensitive and perceptive essay about *Sunrise* by Dorothy B. Jones—included in Lewis Jacobs's 1960 anthology *Introduction to the Art of the Movies*—that drove me to see that film in the first place. Yet apart from Jones and a couple of short reviews, the most enthusiastic writing I could find about the movie was in French, most of it in the pages of *Cahiers du Cinéma*. According to a poll of that magazine's critics in 1958, Murnau was the greatest of all film directors and *Sunrise* (1927) was his greatest film.

Part of what continues to make it great, in my opinion, is a particular utopian moment in film history—the end of the silent era, when movies reached a certain pinnacle of visual expressiveness that was tied in that era to a dream of universality, a belief that cinema could speak an international tongue. Properly speaking, *Sunrise* is not so much a silent picture as a pretalkie, existing in a netherworld between sound and silence; it has a very beautiful soundtrack of music (credited to Hugo Riesenfeld) and selective sound effects that for me is an essential part of its magic.

It was the first Hollywood picture of a remarkable German director who already had seventeen features to his credit (only nine of which survive today), made at a time when both American and German cinema could be said to be enjoying a particular renaissance. It combined many of the most impressive features of filmmaking in both countries, yielding a fable that was deliberately transnational—a collaboration between German craft and American technology, a German story (by Hermann Sudermann) and script (by Carl Mayer) performed by American actors that could theoretically be set almost anywhere. The three leading characters are simply described in the credits as The Man (George O'Brien), The Wife (Janet Gaynor), and The Woman from the City (Margaret Livingstone). A European art movie made with the unlimited resources of a major Hollywood studio, Fox, *Sunrise* fared poorly at the box office but was enough of a prestige item to garner three Oscars the first year of the Academy Awards—for best actress, best cinematography, and "artistic quality of production"—and went on to become a major influence in the careers of directors John Ford and Howard Hawks.

Much as *Kane* is grounded in theater and radio, the aesthetics of *Sunrise* have a good deal to do with painting and music, brought together in a remarkably interactive way that suggests another utopian dream—a definition of cinema as the meeting point between those arts. Subtitled *A Song of Two Humans,* the film is structured in three movements, beginning and ending with slow tempi in a country setting that are separated by a city scherzo; apart from the happy ending, which functions like a coda, the three movements might be described as melodramatic, comic, and tragic, in that order—accompanied by a painterly control of light passing from night to day in the first movement, from day to night in the second, and from night to day in the third.

The Man, a simple farmer, is having a torrid affair with a vacationing City Woman, who signals to him by whistling to meet her for a night of lovemaking in the marshes. Trying to convince him to move with her to the City, she proposes that he drown his Wife in the nearby lake; but when he tries to carry this plan out the next day, en route to the City, he recoils in horror and succeeds only in terrifying the Wife. Over a day and evening in the City, the married couple become reconciled and fall in love all over again; but when a storm breaks out on their way back across the lake, the Wife apparently drowns—until a fisherman finds her, still alive, and the City Woman is sent packing as dawn breaks.

With a story this elemental, inflections are everything, and Murnau's richly imaginative and complex mise-en-scène synthesizes performances, sets, camera movements, and special effects (including many different kinds of superimposition) to spell them out, combining aspects of music and painting in the process. Early on, when the Man walks across the meadow to meet the City Woman in the marshes, the camera eerily takes on an independent intelligence, first following the Man, then accompanying him, and finally rushing ahead of him to arrive at the City Woman by a separate route before he does. Her evocations of the City when they meet are sexually charged expressionist visions rendered through double exposures and camera gyrations, and the overlaps and distortions of the music heard convey the same cacophony. (Much later in the film, the passing of lanterns outside her bedroom window create a painterly equivalent to a glissando.) Even the intertitles are integrated graphically in the visual design: the City Woman's line "Couldn't she get drowned?" sinks and wavers like a body receding below a lake surface covered by mist—an effect complemented at the very end of the movie, when the watery and wavery title "Finis" dries and stiffens from the heat of the rising sun.

Some actions are deliberately and musically protracted to create an ominous mood; when the Man slowly advances toward his Wife in the boat to throw her overboard, Murnau had twenty pounds of lead placed in George O'Brien's shoes to ensure that his movements were sufficiently heavy and slurred. In the justly celebrated trolley ride taken by the couple into the City, the orchestration of O'Brien and Gaynor's exquisite acting (outlining her fear and his remorse) with the shifting landscapes behind them suggests both a fusion of melody with harmony and a powerful *modulation* between the "minor" key of the film's first movement and the "major" key of its second. The city itself—a gargantuan set constructed on the Fox backlot, teeming with choreographed activity—is made to conform to a frightened rural couple's perception of its size, noise, confusion, and scale, and the Luna Park they visit in the evening is an even more delirious expressionist construction. (To heighten a sense of depth at an outdoor cafe, Murnau not only used a set with forced perspectives and larger light fixtures in the foreground than in the background; he also placed dwarfs at the back tables on a terrace.)

"They say that I have a passion for 'camera angles,'" Murnau wrote in 1928.

To me the camera represents the eye of a person, through whose mind one is watching the events on the screen. It must follow characters at times into difficult places, as it crashed through the reeds and pools in Sunrise at the heels of the Boy, rushing to keep his tryst with the Woman of the City. It must whirl and peep and move from place to place as swiftly as thought itself, when it is necessary to exaggerate for the audience the idea or emotion that is uppermost in the mind of the character. I think the films of the future will use more and more of these 'camera angles,' or as I prefer to call them these 'dramatic angles.' They help to photograph thought.

Though all of Murnau's surviving films "photograph thought" in one manner or another, this only begins to describe their compositional and structural brilliance and their stylistic diversity. This highly cultivated director—who made only three pictures after Sunrise before dying in a car accident—was equally at home in the natural locations of Nosferatu and Tabu (his last feature) and the studio sets of Faust and Sunrise, and the intricate editing patterns of Tartuffe are as central to his style as the elaborate camera movements in The Last Laugh. The thoughts he photographed could be shared as well as individual, especially in Sunrise—the shared city visions of the Man and City Woman are quite distinct from the shared perceptions of the City experienced by the Man and the Wife. When the Man and Wife get tipsy on wine at the Luna Park cafe, the blurred fairy creatures circling over their heads offer a precise expression of their common romantic giddiness.

Even more striking is the embodiment of the couple's enraptured state as they sail home across the lake, when a passing raft with silhouetted figures dancing around a bonfire perfectly captures their wild and exalted bliss, and the Wife ecstatically rocks her head back and forth in time to the music. For all the dated and melodramatic aspects of Murnau's eccentric stylization, the erotic charge of the Man's two relationships—a sexual object for the City Woman, a dominating figure to his Wife—remains startling in its directness. In more ways than one, Sunrise triumphs as a masterwork of thought and emotion rendered in terms of visual music, where light and darkness sing in relation to the polarities of day and night, fire and water, sky and earth, city and country, man and woman, reality and desire, good and evil, nature and culture, love and death.

Sunset Boulevard (1950)

by Morris Dickstein

BILLY WILDER WAS NEVER A FAVORITE of auteurist critics. His mixture of ferocious satirical comedies, romances, and melodramas seemed too eclectic for any personal style or themes. Wilder lacked the obsessions of a Hitchcock, a Ford, or a Hawks, as well as their strong visual instincts. He seemed to belong not with the strong directors who imposed their visions but with the literate screenwriters—Joseph Mankiewicz, Preston Sturges—who had begun directing to protect their own scripts, whose gift was in words rather than pictures. Notwithstanding his fabled cynicism, he seemed like the ultimate Hollywood insider, a crowd-pleasing craftsman, sentimental for all his surface toughness, coarse and vulgar despite his European sophistication.

Or so at least the indictment ran.

From this viewpoint *Sunset Boulevard* (1950) was very much an insider's film, in David Thomson's words, "one of Hollywood's most confused pieces of self-adulation." Though Louis B. Mayer cursed Wilder out—"You bastard," he said after an early screening, "you have disgraced the industry that made you and fed you"—*Sunset Boulevard* was the kind of "quality" production that won Academy Awards, not plaudits from *Cahiers du Cinéma*. For some, the limitations of *Sunset Boulevard* were confirmed by its grab-bag of cinematic effects. The movie begins in the dark world of the film noir, with its title printed in block letters along a curbside, the camera tracking feverishly down a deserted street, and a caravan of police cars and motorcycles pulling up at the mansion of silent film star Norma Desmond to investigate a murder. All this is accompanied by Franz Waxman's thriller music and, soon, the Chandleresque voice-over of a man detailing the circumstances of his own death. The speaker is Joe Gillis, Norma's much younger factotum and gigolo, whose body lies floating, face down, in her pool.

But as the flashback begins, the film modulates into a breezy, knowing satire of contemporary Hollywood, full of references to actual people and places. The look and tension of noir filmmaking seem completely forgotten. After a perfunctory chase in which two men try to repossess Joe's car, we shift gears yet again when he takes refuge in Norma Desmond's seemingly deserted "Sunset castle," which, like her, is a decaying remnant of the silent film days of the 1920s. Here the most puzzling thing at first is Gloria Swanson's strident, mannered, operatic performance, which starts as high Camp with the obsequies for a pet monkey and culminates with a Grand Guignol mad-scene worthy of Callas or Sutherland. Under Wilder's direction, Swanson makes no attempt to humanize Norma, to play her from the inside for pathos or sympathy. Though Swanson tells William Holden that "we didn't need dialogue—we had faces," her own face is often a garish mask of self-absorbed posturing and melodrama: precisely what the 1940s saw when it glanced back at the silent film era.

Besides Swanson's dramatics, the other famous oddity of *Sunset Boulevard* is Holden's postmortem narrative, which seems like a send-up of the flashback technique favored by many noir directors—including Wilder himself in *Double Indemnity*—in the decade following *Citizen Kane*. The witty, sarcastic tone of *Sunset Boulevard*—beautifully maintained by William Holden's rueful narration—makes light of the shadow of fatality and inevitability that broods over the noir world, though Joe Gillis is as fatefully hooked as Walter Neff in *Double Indemnity*. Veering from bemused comedy to Camp artifice, the film scarcely can sustain the self-enclosed intensity of the noir vision.

But our view of *Sunset Boulevard* is skewed by Wilder's reputation as a satirist and by its own renown as the best movie ever made about Hollywood. Far from damaging the movie by hamming it up, Gloria Swanson burns up the screen from the first moment she appears. Next to Holden's cool, laid-back, "modern" movie-acting, which depends so much on the inflections of his voice, her performance is so visual, so gestural, that it revives the spirit of silent film single-handedly. There's something lifeless about the scenes without her or Erich von Stroheim, her devoted caretaker, especially the few between Holden and the kids his own age, the "normal" world to which he is presumably trying to escape. *Sunset Boulevard* is an ingenious adaptation of the genre conventions of noir to its Hollywood subject. Though Wilder, unlike many of his fellow émigrés, never seemed much like a German director, here he reaches back through noir to its primary source, the expressionism of horror and Gothic, to convey his sense of two Hollywood generations, both out of touch with anything real: one immured narcissistically in its past glories, the other trapped in the tawdry superficiality of the present.

Wilder uses Gothic elements to give his Hollywood a mythic dimension beyond the reach of satire. When Joe lands in Norma's driveway he is like a child who has stumbled into the Old Dark House, except that his life in the daylight world has effectively reached a dead end: he can't pay his rent, can't keep his car (his "legs"), can't sell his scripts, can't even put new heels on his shoes. He is first taken for the undertaker who will see to the burial of the pet monkey; instead he becomes the "stray dog" who'll take the animal's place. After being admitted by Cerberus (Stroheim), the guardian of the gates, he encounters Norma first as a disembodied voice from the balcony above, then as a mysterious pair of eyes peering through a bamboo screen. Despite the initial misunderstanding, her first words to him have an aura of fatality that he will never shake off: "You there, why are you so late? Why have you kept me waiting so long?"—as if, like Sleeping Beauty, she has been waiting for someone like him to bring her back to life.

We learn eventually that despite the grand scenes she loves to play, Norma is one of the living dead, like the "Waxworks" from silent film days with whom she plays those funereal games of bridge. Joe himself describes her as a sleep-walker whom it would be dangerous to awaken—exactly what he later tries to do. She is surrounded by reflections of her own image, embalmed in her own illusion that she is still a great star. In this she is abetted, of course, by her loyal retainer, Stroheim, once her husband and director, whose willing emasculation foreshadows Joe's own humiliating bondage and dependency. Norma sucks vitality from Joe as she drinks in a half-demented energy from the fans she imagines awaiting her "return." She is more than the *femme fatale* of 1940s movies whose sexual allure is bound up with treachery and entrapment—who, seen from the outside, is a projection of male anxiety, a deep-seated fear of women's sexual needs. She is the figure who lies behind film noir: the fatal woman of Gothic, *la belle dame sans merci*. *Sunset Boulevard* makes no sense unless we see Norma as a vampire: this is what Swanson's garish, histrionic performance finally comes to.

Once we realize this, the other Gothic details fall into place: the dead monkey, the rats nibbling around in the empty pool, the vaguely haunted house that entombs another era, the giddily expressionist close-ups of Stroheim's white-gloved fingers playing the wheezing organ. Pauline Kael once drew attention to the expressionist elements in *Citizen Kane*—including cinematographer Gregg Toland's debt to the camera work of Karl Freund, and Welles's own outsized acting, which substitutes virtuosity for intimacy and showiness for inwardness. Numerous elements from *Kane* reappear in *Sunset Boulevard*. The brooding castle in both films suggests emotional isolation, loss of touch with reality, and the failure of money to buy love. The May-December romance of Kane and Susan Alexander is distantly echoed in Norma's purchase of Joe and her failure to hold him.

Above all, both films use deep-focus imagery to convey power relationships involving love, money, and personal vanity. When, deep in the frame, Joe walks in while Norma is calling her rival, Betty, or when Joe sends Betty away and the camera moves up slightly to show Norma peering down at the scene from above, as she did when Joe first arrived, these shots, effective as they are, are almost embarrassingly reminiscent of Toland and Welles. If *Citizen Kane* is the best German film ever made in America, *Sunset Boulevard* is one of the best Wellesian films ever made in Hollywood. In his next film, *Ace in the Hole* (1951), Wilder would focus even more savagely on the other part of the Kane world of unscrupulous yellow journalism and media manipulation.

Despite Wilder's intense dislike of formula and genre films, *Double Indemnity*, *Sunset Boulevard*, and *Ace in the Hole* make up a trilogy that marks Wilder's significant contribution to film noir. What Neal Sinyard and Adrian Turner say of Fred MacMurray's role in the first of these films could easily be applied to the other two: "Neff is the first of Wilder's morally weak heroes who, through motives which drift between greed, ambition, vanity and sexual enslavement, finds himself in a situation which he becomes powerless to control but which he has to see through to its tragic conclusion." Each of these men begins by calling the shots; each is caught in a triangular web he tried to control; each is finally killed by a woman he thought he could use and dominate. Wilder's seeming pastiche of noir turns out to be his creative attempt to work within its terms, to take them to extremes.

Though he calls himself a heel more than once, and repels his bright-eyed young girlfriend out of sheer self-loathing, William Holden plays the cynic as victim rather than villain. Like MacMurray in *Double Indemnity*, he falls into the hands of a predatory woman who uses him more than he uses her. The turning point for Joe Gillis comes on New Year's Eve after he has made his strongest bid to escape. Norma cuts her wrists with his own razor, and, out of guilt and sympathy, he returns to berate or comfort her.

Lying in bed with her arms outstretched she plays her greatest scene, and at the stroke of midnight, as the strains of "Auld Lang Syne" waft into the room, she reaches up and pulls him toward her with nails that look like talons and a mouth that, as the image slowly fades, looks as if it could as easily sink teeth into his neck as kiss him on the lips. With this dissolve, in the best Hollywood fashion, their affair truly begins. It's hard not to read this as a classic male fantasy, a fear of regression and entrapment which is film noir's Gothic inheritance.

One of the most vampirish myths of the fin-de-siécle era plays a key role in *Sunset Boulevard*, the story of Salome, which is the subject of the interminable script which Norma is preparing for her return. "She demands his head on a golden tray, kissing his cold, dead lips," she says, summarizing the script yet also foreshadowing her own story. Gillis edits this "silly hodgepodge of melodramatic plots" for her and plays his appointed role in the real-life version. Norma sends the final script over to DeMille, who had directed her (and Swanson) in her greatest successes, and DeMille at that moment just happens to be shooting *Samson and Delilah*, another clear parallel to Norma's sapping of Joe's strength. Yet Norma is also Miss Havisham, the Gothic recluse in Dickens's *Great Expectations* whose house was a shrine to the frozen past but who also contributed to young Pip's coming-of-age.

Such literary allusions in *Sunset Boulevard* all point to themes of imprisonment, sexual bondage, and feminine hysteria and madness. Norma's house (like Norma herself) "seemed to have been stricken with a kind of creeping paralysis" which left it "out of beat with the rest of the world." Yet Wilder's references to real people and their film careers, from Stroheim, Swanson, and DeMille to Alan Ladd and Betty Hutton, gives this self-enclosure another dimension, referring not simply to silent film days and Norma's madness but also to the narcissistic illusions of the star system and the film world. Norma lives to be seen. Joe becomes her audience even more than her lover, and she constantly performs for him—coy little routines that were old before he was born. No wonder the film has been taken for an allegory of an aging Hollywood trying to capture the attention of a younger generation. Working on her script, Joe finds that "it wasn't so simple getting some coherence into those wild hallucinations of hers." At the end, when he tells her the truth and tries to walk out, he is closing her down, destroying the one thing that makes life bearable for her.

There is an undeniable grandeur in Norma's illusions, as staged by Stroheim, that cannot be matched by Joe's sardonic, up-to-date realism. When Norma/Salome sheds her veil as she dances with Joe at her New Year's party for two, Stroheim picks it up with a look of dogged devotion and kinky romanticism. When Joe drives a stake through Norma's heart, he destroys himself as well. Joe's bland young sweetheart, Betty, finds that she cannot lure him away from Norma and back to his earlier, uncomplicated self. Betty's normality, like Joe's cynical realism, is no match for Norma's baroque self-dramatization. Having fixed her nose but lost all desire to become a star, Betty is content to remain behind the camera. But Norma understands that ego, illusion and performance are essential to art, even her kind of bad art.

Norma and Joe are made for each other, feeding upon each other as performer and audience, actress and writer, grande dame and cheap gigolo. Both are prisoners in a castle without locks, both are in the "sunset" of their careers. Yet Joe is already compromised before they meet—Betty had been the first to tell him so, the first woman to betray him—while Norma, in the half-mad recesses of her suffocating narcissism, preserves a kind of hysterical integrity. Joe wonders, "How could she breathe in that house so crowded with Norma Desmonds, more Norma Desmonds, and still more Norma Desmonds?" Yet in her final scene she is a star again, as Stroheim is able to direct her again, nourishing her illusions as devotedly as ever. As writers from Shakespeare to Henry James have suggested, there is not so wide a gap between madness and art.

Wilder grasped that Hollywood itself could be a scene of Gothic isolation and solipsistic emotion. He showed the grandeur that could emerge from the parasitical relations between actors and writers, performers and directors, stars and stargazers—cannibals all. Like most noir films, with their dark motives and circular structures, *Sunset Boulevard* makes corruption and betrayal seem inescapable. Yet Wilder pays tribute to what can emerge from this hothouse world, just as he does honor to the film formulas he lightly parodies. As Hollywood keeps reinventing itself, as Wilder's own films become relics of a distant age, his barbed tribute stings and sings with even more authority.

The Thief of Bagdad (1924)

by Joe Morgenstern

IN THE VERY FIRST SCENE OF *The Thief of Bagdad*, it is written in the stars—literally written in the starry sky of a desert night—that "happiness must be earned." Truer words were never twinkled for Douglas Fairbanks's thief, an uncommonly rambunctious commoner who embarks on a succession of physical and moral tests to make himself worthy of a beautiful princess. For us, though, more than two hours of happiness are there for the taking in this Arabian Nights fantasy, which was made in 1924 and still stands as a shining achievement of the silent era.

The movie is actually much longer than two hours; the running time was originally 155 minutes, though it's shorter by sixteen minutes in a luminous version now available on DVD. Fairbanks, who also produced and wrote the script (under the pseudonym of Elton Thomas), sets the tone with a performance that is fearlessly extravagant and hugely endearing for its self-delight. Like his collaborators in the ambitious production, which was directed by Raoul Walsh, the actor seems to have been thrilled to the point of giddiness with the medium's possibilities. Clad only in pantaloons, headband, and earrings, with a pencil mustache punctuating his smile, Fairbanks leaps, swaggers, and dances through the streets of a Bagdad that clearly knows the thief, Ahmed, and finds him dangerously entertaining. At one moment he climbs a magician's magic rope, then levitates on a balcony while stealing a quick meal. At another he eludes his pursuers by scampering over the backs of worshipers at prayer. At all times he's a prodigy of motion and a delighted witness to his own one-man show.

Silent films at their melodramatic worst can drive modern audiences to distraction with prosaic intertitles that explain what should have emerged wordlessly. But the silent version of *The Thief of Bagdad* (a fine sound version, starring Sabu, was produced in sumptuous Technicolor by Alexander Korda in 1940) is a model of narrative clarity, with little need for elaborate titles, and no need at all for what we'd call a "back story," a dutiful detailing of how the hero came to be who he is and why he's doing what he does. It's understood that Ahmed steals because he's a thief and that he steals with such style and verve because he has a virtuoso's gift and loves to use it. (In one cheerfully gratuitous gesture he stands on his head and shakes all of his newly purloined coins from his pockets.)

It's just as readily understood that the thief, having stolen the princess's heart, can keep it, and prevail over his royal rivals, only by going on a journey of spiritual transformation. And what a journey it is, even to the jaded eyes of those of us who live in digitally enhanced times, when anything that can be imagined can be put on the screen. The imaginings in *The Thief of Bagdad* were those of William Cameron Menzies, one of the most influential visual artists in the history of the motion picture medium and the first man to earn the title of production designer. (Fifteen years later he did *Gone With the Wind* and won an Oscar for outstanding use of color.)

Menzies's sets for *The Thief of Bagdad* were, first and foremost, enormous. (Shot in black and white, the movie was, according to the custom of the day, tinted in several different colors to correspond with the moods of specific scenes or sequences.) Long before the silver screen stretched itself wide to compete with TV, these environments were notable for their verticality—palace chambers that reached toward cloudless skies, palace gates that rose and fell within soaring chevroned walls. More than that, though, Menzies's designs were works of artistic distinction that caught and held the eyes of moviegoers who may have cared not at all about art but who responded to the power of his sweeping lines. Sometimes *The Thief* fills its screen to bursting with exotic creatures or swarming troops (real animals and real troops, not glibly digitized phantasms) but there's rarely any clutter. Bold graphic elements—a diagonal slash of a stairway, a verti cal string of giant beads alongside a huge cubist face—enhance the strangeness of a world in which Ahmed struggles with his fabulous adversaries.

It's a world that changes before our own startled eyes from comically energetic to mysteriously lyrical. As a cynical, swashbuckling thief, Douglas Fairbanks finds plenty of time for shameless fun: riding the rails, as it were, of a palanquin into the palace; peering down at the princess from a vantage point atop a tree in her garden; pitching from the back of a bucking horse into a royal rose bush. (The thief has no way of knowing that by touching the bush's magic petals he has confirmed himself as his beloved's only legitimate suitor.) Once Ahmed gets religion, however, once he plunges into his perilous tasks, the pace turns slow and dreamlike and the hero is often dwarfed by the stunning scenery.

Few people who aren't filmmakers or film-school students watch silent films these days, and sometimes film students do so reluctantly. (Sometimes film students are reluctant to watch anything that isn't in color, or anything produced before the generation of Spielberg, Scorcese, Coppola, and De Palma.) Yet it's not just educational, it's downright thrilling, even now, to watch the gleeful thief do battle with dragons and flying monsters; to follow him to the bottom of the sea, where he turns his back, regretfully but virtuously, on a bevy of sexy sirens; to see him sally forth at a tree-skimming gallop astride a flying horse, or soar off for a happy ending with his beloved aboard a flying carpet big enough to cover a bedroom. When *The Thief of Bagdad* opened in the late winter of 1924, the *New York Times* called it "a feat of motion picture art which has never been equaled and one which itself will enthrall persons time and again." I speak as one of those persons when I say that for once a movie critic got it absolutely right.

Tokyo Story (1953)

by Kevin Thomas

WHEN THE LATE YASUJIRO OZU'S *Tokyo Story* (1953) was recently picked up by an American distributor, Manhattanites discovered what local film buffs have long known that Ozu, who died in 1963 at sixty, was one of the all-time great directors. (Because of Los Angeles's sizable Japanese American community, Japanese films were exhibited continuously here from about 1910 to 1990, with the exception of the World War II years.) However, we can indeed be grateful that Dan Talbot of New Yorker Films bought this sublime film and only hope he will be able to obtain more of Ozu's fifty-four films.

This is because that oft-quoted belief that Ozu is "too Japanese" for foreigners still persists, the proof of which is that once again the Kabuki Theater, local show-case for Ozu's longtime employer Shochiku Films, has been presenting a series of Ozu films without contacting the press, assuming there would be no interest in these "old" films. . . .

Often regarded as Ozu's greatest film and said to be his favorite, *Tokyo Story* is a masterpiece of subtlety and simplicity. Long before the term "generation gap" was coined Ozu probed it profoundly and furthermore protested the deteriorating quality of overpopulated urban life.

Tokyo Story tells of a kindly elderly couple (Chishu Ryu, Chieko Higashiyama) living in a port town near Hiroshima, who make their first trip to Tokyo to visit their married children, whom they have not seen in many years.

Upon their arrival they discover that their eldest son (So Yamamura), a doctor, is not as successful as they had imagined. Moreover, both the son, whose office is in his home in a grim industrial area, and the daughter (Haruko Sugimura), who lives behind the very modest beauty shop she operates with her husband, scarcely have room to put up their parents let alone time to entertain them.

In a sense *Tokyo Story*, which was written by Ozu with his perennial collaborator, Kogo Noda, can be taken as a stricture against children who neglect their parents and forget they aren't going to live forever. But this is just a starting point. Like all great artists Ozu is openly committed—in his instance to tradition—but is capable of viewing individuals and situations in the round and with compassion.

Therefore, both the son and the daughter can be seen as being basically good people, although there's a hard veneer of insensitivity and selfishness hiding the woman's vulnerability. (The remarkable Miss Sugimura always plays such women to perfection.) Anyway, circumstances beyond their control have changed them from what their parents had remembered and made them self-absorbed in their own struggles for survival.

Change, and beyond it, the fleetingness of life itself is what Ozu laments so eloquently while always counseling acceptance of the inevitable. Typically for Ozu, the elderly mother advises her widowed daughter-in-law (Setsuko Hara), who has been kinder to the couple then their own flesh and blood, to marry again. Also typically, the couple, once home, become reconciled to the way their children are now and are grateful that they have turned out as well as they have.

As always, Ozu frames this most moving of domestic dramas (which incidentally is not without humor) with his customary austerity so as to avoid sentimentality and at the same time to create a sense of overpowering evocativeness. For example, one of his characters receives word of another's dying while the construction of a skyscraper is seen and heard in the background.

As always in an Ozu film the acting is ensemble playing at its finest. Chishu Ryu, who was only forty-seven when he played this elderly man and has been in all but two of Ozu's films, is ever the director's alter ego, the epitome of quiet and dignified resignation. A veteran stage star, Chieko Higashiyama, as the elderly wife, has a warmth, dignity, and presence that brings to mind Ethel Barrymore at her finest.

Top Hat (1935)

by Carrie Rickey

IN THE CONTEXT OF CONTEMPORARY music videos where jump cuts punctuate hip-hop rhythms, where lyrics and garb leave little to the imagination and where dance moves simulate sexual gyrations, Fred Astaire and Ginger Rogers may strike some as quaint relics of mummified Victorianism.

Revisit their stylized series of 1930s musicals and you're spellbound by movies that are, like the standards they introduced, incomparably sinuous and melodic. Astaire and Rogers are the guerrillas of eros, holding the camera hostage and dancing with it in real time.

At the moment when talking pictures were relatively new and synchronization of sound and image was imperfect, shooting a dance number in a single take— as Astaire insisted—was revolutionary. No cheating. No shooting dances (or body parts) in segments. One of the beauties of their moves is that of whole figures navigating real space. Another beauty: clothes that are suggestively tailored rather than explicit. Likewise the music and lyrics, alternatingly playful and plaintive (written by the likes of Irving Berlin, the Gershwins, and Cole Porter), all variations on one of life's Two Big Themes. These would be Seduction and Love, which are a lot more enduring, not to mention universal, than simulated sex.

From flirtation to consummation to transcendence, Astaire and Rogers express the variety of romantic and sexual experience without ever taking their clothes off.

While neither the most rhapsodic of their films (that would be *Swing Time*) nor the giddiest (that would be *Follow the Fleet*), *Top Hat* (1935) is the most iconic.

This, the fourth musical of the nine they made together during the 1930s, is the Irving Berlin tunefest in which Astaire, that man about town, and Rogers, that girl next door, become Astairogers, avatars of continental sophistication and romance who dance away Depression woes. (Not bad for vaudeville workaholics respectively born in Omaha, Nebraska, and Independence, Missouri.)

Their RKO colleague Katharine Hepburn famously cracked of the partnership between the insouciant patrician and the saucy prole that "she gave him sex and he gave her class." Well, yes. But just as essential to the irresistible alchemy of Astairogers is how physically and temperamentally the two complement each other. You'd draw him as a straight line; her as corkscrew curl. His character is unfailingly direct; her characters think the shortest distance between two points is around the world. (Or in the case of *Top Hat,* these two Americans on adjacent floors of an English hotel find that the shortest distance between them is to fly from London to Lido.) Another fundamental of their appeal is how, against some of the most artificial and stylized sets ever imagined, they project a healthy naturalism—like apples in an orchard of candied fruit.

Their *Top Hat* characters are Jerry Travers, a Broadway dancer making his London debut, and Dale Tremont, an American mannequin modeling the diaphanous wares of Beddini (Erik Rhodes), a tony designer. Jerry and Dale travel in society but are not of it, functioning as entertainers to the aristocracy and thus retaining at least a centimeter of ironic distance from the swells who wear dinner clothes in the daytime and who are blissfully untouched by that economic debacle called the Depression. It goes without saying that Jerry and Dale work for a living while the rich play. It also goes without saying that Jerry and Dale have considerably more fun than those top-hatted boulevardiers.

The title number is performed on a theater stage as Astaire/Jerry, a drill sergeant in fancy dress, shoots down a chorus line of similarly clad men who ape his moves. His taps firing like gunshot, Jerry symbolically shoots to death these mimickers with his cane, asserting his individualism and symbolically ridding the field of professional and romantic competition (which presages his elimination of Dale's other swains).

Musically and narratively, the film is about a guy who imagines himself a lone eagle but who is in fact a lovebird. Esconced in his producer's fancy hotel apartment, Jerry sings and dances "No Strings" ("I'm fancy-free/and free for anything fancy"), only to hear from management that he's disturbed the sleep of Dale, slumbering upon what resembles a white lacquer Ark built for a Moderne Noah. When lovely Dale herself disturbs Jerry's Terpsichorean reverie, he instantly changes his tune about permanent attachments.

Choreographically, the film opposes Jerry's unfettered joy in dancing solo with his unexpected ecstasy in dancing duets. The operative metaphor of the duets is romance as force of nature. Jerry pursues the elusive Dale to a park where a sudden storm has the pair seeking refuge under a gazebo. He serenades her with "Isn't It a Lovely Day to Be Caught in the Rain?" The change in the weather musically and emotionally conveys his change of heart. He explains that lightning and thunder are the effect of a cloud kissing another cloud, generating romantic electricity.

At first she resists his pickup line, and also his two-step. But Astaire and Rogers are lightning and thunder. For every lightning patter of his feet, she responds with a thunderous echo, trying to top him. For minutes they do not touch. But in this-try-and-catch-me duet, he does catch her, sweeping her into his arms, consummating their dance romance.

The weather motif is echoed in "Cheek to Cheek," the floatiest of all their numbers, by Rogers's feathered frock, which makes her resemble a cumulus cloud partnered with a lightning bolt.

Astaire and Rogers were among the first to bring eloquent physical movement to moving pictures. To watch *Top Hat* is to know that they remain the greatest.

Touch of Evil (1958)

by Michael Sragow

ORSON WELLES'S TOUCH OF EVIL takes viewers on a jolting ride through a seedy town on the U.S.-Mexico border, circa 1957. At every turn, the glamorous stars—Charlton Heston and Janet Leigh, as a determined Mexican prosecutor and his new American wife—come up against a couple of charismatic grotesques: a baggy-pants crime boss named Grandi, played by Akim Tamiroff, and a tainted American police captain named Quinlan, played by Welles himself. Their jeopardy-riddled journey makes for one of the freest, riskiest, and raciest melodramas ever financed by a Hollywood studio.

The picture opens with a mind-blowing traveling shot that starts at the level of a belt-buckle and then swings left and right and up, as a quick and shadowy figure sets a time bomb and places the device in the trunk of a car. Continuing in one unbroken shot, the camera pulls away into a panoramic view of the border town of Los Robles, then floats down to follow Mr. and Mrs. Vargas (Heston and Leigh) as they prepare to cross from his country to hers on foot. ("You folks are American citizens?" the border guard asks pointedly, before congratulating Vargas on a bust.) The Vargases reach the checkpoint just as the millionaire and the blonde in the car do—and the blonde complains, "I've got this ticking noise in my head. . . ."

The Vargases kiss. Welles cuts—and Kaboom! Welles nails down the movie's mood, setting, plot, and even its racial friction in one audacious piece of virtuoso camera choreography. (The shot clocks in at three minutes and twenty seconds.)

For four decades, movie lovers savored this shot despite opening credits that Universal Studios draped over it in 1958—along with a Henry Mancini score that added to the surface excitement while diluting the atmosphere and obscuring the ticking-bomb progress of the car. But in 1998, producer Rick Schmidlin hired editor and sound designer Walter Murch to put *Touch of Evil* into the audiovisual shape Welles had outlined in a fifty-eight-page memo protesting the studio editing of the film. In the Murch reedit, available on DVD, you get to see this sequence—one of the most influential in movie history—*without* opening credits and *with* an ominous aural backdrop, including the doomed vehicle's car radio that operates like a tracer in the viewer's mind.

When this keen-witted version opened theatrically, some fans missed the Universal-cum-Mancini credit sequence; the hardscrabble splendor of the reediting didn't jibe with their memories of the cheap-to-sublime thrills they had when discovering this movie classic in a 1950s drive-in or on 1960s late-night TV. Of course, in 1998, Murch anticipated the controversy; as he told me then, the traveling shot had become "the Ten Commandments for a number of filmmakers" even in its tarted-up state. But, as Murch went on to explain, "Universal had dropped those titles on it simply, I think, because that's the only way they could deal with a three-minute shot. And because you had titles, Henry Mancini had to write 'title music.' We replaced the Mancini music with the kind of aural tapestry that Welles wanted: complicated, overlapping sounds from car radios, nightclubs, tourist traps, strip clubs." (In the course of their work, Murch and Schmidlin obtained an additional twelve-page memo and nine pages of music notes and also referred to production records and Welles's personal copy of his final shooting script.)

Admirers of Welles in general and this movie in particular may disagree on the merits of the studio edit and the Murch reedit. Both versions *should* remain in release. But the dynamism and solidity of the 1998 *Touch of Evil* go way beyond the opening sequence and only augment the strengths that won the film its first renown.

When Welles signed on with Universal to direct and write as well as act in *Touch of Evil*, he wasn't slumming—after nearly a decade abroad, he was fighting for the chance once again to become an American artist working in America. He thoroughly revamped the script, based on a serviceable *policier* called *Badge of Evil* (written by Robert A. Wade and H. Billy Miller under the pseudonym Whit Masterson). He made anti-Mexican racism a key issue, told the story from three different points of view, and brought a tragic dimension to his heavy of heavies—Quinlan, an obsessive police captain with an adoring henchman, an instinct for finding culprits, and a penchant for framing them. (Quinlan proved to be one of his signature roles as an actor and persona: the archetype of the big man whose own excesses help bring him to his knees.) Reversing the racial makeup of two key characters, Welles turned the putative hero (Heston) into a Mexican supernarc and his new wife (Leigh) into a spunky Anglo from Philadelphia, the City of Brotherly Love.

But Welles did his most glorious work during shooting on the backlot and in Venice, which stood in for the border town of Los Robles. It was, for him, a homecoming. "When Welles went to Europe," Pauline Kael wrote in her rave review of Welles's 1966 *Falstaff*, "He lost his greatest asset as a movie director: his sound" and "compensated by developing greater visual virtuosity."

Back in America for *Touch of Evil*, Welles took his camera wizardry to new heights while cooking up a soundtrack as dense, unruly, and alive as *Citizen Kane*'s. (The climactic bugging of Captain Quinlan eerily resembles Murch's sound-and-image wizardry on Francis Coppola's surveillance thriller *The Conversation*.) And Welles managed to meld old colleagues like Joseph Cotten, Ray Collins, Tamiroff, and Marlene Dietrich, young stars like Leigh and Heston, and seasoned Hollywood hands like Joseph Calleia into a *melodramatis personae* vivid enough to anchor a gutter-baroque extravaganza. Dietrich, in particular, is sensationally mordant, predicting Quinlan's fate in her Tarot cards—"Your future's all used up"—and later delivering his epitaph: "He was some kind of a man."

All those creative priorities are reflected in Welles's fifty-eight-page memo, which Universal wisely duplicates on the DVD. Near the top Welles writes, "I assume that the music now backing the opening sequence of the picture is temporary" and goes on to sketch his inventive ideas for the aural texture. But he soon argues with amazing force and specificity against new cutting rhythms, studio-inserted additions, and, in particular, a glued-together sequence that he designed to play out in two pieces. Welles's goal is always to maintain the integrity he built into the screenplay. "What's vital," he writes, "is that both stories—the leading man's and the leading woman's—be kept equally and continuously alive."

As Welles describes his "original storyline," it's all about the testing of a honeymoon couple by a violent incident that engages the man's professional conscience and subjects the wife "to a series of indignities which irritate and bewilder her and which her husband fails to completely appreciate."

The Murch-Schmidlin reediting restores that critical male-female balance, thus intensifying the payoff to Susan Vargas's frightful night in a motel—a precursor to Leigh's nightmare motel stay in *Psycho*—and heightening her perilous confrontations with Akim Tamiroff's comic-grotesque crime boss. And some deft celluloid surgery near the end of the reedit deepens what Curtis Hanson (the director/cowriter of *L.A. Confidential*)—a fan of the 1958 version—once told me was "the most heartfelt love story in Welles's body of work, between the corrupt but larger-than-life Captain Quinlan, played by Welles, and his partner, played by Joseph Calleia. Quinlan is assisted, idolized, loved by his heartsick deputy, who would rather die for him than betray him—and who ultimately does both." As this version of *Touch of Evil* makes dark-crystal-clear, it's a classic because its brave emotions match its towering bravura.

Trouble in Paradise (1935)

by Richard Schickel

VENICE. A PRETTY CANAL. A GONDOLIER'S SONG. We are primed for romantic enchantment. Until it is revealed that he is not poling a pair of embracing lovers through the languid waters. What he's propelling is a garbage scow. And his song underscores a sequence in which a second story man KOs a victim in a hotel room and scuttles over the balcony.

The camera then tracks across some Venetian facades as the gondolier's song is picked up by an underscoring orchestra. It comes to rest on another balcony, where it finds a "baron" (Herbert Marshall). He is planning a seductive dinner for a "countess" (Miriam Hopkins). It is causing him a certain distress. "Beginnings are so difficult" he complains—ironically, considering that sequence in which he is participating is one of the most famous and justly admired beginnings in movie history. The obliging waiter, naturally, proposes cocktails as an icebreaker. The baron agrees, though why such an obviously practiced roue does not automatically think of a nice, dry Martini as the ideal choice for such occasions is not explained.

Somehow, the cocktails silently mutate into champagne, mostly, one imagines, to accommodate this inspired dialogue. "And waiter," the baron says, "you see that moon? I want to see that moon in that champagne." "Moon in champagne," the fellow solemnly notes on his order pad. "As for you, waiter," he adds, "I don't want to see you at all."

We now settle in for what is surely the wittiest seduction scene in movie history. With one clue and another, we're already pretty certain the baron and his inamorata are not what they're pretending to be. Now we learn that he's the notorious society thief, Gaston Monescu, specializing in jewels but not averse to lifting cash and, for all we know, bearer bonds and fur coats, and that his inamorata is just plain Lily (no last name given) and that she, too, is a thief, every bit Gaston's equal, except in the strong-arm department. For it is, in fact, Gaston we have just witnessed bonking the conk of a rich ninny—M. Filibia (Edward Everett Horton)—and making off with his overstuffed wallet, an act that will have consequences further down the plot line.

Before they reveal their true identities the pair practice their skills on one another. She has stolen his wallet. He shakes it out of her. He then gallantly returns her pin to her. "It has one very good stone," he observes. She asks him for the time. He gropes for his pocketwatch, which she then retrieves from her purse. It was five minutes slow, she says, "but I regulated it." He confesses to having her garter, which he has no intention of returning. She clutches at her skirt. He removes it from a pocket and kisses it lightly. Whereupon, she hurls herself into his arms. "Darling!" she cries. A moment later we see his arm hanging the "Do Not Disturb" sign on his suite's door. Fade out.

At the time *Trouble in Paradise* was released (1932), some earnest souls thought of its opening as a sort of Depression-era comment on the movie that was to follow—wasn't romance among the well-heeled and well-spoken "garbage" when millions were out of work? Some considered it more narrowly—as a very extended example of the "Lubitsch touch," in this case virtually a full-body massage—all grace, lightness, and ingratiation.

But however you analyzed the opening of *Trouble in Paradise,* anyone could see that the director and the screenwriter, Samson Raphaelson, continually grounded its deftness in a harsher reality. Besides that garbage scow, there was the fairly brutal robbery and a phone call to the baron's suite, in which a friend or relative of Lily is shown to be distinctly *declassé.* You also had to admire the fact that they extended its deliciously ambiguous tone for a breathtaking fifteen minutes.

Lubitsch and Raphaelson could not, of course, sustain that tone for the movie's entire running time (which was just under an hour and half). This is not to be taken as criticism. It is more sensible to be grateful for what we have received, especially since the rest of the movie is very good indeed.

They make the transition to Paris, where the movie will settle down, jarringly—a shot of the Eiffel Tower, with animated radio waves emanating from it introduces a slightly lame satire on radio commercials and advertising signage. The tone of this brief passage signals a general shift in the movie's mood—it becomes just slightly nervous, a trifle too busy, and somewhat digressively developed. Occasionally, it seems to have too much on its mind.

I am bound to admit that Lubitsch would have disagreed with this judgment. In his marvelously detailed study of the director's American movies, William Paul quotes him thus: "As for pure style I think I have done nothing better or as good as *Trouble in Paradise*." Paul buttresses this comment with a rich sampling of critical writing that rings changes on the notion that this is a near-to-perfect comedy.

To see why it doesn't quite fit that description, it's necessary to undertake that most boring of critical tasks, a plot summary. I'll try to be brief. The advertising sequence takes us to Mariette Colet (Kay Francis), heiress to the Colet perfume empire, whose products the ads are satirically promoting. We meet her as her board of directors proposes wage cuts. She is more interested in her luncheon engagement and rejects their idea. But on her way to lunch she pauses to buy a purse, which is her most interesting moment in the movie. The clerk shows her something undistinguished for 3,000 francs. No, she says, it's too expensive. She spots something exquisite. It's price is 125,000 francs, but she snaps it up. This is possibly one of the clearest statements of value Lubitsch ever made. Junk is always overpriced; something beautiful is always a bargain.

In any event, the purse moves the plot. Gaston, now in Paris with Lily (and not doing terribly well), steals it at the opera and returns it to Mariette for a reward (the living room of her very elegant deco house is crawling with poor people, among them a left-wing radical who keeps crying "phooey" to Mariette's wealth). Gaston dismisses the radical (with some blunt comments in his native—possibly Romanian—tongue), returns the purse, and is rewarded with a job as Mariette's private secretary.

He proves adept at straightening out her tangled affairs, all the while supervising what seems to be a superfluous diet and exercise program for Mariette. He even brings Lily on as his assistant, and they begin planning what could be their best score. But Gaston has fallen in love with Mariette, Lily finds out, and, driven by jealousy, attempts to go through with the robbery. Mariette discovers her but forgives her and permits the thieves to escape. In the movie's last scene they reprise their earlier pickpocket competition and we see that they have made off with 100,000 francs, a pearl necklace, and, yes, the purloined purse that caused all the *Trouble in Paradise*.

And, you ask, what's wrong with that? To which, I reply, nothing. But in pursing the movie's main line I have left out a few details. Mostly these involve M. Filibia and a character known only as the Major (Charles Ruggles). They are Mariette's suitors, but the former is silly and the latter is rather stiffly British. Both are highly conventionalized comic figures of their day, and both are unfunny. Indeed, they are straw men. One can't imagine Mariette having the slightest interest in either of them, and, indeed, she is dismissive, almost rude to them, throughout the movie. Filibia at least has a function—he has eventually to remember who it was that knocked him out and stole his money in Venice, which, with many a furrowed brow, he finally does.

The relationship between Gaston and Adolphe J. Giron (C. Aubrey Smith) has a little more bite. He's the chairman of the company's board, whose claim to competence is based largely on his forty-year relationship with the Colet family. Each instinctively understands the other to be a crook (Giron is an embezzler), and a nice tense scene of recognition and accusation is played out between them. Recounting the encounter to Mariette, Gaston allows a certain class resentment to show. He has worked his way up from nothing, he's "a self-made crook," but that cuts no ice with the upper classes. As he observes, membership in the social register allows you to escape jail. It is what the movie has in the way of social commentary, but the observation is scarcely original, and it is, perhaps sensibly, rather thrown away by Marshall.

He and Mariette also rather throw away their romantic possibilities. This occurs in another famous sequence that is the movie's emotional center. Their rooms in Mariette's palatial home are adjoining. There is, as far as we know, no internal door connecting them. There comes a moment when she has to go out for a boring dinner party at the Major's. She would rather stay home and, at last, go to bed with Gaston. He thinks, however, that she should go to the party and return early. Their positions, however, shift in the course of a discussion to which we are not privy. What happens is that one or the other of them emerges from time to time to instruct the befuddled butler either to let her car go or stay. What's funny—and never explained—is that sometimes he speaks to this functionary from her room, while sometimes she speaks to him from his room. And vice versa. Romantic confusion has rarely been so wittily emblematized as it is in this sequence.

The sequence concludes yearningly—with shots of his chaste bed, first seen in a mirror, then with their embracing silhouettes projected onto it. She says there's no need to hurry their consummation—they have days, weeks, months to enjoy themselves. But Gaston—and we in the audience—are beginning to suspect otherwise. Lily is on to them. M. Giron awaits below, prepared to unmask Gaston. And at the party, M. Filibia will finally make the connection between Madame Colet's secretary and the man who robbed him in Venice.

But it is a beautifully designed and perfectly paced bit of moviemaking, dryly witty, yet touched by romantic loss. Despite our fondness for Lily, we really want Gaston to attain his heiress—at least for a night. And we want Mariette, at last, to have a man worthy of her. Much as we like Lily we can't help suspecting that Gaston and Mariette are in some ways better matched souls.

Let me put that another way: Gaston and Mariette hint at the possibility of transcendence, of a respectable life for him, of a life less sunk in boredom and social irrelevance for her. Gaston and Lily are bound only for the criminal margin, for lives perpetually on the run.

That, naturally, is a subject for debate. So is Gilbert Adair's contention (in *Flickers*), that *Trouble In Paradise* is "a masterpiece of delivery, the most mellifluous, the most perfectly spoken film in the history of the American cinema." I think it does not quite achieve that status. Mariette is supposed to be a somewhat careless, even ditsy, rich lady, who is brought to common sense by Gaston, rather as Claudette Colbert would be by Clark Gable in *It Happened One Night*. But that kind of lightness was not in Kay Francis's range. She's rather a sober presence in the movie, better at yearning than she is at brittle exchanges.

Something similar could be said of Marshall. Bright, brisk Miriam Hopkins draws the incisiveness out of him. So do the minor characters who suspect his bona fides. But when he's around Francis he tends to moo his lines, suggesting a *weltschmerz* to which his character is not, perhaps, entirely entitled. I prefer the smart, edgy, *knowingness* of Miriam Hopkins's performance and feel, putting it simply, that the movie's Francis-Marshall nexus is just a bit softer, creamier, than I prefer.

One could, however, as easily argue the opposite, namely, that the Gaston-Mariette romance is from the start foredoomed, and that they know it. Read in that light, their relationship gains a certain poignancy from their implicit acknowledgement that the social distance between them is too great to bridge more than temporarily.

But if Lubitsch was, in this, his first talking picture comedy, just a little more jittery, a little less sure of himself, than he soon would be, it is unimportant. He would soon do better. Indeed, the movie I consider Lubitsch's masterpiece, *The Shop Around the Corner,* is actually more sentimental. But by then, the calmness of his formalism—it's a movie of impeccably edited medium shots, and also one that observes the unity of place more rigorously—somehow dries out its potential for sogginess.

But grateful for its many delights, one eagerly forgives the occasional insecurities of *Trouble in Paradise,* particularly when you realize that the main line of American moviemaking was already veering away from Lubitsch. This was the era of *The Public Enemy* and *Scarface,* of *I Was a Fugitive from a Chain Gang* and *Red Dust.* The movies were embracing a grittier realism, a more wisecracking, more "American" style of dialogue.

Lubitsch, though, stuck to his path. He would never make a full-length movie set in contemporary America (the exception is his great, brief contribution to the anthology film, *If I Had a Million*). He would also cling very largely to the *Mittel-European* playwrights he loved to adapt, to the French settings—or rather the backlot versions of them—that he loved to explore. Interestingly, he would be fired by Paramount because, as William Paul tells us, only two of the pictures he made in his eleven years on the lot made money.

It was probably the critics, adoring his elegance, who kept him alive, and bless them for that. Without their efforts—Lubitsch is one of the few directors who seems never to have suffered a "reconsideration"—we would not have such timeless delights as *The Shop Around the Corner, Bluebeard's Eighth Wife, Ninotchka, Heaven Can Wait,* and *Cluny Brown* to light our weary way. Indeed, it is only lately that one has begun to fear for his posthumous reputation. The anonymous (and historically ignorant) studio lords of the videotape and the DVD ignore him. Most of Lubitsch's movies are not available in these formats. We desperately need them—for their own delicious sakes, but also for the reminder they offer of a witty and romantic imaginary world that never was but should have been.

Ugetsu Monogatari (1953)

by Gerald Peary

UGETSU MONOGATARI (TALES OF THE RAINY MOON) is set during a civil war in sixteenth-century Japan, the same type of mindless, never-ending anarchy of the Thirty Years War in Bertolt Brecht's *Mother Courage.* In both cases, the various warring parties are interchangeable in their raping, pillaging, banditry, and forced recruiting; and the best thing for the populace to do is hide their food, women, and army-aged men whenever the gunfire of approaching battalions is heard in the distance.

Still, as in *Mother Courage,* the war in *Ugetsu* leaves opportune pockets of time to work and raise a family, and, if you are material and ambitious, affords chances to make a pile of money and get ahead. So it is that two dirt-poor peasants, a potter named Genjuro (Masayuki Mori) and a neighbor farmer named Tobei (Eitaro Ozawa), become obsessed with the possibilities of success when an army marches through their village. Genjuro decides that riches await in the nearby city of Kyoto, swollen in population because of the fighting, where he can sell his wares at escalated prices. Tobei, who accompanies Genjuro to assist in the merchandising, becomes deluded that his real destiny is to be a powerful samurai.

So much hubris! As with many great and complex films, this 1953 masterpiece by Kenji Mizoguchi (1989–1956) lends itself first to the simplest of readings: as a parable—spiritually Buddhist and politically conservative—teaching us that we must know, and accept, our place on earth. In the fairyland settings of this period movie, a kind of Jack and the Beanstalk tale evolves of these two rubes who, swell-headed, reject what they are pledged to accomplish at the marketplace, to earn a little money for their families. Instead, away from the common-sense eye of their spouses, they both leap foolishly at fortune's wheel and succumb to dubious worldly temptations.

Tobei, the stupider and cruder of the two, goes scurrying after an army, begging on his knees to be taken in as a samurai. Not unexpectedly, soldiers laugh at this lowest-caste fool, kick him away. But Tobei cannot be stopped. In what would be a grave blasphemy in any culture, he steals the severed head of a genuine samurai who has committed hari-kari and lies that he has slain that noble warrior in combat. (Didn't cowardly Falstaff do something of this ilk, stabbing an already dead man and taking credit?) For this supposed great deed, Tobei is made head of an army troop. He swaggers about in clunky armor and on horseback, bragging about his prowess on the battlefield, forgetting that he is married. We, of course, await his comeuppance.

Genjuro's coup de grace is slower and more subtle, an enthralling part of *Ugetsu.* For a time, Genjuro's nose is to the grindstone, as he sits in the Kyoto market for long hours selling his pots; and his only dream is an unselfish one: to buy a shiny silk kimono for the wife, whom he believes waits devotedly in the mountain village. But everything is shattered, spun out of control, when, at his workspot, he makes the acquaintance of the mysterious, ravishing Lady Wasaka (*Rashomon* star Machiko Kyo). She, with the help of her conniving old nurse, lures him to her country mansion and into a feverish love affair.

Genjuro, smitten, forgets his labors, and he rejects his plain, humble wife for this Circe-like noblewoman. Odysseus could get away with such transgressions, and be reunited with the ever-faithful Penelope; for Genjuro, adultery leads indubitably to marital tragedy.

The universality of Ugetsu, which has become enshrined around the world since it won the Golden Lion at the 1953 Venice Film Festival, results from a resourceful blend of Eastern and classic Western sources. Surely, Greek mythology, The Odyssey, Shakespeare, resonate in the narrative. Also, Tobei's military misadventures were borrowed by Mizoguchi from a favored French short story, "How He Got the Legion of Honor," of Maupassant.

However, much of the dissonant music on the brilliant soundtrack comes from the drums and flutes of Japanese Noh drama. And the chief inspiration for the screenplay by Yoshikata Yoda are tales of the supernatural from Akinari Ueda's 1776 collection. In fact, Ugetsu is probably most heralded for Mizoguchi's startling generic leap from credible, detailed historical drama into eerie ghost story.

The first foray into the otherworldly is entirely unexpected, when Genjuro and Tobei and their two wives and Genjuro's tiny son climb into a canoe which is to take them to Kyoto. But the boat trip is, instantaneously, no picnic, as a thick, mournful fog envelops the Styxlike waters; and a rowboat from a Dantean Hell approaches with a dying man inside. He warns them with his last breaths of stark dangers ahead in the world. (Whatever the Japanese equivalent: they aren't in Kansas anymore!) And later: we the audience catch on before Genjuro does that, with his chancy extramarital romance, he has wandered into a palace of the dead, that the pale, beautiful Lady Wasaka, behind a Noh mask, has come for him from the graveyard.

Can we equate Lady Wasaka, the sharp-toothed succubus who pounces on Genjuro when he delivers pottery to her ghostly estate, with the lethal manipulations of Count Dracula? Considering Mizoguchi's filmic style, he might have been influenced by the first and best Dracula movie, F.W. Murnau's Nosferatu (1922), which the filmmaker could have seen in Japan when in his twenties. Therein, Jonathan Harker, a loving husband with a wife who adores him back home, journeys to Dracula's castle on business matters only to be waylaid by, and imprisoned by, the bloodsucking Count. So it is that the undead Lady Wasaka leaps on her prey, Genjuro, knocks him to the ground, makes him her sexual prisoner.

There's also a love triangle in the Murnau oeuvre that bears striking comparison to Ugetsu, and that's in Sunrise (1927). Amoral and mad for love, the City Woman seduces the farmer Man, who had lived, previous to this assignation, in perfect harmony with his doting Wife. In *Sunrise,* the first sight we have of this temptress is at the finale of a long, dizzying tracking shot through nature, the camera providing a visual and poetic equivalent of the Man, losing his grounding and orientation, staggering toward the object of his desire.

So it is also in *Ugetsu* that Mizoguchi represents Genjuro's loss of his reason and his seduction through a trio of mesmerizing, expressionistic tracking shots: (A) The camera slowly strolls alongside and on a parallel during his disquieting walk with Lady Wasaka and her nurse on a haunted country road. (B) The camera tracks quickly through the vegetation by the mansion, suddenly comes upon Genjuro in an outdoors bath watched over by his mistress. (C) The camera again leaps through space and comes down on a picnic ground by a lake, where Genjuro, now totally gone to *l'amour fou,* declares his devotion to his now bride-to-be: "I wouldn't care if you are a demon! I never imagined such pleasures existed! This is divine! This is paradise!"

Genjuro is a sinner, cheating on his virtuous wife, and his philandering cannot go unpunished. Still, Mizoguchi allows us to see, and feel, what is so energizing about Genjuro's transgressions. Great sex, and in wonderful settings! Nothing like his squalid, one-room house, where his child is under foot. Also, Lady Wasaka compliments him in a significant way his peasant wife never would have thought of: she regards him not as an artisan but as an Artist. "Are there secret formulas?" she asks him worshipfully of his ceramics.

Mizoguchi and women. No filmmaker in the history of cinema has provided so many examples in his work of the suffering of women through the centuries—as concubines, prostitutes, geishas, and as downtrodden wives. Several of his greatest achievements: *The Life of Oharu* (1952), the trek down, down, down of a court lady transformed into the lowest harlot; *Sansho the Bailiff* (1954), in which an aristocratic woman is separated for years from her beloved children as they become plunder of slave traders; and she is prostituted, her feet bound and crippled.

The "progressive" nature of Mizoguchi's sexual politics have been questioned by some feminist thinkers who complain that Mizoguchi's women are male projections: a locus of masochistic tribulations with no revolt or way out. To be a woman is to carry the weight of the world, forever and ever. Further, his female characters break down structurally into the traditional male-defined categories of wives and whores.

Both charges readily apply to *Ugetsu,* and yet there is so much more. The greatness of the film has much to do with Mizoguchi's heartfelt compassion for his women in distress, and his belief that their hardships, so rarely acknowledged by men, deserves our attention and respect. While his movie nominally has two male protagonists, Mizoguchi saves his most intimate camera moments, and his most intense, sympathetic close-ups, for the film's three females, the wives of Tobei and Genjuro and, even, the femme fatale, Lady Wasaka.

"For a man's success, someone has to suffer," wails Ohama (Mitsuko Miura), Tobei's spouse. Abandoned by her now-samurai husband, she wanders lost in the countryside until (we see, but her husband doesn't know) she is gang-raped by a bunch of filthy soldiers. Likewise, we are witness to the horrific thing that happens to Genjuro's wife, Miyagi (Kinuyo Tanaka), at the same moment that her husband, oblivious, is cavorting with his lover. Also in the countryside, Miyagi protects her little boy's supply of food from maddened, starving soldiers. One of them, out of his head, randomly stabs Miyagi and sends her, badly wounded, stumbling off screen.

Cut to the end of the movie: Ohama, who (typical Mizoguchi) has been forced into prostitution, is reunited with her ignoble husband, Tobei. He realizes his idiocy in being a samurai as he begs his wife's forgiveness. This "happy ending" is the only compromise in *Ugetsu*. (It was forced on Mizoguchi by his producers, the regretful filmmaker explained in interviews.) Fortunately for the integrity of the movie, things are not so neatly tied together for Genjuro and Miyagi.

Genjuro has seen the light! He leaves behind Lady Wasaka and races back to his village to be again with his wife. The most famous shot in the movie: Genjuro walks left to right through his darkened, vacated house, and the camera pans left to right with him. Then the camera, independently, reverses and pans right to left. Miraculously, it now catches Miyagi peacefully minding the fire and acting as if Genjuro had never left. "I've warmed sake. You must be tired," she says, a Stepford wife, ignoring his attempts to apologize.

Is Miyagi alive, or a phantom? Many critics writing about *Ugetsu* have said that it's clear that she's dead because we have observed her killed in that earlier episode. Not true! Mizoguchi has her wounded, but the last we have seen of her she's definitely breathing. So watching *Ugetsu* for the first time, we are the ones who are disoriented! We are the ones who look on her intensely, not sure if she is living or undead! And when she sobs and wipes her nose on her kimono sleeve, could this touching human gesture, we wonder, come from an apparition? In contrast, Genjuro quickly accepts that Miyagi is well and waiting for him, because he has not seen her stabbed. He slides into his father role, putting his son to bed and murmurs to himself, contentedly, "Back home! Back home at last!"

Then Genjuro sleeps, and we are left in the room with Miyagi. This is the third occasion in the movie that Mizoguchi has sent his protagonists into a snooze, the women stand awake.

The first time: back in the village, Genjuro and Tobei kept the fire going in Genjuro's kiln for so many hours that they are finally collapsed in a heap on top of each other. "Our men work so hard!" one wife tells the other, admiringly. But Mizoguchi's irony is that the women are still on their feet toiling at the kiln while their husbands doze! It's so "natural" for them that they wouldn't think to notice the gender inequity.

The second time: Genjuro lies in a deep slumber in Lady Wasaka's room. She awakens, rises, and prances happily about because of the new man in her bed. She brings a lamp to gaze at his face. This is the moment that Mizoguchi's nobility of spirit stretches even to this demon-woman, who thirsts for love to combat her loneliness. Just as the rest of (living) humanity.

The final time, the penultimate scene of *Ugetsu*: Miyagi runs to get a blanket, which she places endearingly on her husband. What else is there for her to do? She slowly puts away her shoes, picks up things, and straightens their little home. Then she takes a needle and thread and, sitting so quietly, begins to patch a kimono. It's all devalued "women's work," but in this beautiful, tender sequence Mizoguchi is showing us, with his most respectful camera, how precious it all is. How precious Miyagi is. . .

The next day, Genjuro wakes up happily, but his wife is gone. Disappeared. And he finds out from villagers that she had been mortally wounded by brigands, though she brought their son home before she died.

Yes, Miyagi was a ghost! And now, as Genjuro, alone on earth, works day and night, takes care of his son, and with no plans ever again to leave his mountain village, she speaks to him in plaintive voiceover, "At last you've become the man of my dreams. Alas, I'm not in the same world as you, except in spirit."

A profound ending. Mizoguchi's epiphanic message: Miyagi is all women, toiling invisibly through all history, through all civilizations, while men are too asleep to notice. She is a ghost, as Lady Wasaka is a ghost, as all women on earth—cooking, sewing, minding the children, helping their men—have been ghosts.

Unforgiven (1992)

by Kenneth Turan

THE WESTERN IS BACK. With a vengeance. Saddle up or get out of the way. This is the message of *Unforgiven.*

Even before it won four Oscars, including best picture, best director for Clint Eastwood, and best supporting actor for Gene Hackman, it was obvious that this was not cowboy business as usual. Simultaneously heroic and nihilistic, reeking of myth but modern as they come, it is a western for those who know and cherish the form, a film that resonates wonderfully with the spirit of films past while staking out a territory quite its own.

Produced, directed by, and starring Eastwood, it is hard to imagine *Unforgiven* in anyone else's hands. Starting with his 1959 turn as hard-bitten Rowdy Yates on TV's *Rawhide,* no other active actor/director has made as many westerns, no one else has the connection with and feeling for the genre that only working in it for more than thirty years on both the large and small screens can provide. And going as far back as Sergio Leone's 1964 *A Fistful of Dollars,* Eastwood has delighted in bending boundaries, in pushing the western to areas outside the accepted canon.

Eastwood's westerns, usually employing a variant of the emotionless Man With No Name persona he created for his three films with Leone, reached a kind of apocalyptic crescendo with a trio he directed himself: *High Plains Drifter, The Outlaw Josey Wales,* and *Pale Rider.* Yet he has also done quasimusical westerns (*Paint Your Wagon*), modern-day comic westerns (*Bronco Billy*), and even police dramas that were really westerns in disguise (*Coogan's Bluff*).

So its not surprising that Eastwood recognized the strengths of David Webb Peoples's exceptional *Unforgiven* screenplay, the unexpected turns its plot takes, the power of its idiosyncratic characters, the adroit way it mixes modern and traditional elements. Not only that, Eastwood was shrewd enough to hold on to the script for more than a decade, until, just past his sixtieth birthday, he felt he had weathered enough to do the role properly. "I always thought it was a little gem," he said in an interview just prior to the film's release, "but I figured I had to age into it."

For *Unforgiven,* the story of a reformed gunslinger who reconfronts his past, is very definitely an old-guy western, as elegiac in its own way as such classics as *The*

Wild Bunch and *Ride the High Country*. As *True Grit* was for John Wayne, this is also something of a last hurrah for Eastwood's Man With No Name persona, but because Eastwood is who he is, it is a dark and ominous goodbye, brooding and stormy.

Unforgiven is also, and this is perhaps its most unexpected aspect, a neat piece of revisionism, a violent film that is determined to demythologize killing. Considerable emphasis is placed on how hard it is to kill even one man, on the destructive interior price that must be paid for each and every act of mayhem. If there are thrills to be had here, none of them are to be paid for cheaply.

"I've done as much as the next person as far as creating mayhem in Westerns," Eastwood said, "but what I like about *Unforgiven* is that every killing in it has a repercussion. It really tears people up when they are violent, and I felt it was time for that kind of thing in the world."

Both the time and setting of *Unforgiven*—1880 in Big Whiskey, Wyoming— emphasize this sense of mortality. The frontier West is coming to an end, both physically and spiritually, but that close is leaving considerable frustration in its wake. In the forbidding high country, a flat empty locale under cold blue skies, the West is very much an angry, hostile place, rife with fury and lawlessness.

In Big Whiskey itself, however, the law is a very definite presence. He is the town sheriff, Little Bill Daggett (Gene Hackman) by name, and he is called on in the film's opening moments to adjudicate a dispute at the local whorehouse. A cowboy from a nearby ranch has viciously cut up the face of one of the prostitutes. When the house's owner complains "no one is going to pay good money for a cut-up whore," Little Bill decrees that the cowboy and a friend who accompanied him pay the owner six horses as compensation.

This does not sit well with Strawberry Alice (Frances Fisher), the most outspoken of the prostitutes, who has a harsher, less mercantile punishment in mind. "Just because we let the smelly fools ride us like horses," she says angrily, giving the film a fascinating neofeminist subtext, "doesn't mean we let them brand us like horses." When Little Bill doesn't agree, Alice masterminds a sub rosa scheme to offer $1,000 cash for the death of the two cowboys, no questions asked.

In the normal course of events, none of this would come to the attention of William Munny (Eastwood), a destitute Kansas farmer who, having recently buried his wife, divides his time between raising their two small children and awkwardly rooting around with his recalcitrant hogs.

Munny is not just any farmer, however. Before he met his wife and reformed eleven years previously, he was an alcoholic and "a meaner than hell cold-blooded killer" who was legendary for the heedless death he left in his path. Or so says the self-styled Schofield Kid (Canadian actor Jaimz Woolvett), a callow young blowhard who has heard of Munny's reputation and rides into his yard offering him half the reward if he'll join up with him.

With a face looking so worn and lined it seems to have fallen off of Mount Rushmore, Munny is clearly not eager for his old life. "I'm just a fella now," he tells the Kid with conviction. "I ain't no different than anyone else."

But his impoverished condition is a goad, and Munny ends up enlisting his neighbor and ex-partner, Ned Logan (Morgan Freeman) to join in the quest. As the group heads off for Big Whiskey, the question is twofold. Are they the same men, can they kill the same way, and, more crucial, if they can take one step back down the road to perdition, will they then be able to turn around and return to their quiet lives?

It is one of the pleasures of David Peoples's script, along with period dialogue that mixes menace with a sly and earthy sense of humor, that these kinds of questions come up at all. Peoples, whose résumé includes a shared credit on *Blade Runner* and Jon Else's exceptional atomic bomb documentary, *The Day After Trinity* (which, interestingly enough, he wrote simultaneously with this script), is intent on unromanticizing the West, on portraying shootouts and gunplay as drunken, thuggish violence.

And though he is not interested in creating straight heroes, Peoples has come up with a series of vivid, eccentric characters, from small cameos like a one-armed, three-gun deputy to major roles like dime-novel scribe W.W. Beauchamp (Saul Rubinek) and English Bob, a fancy-pants killer given a nice twist by Richard Harris, who never manage to behave exactly as you'd expect them to.

Most indelible of all, however, is Little Bill, Big Whiskey's sheriff. Ruthless to the point of sadism but possessed of both a sense of justice and a sense of humor, a homebody with a weakness but not an aptitude for carpentry, Little Bill makes up the rules as he goes along. And in playing him Gene Hackman gives one of his most powerful and least mannered performances, displaying an implacable strength and controlled passion that forms the essential counterbalance to Eastwood's own considerable force.

For *Unforgiven* is finally very much an Eastwood film. As an actor he is exactly right in a role that is as comfortable as an old hat, as a producer he has had the sense and nerve to cast this film for ability, not box office, and, perhaps most important, as a director he has infused it all with his sure, laconic, and surprisingly emotional style.

Eastwood has dedicated this film to the two directors who were most influential in his career, Sergio Leone and Don Siegel, and perhaps the best thing that can be said about *Unforgiven* is that these two masters would doubtless both be flattered and approve.

"If I was ever to do a last Western," Eastwood said, "this would be it because it kind of sums up what I feel. Maybe that's why I didn't do it right away. I was kind of savoring it as the last of that genre, maybe the last film of that type for me."

Les vampires (1915)

by Jonathan Rosenbaum

A TEN-PART CRIME SERIAL RELEASED in France in 1915 and 1916, *Les vampires* came out during the same period as *The Birth of a Nation* and *Intolerance*. Yet the odd thing about this conjunction is that, far from being contemporary, D.W. Griffith (1875–1948) and Louis Feuillade (1873–1925) seem to belong to different centuries. While Griffith's work reeks of Victorian morality and nostalgia for the mid–nineteenth century, Feuillade looks ahead to the global paranoia, conspiratorial intrigues, and technological fantasies of the twentieth century, right up to the present moment.

Both filmmakers specialized in melodrama. But the style of acting that we associate with Griffith is so theatrical that we can practically hear the floorboards creaking; Feuillade liked to use actors without much stage experience and trained them in a less grandiloquent, more naturalistic style, usually getting them to perform their own hair-raising stunts. While Griffith depended a great deal on editing, Feuillade was a master of long takes and deep focus, developing a complex mise-en-scène in relation to a stationary camera.

Shot largely in the streets of Paris and its suburbs, in dingy shacks and basements, and in ornate Belle Epoque interiors, *Les vampires* revels in the familiar and the everyday, only to explode with unexpected eruptions that transform this peaceful world into a charged universe of unlimited evil and corruption. Like Feuillade's other serials of the teens, it mixes documentary with fantasy as provocatively as the sound movies of Jean Cocteau, Georges Franju, Jacques Tati, Jean-Luc Godard, Jacques Rivette, François Truffaut, and Leos Carax, but without ever relinquishing any of its credentials as popular entertainment.

Yet for most of the past century, Feuillade's movies were so scarce that they were virtually excluded from film history. *Les vampires* had a New York run at a small theater in late 1915 but apparently didn't receive any notice from the press. (It didn't fare much better in England a few months later, where it opened under the improbable title *Charles de la Rue—Crime Investigator.*) Even after the serial was rediscovered about half a century later, missing all its intertitles, the only U.S. screenings it received were at film festivals and museums. A restoration carried out in the mid-1980s at the Cinémathèque Française by Jacques Champreux, the filmmaker's grandson, finally brought the film back to its original form. But it wasn't until this version became available on video in 1998, and turned up on cable the following year—eighty-three and eighty-four years after its French and U.S. premieres!—that American viewers had a proper chance to discover it on their own.

It's hard to think of another silent masterpiece that has dated less. (For my money, the only other contender is Feuillade's equally great 1918 serial *Tih Minh,* shot on the French Riviera.) Critic David Thomson has called Feuillade "the first director for whom no historical allowances need to be made," and he is probably one of the last as well. Running for about eight hours, though easily and ideally watchable in separate episodes, *Les vampires,* one of the supreme pleasures in movies, unfolds with all the conviction and precision of a fever dream—a quality that is beautifully captured in Olivier Assayas's recent *Irma Vep* (1996), a black comedy about the shooting of a contemporary remake with Hong Kong superstar Maggie Cheung. Feuillade's plot concerns the exploits of an infamous gang of criminals, customarily clad and masked in black, known as the Vampires—not a clan of bloodsuckers, but a band of evildoers who hold most of Paris in their sway.

As full of disguises as a masquerade ball, the serial features so many characters with multiple false identities that part of the fun consists of trying to guess in advance who will turn out to be whom. The voluptuous Irma Vep (Musidora), whom we recognize in her black tights and mask as the leader of the Vampire Gang (her name, in fact, is an anagram of "Vampire"), characteristically creeping over rooftops, also assumes one or more supplementary disguises in each install-ment—as family maid, male secretary, lab assistant, wealthy widow, street tough, switchboard operator, and spiritualist, among others—and when the hero, jour-nalist Philippe Guerande (Edouard Mathé), impersonates someone else as well, the spectator may feel temporarily lost in a sea of characters.

But such confusion is always purposeful in *Les vampires,* where nothing is ever quite what it seems. As critic Annette Michelson has written,

> Haussmann's pre-1914 Paris, the city of massive stone structures, of quiet avenues and squares, is suddenly revealed as everywhere dangerous, the

scene and subject of secret designs. The trap-door, secret compartment, false tunnel, false bottom, false ceiling, form an architectural complex with the architectural structure of a middle-class culture. The perpetually recurring ritual of identification and self-justification is the visiting card; it is, as well, the signal, the formal prelude to the fateful encounter, the swindle, hold-up, abduction or murder.

The dreamlike transitions from normalcy to fantasy are always poetic as well as unpredictable. After shooting a Vampire burglar who falls from a second-story window, a woman looks out the same window, only to find herself lassoed and pulled down into a getaway car that speeds off in a matter of seconds. At a fancy party given for the Paris aristocracy, knockout gas smelling like perfume pours in through a vent, and dozens of guests rush madly for the doors before collapsing where they stand, fluttering to the floor like so many handkerchiefs; doors in the back of the hall open, and Vampires emerge in silhouette to gather up the guests' jewels. Moreno—the head of a rival gang, who briefly holds Irma Vep in his power through hypnosis—is rushing out of a house with her; a trapdoor at the foot of the stairs suddenly opens, and they both fall into an enormous sack held by the police. In a plush hotel room, a bishop presses a button, and a giant cannon emerges from the fireplace, ready to fire a missile into an adjacent nightclub.

These surprises, and many others like them, caused Surrealists like André Breton and Luis Buñuel to celebrate Feuillade's serials, even when they ignored the name of the man who made them. (Other French avant-gardists of the period, however, resented the films' popularity and were more prone to attack Feuillade by name.) Partially because the villains exert a lot more fascination—and usually display much more ingenuity—than the forces representing law and order, one suspects that the Surrealists discovered in *Les vampires* a form of subversion that was fully compatible with their own aesthetic designs, even if Feuillade happened to be a conservative royalist and a tireless workhorse who wrote an estimated 800 scripts and directed 700 of them. (Roughly 500 of these, ranging from one-reelers to full features, still survive at Gaumont, the production company where Feuillade served as artistic director for most of his career.)

Significantly, the Vampires prey only on the rich, and the putative hero comes across as a pampered nincompoop who, before he belatedly collects his wits and defeats the gang in the last episode, has to depend on his mother, various family friends, and a team of other helpers to work out most of the clues and effect most of the rescues. Even when he triumphs at the end, it's his new bride who polishes off the sexy Irma Vep. (Perhaps the most fascinating and ingenious of his helpers are Mazamette—a comic mugger played by Marcel Levesque, who bore a striking resemblance to Feuillade himself—and his son Eustache, played by the popular child actor Bout de Zan.) For most of the serial, the police are fairly ineffectual as well—a point that wasn't lost on the Paris chief of police, who banned the serial for two months in 1916, until Musidora paid him a visit and charmed him into letting the serial resume. (The efficiency of the police takes a quantum leap over the last four episodes, and the forces of good become much more prominent in Feuillade's next serial, *Judex*.)

Up to the last two or three episodes, Feuillade improvised the action on a day-to-day basis, without a script—pursuing a form of "automatic writing" in which some plot twists were determined by vicissitudes in the shooting. Although the First World War is never alluded to, Feuillade started the film only a few weeks after returning from the front and had to kill off one of his characters, Satanas, when the actor playing him, Louis Leubas, was called back. (Two episodes earlier, Feuillade spitefully killed off the Grand Vampire when Jean Aymé, the Swiss actor playing him, repeatedly turned up late for work.) Trusting to chance and instinct, Feuillade allowed the mystery of his surroundings and his own unconscious to seep through, fully justifying the claim made by Henri Langlois, founder of the Cinémathèque Française, in 1965: "I am convinced that surrealism preexisted in cinema. Feuillade's *Les vampires* was already an expression of the 20th century and of the universal subconscious."

Vertigo (1958)

by Kenneth Turan

PROOF OF THE FALLIBILITY OF FILM CRITICS, should it be needed at this late date, is as close as the reviews that greeted Alfred Hitchcock's *Vertigo* when it opened in 1958.

"Another Hitchcock-and-bull story," sneered *Time* magazine; the *New Yorker* said the director "has never before indulged in such farfetched nonsense"; and the *Los Angeles Times* lamented that the film "bogs down in a maze of details." Even the film's few partisans conceded that this was minor Hitchcock at best.

Even seven years later, when iconoclastic British critic Robin Wood had the temerity to call *Vertigo* "one of the four or five most profound and beautiful films the cinema has yet given us," he made sure to follow his statement with the acknowledgement that "this is a claim that may surprise, even amuse, the majority of my readers."

That kind of disclaimer is no longer very much in evidence, as *Vertigo* is conceded to be, in the words of Hitchcock biographer Donald Spoto, the director's "richest, most obsessive, least compromising film." By 1992, when the British Film Institute did its once-a-decade survey of the world's film critics to compile an all-time ten-best list, *Vertigo*, which hadn't been listed in 1962 or 1972, came in at fourth place, bested only by Orson Welles's *Citizen Kane*, Jean Renoir's *Rules of the Game*, and Yasujiro Ozu's *Tokyo Story*.

What's going on here? Why has a film dismissed by the keenest minds of 1958 become an icon of modern cinema? Were they crazy or are we? Or is it simply that *Vertigo* defines the concept of art that is ahead of its time, a motion picture whose virtues resonate much more strongly with contemporary viewers than they could have done four decades past.

For nearly twenty years, from 1967 to 1984, that question was difficult to answer because *Vertigo,* for a variety of reasons, was taken out of theatrical distribution. It returned briefly in 1984, but the print quality was sketchy. Finally, in 1996, after two years of work and a million dollars spent, a restored and revitalized print of *Vertigo* received a nationwide re-release.

By bringing back vivid sights and sounds, restoration partners Robert A. Harris and James C. Katz (whose credits in this area include *Lawrence of Arabia, Spartacus,* and *My Fair Lady*) made it possible for viewers to experience the film in a way that echoed the excitement of its original release.

To best take advantage of 1958's VistaVision format, which utilized side-by-side 35mm negatives, this *Vertigo* went out in 70mm. And Bernard Herrmann's original monaural score was recorded in brilliant DTS digital sound that left no doubt about why it's considered one of the pinnacles of modern film music, unsettling and Wagnerian with hints of something evil this way coming.

As a result, *Vertigo* is revealed as what it probably always was, an audacious, brilliantly twisted movie, infused with touches of genius and of madness. A disturbing meditation on the interconnected nature of love and obsession disguised as a penny-dreadful shocker, it comes off more impressive today than forty years ago because of several factors.

Perhaps most important, the 1960s New Wave, the rise of American independent film, and the proliferation of academic film studies have combined to give considerable cachet to the notion of subjective moviemaking. And though it was made in the heart of the studio system, *Vertigo* is as intensely personal as any entry at Sundance, with some of the biggest stars of the day helping Hitchcock work through the nakedest version of his perennial fascination with glacial blondes and the ghastly jokes of fate.

Hitchcock was able to get away with this because he worked within the context of a thriller plot. *Vertigo* started out as a novel called *D'entre les Morts* (*Between the Dead*) by the French team of Pierre Boileau and Thomas Narcejac, the same pair who'd written the book on which Henri-Georges Clouzot's *Diabolique* was based. In fact, though Hitchcock didn't find out until his celebrated series of interviews with François Truffaut years later, the new novel had been specifically concocted to get the great man's attention.

Vertigo, the film that resulted, focuses on John "Scottie" Ferguson (James Stewart), a San Francisco–based police detective forced into early retirement by the sudden onset of acrophobia, a fear of heights that brings on intense dizziness, or vertigo.

Reduced to spending his spare time with Midge, a sensible ex-girlfriend (played by Barbara Bel Geddes, later known as Miss Ellie of *Dallas*), Scottie is grateful to get a proposition from an old college buddy named Gavin Elster (Tom Helmore), now a wealthy San Francisco businessman.

Elster is concerned about his wife, Madeline. Though he knows it sounds farfetched, Elster feels something or someone has taken possession of Madeline, possibly from beyond the grave, and because he fears for his wife's safety and sanity he wants her followed by someone he knows and trusts.

Scottie, who prides himself on his hardheaded practicality, is dubious at first, but his first glimpse of the blonde and ethereal Madeline, breathtaking in a black evening gown with a teal wrap, changes his mind. One look also tells us what Scottie himself is not ready to admit: he's intoxicated enough to follow this woman anywhere.

Where anywhere turns out to be is one of the many shocks this famously unpredictable plot provides. Yet difficult though its twists are to anticipate, *Vertigo* is most talked about for how, in vintage Hitchcock fashion, it gets its strongest effects not out of surprise but from the more satisfying notion of suspense. The idea is to let the audience in on things the characters don't know and exploit our anticipation of how they'll react when they do find out.

Madeline is played, in one of her strongest and most persuasive performances, by Kim Novak. Projecting a powerful, otherworldly sensuality, she underlines Truffaut's comment to Hitchcock that "very few American actresses are quite as carnal on screen." Its hard to imagine *Vertigo* without her, yet that's what the director was determined to do.

Hitchcock had initially preferred Vera Miles, who'd costarred in his previous *The Wrong Man* with Henry Fonda. But Miles got pregnant and the director was not amused. "It was her third child," he's quoted by biographer Spoto, "and I told her that that one child was expected, two was sufficient, but that three was really obscene. She didn't care for this sort of comment."

Though he was too irked at Miles to use her even though shooting ended up starting so late she became available again, Hitchcock was far from keen on Novak, a top box-office draw who'd come to the project as part of a deal engineered by Lew Wasserman that had her and costar Stewart segue together to *Bell, Book, and Candle.* For one thing, she was independent-minded and had her own ideas about things like wardrobe, a stance the director had little patience with. "My dear Miss Novak," he is famously said to have replied, "you can wear anything you want, anything—provided it is what the script calls for."

Hitchcock, who could be something of a sadist on the set, is said to have taken his revenge by insisting on multiple retakes (one estimate is twenty-four, others say the story is apocryphal) of a scene that called for Novak being dunked in a studio tank. Still, the actress apparently didn't hold a grudge, telling a reporter years later "Hitchcock was dictatorial, but at heart he was a sweet, charming man. He didn't know how to relate to actors as people. He could put you into his plots, but it was a chess game. You were just a piece."

Equally problematic for a long time was how to turn the novel's plot into an acceptable script. Playwright Maxwell Anderson did a first draft with the unpromising title *Darkling I Listen.* Alec Coppel did a second version and ended up sharing screen credit with Samuel Taylor, who also wrote *Sabrina* and came up with the key element that made everyone happy.

Taylor, who never read the original novel, explained in a later interview that he'd told Hitchcock the problem with the Coppel script was "'a matter of finding reality and humanity for these people. You haven't got anybody in this story who is a human being; nobody at all. They're all cut-out cardboard figures.' I told him immediately that I would have to invent a character who would bring Scottie into the world, establish for him an ordinary life, make it obvious that he's an ordinary man. So I invented Midge." Stewart, for one, was so delighted he charged into the director's office and said, "Now we have a movie, now we can go ahead!"

Once Hitchcock began to work, another of the qualities that make him a figure of increasing interest came into play: the impressive amount of craft (acquired by directing dozens of pictures over three decades and almost unknown today) he brought to the table. Hitchcock was a master of every detail of the filmmaking process, meticulous enough to have Novak practice some of her movements to a metronome. His solution to simulating Scottie's vertigo, done by having the camera simultaneously zoom in and track out, was the result, he told Truffaut, of fifteen years of thinking about how best to show dizziness on screen.

So strong was Hitchcock's control of the medium that, working with cinematographer Robert Burks, he was able to bend the city of San Francisco to his will, creating a deliciously ghostly metropolis, nearly deserted and not of this world. He also shrewdly combined studio shots with location work, recreating in carefully measured detail on L.A. soundstages such San Francisco landmarks as Ernie's restaurant and Ranshohoff's department store.

The mission at San Juan Bautista, 90 miles south of the city, is a key *Vertigo* location, but in real life it doesn't have the belltower critical to the plot. So Hitchcock constructed one in the studio and optically superimposed it on the shot. His pure skill as a director is critical in making *Vertigo*'s story plausible and shows why screenwriter Taylor later said, "I don't believe there's anybody who in purely cinematic terms is Hitchcock's equal."

Finally, more than Hitchcock's ability, what connects most impressively to today's audiences is the strange darkness of *Vertigo*'s themes, its moments of obsessive eroticism, its tipping of the hat to sadism, masochism, fetishism, necrophilia, and more garden-variety neuroses. The film's continued ability to unsettle and disconcert without resorting to graphic visuals underlines how modern and timeless its themes and execution remain.

Interestingly enough for a film that became so celebrated, all of *Vertigo*'s creators had problems with the project. Not only had Hitchcock wanted Vera Miles, he grumbled later that the film had not done well at the box office because Jimmy Stewart looked too old. Screenwriter Taylor said he would have preferred Ingrid Bergman for the female lead, and composer Bernard Herrmann said "they never should have made it in San Francisco and not with Jimmy Stewart. I don't think that he would be that wild about any woman. It should have been an actor like Charles Boyer. It should have been left in New Orleans, or in a hot, sultry climate."

Yet notwithstanding all this negativity, *Vertigo* continues to have the strongest possible impact. Because Alfred Hitchcock put so much of himself into the film, *Vertigo* plainly demands an equally strong and equally personal response.

The Wild Bunch (1969)

by Michael Wilmington

SAM PECKINPAH'S THE WILD BUNCH OPENS with perhaps the most startling burst of sustained violence in all of the American cinema: a raging inferno of quick-cut, slow-motion bloodshed, with outlaws and ambushers on the roofs above shooting it out, during a busted railroad office robbery, in five dense minutes of horrific carnage. It is a scene of extraordinary art and impact, exploding off the screen with such force and affecting audiences so viscerally, they sometimes reel back in shock.

The movie closes with another burst of slaughter; an insanely bloody standoff involving four surviving outlaws of the wild bunch, an entire Mexican army contingent, and a Gattling gun passed from hand to hand. In between, Peckinpah shows his antiheroes trapped between a posse of vicious mercenaries and the immoral Mexican Army that buys their rifles; a three-cornered game of demonic intensity, nightmare nihilism, and outrageous compassion. Peckinpah himself describes it simply and tersely: "It's what happens when outlaws go to Mexico."

This is a movie that overwhelms and incites. Though *The Wild Bunch* is set in 1913, at the end of the Western frontier period, it has a more profound sense of the present than all but a handful of films set in 1969, the year it was released. It is contemporary: it's about the period in which it was shot, America during the height of the Vietnam War, with all its violence and malaise—and it foreshadows America right now.

The movie throbs with the intensified vision, the paranoia, the cockeyed fatalism and courage of men who live near death: soldiers, outlaws, cops. And once Peckinpah—and his brilliant cinematographer, Lucien Ballard, and editor Lou Lombardo—stun you with *The Wild Bunch*'s opening credit sequence (Pike Bishop's gang masquerading as soldiers as they stroll toward the office they're going to rob) and sweep you into the five minute cataclysm, the movie never lets you off the hook.

The Wild Bunch is an American masterpiece, one of the greatest ever produced in the Hollywood system. But for years it was also a mutilated classic, shorn of crucial scenes in its first release. (The 1995 theatrical run of the original, a 144-minute director's cut, was a cause for celebration.) Few that followed it, even among its many imitators, have its sense of tragedy and loss, its depth, melancholy and lyricism, or its savagery and dark wit. Even Peckinpah's directorial credit is thrilling: a freeze-frame on a macabre close-up of William Holden as outlaw chief Bishop, caught in splotches of color, right after growling to his men: "If they move, kill 'em," with an ominous Jerry Fielding musical chord crashing down behind him.

What happens next in the movie—the pursuit of Pike's gang to Mexico by a posse led by his erstwhile best friend, Deke Thornton (Robert Ryan), their plunge into the Mexican civil war as gun runners, and their final fateful battle—is really the classic American story of noble outlaws: the bad men who redeem themselves, a staple of the movie western since the days of William S. Hart and, especially, John Ford.

Yet no noble outlaws or "good bad men" were ever quite this bad before, no posse this depraved. It seems at first a movie without heroes. Peckinpah shoves in our faces their flaws and ugliness, from Old Man Sykes's rotten teeth to the Gorch boys' horny sadism. The posse are even worse—and, in fact, the only group that gets any conventional sympathy here are the Mexican villagers with whom the Bunch briefly stay: a dreamlike community whose patriarch has the film's key speech: "We all dream of being a child again, even the worst of us—perhaps the worst most of all."

Fittingly, in the whole course of this most violent of westerns, we never see a child killed—even though smiling kids are around from the beginning. In the title sequence, as the Wild Bunch arrives on horseback, children giggle as they torture a scorpion, dropping it into a mass of ants and then setting them all on fire. The Bunch themselves are like children: whimsical, violent, quick to play and laugh—but also quick to kill. The six actors who play Pike's gang—Holden as Pike, Jaime Sanchez as Angel, Ernest Borgnine as Pike's right-hand man Dutch Engstrom, Edmond O'Brien as Old Man Sykes, and Warren Oates and Ben Johnson as the likably scabrous Gorch brothers, Lyle and Tector—all had close to their finest hour in the making of this movie. So did Strother Martin and L.Q. Jones as Coffer and T.C., vilest of the posse. And so, in a way, did actor-directors Emilio Fernandez and Alfonso Aura as two memorable Alfonso Bedoya–style psychopaths in the Mexican Army.

Holden, whose great days in *Sunset Boulevard* and *The Bridge on the River Kwai* seemed past by 1969, replaced Lee Marvin (who would have been the perfect *Wild Bunch* star; in the worst mistake of his career, Marvin—who had collaborated brilliantly with Peckinpah in the picaresque 1963 TV comedy *The Losers*—rejected Pike for *Paint Your Wagon* and a bigger payday, claiming that *Wild Bunch* was too much like *The Professionals*. But even though Holden lacks Marvin's grinning menace and joyous hard-guy athleticism, in the end he makes Pike his own anyway: a weaker, wearier, mellower gang boss. By now, one cannot imagine the film without him any more than one can imagine it without Oates, Johnson, O'Brien, or any of the others.

Peckinpah brings out a surface brutishness in Holden and the whole Wild Bunch, but he also reveals vulnerability beneath. Probably more disturbing to some audiences than the violence itself—which consumes only a fraction of the movie—is our mixed response toward these outlaws. Sometimes odious, they're also capable of a twisted, savage bravery and grandeur—and one repeated exchange among the gang becomes their mantra: "Let's Go!" "Why not!" It's an existential adventurer's credo, the movie's main chord. In his role as the reluctant bounty hunter in *Bring Me the Head of Alfredo Garcia,* Warren Oates played Peckinpah and, in *The Wild Bunch,* so does Holden. He has Peckinpah's mustache, swagger, and mannerisms. So *The Wild Bunch* is both self-portrait and ultimate vindication. Throughout the 1960s, after the debacle of his firing from the Steve McQueen movie *The Cincinnati Kid,* Peckinpah had been something of an exile, a wiry Westerner with a hair-trigger temper, a perfectionist feuding constantly with his bosses. *The Wild Bunch* brought him back.

Peckinpah's models here were the John Ford of *My Darling Clementine,* the John Huston of *The Treasure of Sierra Madre,* and, to a greater extent, Akira Kurosawa. Kurosawa had created his legendary action scenes, from *Seven Samurai* on, by shooting simultaneously with three cameras. Throughout *The Wild Bunch,* Peckinpah doubled his mentor's arsenal, using six cameras, and the effects—especially the famous use of slow motion, that agonizing, ecstatic flail as bodies hurtle endlessly in their death throes—create a frenzied immediacy that summons up both the moment of death and the jaws of hell.

Did *The Wild Bunch* go too far? So thought some overoutraged critics and moralists at the time. But it should be obvious by now that *The Wild Bunch,* of all movies, is no shallow exploitation of violence. By rubbing the audience's nose in horror, Peckinpah (like Arthur Penn in the Kurosawa-influenced *Bonnie and Clyde*) resensitized viewers. Other late-1960s movies turned violence into glib entertainment. When Peckinpah let the blood flow, he also let life break out.

If he had a genius for screen violence, he had a talent for tenderness too; Jean Renoir once said Peckinpah knew much of "the music of the soul"; we can see that in rare, gentler pieces like the 1966 TV film of Katherine Anne Porter's "Noon Wine." And so, in the end, he made these deeply flawed, dangerous, near psychopathic, weirdly attractive outlaws come to life as few movie characters ever

have. That's why the Wild Bunch seems so magnificent in their last stroll down
the road to apocalypse. The image burns itself into your memory: the morning
before the last battle, the last walk, the last "Let's go!" "Why not?" and the Wild
Bunch, now beatifically calm, striding warily down the dusty, sunny Agua Verde
street: Borgnine's gun slung casually over a shoulder, Holden's in his left hand,
Oates's in his right, and Ben Johnson's rifle cradled in his arms, like the child that
the worst of us longs to be.

Winchester '73 (1953)

by Gerald Peary

ACCORDING TO SCREENWRITER BORDEN CHASE, the 1950 pre-
view audience at *Winchester '73* tittered seeing the name of James Stewart heading the cast. Who could imagine the folksy, affable actor, so deft at light, romantic
comedy, in an intense black-and-white western? The only occasion he had
appeared even vaguely in the saddle was for a humorous poke at cowboy movies,
Destry Rides Again (1939).

But Stewart had been fishing to do something new on screen; and he enlisted
Universal producer Aaron Rosenberg to champion a western story by Stuart N.
Lake about a totemic rifle being passed hand to hand, a project abandoned by
filmmaker Fritz Lang. And to direct? Someone suggested Anthony Mann, a maker
of "B" movies since 1944, once an assistant director for Preston Sturges.

Who? Of American film critics, only *The Nation's* Manny Farber had taken
notice of the "noir" filmmaker of *T-Men* (1947), *Raw Deal* (1948), and *Reign of
Terror* (1949), and later he would praise Mann's "Germanic rigor, caterpillar intimacy." In 1950, Mann had just completed a Barbara Stanwyck–starring western,
The Furies.

"We saw this picture he made, none of us had heard his name," Stewart said
later. "This was a beautifully directed picture. He was a visual man, and he was
able to make the background, and movement, a part of the story."

Mann, when hired, got his way: a major rewrite by screenwriters Robert L.
Richards and Chase, and a veteran cinematographer, William Daniels, who had
distinguished himself in the 1930s with his lighting of Greta Garbo. Stewart, an

expert horseman from childhood, now taught himself to shoot a repeating rifle. "Knowing how to use something is the only way to realism," Mann said succinctly, praising his actor's dedication. "He worked so hard his knuckles were raw with practicing, so he could do it right." The shoot on location in Arizona was smooth and without studio complaint. When *Winchester '73* was released, the reviews were decent, the film made some money, and James Stewart was accepted as a movie cowboy, especially with, later the same year, his appearance in Delmer Daves's *Broken Arrow.*

Those in the United States who wrote about movies in the 1950s tended to view cinema from a sociological vantage, rarely noticing, or commenting on, directorial style but concentrating their critical judgments on the worthiness of a film's overt themes. Thus, American reviewers were far more taken by the liberal-minded *Broken Arrow,* because it humanized Native Americans in the story of a white man (Stewart) who has an Indian wife and who brokers a peace between Washington and native tribes. In contrast, French film critics around the magazine *Cahiers du Cinéma*—André Bazin and future cineastes Jean-Luc Godard, François Truffaut, Jacques Rivette—celebrated subjective, existential themes over politically correct ones, and they valued much more visual style—editing, rhythm, mise-en-scène—than a well-meaning script.

It was the French who hailed the edgy, pictorially thrilling oeuvre of Anthony Mann, praising his unorthodox use of outdoor locales, especially in his collaborations with Stewart. Truffaut: "It is to Anthony Mann that we owe the purest westerns of the last few years." Godard: "With Mann one rediscovers the western, as one discovers arithmetic in an elementary math class. I have seen nothing so completely new since—why not?—Griffith."

Winchester '73 was the first of five Mann/Stewart westerns, also *Bend of the River* (1952), *The Naked Spur* (1953), *The Far Country* (1955), and *The Man From Laramie* (1955). Mann's personal touches? These were increasingly violent, neurotic, and expressionistic, utilizing Stewart as a man always with a deep secret and obsessed with a tenuous, violent mission, one which, Hamletlike, could backfire, causing psychological and moral damage to he who made the blood spill. A *new* Stewart evolved: fierce, hot-tempered, imploding from demons, who had been glimpsed briefly in the nightmare sequences of *It's A Wonderful Life* (1946) and who, of course, would emerge fully as the irate revenger dragging Kim Novak to the top of the tower in Alfred Hitchcock's *Vertigo* (1958).

Mann on Stewart: "He seemed to have something more burning and exciting on screen that when you met him personally. . . . And his emotion when roused was something we concentrated on, of course, especially after *Winchester '73.*"

Mann's first western with Stewart is often a throwback. Though purposefully stripped of Fordian sentimentality and transcendence, *Winchester '73* has many counterparts in plot, characters, and settings, to the 1930s and 1940s films of John Ford, especially *Stagecoach* and *My Darling Clementine*.

The protagonist, Lin McCadum, has a few brief heated moments; yet except for the firearms and cowboy garb, Lin isn't substantially different from Stewart's benign 1940s roles, nothing like the tainted avenger who prevails in noirish westerns of the 1950s. He's basically a decent, modest, and righteous guy whose quest, though violence must come at the end, holds little moral ambiguity. He's after the evil, remorseless gunslinger who shot his beloved father in the back. That person is Dutch Henry Brown (Stephen McNally) who, we eventually learn, is actually Lin's compulsively criminal brother.

Abel and Cain? Absolutely. Dutch Henry even wears a black hat. But *Winchester '73* is also, consciously, a Sophoclean story of fratricide in the West. It's as an Oedipus tale that the film gets a bit unusual.

"I don't know of any great man who ever had a great son," Mann said tellingly, in a *Cahiers* interview. "This must have been a terrible thing for the son to live with the image of his father." What's amiss with *Winchester '73*'s protagonist—is this a deconstruction of the stalwart western hero?—is that he's deeply stunted. He lived with, and for, his great departed father, quotes, without ever questioning it, his father's wisdom, knows how to shoot so expertly because his father taught him how. He has no wife or love life but hangs out on the range with an elderly man, High-Spade Frankie Wilson (Millard Mitchell), because here, obviously, is a substitute dad.

As for his quotidian existence wandering the range, Lin is completely possessed with tracking down his father's murderer. At various points in *Winchester '73*, we see Lin rejecting food and shelter, also a chance to hang out with a woman of whom he's becoming enamored, because these pleasures would slow his hunt. His ambition beyond the revenge couldn't be more sketchy: "Maybe take up the ranch, find the strays. I haven't thought about it."

Stewart did a decent job describing his simple-motivated character in *Winchester '73*: "I guess he was a plodder, the inarticulate man who tried. . . . But for some reason, I made it. I got through." While Lin proceeds on the generic course of a traditional western—holding off hostile Indians, shooting his way through a bunch of bad-guy underlings, killing his adversary in a one-on-one shootout, getting the girl at the end—it's the idiosyncratic characters in *Winchester '73* who make the terrain appealingly different. Among the film's many virtues are its colorful ensemble, including a charismatic, populist Wyatt Earp

(Will Geer), a man-crazy, promiscuous heroine (Shelly Winters), and a secondary villain of great gusto and bravado (Dan Duryea).

The most radical thing about *Winchester '73* is that its protagonist is not the locus of western myth. What's held in awe, what's fetishized throughout the movie, both by characters who clutch it and fondle it and by Anthony Mann's camera, is that titular rifle. Practically every scene starts and ends by Mann focusing on it in close-up, and it appears in many scenes from which Lin is absent. It's bartered over and fought over by characters, looked on sexually by the heroine, who says (a grand double-entendre!), "You never know when a girl might need a bullet." The glorious gun also literally begins the movie and concludes it.

For those out of the NRA loop: Oliver Winchester's 1873 version of a repeating rifle, for which one could use the same bullets as for a six-gun, was considered the best ever made, and "the Model of 1873" was produced into the 1920s. Concerning rifles, *Winchester '73* becomes philosophical: it's not men that make history but machinery. Firearms. The massacre at Little Big Horn is explained here as having occurred not because Custer and his troops were surrounded but because the Sioux tribe were blessed with repeating rifles, the cavalry strapped with archaic Springfields. Men without guns in *Winchester '73* describe themselves, anxiously, as "naked," and virtually all the scenes are brilliantly choreographed one-upmanship dances of pistols and rifles. The most memorable: the target-shooting contest in Dodge City pitting the two estranged brothers; the climactic gun battle of the same brothers, repeating rifle versus repeating rifle, ricocheting bullets among mountain rocks.

"The gun which passed from hand to hand allowed me to embrace a whole epoch, a whole atmosphere," Anthony Mann said. "I really believe that it contains all the ingredients of the western, and that it summarizes them." A French critic astute about Anthony Mann nevertheless complained, when describing *Winchester '73*, of "the very premise requiring that many key scenes take place in the hero's absence. . . . The hero is upstaged throughout the film by the prop and its successful owners." What it criticized is, of course, that what makes *Winchester '73* so enthralling—an abiding, nonpareil genre classic.

The Wizard of Oz (1939)

by Peter Keough

THE TERROR INSTILLED IN ME AS A CHILD by repeated viewings of *The Wizard of Oz,* I now realize, drove me to become a film critic.

Every holiday season the film would be broadcast on television, and with the rest of the family I would be obliged to watch. Was I the only one who had nightmares about twisters languidly, inexorably lolling across the Kansas greyness, the phallic funnels looming over the womblike shelter of the storm cellar, shut tight to Dorothy's beseeching? The macabre spectacle of the Wicked Witch of the East's feet, robbed of their Ruby Slippers, shriveling up under Dorothy's house? Or the Winged Monkeys, their formations filling the sky like a cross between Goya's *Sleep of Reason* and the Luftwaffe, off to their hideous dismemberment of the Scarecrow? Or the appalling realization that one's entire experience, in living color yet (though in its earliest TV broadcasts, in even eerier black and white), might be no more than a dream? These were things, like sex and death (*Goldfinger* and *Bambi* did the job for those two), that no one spoke about. Year after year I watched, the terrors unspoken, until the ritual of film reviewing would sublimate them.

Years later, my fate as a critic sealed, I returned to *Oz* to see what all the fuss was about. Released in a newly restored version, the film was being shown in a large theater filled with an audience consisting mostly of hundreds of prepubescent girls dressed in Dorothy's blue polka dot gingham dress. It was the first time I saw it, as they say, the way it was meant to be seen, on a big screen and in a big dark hall with hundreds of strangers. Would *Oz,* like the genial shaman of the title, prove a humbug? Would it disperse into smoke and mirrors and, with it, the whole artifice of movies which I revered?

The artifice proved shaky all right, but it wasn't *Oz's* fault. Because of some projector problem we had to be content with a postage-stamp image on the big screen that was about the same size as that on a large TV in a sports bar. So much for six decades of technological development. And the preteen audience seemed more respectful than awed. No crying, squealing, or laughter, a few clap-alongs with the tunes ("Ding Dong! The Witch Is Dead" a particular crowd-pleaser), and only polite applause when the Wicked Witch of the West was melted.

Gradually, though, the magic, long gone beyond kitsch to archetype by cease-less repetition and cultural recycling, drew me in, but the innocence of my child-hood responses had darkened with rueful experience. The cyclone no longer got a rise out of me, but the grey wastes of Kansas, as bleak as the Oklahoma Dustbowl in John Ford's *The Grapes of Wrath* released in 1940, the following year, seemed horrifying enough. Against that backdrop, surrounded by the dilapidated barnyard, Dorothy's rendition of "Somewhere Over the Rainbow" echoes over the years as a stinging reproach to false optimism and lost illusions. The miracle of Judy Garland's performance lies in her utter lack, not only of makeup and super-ficial beauty, but of irony. And, of course, that homespun, limpid beauty would slowly be laid to waste in the tragedy that was Garland's life.

But her Dorothy lives on, an icon free to be picked apart by fans and critics, such as myself, desperate to retrieve her wonder. When amazement fails, there's always analysis, and few films are as rife with archetypal resonance and histori-cal, cultural, and personal reverberations as *Oz*. Some essay questions for discus-sion: How does Dorothy's quest with her three needy, dysfunctional friends relate to current pop-psychological issues of empowerment and passive aggression? Is the film a Freudian, feminist, or Marxist allegory? Is the man behind the curtain a metaphor for the dubious magic of the motion picture industry itself?

Well, so be it. The key to growing up, as Dorothy realized, is discovering that one's fears and desires are mostly special effects and hokum, and resigning one-self to the fact that, except for an inconsequential sojourn for a couple of hours to a gaudy two-dimensional somewhere over the rainbow, there is indeed no place like home, the humdrum monochrome of the familiar, oppressive, and hopeless that one returns to after the flickering illusion is over.

That home, Dorothy's Kansas, is ruled over by the tyrannical local landowner Almira Gulch (the oddly sexy Margaret Hamilton, later to sell us Maxwell House coffee), a barren matriarchy (that Auntie Em is a cold-blooded taskmaster, despite her crullers) served by bumbling, ineffectual males (I still laugh at Uncle Henry's line, "Oh, she bit her dog, eh?"). The scenario is ripe for revolution, but when the sole spirit of male rebellion, Toto, asserts himself, Gulch sentences him to death. This summons the fertilizing male principle—that inevitable cyclone—that pro-pels Dorothy, home and all, into a realm of endless possibility, where the conflict between independence and conformity can be resolved through kitschy fantasy and some catchy production numbers.

Oz, though, is merely Kansas transformed through Dorothy's polymorphously perverse wish fulfillment (she is, after all, the sixteen-year-old Judy Garland) and early Technicolor. In this Utopia, she has slain the mother-oppressor, the Witch of the East, usurped that tyrant's power in the form of the Freudianly ripe ruby footwear (with the intervention of dotty Billie Burke's oddly detached Good Witch of the North), but still requires patriarchal assistance to defeat the vengeful Wicked Witch of the West (Hamilton, again, seductive in green).

That includes the three Kansas farmhands metamorphosed into types of their own inadequacy. The Scarecrow, played with rubber-limbed grace and guileless guile by Ray Bolger ("I think I'll miss you most of all," says Dorothy, and she may be right) is a stuffed man who wants brains who is nonetheless the brains of the outfit. The Tin Man, played by the gently melancholy Jack Haley, is a hollow man who bemoans his heartlessness, though his crying often threatens to rust him into immobility. And the Cowardly Lion, played by Bert Lahr, the only actor who could get away with rhyming "rhinoceros" with "imposseros!" is a mincing bully who wears a suffocating ninety-pound costume that does not conceal the "dandy-lion" terrified within. While these three hide their potency behind the guise of debility, the goal of their quest, the Wizard himself (Frank Morgan, in one of five roles—think of how the film would have played if the dyspeptic W.C. Fields had not held out for more money for the part), veils his powerlessness under the veil of omnipotence.

Or is it powerlessness? Of all the images in *Oz,* that of the disembodied bulbous head crossed by fire and brimstone still disturbs. When he is exposed by the indefatigable Toto, the Wizard reveals that ultimate Hollywood secret: that the reality doesn't matter as much as the image, that illusion is as honest as truth if believed in, if only for 101 minutes of screen time.

To create the illusion that is *The Wizard of Oz,* many labored behind that curtain, beginning with L. Frank Baum, who wrote the book in 1900, and including four directors (Richard Thorpe, Victor Fleming, George Cukor, and Victor Fleming), ten screenwriters, and hundreds of actors, musicians, craftsmen, and dwarves. Perhaps the most wonderful thing about *Oz* was that it got made at all, a process of creative cooperation and chaos motivated by vanity, greed, and longing into the most enduring figment of our pop-culture pantheon. The doubts of former frightened children aside, it remains as profound an epic as *The Odyssey* and *The Inferno,* as intimate as a girl waking from a dream.

Written on the Wind (1956)

by J. Hoberman

THE MOST VIOLENT AND HYPERBOLIC of family melodramas, Douglas Sirk's *Written on the Wind* may be the quintessential American movie of the 1950s. The film turns a cold eye on the antics of the degenerate superrich, with Robert Stack and Dorothy Malone as two overaged juvenile delinquents, one a lush, the other a nympho, the wayward offspring of a Texas oil billionaire. Trash on an epic scale, it's a vision as luridly color-coordinated, relentlessly high-octane, and flamboyantly petit bourgeois as a two-toned T-bird with ultrachrome trim.

Written on the Wind has risen steadily in critical esteem since the Sirk revival of the early 1970s. The film is not only the ancestor of *Dallas, Dynasty,* and the other imperial soaps that ruled prime time during Reagan's first term, but, in its delirious pessimism, it's the Hollywood corollary to Allen Ginsberg's *Howl.* But then who in America would have been sufficiently alienated to appreciate Sirk's brilliance at the time of the movie's original release?

To watch *Written on the Wind* is to enter a semiotic jungle and encounter a ferocious irony. Sirk, who achieved his greatest success directing glossy soap operas for Universal, was one of the century's more drastically displaced persons. In his youth, he studied with the great art historian Erwin Panofsky and translated Shakespeare's sonnets, knew Brecht and staged Kurt Weill's last German production. Sirk was a European intellectual, and, if not exactly Adorno in Hollywood, he was nevertheless temperamentally suited to appreciate the exuberant one-dimensionality, the fantastic *Ersatzkeit* of his adopted culture. Long after he returned to Europe, Sirk maintained that he would have made his Hollywood swan song, the monstrous *Imitation of Life,* for the title alone.

Written on the Wind is not simply kitsch—it has a lurid classical grandeur that suggests Norman Rockwell redecorating Versailles (or Jacques-Louis David painting Vegas). Sirk dots the screen with stylized patches of hot canary and flaming turquoise, doubles the image with reflections, skews it with shock tilts, slashes it with flagrantly unmotivated shadows. *Written on the Wind* is the original Technicolor noir. It's fabulously ill, it reeks of autumnal rot. "It is like the Oktoberfest," Sirk's admirer Rainer Werner Fassbinder once wrote. "Everything is colorful and in motion, and you feel as alone as everyone [else]." And, as with the Oktoberfest, a good many of the characters are stumbling around sloshed.

The movie is at once overexcited and detached, embodying a distinctively contemporary attitude that some have associated with the postmodern. Although Sirk keeps things hyper with much brisk cutting on movement, his camera consistently dollies back, transforming point-of-view shots into two-shots, to emphasize relationships and prevent easy identification with his characters. Throughout, Sirk deploys mirrors and rear-screen projection in the service of a distanced antinaturalism. Nature is even phonier than the barren forest of oil rigs that signifies the Hadley wealth; it's like a museum diorama in which everything has its didactic place. A tree exists only to show the initials that were romantically carved there fifteen years before and have been perfectly preserved ever since.

There's a monumental Edward Hopper quality to the town pharmacy—the emptiness, the stylized light pattern, the thicket of banners emblazoned "Buy Quality Drugs Here"—that epitomizes the film's frantic affect and seductive flatness. It is in that drugstore that *Written on the Wind* has its natural home. The images are as flashy and iconic as the cover design of a paperback novel. Everything in the film is exaggerated, heightened, concentrated—and theoretical. The lizardlike, liver-spotted patriarch of the Hadley clan (Robert Keith) sits beneath his painted image; his drunken son (Stack) careens through a rear-screen projected wasteland that might have inspired Antonioni's *Red Desert*; his daughter (Malone) makes love to a photo of the film's star and universal object of desire (Rock Hudson), a Hadley serf who spurns her advances because he's in love with her sister-in-law (Lauren Bacall).

Sirk is less a director of actors than a master of blocking, arranging his performers in stylized postures as though they were modeling for liquor advertisements or the Anaheim Palace of Living Art. Malone, who drives a flaming red sports car to the weak-willed Stack's glaring yellow one, is a human jukebox, a virtual taxonomy of 1950s come-hither looks, an outrageous erotic construction (based, it becomes apparent, on sexual frustration). Brandishing her tits and licking her lips (she's obviously inherited the lizard's hyperactive tongue), she's Hadleyworld's J.R., the spirit of wanton destruction. The tormented Stack crowds the screen while flinching away from the camera—with his constricted delivery and crooked gait, he's a walking metaphor for tortured ambivalence. Bacall awakes on her wedding night to find him lying aslant—like some corn-fed Adonis who's been slain in the marriage bed. (Then, in one of the film's most haunting images, she adjusts his pillow to discover the pearl-handled revolver he's tucked underneath.)

A genius at juggling volumes, doling out light, positioning the camera, Sirk is also supremely tactile, with a sculptor's flair for juxtaposing unexpected textures. Everything in *Written on the Wind* feels sealed in plastic, airbrushed to the point of reflection. The sets are a hermetic succession of furniture showrooms. Like Frank Tashlin, Sirk anticipates the commodity artists of the 1980s. *Written on the Wind* revels in the spectacle of immaculate consumption; it feasts on the decor of a posh Miami Beach hotel. The suite, which Stack has furnished for Bacall with an absurd abundance of fruit, flowers, gowns, handbags, and silk underwear, is a cross between a midwestern funeral parlor and a djinn's palace. It's the setting in which the Bacall character experiences *herself* as a commodity, becomes fascinated and ashamed, and flees—but not very far.

No director has ever made more expressive use of decor or the objective correlative. *Written on the Wind* creates a shorthand lingo of fast cars, cigarettes, and booze. This is a universe where people dress like mood rings and surround themselves with totemic fetishes: the model oil-rig phallus that dominates the patriarch's desk, the silver poodles that guard Bacall's calendar, the crimson anthuriums and *étagère* of perfume bottles that decorate Malone's boudoir. (In this strategy, Sirk's most perceptive disciple is not Fassbinder but Errol Morris, who uses the telling personal effect to turn a talking head into a talking sarcophagus.) Nothing is funnier than the little bits of world culture, ancient statutes, and abstract paintings Sirk scatters as *tchotchkes* throughout the Hadley mansion and the film.

"What used to take place in the world of kings and princes has since been transposed into the world of the bourgeoisie," Sirk told Jon Halliday in a long and justly celebrated interview. The Hadleys are Sirk's embodiment of America, a small-town family grown rich beyond measure. But rather than said burghers, these yokels are laughably (and magnificently) petit bourgeois—the emotionally deprived rich kids acting out their domineering father's rapacious desires, one craving sex, the other seeking oblivion.

In opposition to these hysterical Hadleys are the ostensibly normal Bacall and Hudson. While the Hads are weak, passionate, and rebellious, the Had-nots are moralizing, smug, and pantingly eager to please the old man. The supposedly independent Bacall is all too cooperative; once married into the family, she makes her reports directly to Dad. Hudson, the film's nominal hero, is no less ambiguous—his overweening virtues serve to cripple Stack even as they stifle Malone. Hudson is little more than a broad-shouldered absence and, despite his evident resentment, the father's tool—the foreman in the firm's *Metropolis*-blunt class structure. (Below him are the lustful white workers Malone vainly tries to pick up and the subterranean black slaves who exist only to open doors and pour drinks.) Indeed, Hudson is actively fawning on the old man, as a sinister police car simply marked "Hadley" drives up with Malone and her latest lower-class swain in tow.

Where the Hads are direct, the Had-nots are devious. Hudson submits to the father's rule, using Malone to act out his Oedipal desires. Here, as Fassbinder pointed out, "the good, the 'normal,' the 'beautiful' are always utterly revolting; the evil, the weak, the dissolute arouse one's compassion." One cares for the grotesque Malone because her continually thwarted sexuality poses the greatest threat to the patriarchal order. Indeed, in the film's most hilarious excess, her inflamed strip-mambo literally knocks the father dead. By contrast, Stack can only desecrate the rule of the father, as when, in a paroxysm of impotence, he smashes a bottle of bootleg cornmash against the side of Dad's big white house. Even so, his character manages to find a place in the chain of patriarchal oppression when his violence aborts Bacall's pregnancy.

Written on the Wind is not simply epic trash but meta-trash. As the pulp poetry of the title suggests, it's about the vanity of trash, set in a world Sirk finds poignantly innocent. (There's a wonderful, if belated, gag that no one is quite sure exactly where Iran is.) This is the land of simulacrum, a hall of mirrors in which the reflection of an image substitutes for the image itself. Malone disposes of both male Hadleys (freeing Hudson to possess the film's only possible mother, which is to say, Bacall) and sentences herself to eternal sexual frustration. She's left to fondle her father's oil-rig dildo, the image of the dead patriarch smiling benignly from above, as Hudson and Bacall make their escape. The last shot is of a black servant closing the gate; you expect him to roll up the lawn and strike the set.

Contributors

John Anderson is the chief film critic for *Newsday*.

David Ansen is a movie critic and senior editor at *Newsweek*.

Gary Arnold has been the movie critic of the *Washington Times* since 1989. He lives in Arlington, Virginia.

Jami Bernard is a film critic for the *New York Daily News*.

Peter Brunette is a film critic for indiewire.com and has written or edited six books on film history.

Jay Carr is the film critic of the *Boston Globe* and *New England Cable News*.

Godfrey Cheshire's film criticism appears in *The Independent Weekly* (www.indy-week.com).

David Denby is a film critic and staff writer for the *New Yorker* and was for twenty years film critic of *New York* magazine. He is the author of *Great Books*.

Morris Dickstein teaches English and film studies at the Graduate Center of the City University of New York. His books include a study of the 1960s, *Gates of Eden* (Harvard, 1997), and a social history of American fiction after the Second World War, *Leopeard in the Temple* (Harvard, 2002). His film criticism has appeared in *The Nation*, *The Bennington Review*, *American Film*, and *Partisan Review*, where he is a contributing editor.

Roger Ebert is the film critic of the *Chicago Sun-Times* and author of *The Great Movies* (2002).

Judy Gerstel is currently an editor and columnist for the *Toronto Star*. She formerly served as film critic for the *Star* and the *Detroit Free Press*.

J. Hoberman is the senior film critic for the *Village Voice*. His books include *Bridge of Light: Yiddish Film Between Two Worlds*, *The Red Atlantis: Communist Culture in the Absence of Communism*, and *Midnight Movies* (written with Jonathan Rosenbaum), as well as monographs on the films *42nd Street* and *Flaming Creatures*.

Richard T. Jameson has served as film critic for *7 Days* magazine, *The Weekly* (Seattle), and *Mr. Showbiz* online magazine, among others. He has also been editor of the film journals *Movietone News* and *Film Comment,* as well as a National Society of Film Critics collection *They Went Thataway: Redefining Film Genres* (1994).

Dave Kehr is a New York–based film writer.

Peter Keough has been the film editor of the *Boston Phoenix* since 1989.

Andy Klein currently reviews films for the New Times chain and KPCC radio, was film editor and chief film critic for the *Los Angeles Reader,* and has reviewed for the *Los Angeles Herald-Examiner,* AP Radio News, *Salon, Movieline,* and Microsoft Cinema online.

Emanuel Levy is the chief film critic for *Screen International* and a tenured film professor at Arizona State University. He is the author of seven books, including the biography *George Cukor, Master of Elegance, Cinema of Outsiders: The Rise of American Independent Film*, and *Citizen Sarris, American Film Critic*. His biography of the Broadway and Hollywood director Vincente Minnelli will be published in 2003 for the centennial of Minnelli's birth.

Todd McCarthy is chief film critic of *Variety,* is the author of the biography *Howard Hawks,* co-wrote and co-directed the documentary, *Visions of Light: The Art of Cinematography,* and wrote the documentary, *Preston Sturges: the Rise and Fall of an American Dream.*

Joe Morgenstern is the film critic of the *Wall Street Journal.*

Rob Nelson is the film editor and lead film critic at *City Pages* in Minneapolis. He is the recipient of three editorial awards from the Association of Alternative Newsweeklies. His work has also appeared in *CinemaScope, Spin, Village Voice,* the *Boston Phoenix, The Independent Film and Video Monthly, Isthmus,* and *Mother Jones.*

Gerald Peary is a film critic for the *Boston Phoenix* and head of the film program at Suffolk University, Boston. He is the author of eight books on cinema, the latest of which is *John Ford: Interviews*. He was a Fullbright Scholar in Belgrade studying Yugoslavian film comedy and an acting curator of the Harvard Film Archive.

Terrence Rafferty is critic at large for *GQ* magazine. His work has also appeared in *Sight and Sound, The Atlantic, Village Voice, The Nation,* the *New York Times,* and the *New Yorker,* where he was a staff member for ten years. A selection of his writing on film, *The Thing Happens,* was published in 1993.

Peter Rainer is the film critic for *New York* magazine. He is also chairman of the National Society of Film Critics and the editor of the critics' anthology *Love and Hisses.* A 1998 finalist for the Pulitzer Prize in Journalism, he discusses movies regularly for "Film Week," aired over Minnesota Public Radio, and has written and co-produced the *A&E Biography* documentaries on Sidney Poitier and the Hustons. He has also been the film critic at *New Times Los Angeles* and the *Los Angeles Herald Examiner,* and, as a staff critic for six years, contributed film reviews and commentary to the *Los Angeles Times.* His writing has also appeared in the *New York Times Magazine, Vogue, GQ, Esquire, Premiere,* and *Mademoiselle,* and he has appeared frequently as a film commentator on such shows as *Nightline* and *ABC World News Tonight.* He has also taught film criticism in the graduate division of the University of Southern California Film School and served on the juries for the Venice and Montreal film festivals.

Carrie Rickey is a film critic at the *Philadelphia Inquirer.*

Eleanor Ringel reviews movies for the *Atlanta Journal Constitution,* has been a regular columnist for *TV Guide,* and has won prizes from Sigma Delta Chi for criticism.

Jonathan Rosenbaum is the film critic for the *Chicago Reader.* His books include *Moving Places, Midnight Movies* (with J. Hoberman), *Film: The Front Line 1983, This is Orson Welles* (editor), *Placing Movies, Movies as Politics, Greed, Dead Man, Movie Wars,* and *Abbas Kiarostami* (forthcoming, with Mehrnaz Saeed-Vafa).

Andrew Sarris is a film critic for the *New York Observer,* a professor of film at The School of the Arts, Columbia University, and the author of several books on film history.

Richard Schickel reviews movies for *Time* magazine. He is the author of many books, among them: *The Disney Version, D.W. Griffith: An American Life, Intimate Strangers, The Culture of Celebrity, Brando: A Life in our Times, Clint Eastwood: A Biography,* and *Matinee Idylls.* He was recently awarded the Maurice Berry Prize for his contributions to film criticism, and is the producer-writer-director of over thirty television series.

Matthew Seitz is a film critic for the *New York Press,* a television critic for the *Star-Ledger* of Newark, New Jersey, and a contributor to *Sound & Vision* monthly.

Henry Sheehan has been the film critic of the *Orange County Register* since 1993. Before that, he wrote about the movies for the *Los Angeles Reader, Boston Phoenix,* and many other publications.

Robert Sklar reviews films for the *Forward*, a New York weekly, and is the author of several books on film, most recently *A World History of Film.*

Michael Sragow is the movie critic of the *Baltimore Sun* and contributes revival notes to the *New Yorker.* He is editing a collection of James Agee's writing for the Library of America and working on a biography of director Victor Fleming.

David Sterritt is a film critic for the Christian Science Monitor and a film professor at Long Island University and Columbia University. A slightly different version of his article on *Breathless* appeared in the *Chronicle of Higher Education.*

Charles Taylor is a regular contributor to the web magazine *Salon.* His writing has also appeared in the *New Yorker, Details, Film Comment,* and *Sight and Sound.*

Kevin Thomas of the *Los Angeles Times* is the longest-running film critic for an American newspaper.

Peter Travers is the film critic of *Rolling Stone* magazine.

Kenneth Turan is the film critic for the *Los Angeles Times* and a regular contributor to National Public Radio's "Morning Edition." His latest book, *Sundance to Sarajevo: Film Festivals and the World they Made* will be published in spring 2002.

James Verniere is the film critic of the *Boston Herald.*

Armond White, film critic for *New York Press,* is author of *Resistance: Ten Years of Pop Culture that Shook the World* and the upcoming *Heroic Conscience: Ethics vs. Hollywood.*

Michael Wilmington is the film critic of the *Chicago Tribune.*

William Wolf is the editor-in-chief of the online magazine *wolfentertainmentguide.com* and is a member of the Online Film Critics Society. He teaches film courses at New York University in the English and French departments and for the NYU School of Continuing and Professional Studies, and is the author of *Landmark Films: The Cinema and Our Century* and *The Marx Brothers.*

Index

Numbers in **bold** indicate the first page in each film's main entry.

Permissions

"2001: A Space Odyssey" by James Verniere. Reprinted by permission of the author.

"42nd Street" by Emanuel Levy. Reprinted by permission of the author.

"The 400 Blows" by Peter Brunette. Reprinted by permission of the author.

"All About Eve" by Peter Travers. Reprinted by permission of the author.

"Annie Hall" by Jay Carr. Reprinted by permission of the author.

"Ashes and Diamonds" by Peter Keough. Reprinted by permission of the author.

"L'Atalante" by Terrence Rafferty. Originally appeared in the *New Yorker*, November 5, 1990. Reprinted by permission of the author.

"The Bank Dick" by Henry Sheehan. Reprinted by permission of the author.

"The Battleship Potemkin" by Roger Ebert. Originally appeared in the *Chicago Sun-Times*. Reprinted by permission of the author.

"The Birth of a Nation" by Dave Kehr. Reprinted by permission of the author.

"Blow-Up" by Andrew Sarris. Originally appeared in the *Village Voice*, December 29, 1966. Reprinted by permission of the author.

"Bonnie and Clyde" by Richard Schickel. Reprinted by permission of the author.

"Breathless" by David Sterritt. A slightly different version of this essay appeared in the *Chronicle of Higher Education* in April, 2000.

"Bringing Up Baby" by Morris Dickstein. Copyright © 2002 Morris Dickstein, written especially for this volume.

"Casablanca" by Jay Carr. Originally appeared in the *Boston Globe*, April 26, 1992. Reprinted by permission.

"The Chant of Jimmie Blacksmith" by Joe Morgenstern. Reprinted by permission of the author.

"Children of Paradise" by Jay Carr. Originally appeared in the *Boston Globe*, February 23, 1992. Reprinted by permission.

"Chinatown" by James Verniere. Reprinted by permission of the author.

"Citizen Kane" by Godfrey Cheshire. Reprinted by permission of the author.

"Close Encounters of the Third Kind" by Matthew Seitz. Reprinted by permission of the author.

"Closely Watched Trains" by Richard Schickel. Reprinted by permission of the author.

"Close-up" by Jonathan Rosenbaum. Reprinted by permission of the author.

"Dance, Girl, Dance" by Carrie Rickey. Copyright © 2002 Carrie Rickey.

"The Decalogue" by Michael Wilmington. Originally appeared in the *Chicago Tribune*, March 22, 1996. Copyright © 1996 *Chicago Tribune*.

"The Diary of a Country Priest" by Henry Sheehan. Reprinted by permission of the author.

"Diner" by Peter Rainer. Originally appeared in the *Los Angeles Herald Examiner*, May 7, 1982. Reprinted by permission of the author.

"Do the Right Thing" by David Sterritt. Reprinted by permission of the author.

"La Dolce Vita" by Roger Ebert. Originally appeared in the *Chicago Sun-Times*. Reprinted by permission of the author.

"Double Indemnity" by Matthew Seitz. Reprinted by permission of the author.

"Duck Soup" by William Wolf. Reprinted by permission of the author.

"Easy Rider" by William Wolf. Reprinted by permission of the author.

"Enter the Dragon" by Michael Sragow. Reprinted by permission of the author.

"The Entertainer" by Charles Taylor. Reprinted by permission of the author.

"The Exorcist" by Terrence Rafferty. Originally published in the *New York Times*, September 17, 2000. Copyright © 2000 by the New York Times Co. Reprinted by permission.

"Faces" by Andrew Sarris. Originally appeared in the *Village Voice*, November 28, 1968. Reprinted by permission of the author.

"Fargo" by Peter Travers. Originally published in *Rolling Stone,* March 21, 1996. Reprinted by permission of the author.

"Frankenstein and The Bride of Frankenstein" by Richard T. Jameson. Reprinted by permission of the author.

"The General" by Roger Ebert. Originally appeared in the *Chicago Sun-Times*. Reprinted by permission of the author.

"The Godfather and The Godfather Part II" by Michael Sragow. Reprinted by permission of the author.

"Gone with the Wind," by Eleanor Ringel. First published in the *Atlanta Journal-Constitution*, June 26, 1998, under the title "Almost 60, 'Wind' Remains a Force." Reprinted with permission from the *Atlanta Journal* and the *Atlanta Constitution*.

"The Gospel According to St. Matthew" by Rob Nelson. Reprinted by permission of the author.

"The Graduate" by Jami Bernard. Reprinted by permission of the author.

"On the Waterfront" by Robert Sklar. Reprinted by permission of the author.

"Open City" by Peter Brunette. Reprinted by permission of the author.

"The Palm Beach Story" by David Ansen. Reprinted by permission of the author.

"Pandora's Box" by Charles Taylor. Reprinted by permission of the author.

"The Passion of Joan of Arc" by Roger Ebert. Originally appeared in the *Chicago Sun-Times*. Reprinted by permission of the author.

"Pather Panchali, Aparajito, The World of Apu" by Gary Arnold. Reprinted by permission of the author.

"The Piano" by Judy Gerstel. Reprinted by permission.

"Psycho" by Charles Taylor. Reprinted by permission of the author.

"Public Enemy" by John Anderson. Reprinted by permission of the author.

"Pulp Fiction" by Jami Bernard. Reprinted by permission of the author.

"Raging Bull" by Jami Bernard. Reprinted by permission of the author.

"Rashomon" by Andy Klein. Reprinted by permission of the author.

"Rebel Without a Cause" by Jay Carr. A shorter version of this piece was printed in the *Boston Globe*. Reprinted by permission of the author.

"The Rules of the Game" by Jay Carr. Originally published under the title "Retrospective" in *Foreign Affairs*. Reprinted by permission of the author.

"Schindler's List" by Jay Carr. Reprinted by permission of the author.

"The Searchers" by Peter Travers. Originally published in *Rolling Stone,* June 10, 1996. Reprinted by permission of the author.

"The Seven Samurai" by John Anderson. Reprinted by permission of the author.

"The Seventh Seal" by Peter Keough. Reprinted by permission of the author.

"Singin' in the Rain" by Judy Gerstel. Reprinted by permission.

"Star Wars" by Matthew Seitz. Reprinted by permission of the author.

"La Strada and Nights of Cabiria" by Gary Arnold. Derived from pieces originally published in the *Washington Times* on January 16, 1996, and November 1, 1997. Reprinted by permission of the author.

"Sunrise" by Jonathan Rosenbaum. Reprinted by permission of the author.

"Sunset Boulevard" by Morris Dickstein. A longer version of this story was first published in *Grand Street* (Spring 1998). Reprinted here by permission of the author. Copyright © 1988, 2002 by Morris Dickstein.

"The Thief of Bagdad" by Joe Morgenstern. Reprinted by permission of the author.

"Tokyo Story" by Kevin Thomas. Originally published under the title "A Family Reunion" in the *Los Angeles Times*. Copyright © 1972 *Los Angeles Times*. Reprinted with permission.

"Top Hat" by Carrie Rickey. Copyright © 2002 Carrie Rickey.

"Touch of Evil" by Michael Sragow. Reprinted by permission of the author.

"Trouble in Paradise" by Richard Schickel. Reprinted by permission of the author.

"Ugetsu Monogatari" by Gerald Peary. Reprinted by permission of the author.